Fodor's 1st Edition

Kenya and Tanzania

The Guide for All Budgets, Where to Stay, Eat, and Explore On and Off the Beaten Path

D1302302

When to Go,
What to Pack

Post-it® Flags,
Web Sites, and More

Fodor's Travel Publications • New York, Toronto, London, Sydney, Auckland
www.fodors.com

Fodor's Kenya and Tanzania

EDITOR: Mark Sullivan

Editorial Contributors: Kim Beury, Christine Cipriani, Mary Anne Fitzgerald, Tara Fitzgerald, Melissa Shales, Delta Willis.
Editorial Production: Tom Holton
Maps: David Lindroth, *cartographer*; Bob Blake, *map editor*
Design: Fabrizio La Rocca, *creative director*; Guido Caroti, *art director*; Jolie Novak, *senior picture editor*; Melanie Marin, *photo editor*
Cover Design: Pentagram
Production/Manufacturing: Colleen Ziemba
Cover Photograph: Michael K. Nichols/National Geographic

Copyright

Important Tip

Although all prices, opening times, and other details in this book are based on information supplied to us at press time, changes occur all the time in the travel world, and Fodor's cannot accept responsibility for facts that become outdated or for inadvertent errors or omissions. So **always confirm information when it matters,** especially if you're making a detour to visit a specific place.

Special Sales

Fodor's Travel Publications are available at special discounts for bulk purchases for sales promotions or premiums. Special editions, including personalized covers, excerpts of existing guides, and corporate imprints, can be created in large quantities for special needs. For more information, contact your local bookseller or write to Special Markets, Fodor's Travel Publications, 280 Park Ave., New York, NY 10017. Inquiries from Canada should be directed to your local Canadian bookseller or sent to Random House of Canada, Ltd., Marketing Department, 2775 Matheson Boulevard East, Mississauga, Ontario L4W 4P7. Inquiries from the United Kingdom should be sent to Fodor's Travel Publications, 20 Vauxhall Bridge Road, London SW1V 2SA, England.

CONTENTS

Maps

ON THE ROAD WITH FODOR'S

The more you know before you go, the better your trip will be. East Africa's most fascinating small museum (or its most chaotic outdoor market or trendiest seafood restaurant) could be just around the corner from your hotel, but if you don't know it's there, it might as well be on the other side of the globe. That's where this book comes in. It's a great step toward making sure your next trip lives up to your expectations. As you plan, check out the Web as well. Guidebooks have been helping smart travelers find the special places for years; the Web is one more tool. Whatever reference you consult, be savvy about what you read, and always consider the source. Images and language can be massaged to make places appear better than they are. And one traveler's quaint is another's grimy. Here at Fodor's, and at our on-line arm, Fodors.com, our focus is on providing you with information that's not only useful but accurate and on target. Every day Fodor's editors put enormous effort into getting things right, beginning with the search for the right contributors—people who have objective judgment, broad travel experience, and the writing ability to put their insights into words. There's no substitute for advice from a like-minded friend who has just come back from where you're going, but our writers, having seen all corners of Kenya and Tanzania, are the next best thing. They're the kind of people you'd poll for tips yourself if you knew them.

Kim Beury has written about Kenya and Tanzania since the mid-1980s, when she traveled to the region with the Peace Corps to teach high school in the foothills of Mt. Kilimanjaro. (Always up for a challenge, she also climbed the legendary peak.) She has spent much time in East Africa, floating in hot-air balloons over the Serengeti and riding the Tazara Railway the entire route from Tanzania to Zambia. She holds a master's degree in international development focused on improving qualities of life in developing countries. The freelance writer and public relations professional penned our Dar es Salaam chapter.

Mary Anne Fitzgerald is the author of two books: *Nomad,* an account of her adventures in Africa, and *My Warrior Son,* which tells about her life with a Maasai boy she adopted. Born in South Africa, she has worked as a Nairobi-based correspondent for London's *Financial Times, Independent,* and *Sunday Times.* During the course of her journalistic career she has written numerous travel pieces for a variety of newspapers and magazines. She now divides her time among Kenya, Europe, and the United States.

Kenyan-born **Tara Fitzgerald** has lived and breathed the country she writes about. Raised among the Samburu people of northern Kenya, she later ran a nongovernmental organization there in an office at the foot of Mt. Kenya. She now works in Somalia for the United Nations, reintegrating 250,000 refugees back into their local societies.

An award-winning freelance travel writer and editor, **Melissa Shales** was brought up in Zimbabwe. She studied history and archaeology before turning her passion for travel into a career that has taken her much of the way around the world. She has commissioned and edited nearly 100 guides and written more than 20, including books on Kenya, Tanzania, Morocco, South Africa, and Zimbabwe. Although she's based in England, Africa is in her blood.

Delta Willis searched for fossils alongside Richard Leakey for her book *The Hominid Gang,* and organized Stephen Jay Gould's first trip to Africa. Drawn to Kenya in 1977 by her work for Survival Anglia Ltd., the British producer of natural history films, she is currently researching *In the Shadow of Sultans,* about life in Zanzibar.

Don't Forget to Write

Your experiences—positive and negative—matter to us. If we have missed or misstated something, we want to hear about it. We follow up on all suggestions. Contact the Kenya and Tanzania editor at editors@fodors.com or c/o Fodor's, 280 Park Avenue, New York, New York 10017. And have a fabulous trip!

Karen Cure

Karen Cure
Editorial Director

Kenya and Northern Tanzania

KEY

Rail Lines

0   140 miles

0   210 km

N

SOMALIA

ETHIOPIA

SUDAN

UGANDA

El Wak

Wajir

Moyale

Marsabit Nat. Res.

WOYAMDERO PLAIN

BILESHA PLAINS

D500

C80

C81

A3

A3

Lake Chew Bahir

Losai Nat. Res.

Rahole Nat. Res.

Kora Nat. Res.

Meru Nat. Park

Garissa

North Horr

Loyangalani

Chalbi Desert

Mathews Range

Buffalo Springs Nat. Res.

Shaba Nat. Res.

Samburu Nat. Res.

Isiolo

Meru

Mt. Kenya Nat. Park

Mt. Kenya

Embu

Ol Doinyo Sabuk

Thika

Sibiloi Nat. Park

Kaobi Fora

Allia Bay

Lake Turkana

Baragoi

Marallal

Marsal National Sanctuary

Lake Bogoria Nat. Res.

Nanyuki

Nyeri

Aberdare Nat. Park

A2

A104

South Island Nat. Park

Lokichar

S. Turkana Nat. Res.

Saiwa Swamp Nat. Pk.

GREAT RIFT VALLEY

Nyahururu

Nakuru

Naivasha

B4

A1

Lodwar

LOTIKIPI PLAIN

A1

Kitale

Mt. Elgon Nat. Park

Webuye

Eldoret

Kakamega Nat. Res.

Kakamega

Kisumu

Kericho

Kisii

Lake Nakuru Nat. Park

Narok

B1

C57

Mbale

Busia

Bugembe

Homa Bay

Ruma Nat. Park

Kolido

Lira

Jinja

Kampala

Entebbe

EQUATOR

Lake Kyoga

Lake Victoria

Gulu

Nakasongola

Masindi

Nairo

Ewaso Ngiro

A1

A2

A42

A2

B9

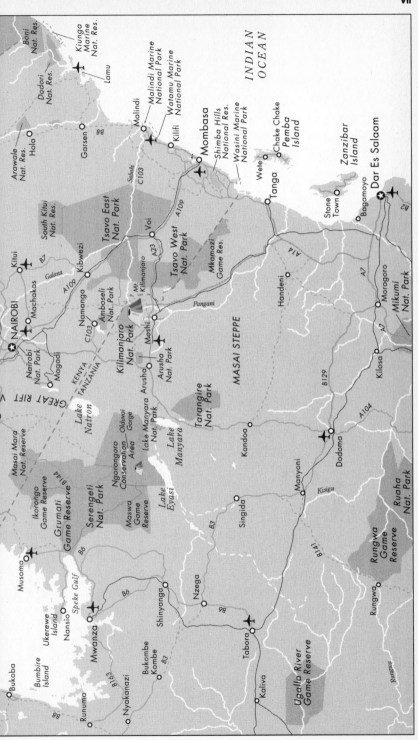

Tanzania and Zanzibar

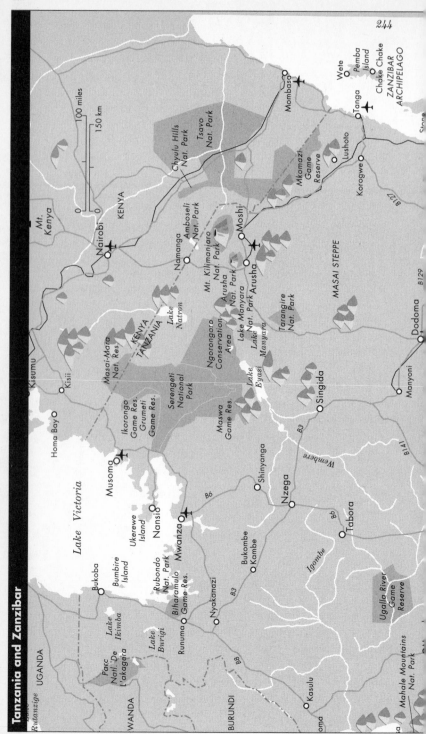

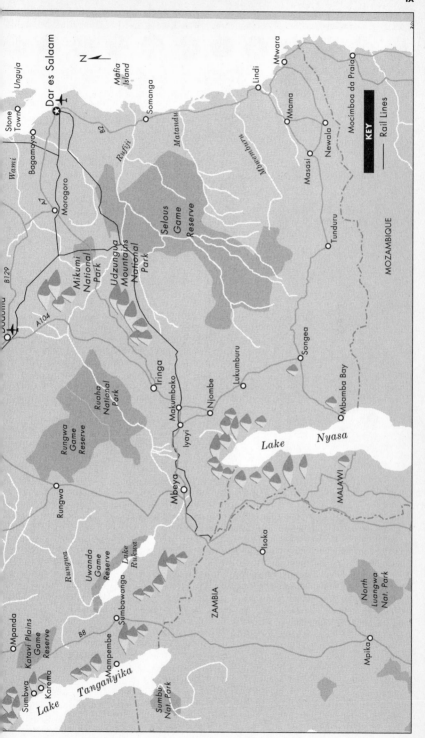

World Time Zones

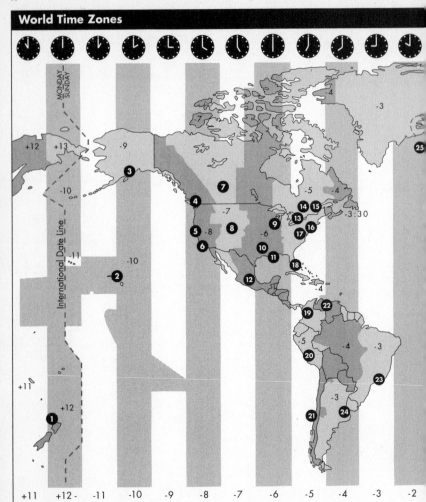

Numbers below vertical bands relate each zone to Greenwich Mean Time (0 hrs.).
Local times frequently differ from these general indications,
as indicated by light-face numbers on map.

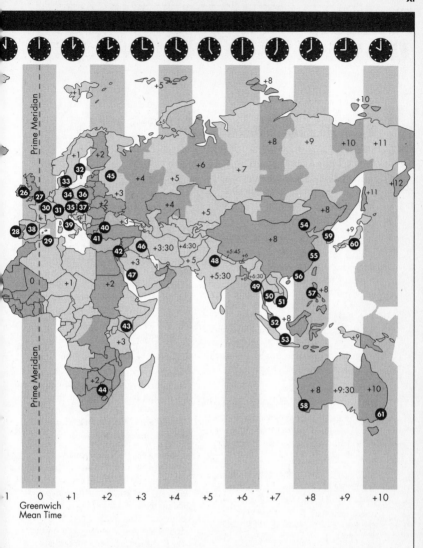

ESSENTIAL INFORMATION

AIR TRAVEL

TO KENYA

In addition to Kenya Airways, many international carriers fly into Kenya each day. European carriers British Airways, KLM, Swissair, and Sabena all offer daily flights. Gulf Air and Emirates offer reasonably priced flights from Europe that stop in the Middle East. There are no direct flights from the United States, so you will need to make a connection in Europe. Northwest Airlines connects with KLM, American Airlines connects with British Airways, and Virgin Atlantic connects with Kenya Airways. If you are coming from Australia or New Zealand, connect in South Africa, Europe, or the Middle East.

TO TANZANIA

Most international flights land in Dar es Salaam, but some carriers also land at Kilimanjaro International Airport. KLM offers the only daily flights to Dar es Salaam.

➤ TO KENYA & TANZANIA: **Air France** (☎ 800/237–2747 in the U.S., 0845/084–5111 in the U.K., WEB www.airfrance.com). **British Airways** (☎ 800/247–9297 in the U.S., 0845/779–9977 in the U.K., WEB www.british-airways.com). **Emirates** (☎ 212/758–3944 in the U.S., 0870/243–2222 in the U.K., WEB www.emirates.com). **Gulf Air** (☎ 888/359–4853 in the U.S., 0870/777–1717 in the U.K., WEB www.gulfairco.com). **KLM** (☎ 800/343–2506 in the U.S., WEB www.klm.com). **Kenya Airways** (☎ 800/343–2506 in the U.S., 0178/4888233 in the U.K.). **South African Airways** (☎ 800/722–9675 in the U.S., 0870/747–1111 in the U.K., WEB www.flysaa.com). **Swiss Air** (☎ 800/221–4750 in the U.S., 0845/601–0956 in the U.K., WEB www.swissair.com).

➤ WITHIN KENYA: **Air Kenya** (☎ 02/502–601). **Boskovic Air Char-** ter (☎ 02/501–210). **Kenya Airways** (☎ 02/210–771). **Tropicair** (☎ 0176/32890).

➤ WITHIN TANZANIA: **Air Tanzania** (☎ 022/210–245). **Precision Air** (☎ 022/213–0800). **Regional Air** (☎ 027/250–4477).

BOOKING

When you book **look for nonstop flights** and **remember that "direct" flights stop at least once.** Try to avoid connecting flights, which require a change of plane. For more booking tips and to check prices and make on-line flight reservations, log on to www.fodors.com.

CHECK-IN & BOARDING

Most carriers require you to check in two hours before your scheduled departure time for domestic flights and 2½ to 3 hours before international flights. Always **ask your carrier about its check-in-policy.**

Assuming that not everyone with a ticket will show up, airlines routinely overbook planes. When everyone does, airlines ask for volunteers to give up their seats. In return, these volunteers usually get a certificate for a free flight and are rebooked on the next flight out. If there are not enough volunteers, the airline must choose who will be denied boarding. The first to get bumped are passengers who checked in late and those flying on discounted tickets, so **get to the gate and check in as early as possible,** especially during peak periods.

Always **bring a government-issued photo I.D. to the airport;** even when it's not required, a passport is best.

CUTTING COSTS

The least expensive airfares to Kenya and Tanzania must usually be purchased in advance and are nonrefundable. It's smart to **call a number of airlines,** and when you are quoted a good price, **book it on the spot**—the same fare may not be available the next day. Always **check different routings** and look into using different airports. Travel agents, especially low-fare specialists (☞ Discounts & Deals, *below*), are helpful.

Consolidators are another good source. They buy tickets for scheduled international flights at reduced rates from the airlines, then sell them at prices that beat the best fare available directly from the airlines, usually without restrictions. Sometimes you can even get your money back if you need to return the ticket. Carefully read the fine print detailing penalties for changes and cancellations, and **confirm your consolidator reservation with the airline.**

➤ CONSOLIDATORS: **Cheap Tickets** (☎ 800/377–1000). **Discount Airline Ticket Service** (☎ 800/576–1600). **Unitravel** (☎ 800/325–2222). **Up & Away Travel** (☎ 212/889–2345). **World Travel Network** (☎ 800/409–6753).

ENJOYING THE FLIGHT

The flight to East Africa is a long one, and the cabin staff makes an effort to allow passengers to sleep. To avoid dehydration, drink at least one glass of water per hour in flight and limit your alcohol and caffeine intake. It is a good idea to get up and walk about once an hour to maintain your circulation. For additional jet-lag tips consult *Fodor's FYI: Travel Fit & Healthy* (available at bookstores everywhere).

For more legroom, **request an emergency-aisle seat.** Don't sit in the row in front of the emergency aisle or in front of a bulkhead, where seats may not recline. If you have dietary concerns, **ask for special meals when booking.** These can be vegetarian, low-cholesterol, or kosher, for example. Internal flights are generally very short so only snacks are provided, if any food is served at all.

None of the major airlines allow smoking on the flight. No domestic airlines allow smoking, although some charter companies may allow you to smoke.

FLYING TIMES

The trip from Europe to East Africa lasts between eight and nine hours.

Flights from South Africa last about five hours. Your actual travel time may be significantly longer if your flight has a layover.

HOW TO COMPLAIN

If your baggage goes astray or your flight goes awry, complain right away. Most carriers require that you **file a claim immediately.**

➤ AIRLINE COMPLAINTS: U.S. Department of Transportation **Aviation Consumer Protection Division** (✉ C-75, Room 4107, Washington, DC 20590, ☎ 202/366–2220, 🌐 www.dot.gov/airconsumer). **Federal Aviation Administration Consumer Hotline** (☎ 800/322–7873).

RECONFIRMING

It's a good idea to **reconfirm international flights** to and from East Africa at least 72 hours before departure. Internal flights should be reconfirmed at least 48 hours before departure, particularly if you are trying to connect with an international flight.

AIRPORTS

Kenya's two major international airports are Jomo Kenyatta International Airport, about 16 km (10 mi) southeast of Nairobi, and Moi International Airport, 16 km (10 mi) west of Mombasa. Most charter flights depart from Wilson Airport, just south of Nairobi. The majority of international flights come into Nairobi, where you can find connections to Mombasa.

Tanzania has three international airports, Dar es Salaam International Airport, about 17 km (10 mi) outside town; Zanzibar International Airport, which serves the island of Unguja; and Kilimanjaro International Airport, equidistant between Arusha and Moshi in the northern part of the country. The majority of international flights head to Dar es Salaam, although if you are going on safari in the north, you may wish to consider flying straight into Kilimanjaro International Airport.

➤ KENYA AIRPORTS: **Jomo Kenyatta International Airport** (☎ 02/822–111). **Moi International Airport** (☎ 011/433–211). **Wilson Airport** (☎ 02/501–943).

➤ Tanzania Airports: **Dar es Salaam International Airport** (☎ 022/212–4169). **Kilimanjaro International Airport** (☎ 027/254–4125). **Zanzibar International Airport** (☎ 024/223–2001).

BIKE TRAVEL

Bicycles are an increasingly common sight on roads in East Africa. The combination of reckless drivers and the lack of bike lanes makes this a dangerous means of transportation. A better option for avid cyclists is the cycling safaris that tour operators are beginning to lead near Mt. Kenya and other national parks. You can also rent bicycles to explore the scenic wonders of places like Hells Gate National Park.

BIKES IN FLIGHT

Most airlines accommodate bikes as luggage, provided they are dismantled and boxed. Airlines sell bike boxes, which are often free at bike shops, for about $5 (it's at least $100 for bike bags). International travelers can sometimes substitute a bike for a piece of checked luggage at no charge; otherwise, the cost is about $100. Domestic and Canadian airlines charge $25–$50.

BOAT & FERRY TRAVEL

Several ferries travel between Dar es Salaam and Zanzibar. The fastest trip, lasting about 75 minutes, is on hydrofoils operated by Sea Express and Azam Marine. Sea Express has daily departures from Dar es Salaam at 8, 10, noon, 2:30, and 4:30, with returns at 7, 10, noon, 2:30, and 4:30. Azam Marine departs from Dar es Salaam at 8, 1:15, and 4, returning at 7, 1:30, and 4. Tickets are about $35.

The slowest trip is made by Flying Horse on a ship affectionately known as *Yongo,* a Swahili word for "millipede." It costs about $10.

➤ Boat & Ferry Information: **Azam Marine** (☎ 054/233–046). **Flying Horse** (☎ 054/233–031). **Sea Express** (☎ 054/233–002).

BUS TRAVEL

Because the roads in East Africa are not always in the best condition, traveling by bus is an option only if you have a lot of time. Regular buses running between Dar es Salaam and Arusha, for example, take at least nine hours. Buses marked EXPRESS are usually not much faster, but the small added expense means you'll be guaranteed a seat and a bit more comfort.

For travel between Kenya and Tanzania, use reputable companies such as Davanu Shuttle and Riverside Shuttle, which offer daily service. Buses leave Nairobi and Arusha at 8 AM and 2 PM. The five-hour journey costs $20 to $25.

➤ Bus Information: **Davanu Shuttle** (✉ University Way, Nairobi, ☎ 02/222-002). **Riverside Shuttle** (✉ Koinange St., Nairobi, ☎ 02/219–020).

BUSINESS HOURS

Business hours throughout Kenya and Tanzania are generally open weekdays from 8 to 5. Most businesses, particularly outside the larger cities, close for lunch between 1 and 2. Some businesses are also open Saturday from 8:30 to 1.

BANKS & OFFICES

Kenya governmental offices are open weekdays from 8 or 8:30 to 5, closing for lunch between 1 and 2. Office hours in Tanzania are a little earlier, usually from 7:30 to 3:30. Banks in both countries are generally open weekdays from 9 to 3. In Nairobi banks are open from 9 to 11 on the first and last Saturdays of the month, while those in other parts of the country are open every Saturday. Bank branches at Jomo Kenyatta International Airport and Moi International Airport are open around the clock. Large cities have currency exchange offices that are open weekdays from 9 to 5.

GAS STATIONS

Hours for gas stations vary, depending on the location of the station and the demand for fuel. As a rule, fuel will be available from 7 to 7. Gas stations are open longer hours along major highways.

MUSEUMS & SIGHTS

In both Kenya and Tanzania, museums in larger cities are open from

9:30 to 6 every day of the year, including public holidays. Other museums tend to have shorter hours.

PHARMACIES

Most pharmacies are open normal business hours, although some pharmacies will remain open until 9 or 10. In Nairobi the *Daily Nation* publishes a list of pharmacies that stay open late.

CAMERAS & PHOTOGRAPHY

East Africa, with its majestic landscapes, is a photographer's dream. Photos of elephants lumbering past Mt. Kenya and Maasai villagers near Mt. Kilimanjaro are sure to be among your favorites. Residents of Kenya and Tanzania seem amenable to having picture-taking tourists in their midst, but you should always **ask permission before taking pictures of individuals.** Don't photograph airports, government buildings, naval bases, or military camps.

The sun is more intense this close to the equator, so **purchase faster film** to help prevent overexposure. A filter and lens hood will help to reduce the glare. For the best light it is advisable to shoot photos early in the morning or in late afternoon. Do **invest in a telephoto lens to photograph wildlife**: even standard zoom lenses of the 35–88 range won't capture a satisfying amount of detail.

The *Kodak Guide to Shooting Great Travel Pictures* (available at bookstores everywhere) is loaded with tips.

➤ PHOTO HELP: **Kodak Information Center** (☎ 800/242–2424).

EQUIPMENT PRECAUTIONS

Don't pack film and equipment in checked luggage, where it is much more susceptible to damage. X-ray machines used to view checked luggage are becoming much more powerful and therefore are much more likely to ruin your film. Carry an extra supply of batteries, and **be prepared to turn on your camera or camcorder** to prove to security personnel that the device is real. Always **ask for hand inspection of film,** which becomes clouded after repeated exposure to airport X-ray machines,

and **keep videotapes away from metal detectors.**

In addition, **take a camera bag** to protect your camera against rough conditions. Lens tissues are useful for wiping off any dust. Do not leave film in the glove compartment or on the dashboard, as the intense heat will spoil it sooner than you think.

FILM & DEVELOPING

Film, usually Kodak or Fuji, is widely available in heavily touristed areas. You will find that 64-, 100-, 200-, and 400-speed film is readily available, while 800-speed film is harder to come by. Beware of expired film.

CAR RENTAL

If you are traveling long distances, renting a car is often a good idea. They are available in Nairobi and Dar es Salaam, as well as many other cities. It's a good idea to **reserve a car before beginning your trip,** as you may find that the type of car you want is not available at the last minute. If you will be leaving the major highways, think about renting a four-wheel-drive vehicle.

You might **consider hiring a driver** who can also serve as a guide. Remember that in addition to the cost of the car, you must also pay for the driver's food and accommodations. Drivers work between 8 and 6. If you want them to work later, you must pay a nominal overtime fee.

➤ MAJOR AGENCIES: **Alamo** (☎ 800/522–9696; 020/8759–6200 in the U.K., WEB www.alamo.com). **Avis** (☎ 800/331–1084; 800/879–2847 in Canada; 02/9353–9000 in Australia; 09/525–1982 in New Zealand; 0870/606–0100 in the U.K., WEB www.avis. com). **Budget** (☎ 800/527–0700; 0870/156–5656 in the U.K., WEB www.budget.com). **Dollar** (☎ 800/800–6000; 0124/622–0111 in the U.K., where it's affiliated with Sixt; 02/9223–1444 in Australia, WEB www. dollar.com). **Hertz** (☎ 800/654–3001; 800/263–0600 in Canada; 020/8897–2072 in the U.K.; 02/9669–2444 in Australia; 09/256–8690 in New Zealand, WEB www.hertz.com) **National Car Rental** (☎ 800/227–7368; 020/8680–4800 in the U.K., WEB www. nationalcar.com).

CUTTING COSTS

To get the best deal, **book through a travel agent who will shop around.** Also **price local car-rental companies,** although the service and maintenance may not be as good as those of a major player. Remember to ask about required deposits, cancellation penalties, and drop-off charges if you're planning to pick up the car in one city and leave it in another. If you're traveling during a holiday period, also make sure that a confirmed reservation guarantees you a car.

➤ KENYA AGENCIES: **Central Car Hire** (✉ Standard St., Nairobi, ☎ 02/222–888). **Concorde Car Hire** (✉ Ring Rd., Nairobi, ☎ 02/448–953 or 02/448–954). **Let's Go Travel** (✉ Waiyaki Way, Nairobi, ☎ 02/447–151 or 02/441–705).

➤ TANZANIA AGENCIES: **Chemah Brothers** (✉ Shangani Rd., Stone Town, ☎ 024/233–385). **Serena Car Hire** (✉ India St., Arusha, ☎ 027/255–6593). **Takims Holidays Tours** (✉ Simeon Rd., Arusha, ☎ 027/250–8026, WEB www.takimsholidays.com).

INSURANCE

When driving a rented car you are generally responsible for any damage to or loss of the vehicle as well as for any property damage or personal injury that you may cause. Before you rent, see what coverage your personal auto-insurance policy and credit cards provide.

All car rental agencies will require you to pay a hefty deposit. On top of this, companies offer you the option of taking out collision damage insurance and theft protection insurance. It is well worth taking out both types of insurance, as the cost of an accident or theft could be considerable. If you take out insurance with the rental agency, find out exactly what it covers, as some policies do not offer medical coverage.

REQUIREMENTS & RESTRICTIONS

Drivers in Kenya are required to be over 23 and under 70 with a valid license that has been held for a minimum of two years. An international driver's license is required in Tanzania. Many agencies restrict where you can travel, so ask about the areas you plan to visit. Most won't allow you to take vehicles across the border between Kenya and Tanzania, although some of the larger companies will let you do it for an extra fee. They will arrange all the paperwork for you.

SURCHARGES

Before you pick up a car in one city and leave it in another, **ask about drop-off charges or one-way service fees,** which can be substantial. Note, too, that some rental agencies charge extra if you return the car before the time specified in your contract. To avoid a hefty refueling fee, **fill the tank just before you turn in the car,** but be aware that gas stations near the rental outlet may overcharge.

Surcharges vary from company to company, so it is worthwhile to **take the time to read the small print.** Some agencies offer what they call an unlimited mileage rate but charge the normal rate at a certain point. Always **check that the unlimited mileage rate is really unlimited.**

CAR TRAVEL

Driving in East Africa can be a hair-raising experience. There are too few police officers to enforce the rules of the road, and many drivers hit the streets without licenses or insurance. Vehicles are often overloaded or dilapidated. On top of all that you must contend with trailers fish-tailing across the roadway and buses racing each other to the next stop.

That said, driving in your own vehicle gives you a freedom to explore areas that would otherwise be extremely difficult to reach. The highway systems are reasonably well maintained. Once you move off these main arteries, many roads are unpaved. If you plan to take any of these routes, renting a four-wheel-drive vehicle is a good idea. You should **make sure your car has a spare tire and a jack.** If you are traveling to more remote areas, you should bring food and water, as well as extra fuel. If you break down, other drivers will generally come to your help.

AUTO CLUBS

The Automobile Association of Kenya extends privileges to members of the American Automobile Association in the United States and the Automobile Association in Britain. Contact a local office in your home country for more information.

➤ IN AUSTRALIA: **Australian Automobile Association** (☎ 02/6247–7311).

➤ IN CANADA: **Canadian Automobile Association** (☎ 613/247–0117).

➤ IN NEW ZEALAND: **New Zealand Automobile Association** (☎ 09/377–4660).

➤ IN THE U.K.: **Automobile Association** (☎ 0990/500–600). **Royal Automobile Club** (☎ 0990/722–722 for membership; 0345/121–345 for insurance).

➤ IN THE U.S.: **American Automobile Association** (☎ 800/564–6222).

EMERGENCY SERVICES

In both Kenya and Tanzania dial 999 in case of an emergency on the road. The Automobile Association operates in both countries and provides roadside services to members of affiliated groups.The Kenya Tourism Federation's Tourist Safety and Communication Centre helps visitors deal with all types of emergencies.

➤ KENYA CONTACTS: **Automobile Association of Kenya** (☎ 02/825–060 or 02/825–067 in Nairobi). **Safety and Communication Centre** (☎ 02/604–767 in Nairobi).

➤ TANZANIA CONTACTS: **Automobile Association of Tanzania** (☎ 022/112363 or 022/127–727).

GASOLINE

Fuel is readily available in East Africa. You will find a selection of gas stations in larger towns and along major highways. There are two types of gasoline—regular and premium—in addition to diesel. Unleaded gas is not available. At press time, petrol in Kenya was Ksh 54 per liter of regular, Ksh 55 per liter of premium. In Tanzania regular petrol was Tsh 548 per liter, while premium was Tsh 606 per liter. All stations are full service,

meaning they pump the gas for you. Some stations accept credit cards, although you will find this is more common in Kenya than in Tanzania. Stick with larger companies when refueling, as independent stations have been known to water down the fuel.

ROAD MAPS

Tourist Safari and Nelles both produce good-quality maps of the region. All are readily available in bookshops and many tourist outlets.

RULES OF THE ROAD

The speed limit on major highways is 100 kph (62 mph). The speed limit in urban areas is 50 kph (31 mph). Police never enforce seat belt regulations and rarely enforce drunk-driving laws. Americans and Canadians should remember to **drive on the left side** of the road.

CHILDREN IN KENYA
AND TANZANIA

Traveling to East Africa with children, especially small ones, can be a tiring experience. It is generally well worth the effort, however. Children are welcomed most places, apart from a few exclusive lodges. In the chapters, places that are especially good for children are indicated with a rubber ducky icon 🦆.

If you are renting a car, don't forget to **arrange for a car seat** when you reserve. For general advice about traveling with children, consult *Fodor's FYI: Travel with Your Baby* (available in bookstores everywhere).

FLYING

If your children are two or older, **ask about children's airfares.** As a general rule, infants under two not occupying a seat fly at greatly reduced fares or even for free. When booking, **confirm carry-on allowances** if you're traveling with infants. In general, for babies charged 10% of the adult fare you are allowed one carry-on bag and a collapsible stroller; if the flight is full, the stroller may have to be checked or you may be limited to less.

Experts agree that it's a good idea to use safety seats aloft for children weighing less than 40 pounds. Airlines set their own policies: U.S.

carriers usually require that the child be ticketed, even if he or she is young enough to ride free, since the seats must be strapped into regular seats. Do **check your airline's policy about using safety seats during takeoff and landing.** And since safety seats are not allowed everywhere in the plane, get your seat assignments early.

When reserving, **request children's meals or a freestanding bassinet** if you need them. But note that bulk-head seats, where you must sit to use the bassinet, may lack an overhead bin or storage space on the floor.

FOOD

The majority of restaurants in Kenya and Tanzania welcome children, and a number even offer children's menus. In major cities such as Dar es Salaam, Mombasa, and Nairobi you will be able to locate branches of popular South African fast-food chains such as Nandos, Steers, and Chicken Inn.

LODGING

Most hotels in East Africa do not charge for children under the age of two. Children under 12 who share their parents' rooms will generally be charged half the adult rate. Some lodges in and around the national parks do not allow children below a certain age, as they don't want to disturb the game-viewing atmosphere. It is wise to **check a hotel's policy toward children.**

PRECAUTIONS

Talk with your doctor before travel-ing with small children to areas where there is a danger of malaria. Discuss the best prophylactics for younger children. The best way to prevent malaria is to **keep children from being bitten by mosquitoes.** Travel with mosquito netting in case this is not provided by a hotel. Remember to **bring child-friendly insect repellent** with you, as this is not easily found in either Kenya or Tanzania.

SUPPLIES & EQUIPMENT

Baby formula and diapers are easily found in supermarkets in urban areas. They tend to be quite expensive, so consider bringing your own. Baby formula brands on the market include Nestlé and Sma. Diaper brands avail-able include Pampers, Bébé Dou, and Huggies.

TRANSPORTATION

Car rental firms do not generally have child car seats available. **If you need a car seat, bring your own.** There is no enforcement of regulations regarding child safety in vehicles. Use your own judgment as to what are acceptable safety precautions for your child.

COMPUTERS ON THE ROAD

If you're traveling with a laptop computer, **carry a spare battery and adapter.** Replacements are difficult to find. Never plug your computer into any socket before asking about surge protectors. Many hotels experience extreme electrical fluctuations that can short out your adapter or even destroy your computer.

CONSUMER PROTECTION

Whenever shopping or buying travel services in Kenya and Tanzania, **pay with a major credit card** so you can cancel payment or get reimbursed if there's a problem. If you're buying a package or tour, always **consider travel insurance** that includes default coverage (☞ Insurance, *below*).

➤ BBBs: **Council of Better Business Bureaus** (✉ 4200 Wilson Blvd., Suite 800, Arlington, VA 22203, ☎ 703/276–0100, ℻ 703/525–8277, 🌐 www.bbb.org).

CUSTOMS & DUTIES

When shopping, **keep receipts** for all purchases. Upon reentering the coun-try, **be ready to show customs officials what you've bought.** If you feel a duty is incorrect or object to the way your clearance was handled, note the inspector's badge number and ask to see a supervisor. If the problem isn't resolved, write to the appropriate authorities, beginning with the port director at your point of entry.

IN KENYA & TANZANIA

Visitors may bring cameras, film, and binoculars, all of which must not be sold during their stay in Kenya, as well as nonconsumable provisions and nonalcoholic beverages in such quantities as are consistent, in the opinions of the authorities, with their visit. Those over 18 are entitled to up

250 grams of tobacco and cigarettes, 1 liter of wine or spirits, and a half liter of perfume or eau de toilette of which no more than a quarter may be perfume. The same limits apply to Tanzania, but you are only entitled to bring in 250 ml of perfume. It is possible to bring pets into Kenya provided they have a veterinary certificate.

Gifts are subject to duty, while firearms, illicit drugs, and obscene literature are prohibited.

➤ INFORMATION: **Kenya Customs Department** (✉ Box 30007, Nairobi,☎ 02/715–540). **Tanzania Customs Department** (✉ Box 9053, Dar es Salaam, ☎ 022/212–7783).

IN AUSTRALIA

Australian residents who are 18 or older may bring home $A400 worth of souvenirs and gifts (including jewelry), 250 cigarettes or 250 grams of tobacco, and 1,125 ml of alcohol (including wine, beer, and spirits). Residents under 18 may bring back $A200 worth of goods. Prohibited items include meat products. Seeds, plants, and fruits need to be declared upon arrival.

➤ INFORMATION: **Australian Customs Service** (✉ Box 8, Sydney, NSW 2001, Australia, ☎ 02/9213–2000, FAX 02/9213–4000, WEB www.customs.gov.au).

IN CANADA

Canadian residents who have been out of Canada for at least seven days may bring home C$750 worth of goods duty-free. If you've been away fewer than seven days but more than 48 hours, the duty-free allowance drops to C$200; if your trip lasts 24–48 hours, the allowance is C$50. You may not pool allowances with family members. Goods claimed under the C$750 exemption may follow you by mail; those claimed under the lesser exemptions must accompany you. Alcohol and tobacco products may be included in the seven-day and 48-hour exemptions but not in the 24-hour exemption. If you meet the age requirements of the province or territory through which you reenter Canada, you may bring in, duty-free, 1.14 liters (40 imperial ounces) of wine or liquor *or* 24 12-ounce cans or bottles of beer or ale. If you are 19 or older you may bring in, duty-free, 200 cigarettes and 50 cigars. Check ahead of time with the Canada Customs Revenue Agency or the Department of Agriculture for policies regarding meat products, seeds, plants, and fruits.

You may send an unlimited number of gifts worth up to C$60 each duty-free to Canada. Label the package UNSOLICITED GIFT—VALUE UNDER $60. Alcohol and tobacco are excluded.

➤ INFORMATION: **Canada Customs Revenue Agency** (✉ 2265 St. Laurent Blvd. S, Ottawa, Ontario K1G 4K3, Canada, ☎ 204/983–3500 or 506/636–5064; 800/461–9999 in Canada, WEB www.ccra-adrc.gc.ca).

IN NEW ZEALAND

Homeward-bound residents 17 or older may bring back $700 worth of souvenirs and gifts. Your duty-free allowance also includes 4.5 liters of wine or beer; one 1,125-ml bottle of spirits; and either 200 cigarettes, 250 grams of tobacco, 50 cigars, or a combination of the three up to 250 grams. Prohibited items include meat products, seeds, plants, and fruits.

➤ INFORMATION: **New Zealand Customs** (Custom House, ✉ 50 Anzac Ave., Box 29, Auckland, New Zealand, ☎ 09/300–5399, FAX 09/359–6730), WEB www.customs.govt.nz.

IN THE U.K.

From countries outside the European Union, including Africa, you may bring home, duty-free, 200 cigarettes or 50 cigars; 1 liter of spirits or 2 liters of fortified or sparkling wine or liqueurs; 2 liters of still table wine; 60 milliliters of perfume; 250 milliliters of toilet water; plus £145 worth of other goods, including gifts and souvenirs. If returning from outside the EU, prohibited items include meat products, seeds, plants, and fruits.

➤ INFORMATION: **HM Customs and Excise** (✉ St. Christopher House, Southwark, London, SE1 OTE, U.K., ☎ 020/7928–3344, WEB www.hmce.gov.uk).

IN THE U.S.

U.S. residents who have been out of the country for at least 48 hours (and who have not used the $400 allowance or any part of it in the past 30 days) may bring home $400 worth of foreign goods duty-free.U.S. residents 21 and older may bring back 1 liter of alcohol duty-free. In addition, regardless of your age, you are allowed 200 cigarettes and 100 non-Cuban cigars. Antiques, which the U.S. Customs Service defines as objects more than 100 years old, enter duty-free, as do original works of art done entirely by hand, including paintings, drawings, and sculptures.

You may also mail or ship packages home duty-free: up to $200 worth of goods for personal use, with a limit of one parcel per addressee per day (except alcohol or tobacco products or perfume worth more than $5); label the package PERSONAL USE and attach a list of its contents and their retail value. Do not label the package UNSOLICITED GIFT or your duty-free exemption will drop to $100. Mailed items do not affect your duty-free allowance on your return.

➤ INFORMATION: **U.S. Customs Service** (✉ 1300 Pennsylvania Ave. NW, Room 6.3D, Washington, DC 20229, WEB www.customs.gov; inquiries ☎ 202/354–1000; complaints c/o ✉ 1300 Pennsylvania Ave. NW, Room 5.4D, Washington, DC 20229; registration of equipment c/o Office of Passenger Programs, ☎ 202/927–0530).

DINING

East Africa has an impressive array of dining options, with restaurants offering everything from fast food to international cuisine. Many of the best restaurants in Kenya are in Nairobi, where you can satisfy a craving for almost any type of food. In Tanzania you will find a few excellent restaurants in Arusha and Dar es Salaam. The cost varies considerably, but meals are generally inexpensive by U.S. and European standards. A meal at an outstanding restaurant might run to $25 for a three-course dinner. The restaurants we list in this guide are the cream of the crop in each price range. Restaurants are

indicated by a ✗ icon. Properties indicated by a ✗🏠 icon are noted equally for their restaurants and their rooms.

MEALS & SPECIALTIES

East African food is simple and filling. Kenyans love meat, and their national dish is a type of barbecue called *nyama choma*. Other staples are *ugali*, a stiff corn porridge eaten with beef or chicken stew, and *sukuma wiki*, a tasty type of cooked greens. A tasty Kikuyu dish is *irio*, a hash of beans, corn, potatoes, and greens. On the coast try traditional dishes flavored with coconut and spices. The Indian *samosa*, a pastry filled with ground meat or vegetable, and the *chapati*, a thin skillet bread, are common throughout Kenya and Tanzania. The *mandazi*, a flat doughnut, is a popular breakfast dish. It's very tasty when fresh but quickly becomes hard and stale.

MEALTIMES

Restaurants typically open around noon for lunch and 6:30 or 7 for dinner. Unless otherwise noted, the restaurants listed in this guide are open daily for lunch and dinner.

RESERVATIONS & DRESS

Reservations are always a good idea: we mention them only when they're essential or not accepted. Book at upscale restaurants as far ahead as you can, and reconfirm as soon as you arrive. We mention dress only when men are required to wear a jacket or a jacket and tie.

WINE, BEER & SPIRITS

East Africa brews a selection of beers—White Cap, Tusker, and Pilsner—sold in bottles and cans. Tusker also has a draft beer, but it's available in very few bars and restaurants. Castle, a South African company, recently opened a brewery in Nairobi, so Castle, Ranger, and Lion brands are widely available. Kenya has a developing wine industry. Wines from the Lake Naivasha area are said to be quite respectable. There is also a wide selection of good imported wines available from South Africa, Europe, and Australia.

DISABILITIES & ACCESSIBILITY

East Africa is not an easy destination for travelers with disabilities. Very few tourist attractions are geared toward the needs of travelers with walkers or wheelchairs. Only the more expensive hotels and lodges have rooms that are accessible. At press time the Kenya Disabled Development Society was conducting research into which hotels were accessible. It plans to compile its findings and to make them available on its Web site.

➤ LOCAL RESOURCES: **Kenya Disabled Development Society** (☎ 035/22441, WEB www.netkenya.com/accessible/destinations).

LODGING

When discussing accessibility with an operator or reservations agent, **ask hard questions.** Are there any stairs, inside *or* out? Are there grab bars next to the toilet *and* in the shower/tub? How wide is the doorway to the room? To the bathroom? When in doubt, **opt for newer accommodations.**

➤ COMPLAINTS: **Aviation Consumer Protection Division** (☞ Air Travel, *above*) for airline-related problems. **Civil Rights Office** (✉ U.S. Department of Transportation, Departmental Office of Civil Rights, S-30, 400 7th St. SW, Room 10215, Washington, DC 20590, ☎ 202/366–4648, FAX 202/366–9371, WEB www.dot.gov/ost/docr/index.htm) for problems with surface transportation. **Disability Rights Section** (✉ U.S. Department of Justice, Civil Rights Division, Box 66738, Washington, DC 20035-6738, ☎ 202/514–0301 or 800/514–0301; 202/514–0383 TTY; 800/514–0383 TTY, FAX 202/307–1198, WEB www.usdoj.gov/crt/ada/adahom1.htm) for general complaints.

TRAVEL AGENCIES

In the United States, the Americans with Disabilities Act requires that travel firms serve the needs of all travelers. Some agencies specialize in working with people with disabilities.

➤ TRAVELERS WITH MOBILITY PROBLEMS: **Access Adventures** (✉ 206 Chestnut Ridge Rd., Scottsville, NY 14624, ☎ 716/889–9096, dltravel@prodigy.net), run by a former physical-rehabilitation counselor. **CareVacations** (✉ No. 5, 5110–50 Ave., Leduc, Alberta T9E 6V4, Canada, ☎ 780/986–6404 or 877/478–7827, FAX 780/986–8332, WEB www.carevacations.com), for group tours and cruise vacations. **Flying Wheels Travel** (✉ 143 W. Bridge St., Box 382, Owatonna, MN 55060, ☎ 507/451–5005 or 800/535–6790, FAX 507/451–1685, WEB www.flyingwheelstravel.com).

DISCOUNTS & DEALS

Be a smart shopper and **compare all your options** before making decisions. A plane ticket bought with a promotional coupon from travel clubs, coupon books, and direct-mail offers or on the Internet may not be cheaper than the least expensive fare from a discount ticket agency. And always keep in mind that what you get is just as important as what you save.

DISCOUNT RESERVATIONS

To save money, **look into discount reservations services** with toll-free numbers, which use their buying power to get a better price on hotels, airline tickets, even car rentals. When booking a room, always **call the hotel's local toll-free number** (if one is available) rather than the central reservations number—you'll often get a better price. Always ask about special packages or corporate rates.

When shopping for the best deal on hotels and car rentals, **look for guaranteed exchange rates,** which protect you against a falling dollar. With your rate locked in, you won't pay more, even if the price goes up in the local currency.

➤ AIRLINE TICKETS: ☎ **800/AIR–4LESS.**

➤ HOTEL ROOMS: **Players Express Vacations** (☎ 800/458–6161, WEB www.playersexpress.com). **Travel Interlink** (☎ 800/888–5898, WEB www.travelinterlink.com). **Turbotrip.com** (☎ 800/473–7829, WEB www.turbotrip.com).

PACKAGE DEALS

Don't confuse packages and guided tours. When you buy a package, you travel on your own, just as though you had planned the trip yourself. Fly/drive packages, which combine airfare and car rental, are often a good deal.

ELECTRICITY

To use your electrical devices, **bring a converter and adapter.** East Africa uses the the 220/240-volt, 50-Hz electrical system. Sockets are usually the three-square-pin variety, although some hotels still have three-round-pin sockets. The power supply can be unpredictable, depending on the season, with outages during the rainy season and power rationing during droughts. Power surges are a common occurrence.

If your appliances are dual voltage, you'll need only an adapter. Don't use 110-volt outlets, marked FOR SHAVERS ONLY, for high-wattage appliances such as blow-dryers. Most laptops operate equally well on 110 and 220 volts and require only an adapter.

EMBASSIES

➤ AUSTRALIA: **Australian High Commission** (✉ ICIPE House, Riverside Dr., Nairobi, ☎ 02/445–0340).

➤ CANADA: **Canadian High Commission** (✉ Comcraft House, Haile Selassie Ave., Nairobi, ☎ 02/214–804; ✉ 38 Mirambo St., Dar es Salaam, ☎ 022/211–2831).

➤ UNITED KINGDOM: **British High Commission** (✉ Upper Hill Rd., Nairobi, ☎ 02/714–699; ✉ Social Security House, Samora Ave., Dar es Salaam, ☎ 022/211–7659).

➤ UNITED STATES: **Embassy of the United States of America** (✉ Mombasa Rd., Nairobi, ☎ 02/537–800; ✉ 140 Msese Rd., Dar es Salaam, ☎ 022/266–6010).

EMERGENCIES

In Kenya and Tanzania the emergency number for police, fire, and ambulance services is 999. Be aware that emergency workers could take a long time to respond. There are a number of private ambulance services in both countries.

Flying Doctors and AAR Health Services provide services outside the major urban areas in both Kenya and Tanzania.

In Kenya another option is calling the Kenya Tourism Federation's Safety and Communication Centre. The office was established to help tourists deal with situations ranging from illnesses to accidents.

➤ KENYA CONTACTS: **AAR Health Services** (☎ 02/717–374 or 02/717–375). **Flying Doctors** (☎ 02/501–280 or 02/502–699). **Safety and Communications Centre** (☎ 02/604–767).

➤ TANZANIA CONTACTS: **AAR Health Services** (☎ 022/213–0336 or 02/213–0340). **Flying Doctors** (☎ 022/211–6610).

ETIQUETTE & BEHAVIOR

East Africans, as a rule, are a reserved and religious people. You should **dress conservatively,** as wearing revealing clothing is considered very disrespectful. In Muslim areas, such as cities along the coast, women should cover their shoulders and knees, while men should avoid wearing shorts. Overt displays of affection between people of the opposite sex are frowned on.

If you are unhappy with something, **discuss your dissatisfaction calmly and clearly.** East Africans do not respond well to displays of anger, which often make people less inclined to help resolve a problem. There is a great respect for age in East Africa, where people consider it a great achievement to have experienced so much—being a grandmother is a greater honor than being a mother. To address a woman as Mama or Mzee indicates a respect for her age. East Africans are well known for their hospitality. If you are invited to visit someone's home, be careful not to eat before you go. You will be offered food no matter what time of the day you visit, and it would be an insult to turn it down.

BUSINESS ETIQUETTE

A greeting is very important in East Africa, where it is an elaborate interaction that sets the tone for the rest of the meeting. When meeting someone, shake hands and take time to inquire about the person's health and family. Even when dealing with phone operators, take a moment to greet them and ask how they are. Business cards are of great importance in East Africa, as they are a sign of status. Take care to **dress smartly when conducting business.** Men should wear suits, and women should wear business attire. If you invite a colleague for a meal, you should expect to pay.

GAY & LESBIAN TRAVEL

Homosexuality is illegal in Kenya and Tanzania, and penalties for homosexual acts are harsh. Kenya President Daniel Moi has been extremely outspoken about his hatred of gays, calling them a "scourge." Gay groups exist, but they keep a low profile. There are no gay bars or clubs in either country.

In practice you are unlikely to face any problems traveling as a same-sex couple, although you should be discreet and avoid any public demonstrations of affection.

➤ GAY- & LESBIAN-FRIENDLY TRAVEL AGENCIES: **Different Roads Travel** (✉ 8383 Wilshire Blvd., Suite 902, Beverly Hills, CA 90211, ☎ 323/651–5557 or 800/429–8747, FAX 323/651–3678, lgernert@tzell.com). **Kennedy Travel** (✉ 314 Jericho Turnpike, Floral Park, NY 11001, ☎ 516/352–4888 or 800/237–7433, FAX 516/354–8849, WEB www. kennedytravel.com). **Now Voyager** (✉ 4406 18th St., San Francisco, CA 94114, ☎ 415/626–1169 or 800/255–6951, FAX 415/626–8626, WEB www.nowvoyager.com). **Skylink Travel and Tour** (✉ 1006 Mendocino Ave., Santa Rosa, CA 95401, ☎ 707/546–9888 or 800/225–5759, FAX 707/546–9891, WEB www.skylinktravel. com), serving lesbian travelers.

HEALTH

Kenya has no legal requirement for any vaccinations to enter the country, although you will need to prove you've had a yellow fever inoculation if you are entering the country from an infected country. You will need a yellow fever inoculation to enter Tanzania.

FOOD & DRINK

Be careful about what you eat and drink. As in other developing countries around the world, you can reduce your chances of contracting traveler's diarrhea if you **stay away from salads** and **avoid fruit unless you can peel it yourself.** Avoid unpasteurized milk and dairy products as well as food that has been left sitting around at room temperature. It's a good idea to **stick to bottled water.** Make sure that you drink water from bottles where the seal has not been broken. Always **avoid ice** unless you know it was made with purified water.

MEDICAL PLANS

No one plans to get sick while traveling, but it happens, so **consider signing up with a medical-assistance company.** Members get doctor referrals, emergency evacuation or repatriation, hot lines for medical consultation, cash for emergencies, and other assistance.

➤ MEDICAL-ASSISTANCE COMPANIES: **International SOS Assistance** (WEB www.internationalsos.com; ✉ 8 Neshaminy Interplex, Suite 207, Trevose, PA 19053, ☎ 215/245–4707 or 800/523–6586, FAX 215/244–9617; ✉ 12 Chemin Riantbosson, 1217 Meyrin 1, Geneva, Switzerland, ☎ 4122/785–6464, FAX 4122/785–6424; ✉ 331 N. Bridge Rd., 17-00, Odeon Towers, Singapore 188720, ☎ 65/338–7800, FAX 65/338–7611).

OVER-THE-COUNTER REMEDIES

Over-the-counter pain relievers such as Tylenol and Panadol are readily available in pharmacies and supermarkets. Medications for traveler's diarrhea such as Pepto-Bismol and Immodium are available in most pharmacies. Chamomile tea is good for upset stomachs, but herbal teas are not always easy to find in East Africa. Bring a supply with you for such eventualities.

PESTS & OTHER HAZARDS

Malaria is common throughout most of East Africa. Consult a doctor at least one month before departure for the most up-to-date advice on malaria prophylactics. Taking antimalarial pills does not eliminate all risk because drug-resistant strains have developed in recent years. The best way to prevent malaria is to **avoid being bitten by mosquitoes.** In the evenings you should **cover your arms and legs** and **apply plenty of insect repellent.** Burning mosquito coils at night also helps to ward off mosquitoes; coils can be purchased everywhere. Always sleep under a mosquito net.

Do **avoid swimming in stagnant water,** as lakes and ponds are often infected with schistomiasis, a disease carried by parasites that burrow into your skin. If you have been in water that is doubtful, dry yourself off vigorously so as to dislodge any parasites before they can burrow into your skin.

The region has a high incidence of sexually transmitted diseases, including a penicillin-resistant strain of gonorrhea. East African countries have a high incidence of AIDS. The major modes of transmission are sexual intercourse, dirty syringes, and blood transfusions using contaminated equipment. If you need an injection, have the new syringe unwrapped in front of you. If you need a blood transfusion, consult your embassy. Most keep lists of recommended hospitals.

The sun in East Africa is strong and can burn surprisingly quickly, even on a cloudy day. Always use a good sunscreen, wear a hat, and cover areas of your body that are not normally exposed to the sun. Be particularly careful with children. Prevent heat exhaustion by drinking plenty of water. Most people need to drink at least 2 liters of water per day.

You run the possibility of altitude sickness when you venture to higher elevations. Symptoms, which usually develop within 24 hours, include headaches, fatigue, dizziness, and loss of appetite. The best way to deal with mild symptoms is to rest at the same altitude until you feel better. If symptoms persist or become worse, you should descend to a lower altitude.

SHOTS & MEDICATIONS

The U.S. Centers for Disease Control and Prevention recommends that travelers to East Africa be immunized for hepatitis A and B, typhoid, and yellow fever. You also need a booster for tetanus-diphtheria, measles, and polio. If you will have contact with animals, it also recommends a rabies vaccination. For the latest information check out the organization's Web site.

➤ HEALTH WARNINGS: **National Centers for Disease Control and Prevention** (CDC; National Center for Infectious Diseases, Division of Quarantine, Traveler's Health Section, ✉ 1600 Clifton Rd. NE, M/S E-03, Atlanta, GA 30333, ☎ 888/ 232–3228 or 877/394–8747, ℻ 888/ 232–3299, 🌐 www.cdc.gov).

INSURANCE

The most useful travel-insurance plan is a comprehensive policy that includes coverage for trip cancellation and interruption, default, trip delay, and medical expenses (with a waiver for preexisting conditions).

Without insurance you will lose all or most of your money if you cancel your trip, regardless of the reason. Default insurance covers you if your tour operator, airline, or cruise line goes out of business. Trip-delay covers expenses that arise because of bad weather or mechanical delays. Study the fine print when comparing policies.

If you're traveling internationally, a key component of travel insurance is coverage for medical bills incurred if you get sick on the road. Such expenses are not generally covered by Medicare or private policies. U.K. residents can buy a travel-insurance policy valid for most vacations taken during the year in which it's purchased (but check preexisting-condition coverage). British and Australian citizens need extra medical coverage when traveling overseas. British citizens need extra medical coverage when traveling abroad. Australian citizens need extra medical coverage when traveling abroad.

Always **buy travel policies directly from the insurance company**; if you buy them from a cruise line, airline, or tour operator that goes out of business, you probably will not be covered for the agency or operator's default, a major risk. Before making any purchase, **review your existing health and home-owner's policies** to find what they cover away from home.

➤ TRAVEL INSURERS: In the U.S.: **Access America** (✉ 6600 W. Broad St., Richmond, VA 23230, ☎ 800/284–8300, ⨳ 804/673–1491, ⟦WEB⟧ www.etravelprotection.com), **Travel Guard International** (✉ 1145 Clark St., Stevens Point, WI 54481, ☎ 715/345–0505 or 800/826–1300, ⨳ 800/955–8785, ⟦WEB⟧ www.travelguard.com).

➤ INSURANCE INFORMATION: In the U.K.: **Association of British Insurers** (✉ 51–55 Gresham St., London EC2V 7HQ, U.K., ☎ 020/7600–3333, ⨳ 020/7696–8999, ⟦WEB⟧ www.abi.org.uk). In Canada: **RBC Travel Insurance** (✉ 6880 Financial Dr., Mississauga, Ontario L5N 7Y5, Canada, ☎ 905/791–8700, 800/668–4342 in Canada, ⨳ 905/816–2498, ⟦WEB⟧ www.royalbank.com). In Australia: **Insurance Council of Australia** (✉ Level 3, 56 Pitt St., Sydney NSW 2000, ☎ 02/9253–5100, ⨳ 02/9253–5111, ⟦WEB⟧ www.ica.com.au). In New Zealand: **Insurance Council of New Zealand** (✉ Level 7, 111–115 Customhouse Quay, Box 474, Wellington, New Zealand, ☎ 04/472–5230, ⨳ 04/473–3011, ⟦WEB⟧ www.icnz.org.nz).

LANGUAGE

English and Swahili are the official languages of both Kenya and Tanzania. More than 40 other tribal languages are spoken in Kenya, while more than 120 other languages can be heard in Tanzania. Most East Africans are multilingual, learning their local language as youngsters and adding Swahili, English, and sometimes other languages as they progress through school. English is spoken in the cities and national parks, but Swahili is prevalent in rural areas. Swahili is relatively easy to pronounce, and verbs need not be conjugated for people to understand your meaning. A simple phrasebook comes in handy, especially for negotiating prices. Throughout Kenya and Tanzania locals greatly appreciate any efforts to communicate in Swahili or local languages.

LODGING

The lodgings we list are the cream of the crop in each price category. We always list the facilities that are available—but we don't specify whether they cost extra: when pricing accommodations, always ask what's included and what costs extra.

Assume that hotels operate on the **European Plan** (EP, with no meals) unless we specify that they use either the **Continental Plan** (CP, with a Continental breakfast), **Breakfast Plan** (BP, with a full breakfast) or the **Modified American Plan** (MAP, with breakfast and dinner) or are **all-inclusive** (including all meals and most activities).

APARTMENT & VILLA RENTALS

If you want a home base that's roomy enough for a family and comes with cooking facilities, **consider a furnished rental.** These can save you money, especially if you're traveling with a group. Home-exchange directories sometimes list rentals as well as exchanges.

➤ INTERNATIONAL AGENTS: **Villas International** (✉ 950 Northgate Dr., Suite 206, San Rafael, CA 94903, ☎ 415/499–9490 or 800/221–2260, ⨳ 415/499–9491, ⟦WEB⟧ www.villasintl.com).

HOSTELS

No matter what your age, you can **save on lodging costs by staying at hostels.** In some 4,500 locations in more than 70 countries around the world, Hostelling International (HI), the umbrella group for a number of national youth-hostel associations, offers single-sex, dorm-style beds, and, at many hostels, rooms for couples and family accommodations. Membership in any HI national hostel association, open to travelers of all ages, allows you to stay in HI-affiliated hostels at member rates; one-year membership is about $25 for adults (C$26.75 in Canada, £9.30 in the U.K., $30 in Australia, and $30 in New Zealand); hostels run about $10–$25 per night. Members have priority if the hostel is full; they're also eligible for discounts around the world, even on rail and bus travel in some countries.

➤ ORGANIZATIONS: **Hostelling International—American Youth Hostels** (✉ 733 15th St. NW, Suite 840, Washington, DC 20005, ☎ 202/783–6161, FAX 202/783–6171, WEB www.hiayh.org). **Hostelling International—Canada** (✉ 400–205 Catherine St., Ottawa, Ontario K2P 1C3, Canada, ☎ 613/237–7884; 800/663–5777 in Canada, FAX 613/237–7868, WEB www.hostellingintl.ca). **Youth Hostel Association of England and Wales** (✉ Trevelyan House, 8 St. Stephen's Hill, St. Albans, Hertfordshire AL1 2DY, U.K., ☎ 0870/8708808, FAX 01727/844126, WEB www.yha.org.uk). **Youth Hostel Association Australia** (✉ 10 Mallett St., Camperdown, NSW 2050, Australia, ☎ 02/9565–1699, FAX 02/9565–1325, WEB www.yha.com.au). **Youth Hostels Association of New Zealand** (✉ Level 3, 193 Cashel St., Box 436, Christchurch, New Zealand, ☎ 03/379–9970, FAX 03/365–4476, WEB www.yha.org.nz).

HOTELS

East African hotels range from luxurious (the Mount Kenya Safari Club offers sunken bathtubs) to spartan. Major hotel chains are well represented in Kenya and Tanzania, including Hilton, Holiday Inn, and Inter-Continental. There are also a number of good-quality African chains represented in both countries, including Block, Lonrho, and Sarova. Each city has a number of clean, safe hotels that are perfect for families or people on a tight budget. They usually offer family rates, children's meals, and an army of baby-sitters. Most hotel rates cover the room only, but some include breakfast.

➤ TOLL-FREE NUMBERS: **Best Western** (☎ 800/528–1234, WEB www.bestwestern.com). **Choice** (☎ 800/221–2222, WEB www.choicehotels.com). **Days Inn** (☎ 800/325–2525, WEB www.daysinn.com). **Holiday Inn** (☎ 800/465–4329, WEB www.basshotels.com). **Inter-Continental** (☎ 800/327–0200, WEB www.interconti.com). **Radisson** (☎ 800/333–3333, WEB www.radisson.com).

Sheraton (☎ 800/325–3535, WEB www.starwoodhotels.com).

PRIVATE HOMES

There are a number of companies that rent private homes throughout the country. Kenya Wildlife Services and Home from Home have a wide range of houses around the country that are quite a bargain.

➤ BOOKING AGENTS: **Home from Home** (✉ Box 15097, Nairobi, ☎ 02/891314, WEB www.kenyasafarihomes.com). **Kenya Wildlife Services** (✉ Box 40241, Nairobi, ☎ 02/501–081, WEB www.kws.org).

TENTED CAMPS

Several companies offer luxury tented safaris. These may consist of permanent large tents with concrete floors and adjoining baths or tents set up for the duration of your stay. Prices vary widely according to the amenities you desire.

➤ OPERATORS: **On Safari** (✉ Box 42562, Nairobi, ☎ 02/890–4540). **Specialised Safaris** (✉ Box 15565, Nairobi, ☎ 0733/609–862).

MAIL & SHIPPING

The mail system in Kenya and Tanzania is not particularly reliable. Although letters generally do not go astray, they can take up to two weeks to reach their destinations abroad. Mail sent to Kenya and Tanzania can take anywhere from four days to a week to arrive.

OVERNIGHT SERVICES

There are a number of reliable courier services available in Nairobi, Mombasa, and Dar es Salaam. DHL, Federal Express, and the United Parcel Service offer daily service. It generally takes 2–3 working days for a parcel to reach overseas destinations.

RECEIVING MAIL

You can receive mail through the poste restante in any town that has a post office. This is generally a reliable method of receiving letters and packages, although you should ask anyone sending you a letter to address clearly in block capitals and to underline your surname. An alternative for American Express clients is to have mail sent to its offices in Nairobi and Mombasa.

➤ CONTACTS: **American Express** (✉ Client Mail Service, Express Travel Group, Box 40433, Nairobi 00100).

MEDIA

East Africa has a well-established and active media. You will find easy access to English-language books, newspapers, and television and radio programs.

NEWSPAPERS & MAGAZINES

Kenya has two good-quality English-language dailies, the *Daily Nation* and the *Standard*. The *East African* is a quality weekly covering the region. Tanzania produces the *Daily News*. Foreign newspapers are widely available in urban areas, while current-affairs magazines such as *Time* and *Newsweek* can also be found in select bookstores.

RADIO & TELEVISION

The Kenyan Broadcasting Corporation has radio transmissions in English throughout the country. In Nairobi and Mombasa you can pick up the Capital FM and Kiss FM music stations. BBC World Service, Voice of America, and Radio Deutsche Welle also transmit English-language programs. Program listings are published in the daily papers.

There are four television channels available in Kenya—KBC, KBC2, KTN, and STV. Many programs are imported from the United States, Europe, and Australia. Some establishments also subscribe to M-Net cable from South Africa, which offers CNN and a variety of sports and movie channels.

Radio Tanzania broadcasts in English as well as Swahili. Local stations broadcast mostly in Swahili.

MONEY MATTERS

Both Kenya and Tanzania are relatively inexpensive for travelers because of the weakness of the local currencies. Because of this, you will generally find that restaurants and hotels cost considerably less than at home. Many upscale hotels, however, charge about as much as similar establishments abroad.

All the admission prices quoted in this book are for adults, and you will generally find substantially reduced rates for children. Prices quoted throughout the book are in local currency where possible. For information on taxes, *see* Taxes, *below.*

ATMS

Before leaving home, **make sure your credit cards can be used in East Africa.** Your bank card may not work or may access only your checking account. Do **ask your bank about a debit card,** which works like a bank card but can be used at any ATM displaying a MasterCard or Visa logo.

Barclays Bank has an extensive network of ATMs that accept Master-Card and Visa. ATMs operated by Standard Chartered Bank accept Visa. You will be hard-pressed to find ATMs outside major towns in either Kenya or Tanzania. ATMs are usually reliable, although they are dependent on the poor telephone system. Withdraw enough cash so that you won't be in trouble if the phone service is interrupted.

CREDIT CARDS

Credit cards are accepted in the upscale hotels and restaurants. Most charge you a commission of between 5% and 15% on any credit-card transaction.

Throughout this guide, the following abbreviations are used: **AE,** American Express; **DC,** Diners Club; **MC,** MasterCard; and **V,** Visa.

CURRENCY

In Kenya the currency is the Kenya shilling (Ksh). Bills are printed in 1,000-, 500-, 200-, 100-, and 50-shilling denominations. Coins are minted in 20-, 10-, 5-, and 1-shilling units.

The currency in Tanzania is the Tanzania shilling (Tsh). The bills are in 10,000-, 5,000-, 1,000-, 200-, and 100-shilling denominations. Coins are minted in 200-, 100-, 50-, 20-, 10-, 5-, and 1-shilling units.

CURRENCY EXCHANGE

For the most favorable rates, **change money through banks.** Although ATM transaction fees may be higher abroad than at home, ATM rates are excellent because they are based on wholesale rates offered only by major banks. You won't do as well at exchange booths in airports or rail and bus stations, in hotels, in restaurants, or in stores. To avoid lines at airport exchange booths, **get a bit of local currency before you leave home.**

➤ EXCHANGE SERVICES: **International Currency Express** (☎ 888/278–6628 for orders, WEB www.foreignmoney. com). **Thomas Cook Currency Services** (☎ 800/287–7362 for telephone orders and retail locations, WEB www. us.thomascook.com).

TRAVELER'S CHECKS

Traveler's checks are widely accepted in major banks and exchange offices. If you are heading to rural areas, it is wise to take cash. If you are taking traveler's checks on your trip, you should take those issued in U.S. dollars, which are accepted everywhere. The most commonly accepted traveler's checks are Thomas Cook, American Express, and those issued through major banks such as Citibank and Bank of America. Lost or stolen checks can usually be replaced within a day, if not immediately.

PACKING

Don't overload yourself with baggage—you can easily get clothes laundered and pressed throughout East Africa. Take a large suitcase that you can leave in your hotel and a smaller bag that you can use for short safaris. On safari you are best off with lightweight clothing, although not necessarily a safari suit, which immediately labels you as a tourist. If you are traveling to the highlands, you will need a warm pair of trousers and a thick sweater, as the evenings can get pretty cold. Some restaurants require men to wear a jacket and tie for dinner, so bring along clothes for such an occasion. Corporate travelers should bring appropriate clothing, as people conducting business in East Africa wear suits.

The sun is strong, so make sure to **pack a good pair of sunglasses and a sturdy hat.** Bring along all the toiletries and cosmetics you will need, as

they may be hard to find in East Africa. If you are traveling with small children, bring your own supply of diapers and baby formula, as these items can be pricey. You should also bring child-friendly insect repellent and sunscreen, as you are unlikely to find them in East Africa. Bring an adapter if you are traveling with electrical appliances such as shavers, hair dryers, or laptop computers.

In your carry-on luggage, **pack an extra pair of eyeglasses or contact lenses and enough of any medication** you take to last the entire trip. You may also ask your doctor to write a spare prescription using the drug's generic name, since brand names may vary from country to country. In luggage to be checked, **never pack prescription drugs or valuables.** To avoid customs delays, carry medications in their original packaging. And don't forget to carry with you the addresses of offices that handle refunds of lost traveler's checks. Check *Fodor's How to Pack* (available in bookstores everywhere) for more tips.

CHECKING LUGGAGE

You are allowed one carry-on bag and one personal article, such as a purse or a laptop computer. Make sure that everything you carry aboard will fit under your seat or in the overhead bin. Get to the gate early, so you can board as soon as possible, before the overhead bins fill up.

If you are flying internationally, note that baggage allowances may be determined not by piece but by weight—generally 88 pounds (40 kilograms) in first class, 66 pounds (30 kilograms) in business class, and 44 pounds (20 kilograms) in economy.

Airline liability for baggage is limited to $1,250 per person on flights within the United States. On international flights it amounts to $9.07 per pound or $20 per kilogram for checked baggage (roughly $640 per 70-pound bag) and $400 per passenger for unchecked baggage. You can buy additional coverage at check-in for about $10 per $1,000 of coverage, but it excludes a rather extensive list of items, shown on your airline ticket.

Before departure, **itemize your bags' contents** and their worth, and label the bags with your name, address, and phone number. (If you use your home address, cover it so potential thieves can't see it readily.) Inside each bag, **pack a copy of your itinerary.** At check-in, **make sure that each bag is correctly tagged** with the destination airport's three-letter code. If your bags arrive damaged or fail to arrive at all, file a written report with the airline before leaving the airport.

PASSPORTS & VISAS

When traveling internationally, **carry your passport** even if you don't need one (it's always the best form of I.D.) and **make two photocopies of the data page** (one for someone at home and another for you, carried separately from your passport). If you lose your passport, promptly call the nearest embassy or consulate and the local police.

ENTERING KENYA

Travelers from the United States, Canada, the United Kingdom, Australia, and New Zealand require tourist visas for their visit to Kenya. A three-month single-entry visa costs $50, while a multiple-entry visa valid for a year costs $100. You can purchase a visa at the airport when you arrive, but it is advisable to secure one before you leave. Check on visa requirements before you depart, as regulations are subject to change.

ENTERING TANZANIA

Travelers from the United States, Canada, the United Kingdom, Australia, and New Zealand require tourist visas for their visit to Tanzania. A three-month single-entry tourist visa costs $50. You can purchase your visa on arrival in Tanzania, but it is advisable to get one before you leave. Check on visa requirements before your trip, as regulations are subject to change. You will need a valid yellow fever vaccination certificate if you plan to visit Zanzibar.

PASSPORT OFFICES

The best time to apply for a passport or to renew is in fall and winter. Before any trip, check your passport's expiration date, and, if necessary, renew it as soon as possible.

➤ AUSTRALIAN CITIZENS: **Australian Passport Office** (☎ 131–232, WEB www.dfat.gov.au/passports).

➤ CANADIAN CITIZENS: **Passport Office** (☎ 819/994–3500; 800/567–6868 in Canada, WEB www.dfait-maeci.gc.ca/passport).

➤ NEW ZEALAND CITIZENS: **New Zealand Passport Office** (☎ 04/494–0700, WEB www.passports.govt.nz).

➤ U.K. CITIZENS: **London Passport Office** (☎ 0870/521–0410, WEB www.ukpa.gov.uk) for fees and documentation requirements and to request an emergency passport.

➤ U.S. CITIZENS: **National Passport Information Center** (☎ 900/225–5674; calls are 35¢ per minute for automated service, $1.05 per minute for operator service; WEB www.travel.state.gov/npicinfo.html).

REST ROOMS

You will find that most rest rooms sport modern flush toilets, although some of the tented camps may offer comfortable "long-drops" (pit latrines). As a rule, you will find public rest rooms are a rarity in most parts of East Africa; and when you find one, it probably won't be very hygienic. If you are in a town, you are best off using the rest room at your hotel.

SAFETY

Street crime is an unfortunate reality in East Africa, although it is more prevalent in urban centers and tourist areas. It ranges from purse snatchings to armed robbery. Be smart and take sensible precautions. Wherever you go, **don't wear expensive clothing, avoid flashy jewelry,** and **never handle money in public places.** It's a good idea to keep your money in a pocket rather than a wallet, which is easier to steal. On buses and in crowded areas, **hold handbags close to the body;** thieves use knives to slice the bottom of a bag and catch the contents as they fall out. **Keep cameras in a secure camera bag,** preferably one with a chain or wire embedded in the strap. Always remain alert for pickpockets, and **don't** walk alone at night, especially in the larger cities. When driving, keep your windows rolled up enough so that thieves don't try to snatch your valuables as you sit in traffic. Always make sure your doors are locked. Do not give a lift to anyone you do not know, even pregnant women or people carrying fuel containers who claim to have broken down.

Before your trip, check with the U.S. State Department (☎ 202/647–5225, travel.state.gov) to see if there are any current advisories about the country you are planning to visit.

WOMEN IN EAST AFRICA

It is not usual for traveling in East Africa to experience extreme sexual harassment. If you do experience harassment, sexual or otherwise, it is best to ignore it. If this fails, state your feelings clearly, calmly, and politely. Avoid walking alone at night, particularly in cities. In more remote areas avoid visiting isolated places where you will be unable to get help.

SENIOR-CITIZEN TRAVEL

To qualify for age-related discounts, mention your senior-citizen status up front when booking hotel reservations (not when checking out) and before you're seated in restaurants (not when paying the bill). When renting a car, ask about promotional car-rental discounts, which can be cheaper than senior-citizen rates.

➤ EDUCATIONAL PROGRAMS: Elderhostel (⊠ 11 Ave. de Lafayette, Boston, MA 02111-1746, ☎ 877/426–8056, FAX 877/426–2166, WEB www.elderhostel.org). Interhostel (⊠ University of New Hampshire, 6 Garrison Ave., Durham, NH 03824, ☎ 603/862–1147 or 800/733–9753, FAX 603/862–1113, WEB www.learn.unh.edu).

SHOPPING

An impressive array of handicrafts can be found throughout East Africa—from traditional baskets to hand-painted beads, from stone carvings to brightly colored sarongs, from paintings to jewelry crafted from precious and semiprecious stones. All of these can be found in department stores, lodge boutiques, and markets throughout the region.

Shops have set prices, although if you are purchasing in large quantities, you may be able to negotiate a discount. Vendors on the streets and market stalls will expect you to bargain, so the first price they quote is anywhere from 70% to 100% more than their lowest price.

SMART SOUVENIRS

There are so many innovative handicrafts in East Africa that you are bound to find some beautiful souvenirs of your trip. Some of the more unusual gifts include colorful Tingatinga paintings and tanzanite gemstones from Tanzania. China plates, ostensibly rescued from the wrecks of ships that plied the trade routes to the East, are abundant in Zanzibar and make for unusual and interesting purchases. In Kenya the glassware produced at the Kitengela Glass Factory is fragile to transport but well worth the effort. The items range from large jugs to tiny beads. The soapstone carvings produced in Kenya are easier to travel with and are a great buy. Beautiful handmade photo albums are expensive but very special.

WATCH OUT

Be wary if you are hoping to buy authentic African relics such as masks and tribal gear. These are sold at exorbitant prices, and unless you can spot a fake, you may end up with an overpriced curio. "Ebony" carvings may well have been finished off with a layer of black shoe polish. Real ebony is heavy, and the black cannot be scratched off.

It is illegal to sell objects made from any part of a bird or animal, such as elephant hair bracelets. If you are approached by anyone on the street offering such items, remember that if you buy one, you might get hit with a stiff fine. Also illegal are items made from seashells, ivory, and turtle shells.

SIGHTSEEING GUIDES

The Kenya Professional Safari Guides Association was recently established with the assistance of Kenya Wildlife Service. The organization aims to provide certification to individuals working in the safari business, from drivers to expert guides.

➤ CONTACT: **Kenya Professional Safari Guides Association** (✉ KWS Complex, Langata Rd., Nairobi, ☎ 02/609–355, FAX 02/609–365).

STUDENTS IN KENYA
AND TANZANIA

➤ IDs & SERVICES: **Council Travel** (CIEE; ✉ 205 E. 42nd St., 15th floor, New York, NY 10017, ☎ 212/822–2700 or 888/268–6245, FAX 212/822–2699, WEB www.councilexchanges.org) for mail orders only, in the U.S. **Travel Cuts** (✉ 187 College St., Toronto, Ontario M5T 1P7, Canada, ☎ 416/979–2406 or 800/667–2887 in Canada, FAX 416/979–8167, WEB www.travelcuts.com).

TAXES

In Kenya and Tanzania a $20 tax is charged for an international flight. This tax is usually included in the cost of your ticket.

A value-added tax of 18% is charged on meals and drinks taken in restaurants in Kenya. A surcharge of 20% is added to restaurant and hotel bills in Tanzania.

TELEPHONES

The phone system in East Africa does work, but it can take a few attempts before your local or international call goes through. Most exchanges are on a direct-dial system, although some remote areas still use operators. Public phones operated by phone cards are common and more reliable than coin-operated phones. There is a burgeoning mobile phone industry in both Tanzania and Kenya, although calls on these networks tend to be expensive.

COUNTRY & AREA CODES

In Kenya the country code is 254; in Tanzania it is 255. When calling from outside the country, drop the "0" from the beginning of the area code.

DIRECTORY & OPERATOR ASSISTANCE

In Kenya, for a local operator dial 900; for an international operator dial 0195 or 0196; for local directory

assistance dial 991 or 992. In Tanzania you can reach a local operator by dialing 991; for an international operator dial 0900.

TIME

East Africa local time is three hours ahead of Greenwich mean time. That makes it eight hours ahead of eastern standard time (seven hours ahead during daylight saving time).

TIPPING

Many restaurants in East Africa include a service charge on their bill. If you wish to provide an addition tip for the waitstaff, 10% of the bill should be adequate. Drivers on safari should be tipped well, especially if you have spent several days with them and they have shown you all the animals you wanted to see. You should tip fishermen who take you snorkeling at the coast, children who help push your car out of the mud, and anyone else who has performed a small but appreciated service.

TOURS & PACKAGES

Because everything is prearranged on a prepackaged tour or independent vacation, you spend less time planning—and often get it all at a good price.

BOOKING WITH AN AGENT

Travel agents are excellent resources. But it's a good idea to collect brochures from several agencies as some agents' suggestions may be influenced by relationships with tour and package firms that reward them for volume sales. If you have a special interest, **find an agent with expertise in that area**; the American Society of Travel Agents (ASTA; ☞ Travel Agencies, *below*) has a database of specialists worldwide.

Make sure your travel agent knows the accommodations and other services of the place being recommended. Ask about the hotel's location, room size, beds, and whether it has a pool, room service, or programs for children, if you care about these. Has your agent been there in person or sent others whom you can contact?

Do some homework on your own, too: local tourism boards can provide information about lesser-known and small-niche operators, some of which may sell only direct.

BUYER BEWARE

Each year consumers are stranded or lose their money when tour operators—even large ones with excellent reputations—go out of business. So **check out the operator.** Ask several travel agents about its reputation, and try to **book with a company that has a consumer-protection program.** (Look for information in the company's brochure.) In the United States, members of the National Tour Association and the United States Tour Operators Association are required to set aside funds to cover your payments and travel arrangements in the event that the company defaults. It's also a good idea to choose a company that participates in the American Society of Travel Agents' Tour Operator Program (TOP); ASTA will act as mediator in any disputes between you and your tour operator.

Remember that the more your package or tour includes the better you can predict the ultimate cost of your vacation. Make sure you know exactly what is covered, and **beware of hidden costs.** Are taxes, tips, and transfers included? Entertainment and excursions? These can add up.

➤ TOUR-OPERATOR RECOMMENDATIONS: **American Society of Travel Agents** (☞ Travel Agencies, *below*). **National Tour Association** (NTA; ✉ 546 E. Main St., Lexington, KY 40508, ☎ 859/226–4444 or 800/682–8886, WEB www.ntaonline.com). **United States Tour Operators Association** (USTOA; ✉ 342 Madison Ave., Suite 1522, New York, NY 10173, ☎ 212/599–6599 or 800/468–7862, FAX 212/599–6744, WEB www.ustoa.com).

TRAIN TRAVEL

The overnight train between Nairobi and Mombasa is a relaxing experience. All first- and second-class compartments convert to sleepers, and meals in the dining room are a part of the atmosphere. The train is not air-conditioned, but the high altitude keeps the train cool until it reaches the coast, early the next morning. Passengers sometimes spot wild animals as the train crosses the Athi Plains.

CLASSES

The overnight train offers first-, second-, and third-class options. A third-class seat means sitting on a wooden bench in a crowded compartment all night. Second-class compartments sleep four people and are just as comfortable as the first-class compartments that sleep two. Sexes are separated unless you book the entire compartment. If you are traveling in a party of four, you can open the door between adjoining first-class compartments. You cannot lock the door of your compartment when you leave for meals, so do not leave valuables inside. Bedding and meals are included in the price of your first- and second-class tickets.

FARES & SCHEDULES

The train leaves Nairobi on Monday, Wednesday, and Friday at 7 PM and is scheduled to arrive at 8:30 AM. The return train leaves Mombasa on Tuesday, Thursday, and Sunday at 7 PM and arrives in Nairobi at 9:25 AM. Trains have been known to arrive up to seven hours late. Tickets can be purchased either in Mombasa or Nairobi.

➤ TRAIN INFORMATION: **Kenya Railways Corporation** (✉ Box 30121, Nairobi, ☎ 02/221–211, FAX 02/340–049).

RESERVATIONS

You must book ahead of time for both first- and second-class tickets. Usually two to three days in advance is sufficient, although during peak travel times such as Christmas it is advisable to book a month or more in advance. Compartment numbers are posted on a notice board about 30 minutes prior to departure.

TRANSPORTATION AROUND KENYA & TANZANIA

Both Kenya and Tanzania are big countries, so you can expect to cover great distances while traveling through them. For speed and convenience, flying between cities is a great idea. Both countries are served by a reliable internal flight industry that serves all the major tourist destinations. For those who have the time and inclination, driving is also a good way to get around, as you have greater freedom to head to less well-traveled areas.

Trains connect only a few destinations, so they are seldom a good option unless you want to experience what is left of the region's once-legendary rail system. Buses, generally overcrowded and uncomfortable, are seldom a pleasant means of transportation. In the larger cities, take taxis between destinations, especially at night.

TRAVEL AGENCIES

A good travel agent puts your needs first. Look for an agency that has been in business at least five years, emphasizes customer service, and has someone on staff who specializes in your destination. In addition, **make sure the agency belongs to a professional trade organization.** The American Society of Travel Agents (ASTA)—the largest and most influential in the field with more than 26,000 members in some 170 countries—maintains and enforces a strict code of ethics and will step in to help mediate any agent-client disputes if necessary. ASTA (whose motto is "Without a travel agent, you're on your own") also maintains a Web site that includes a directory of agents. (If a travel agency is also acting as your tour operator, *see* Buyer Beware *in* Tours & Packages, *above.*)

➤ LOCAL AGENT REFERRALS: **American Society of Travel Agents** (ASTA; ✉ 1101 King St., Suite 200, Alexandria, VA 22314 ☎ 800/965–2782 24-hr hot line, FAX 703/739–7642, WEB www.astanet.com). **Association of British Travel Agents** (✉ 68–71 Newman St., London W1T 3AH, U.K., ☎ 020/7637–2444, FAX 020/7637–0713, WEB www.abtanet.com). **Association of Canadian Travel Agents** (✉ 130 Albert St., Suite 1705, Ottawa, Ontario K1P 5G4, Canada, ☎ 613/237–3657, FAX 613/237–7052,

WEB www.acta.net). **Australian Federation of Travel Agents** (✉ Level 3, 309 Pitt St., Sydney NSW 2000, Australia, ☎ 02/9264–3299, FAX 02/9264–1085, WEB www.afta.com.au). **Travel Agents' Association of New Zealand** (✉ Level 5, Paxus House, 79 Boulcott St., Box 1888, Wellington 10033, New Zealand, ☎ 04/499–0104, FAX 04/499–0827, WEB www.taanz.org.nz).

VISITOR INFORMATION

KENYA

➤ KENYA TOURIST OFFICES: **United Kingdom** (✉ 25 Brook's Mews, Mayfair, London, W1Y IIG, ☎ 020/7355–3144). **United States** (✉ 424 Madison Ave., New York, NY 10017, ☎ 212/486–1300; ✉ 9150 Wilshire Blvd., Suite 160, Beverley Hills, CA 90212, ☎ 213/274–6635).

TANZANIA

➤ TANZANIA HIGH COMMISSION: **United Kingdom** (✉ 43 Hertford St., London, W1Y 8DB, ☎ 020/7499–8951). **United States** (✉ 2139 R St. NW, Washington, DC 20008, ☎ 202/939–6125; ✉ 205 E. 42nd St., New York, NY 10017, ☎ 212/972–9160).

➤ U.S. GOVERNMENT ADVISORIES: **U.S. Department of State** (✉ Overseas Citizens Services Office, Room 4811 N.S., 2201 C St. NW, Washington, DC 20520, ☎ 202/647–5225 for interactive hot line; 301/946–4400 for computer bulletin board, FAX 202/647–3000 for interactive hot line); enclose a self-addressed, stamped business-size envelope.

WEB SITES

Do **check out the World Wide Web** when you're planning your trip. You'll find everything from up-to-date weather forecasts to virtual tours of famous cities. Fodor's Web site, www.fodors.com, is a great place to start your on-line travels.

Web sites such as www.africaonline.com have excellent information about the region. To research Kenya, a good resource is www.kenyaweb.com. For information on Tanzania, try www.tanzania-web.com. For specific information about Zanzibar, log onto www.tanzania-web.com and www.allaboutzanzibar.com.

WHEN TO GO

The tourist year in East Africa is divided into low and high seasons. High season runs from December through March and from June through August. Low season runs from April through May and from September through November. During low season most tour operators offer more reasonable rates. The high season is an expensive time to visit, and beds are at a premium, especially in the lodges.

The weather in East Africa is pleasant throughout the year, with the seasons differentiated mainly by the amount of rainfall. The "long rains" generally fall from April through May and the "short rains" from October through November. During the long rains roads can turn into muddy tracks or wash away completely. Sometimes roads are closed in the national parks in more mountainous areas.

During the short rains it seldom pours all day; after a brief shower the rest of the day is often sunny. Many experienced travelers prefer to visit East Africa during the short rains. The landscape is more spectacular—vivid blooms among the deep green foliage along with dramatic skies make for an interesting backdrop for photography.

In southern Tanzania the rainy seasons vary a bit because of the winds from the Indian Ocean. In the Selous Game Reserve, for example, the weather is usually dry until the end of October; January is wet, and July is spectacular.

Another factor to consider in planning when to take a trip to the region is the timing of the migrations of animals. The most photogenic migration, with up to 1.5 million wildebeest crossing from the Maasai Mara into the Tanzanian Serengeti, takes place from mid-August to the end of September.

CLIMATE

The following are average daily maximum and minimum temperatures for cities in Kenya and Tanzania.

MOMBASA, KENYA

Jan.	87F	31C	May	83F	28C	Sept.	82F	28C
	75	24		74	23		72	22
Feb.	87F	31C	June	82F	28C	Oct.	84F	29C
	76	24		73	23		74	23
Mar.	88F	31C	July	81F	27C	Nov.	85F	29C
	77	25		71	22		75	24
Apr.	86F	30C	Aug.	81F	27C	Dec.	86F	30C
	76	24		71	22		75	24

NAIROBI, KENYA

Jan.	77F	25C	May	72F	22C	Sept.	75F	24C
	54	12		56	13		52	11
Feb.	79F	26C	June	70F	21C	Oct.	76F	24C
	55	13		53	12		55	13
Mar.	77F	25C	July	69F	21C	Nov.	74F	23C
	57	14		51	11		56	13
Apr.	75F	24C	Aug.	70F	21C	Dec.	74F	23C
	58	14		52	11		55	13

ARUSHA, TANZANIA

Jan.	84F	29C	May	72F	22C	Sept.	76F	24C
	50	10		52	11		47	8
Feb.	84F	29C	June	70	21C	Oct.	80F	27C
	51	11		48	9		51	11
Mar.	81F	27C	July	69F	21C	Nov.	81F	27C
	53	12		49	9		51	11
Apr.	77F	25C	Aug.	72F	22C	Dec.	81F	27C
	57	14		48	9		50	10

DAR ES SALAAM, TANZANIA

Jan.	87F	31C	May	85F	29C	Sept.	83F	28C
	77	25		71	22		67	19
Feb.	88F	31C	June	84F	29C	Oct.	85F	29C
	77	25		68	20		69	21
Mar.	88F	31C	July	83F	28C	Nov.	86F	30C
	75	24		66	19		72	22
Apr.	86F	30C	Aug.	83F	28C	Dec.	87F	31C
	73	23		66	19		75	24

FESTIVALS AND SEASONAL EVENTS

➤ JAN.: Held on Jan. 12, **Zanzibar Independence Day** marks the anniversary of when the island gained its independence from Great Britain in 1964.

➤ FEB.: A 1967 pledge by government officials to protect "human dignity and social equality" is remembered in Tanzania on February 5 during a holiday called **Arusha Declaration Day.** The **Eldoret Agricultural Show** shows off the best of local farmers. Similar events are held around Kenya the rest of the year.

➤ APR.: Celebrated in Tanzania on Apr. 26, **Union Day** marks the alliance of Tanganyika and Zanzibar.

➤ MAY: On **International Labour Day,** held May 1, working people march through the streets of Dar es Salaam and other large cities in Tanzania. Marking the birth of Muhammad, the holiday of **Maulidi** brings thousands of Muslims from all over the region to the tiny island of Lamu.

➤ JUNE: Celebrating Kenya's independence from Great Britain, **Madaraka Day** is held on June 1.

➤ JULY: **Saba Saba Day,** a festival marking the founding of the Tanganyika African National Union, is held in Tanzania on July 7. **Mwaka Kogwa,** the celebration of the Shirazi New Year, is held each year in Zanzibar.

July is the month of the **Zanzibar International Film Festival,** which showcases the best films from the region. Also in July, a mammoth event called **Festival of the Dhow Countries** celebrates the diverse cultures of the countries that surround the Indian Ocean.

Kenya's **Safari Rally** disturbs the peace of the bush when vehicles roar along the dusty roads. The grueling three-day circuit starts in the center of Nairobi and winds its way up into the mountains.

➤ AUG.–SEPT.: The annual **wildebeest migration** thunders through Tanzania's Serengeti and Kenya's Maasai Mara National Reserve, attracting lions and cheetahs (and plenty of camera-toting tourists).

➤ OCT.: **Moi Day,** named after the president, is celebrated all over Kenya on Oct. 10. Around this time, jacaranda blossoms blanket the streets of Nairobi, where many roads are lined with these elegant trees. **Kenyatta Day,** remembering those who fought to free Kenya from colonial rule, is held on Oct. 20.

➤ OCT.–NOV.: The holy month of **Ramadan** is the time of year when Muslims fast and reflect. In 2002 it begins on Nov. 6 and in 2003 on Oct. 27. If you plan to arrive in East Africa during Ramadan, try to arrive during the final days, when a huge celebration, **Eid al Fitr,** brings everyone out to the streets.

➤ DEC.: On Dec. 12 **Jamhuri Day** is celebrated with great fanfare in Nairobi. Banks and shops are closed on this day, honoring the country's independence.

1 DESTINATION: KENYA AND TANZANIA

Under African Skies

What's Where

Pleasures and Pastimes

Fodor's Choice

UNDER AFRICAN SKIES

AFRICA IS MYSTIC; it is wild; it is a sweltering inferno; it is a photographer's paradise, a hunter's Valhalla, an escapist's Utopia." These words by Beryl Markham, whose 1943 bestseller, *West with the Night,* chronicled her life as a bush pilot in Kenya, are just as true today. Perhaps the grand landscapes of East Africa—the vast plains of the Serengeti, the soaring heights of Mt. Kilimanjaro, the endless beaches of Zanzibar—require the perspective that only a pilot can bring.

Like the Galápagos Islands, the savannas of East Africa serve as a living laboratory that reveals nature's whimsical experiments in form and function. But here there is one monumental difference—scientists believe that it was in East Africa that humankind emerged. It was in 1959 that anthropologist Mary Leakey found the first hominid skull in Tanzania's Olduvai Gorge, effectively shifting the cradle of mankind from Africa's southern tip to its eastern shores. Few who come here do not feel the powerful tug of roots, an emotional link with the landscape, or feel they have managed to go home again. Richard Leakey, an anthropologist who followed in the footsteps of his parents, reckons we feel an affinity for Africa because it's in our blood. People write of their safari experience as "the odyssey of a lifetime" and feel the odd epiphany, as if by being on this terrain they are "somehow part of eternity."

The yearning that people feel for Africa may also have to do with all that we have squandered in our own nations, including ancient traditions, irreplaceable natural wonders, and the great seasonal migrations of wildlife. Few can witness the extraordinary parade of more than 1.5 million wildebeest thundering across the Serengeti and not be reminded of the buffaloes slaughtered by the thousands in the United States. Conservationists in East Africa have found a great deal of hope with the development of effective strategies for the preservation of endangered creatures. Kenya now has some phenomenal private game preserves, while Tanzania is protecting more of its underwater wonders with marine parks.

In East Africa you will encounter some of the most amazing people you will ever met. The majestic Maasai, adorned with beads and draped with colorful fabrics, welcome you with a smile. They beat Buckminster Fuller with their own version of a dome as a home, and their everyday crafts remind us why Picasso was inspired by so-called primitive art. More efforts are being made to ensure that native cultures are not lost. There is an effort among many lodge owners to preserve the traditions of indigenous peoples, particularly their knowledge of medicinal herbs, their music and dance, and their extraordinary jewelry and art.

There is music in this land—in the melodic Swahili tongue, in a mourning dove's lament, and in golden savanna grasses that weave their own hypnotic song. First-time visitors are profoundly surprised by the timbre of a lion's roar that cuts through the night air. Many an evening has been spent around a campfire listening to roars exchanged in the distance and wondering what these cats might be saying to each other. Then come the sudden silences, which means the lions are on the move in the dark.

Not so long ago just such an eerie quiet was noted at a tented camp on the edge of the Serengeti. The next morning a group on safari happened upon a group of lions feasting on a zebra. Although the kill was first spied by Maasai trackers accompanying the group, the excellent guide reconstructed the kill from clues at the scene. The two large lions had attacked a zebra at a small stream, cleverly disemboweled the carcass to lighten the load, dragged it up onto the banks, and had a late-night snack. Everyone in the group got a chill up the spine when they realized the lions they'd heard the night before had been making a kill less than a half mile from where they slept.

Rather than fear, these intrepid explorers felt exhilaration for having witnessed the event. They saw briefly in the distance the face of one lion, his mouth red with blood, his belly heavy. He turned away to continue his sure-footed retreat and disappeared among the golden grasses.

For years the majority of visitors to East Africa saw sights like this from behind the window of a minivan. Walking safaris, where you leave the safety of the vehicle behind, are becoming increasingly popular among those who want to track elephants and rhinos the old-fashioned way, trade stories around a campfire, and wonder, when they hear the haunting yip of a hyena, who will have the last laugh. In the same way, tented camps are also attractive to those who see little appeal in large lodges.

Travelers also want to know that the land they find so fascinating will be there for their children to discover. The ecotourism bandwagon is full and noisy, and travelers must look beyond slick brochures and colorful Web sites. Seek out tour agencies that cater to small groups, make use of smaller lodges or temporary camps, and offer walking and horseback safaris that leave the landscape undisturbed. Make sure to get off the beaten path because many places, such as Kenya's Amboseli National Park and Tanzania's Ngorongoro Conservation Area, have become too popular for their own good or, for that matter, your own enjoyment. You need not cross these places off your list, but avoid the peak season and stay in a private camp outside the park boundaries.

When you head back to the cities, you remember that Kenya and Tanzania are both developing nations with the usual problems of poverty, crime, and corruption. The Kenyan capital of Nairobi, which has seen its population triple in the last two decades, has such a problem with with muggers and pickpockets that it is half-jokingly referred to as "Nairobbery." Things are much better in Tanzania's largest city, Dar es Salaam, but it's a good idea to consider a guide in these and other urban areas.

But with such natural wonders just a few miles away, you're not likely to be spending much time in the cities. If you're like most travelers, East Africa becomes not only the trip of a lifetime but a memory that beckons you to return. Few people travel to this region only once. On the heels of one long safari, Ernest Hemingway was ready to turn around and go right back, writing, "All I wanted to do was get back to Africa."

— By Delta Willis

WHAT'S WHERE

Nairobi and the Ngong Hills

When Teddy Roosevelt and Ernest Hemingway headed out on safari, their base was always Nairobi. After a long day in the bush, adventurers have long retired to the veranda of the Stanley Hotel or the tables of the Thorn Tree Café to swap stories. Although these landmarks still stand, the quiet colonial city surrounding them has changed markedly. Now home to 2 million people, the sprawling metropolis has many of the same problems that plague other African capitals. Many travelers today head to the nearby Ngong Hills, made famous by author Karen Blixen's *Out of Africa*. Here you'll find Nairobi National Park, which holds more rhinos than any other reserve in East Africa.

Western Kenya

Most travelers pass through Western Kenya on their way to the wonders of Maasai Mara National Reserve, but they're missing one of the most fascinating parts of the country. One feature of Western Kenya that you will find no where else on earth is the Great Rift Valley, a geological formation so huge that it's visible from space. The basins created by this gorge filled with rainwater to create a majestic string of lakes that harbor unique and colorful fish. In between are the soda lakes of Elementeita, Nakuru, and Bogoria that attract flamingos by the tens of thousands.

Northern Kenya

The monolith of Mt. Kenya is one of the first things visitors see in Kenya, as pilots often point it out as they make their descent into Nairobi. As you climb Mt. Kenya, you enter a world of lush rain forest, giant bamboo, strange volcanic rocks, equatorial glaciers, and rolling moorlands, all dominated by the twin peaks of Batian and Nelion, the second and third highest in Africa. To the west is Aberdare National Park, where you might chance upon a family of elephants moving through the forest. To the north is Meru National Park, favored by large herds of buffaloes.

Nothing can prepare you for the extraordinary sight of Lake Turkana, a vast expanse that changes from shimmering silver to luminous blue as clouds skim above the surface. When the wind stirs the particles of algae beneath, the lake reveals why people call it the Jade Sea.

The Kenya Coast

Although much of Kenya entices you with wildlife, the towns along the Kenya Coast attract you with their unique culture. Arab traders who came to these shores more than a millennium ago brought Islam to Africa, and the coastal streets are dominated by men wearing long robes called *khanzus*. Women wear black veils called *bui-buis* that reveal only their sparkling eyes. Not far from Mombasa, the country's principal port, you'll find ruins of ancient villages centered around magnificent mosques. Farther north is Lamu, an astounding city made of stone built on a beautiful archipelago.

Dar es Salaam

As you watch the boats in the harbor, Dar es Salaam brings to mind its roots as a fishing village. Today it's one of East Africa's most important ports. Although Dar es Salaam, home to 3.5 million people, is Tanzania's largest city, it isn't the nation's capital (that honor goes to Dodoma). It is, however, the country's economic and cultural capital. Interesting sites include the National Museum, which contains the famous fossil discoveries by Richard and Mary Leakey.

Northern Tanzania

You'll have to get up pretty early in the morning to experience everything that this breathtaking part of Tanzania has to offer. Towering Mt. Kilimanjaro is loveliest at sunrise, when its snowy peaks are tinged with hues of pink and yellow. This is also the most likely time to spot lions stalking their prey in Ngorongoro Crater. Most guides wake you up at dawn for an early game drive through the grasslands of the Serengeti, the setting for the annual wildebeest migration. It's a good idea to get off the beaten track when visiting Northern Tanzania. Don't overlook the smaller reserves, such as beautiful Arusha National Park, known as *Serengeti Ndogo,* or "Little Serengeti." You'll find everything that the bigger parks have to offer, except the crowds.

Zanzibar

Few names are more exotic than Zanzibar, where the pungent scent of cloves drying in the sun led to its being called the Spice Island. Today this jewel in the Indian Ocean attracts adventurers intent on discovering its ancient cities, pristine rain forests, and boldly colored coral reefs. Here you'll find Stone Town, a maze of narrow streets lined with houses featuring magnificently carved doors studded with brass. Although the main island of Unguja feels untouched by the rest of the world, the nearby islands of Pemba and Mnemba offer retreats that are even more remote.

PLEASURES AND PASTIMES

Beaches

Although a sandy shore isn't the first thing that comes to mind when most people think of Africa, Kenya and Tanzania have some of the finest beaches on the continent. The coast north and south of Mombasa is lined with resorts that fill up on weekends with those intent on finding their place in the sun. A little farther off the beaten path are the islands that dot the Indian Ocean, where you shouldn't be surprised if you find yourself alone on a stretch of silvery sand. Zanzibar has fantastic diving, as does nearby Mafia Island.

Big Game Adventures

East Africa is home to one of nature's biggest spectacles, the annual wildebeest migration. About 1.5 million of the gentle creatures travel the plains in search of grass, followed by thousands of zebras, giraffes, antelopes, and gazelles. Great herds of elephants can still be found in East Africa, as well as groups of rhinos and hippos. Big cats such as lions and leopards are common, but don't overlook the intriguing smaller predators, such as hyenas, jackals, and rare wild dogs. Quite fascinating are the primates, including our nearest relative, the chimpanzee. The experience of seeing wildlife from a vehicle is quite tame compared to a walk on the wild side with an experienced guide, and increasingly you can see animals from horseback, mountain bike, canoe, and hot-air balloon. Binoculars are a must, but remember to bring a zoom lens for your camera. You'll be rewarded with unforgettable sights if you take your time and give the animals plenty of room.

Bird-Watching

East Africa is one of the finest bird-watching destinations in the world. Because of the variety of habitats, you can find myriad species, from the majestic African fish eagles that dominate the shores of Lake Naivasha to the thousands of flamingos that billow and bunch over Lake Manyara to brilliant carmine bee-eaters that add a flash of color to the coast. The Serengeti alone has recorded more than 500 bird species, but lesser-known reserves such as Mt. Elgon and the Kakamega Forest can deliver more birds than you can imagine. In the savannas and near escarpments, look for those crowd-pleasers, the lumbering ostriches.

Fishing

Fishing enthusiasts from all over the world are drawn to the coast of Kenya and Tanzania, where the expansive coral reefs are home to dozens of species. On Zanzibar's Unguja Island you can sail in *ngalawas,* the traditional wooden fishing boats used by locals. On the archipelago's smaller islands you can go deep-sea fishing for everything from wahoo to barracuda. Trout fishing is popular in the rivers around Mt. Kenya, and great Nile perch weighing more than 100 pounds are common in Lake Victoria.

Flora

The trees of East Africa—from the thorny acacias to the purple-blossomed jacarandas—are among the most majestic on the planet. The magnificent African baobabs provide water to elephants in time of drought, while whistling thorn trees, which sing when the wind blows, have a symbiotic relationship with several species of ants. Palm trees provide materials for thatch roofs, while mangroves are where locals find the "jungle crook" used for the hulls of dhows.

Hiking

Hiking is an increasingly popular activity in East Africa, from walking safaris in Hell's Gate National Park to treks up Mt. Kilimanjaro. Nearly everywhere you go you will need a guide, who will not only help you find the wildlife but also fill you in on their habits and histories. Because many areas are filled with dangerous animals like buffaloes, rhinos, hippos, and elephants, you may need an armed escort.

FODOR'S CHOICE

Special Moments

Kenya

Baby an orphaned elephant, Langata. Little elephants and rhinos who have lost their mothers are given tender loving care at Sheldrick Animal Orphanage, on the edge of Nairobi National Park.

See eye to eye with a giraffe, Langata. For an incredible close-up encounter with these leggy creatures, visit the Giraffe Centre. They'll even pose for a photo-op.

Track a rhinoceros, Nairobi National Park. A herd of about 50 endangered black rhinos roams Nairobi National Park, a nature reserve so close to the capital that skyscrapers serve as a backdrop.

Trail a pride of lions, Maasai Mara National Reserve. Few things are more thrilling than trailing hungry lions through the sun-baked savanna. East Africa's most popular game park has the largest population of big cats.

Fly with flamingos, Lake Nakuru National Park. Called "the greatest bird spectacle on earth," this lake is home to thousands of pink flamingos who spend their days slurping up beakfuls of blue-green algae.

Gaze across a gorge, Kerio Valley. Dotted with thorny acacias, prickly euphorbias, and castlelike termite mounds, this spur of the Great Rift Valley is one of the most dramatic sights in Western Kenya.

Swing through the jungle, Kakmega Forest. Seldom-seen animals, including the bush-tailed porcupine, giant water shrew, and hammer-headed fruit bat, can be spotted in the Kenya's last surviving stretch of rain forest.

Climb up a dormant volcano, Mt. Kenya. Some of the trails up this towering peak require a good deal of mountaineering skill, but many routes do not require climbing experience.

Wander through Fort Jesus, Mombasa. Built in the late 16th century by the Portuguese, who were keen to control trade along the African coast, this massive edifice still dominates the coastal city.

Cruise by moonlight, Lamu. There's nothing quite as romantic as floating on the Indian Ocean in a triangular-sailed dhow. It is most magical by moonlight, when the crew entertains you with traditional songs.

Tanzania

Come face to face with history, Dar es Salaam. Gaze at the 1.7-million-year-old hominid skull archaeologist Mary Leakey discovered in Olduvai Gorge at the National Museum.

Find your feathered friends, Tarangire National Park. More than 300 species of birds, including martial and bateleur eagles, have been spotted in this seldom-visited reserve. Near the Tarangire River you'll see yellow-collared lovebirds and long-toed lapwings.

Hike in the highlands, Ngorongoro Conservation Area. For a view of the surrounding countryside, head to the volcano called Ol Doinyo Lengai, known as the "Mountain of God" in the language of the Maasai.

Glide through the golden grasses, Serengeti National Park. Join the hundreds of thousands of gnus searching for greener pastures during the annual wildebeest migration.

Scale Africa's tallest peak, Mt. Kilimanjaro. Many people head to Tanzania with the goal of conquering this mountain. Novices can manage the Marangu Route, while more experienced climbers are challenged by five other trails.

Smile at a crocodile, Katavi National Park. If you want to experience what the Serengeti was like before the invasion of minivans, head to this isolated reserve. It's home to one of the continent's largest concentrations of crocodiles.

Dive into the Indian Ocean, Mafia Island Marine Park. Blue-tipped staghorn coral is but one of the 40 types you'll see in the azure waters surrounding Mafia Island. This amazing undersea world is the country's first marine preserve.

Meet a monkey, Mahale Mountains National Park. In a tropical rain forest on the eastern edge of Lake Tanganyika, this reserve is home to one of the world's largest populations of chimpanzees.

Get off the beaten track, Selous Game Reserve. This raw wilderness, still mostly unexplored, was once described as "the heart of Africa." You'll know why when you see the great herds of buffaloes on the horizon.

Get lost in Stone Town, Zanzibar. Stroll around Stone Town, where you can take in the ancient arches, the brass-studded doors, and the many layers of history. The maze of narrow streets will eventually lead you to the harbor, so not to worry.

Dining

Kenya

Carnivore, Nairobi. Take a bite out of a crocodile at this longtime favorite where waiters carry the sizzling game meat to your table on long skewers and carve whatever you wish onto cast-iron platters. $$$$

Hemingway's, Watamu. With fresh fish straight from the Indian Ocean and vegetables flown in from the fertile shores of Lake Naivasha, the food couldn't be better at this eatery on the northern coast. $$$

Ibis Grill, Nairobi. Cool and contemporary, this hot spot serves international cuisine with a Kenyan twist, such as mignons of ostrich fillet served with a juniper-berry glaze. $$$

Peponi's, Lamu. Set beneath great vines of bougainvillea, this restaurant serves up the best seafood on the northern coast. If you prefer, you can dine on a dhow. $$–$$$

Tamarind, Nyali. Known for its *piri piri* (spicy, buttery prawns grilled over charcoal), this Moorish-style palace serves up unbelievable seafood. It's also the country's most beautiful restaurant, with unparalleled views of the harbor. $$$$

Tanzania

Mezza Luna, Arusha. You'll find more than 200 regional specialities on the menu at this popular eatery run by an Italian family. Wash down the excellent pastas with a good wine from South Africa. $$

Sawasdee, Dar es Salaam. The lights of the harbor sparkle as you enjoy the traditional Thai cuisine at one of Dar es Salaam's finest restaurants. $$–$$$

Serengeti, Dar es Salaam. A champagne breakfast is a Sunday-morning ritual among regular patrons of this longtime favorite. $$–$$$$

Tower Top, Stone Town. Gaze down over the rooftops of Stone Town as you sample spice-scented rice while reclining on soft cushions. $$$

Lodging

Kenya

Beach House, Shela. The vibrant wings of carmine bee-eaters may dazzle you as you gaze from your shuttered window at this immaculate lodging next to Lamu's windswept dunes. $$$$

Mt. Kenya Safari Club, Mt. Kenya. One of the most luxurious hotels in East Africa, this colonial-style lodging set in beautifully tended gardens has hosted everyone from Clark Gable to Tom Cruise. $$$$

Norfolk Hotel, Nairobi. If you are staying in the city of Nairobi, this is the place to be. Dine on a spacious terrace that makes you feel like you're out in the countryside. $$$$

Pemba Channel Fishing Club, Shimoni. Overlooking Wasini Island, this small group of colorfully decorated bandas with private verandas attracts anglers from around the world. $$$$

Serena Beach Hotel, Shanzu Beach. Calling to mind a traditional coastal village, this lodging has generously proportioned rooms decorated with Swahili-style furniture. $$$

Tanzania

Bahari Beach Hotel, Dar es Salaam. A scattering of coral-rock chalets with private balconies overlooking the ocean make up this lodging on a palm-lined beach north of Dar es Salaam. $$

Emerson & Green, Stone Town. Once home to one of the richest men in Zanzibar, this restored mansion on the romantic island of Unguja is known for its romantic rooms draped with yards of colorful fabrics. $$$

Mnemba Island Retreat, Mnemba Island. On a private island in the Indian Ocean, this exclusive retreat is set around a secluded lagoon. Cottages are separated from one another by lush tropical vegetation. $$$$

Royal Palm, Dar es Salaam. You'll forget the hustle and bustle just outside the front doors when you walk into the lobby of this luxurious hotel surrounded by extravagant gardens. Antique furnishings evoke a simpler time. $$$$

Zanzibar Serena, Stone Town. On the tip of the Shangani Peninsula, this luxurious hotel has canopy beds where you can lie in bed with a view of the azure waters of the Indian Ocean. $$$$

Game Lodges

Kenya

Bateleur Camp, Maasai Mara. After a day exploring Maasai Mara, return in the evening to this extraordinary tented camp where you sleep in exquisitely carved mahogany beds and dine on fresh lobster and fine wine. $$$$

Little Governor's Camp, Maasai Mara. Set around a watering hole, this camp near the Mara River is a great place to spot wildlife ranging from elephants and hippos to giraffes and warthogs. $$$$

Ol Donyo Wuas, Tsavo National Park. This hideaway in the Chyulu Hills was a pioneering effort in local conservation. Get up at dawn to go horseback riding among herds of zebras, or simply lie in bed and look at Mt. Kilimanjaro through your toes. $$$$

Olerai House, Lake Naivasha. Run by Iain and Orian Douglas-Hamilton, Africa's leading experts on elephants, this enchanting red farmhouse is one of the best places to learn about these gentle giants. $$$$

Sirikwa Safaris Guest House, Kitale. Run by a mother-and-daughter team, this charming inn is set in the foothills of the Cherengani Hills. Your room has a stone fireplace to keep out the evening chill. $

Tanzania

Katavi Tented Camp, Katavi National Park. Simple but elegant, this scattering of tents is in the middle of one of the most fascinating wilderness areas in Africa. There's a telescope for stargazing and campaign chairs for chats around the campfire. $$$$

Kiriwira Camp, Serengeti National Park. With all the charm of a bygone era, this luxurious camp lets you sink into a high-backed chair as you contemplate the endless savanna. The antique gramophone nearby softly plays Puccini. *$$$$*

Ngare Sero Mountain Lodge, Arusha National Park. The name means "sweet water," which refers to a nearby mountain spring. You must cross a small footbridge to reach the beautiful estate where this lodge is located. *$$$$*

Ngorongoro Crater Lodge, Ngorongoro Conservation Area. Over the top, this lodging with crystal chandeliers and carved paneling has been called the Versailles of Ngorongoro. The pampering of a butler and the luxury of a bathtub are all the more welcome when you return from the bush. *$$$$*

Sand Rivers Selous Lodge. Near the Rufiji River, this isolated lodge has Africa at its doorstep. Constructed of local stone and mahogany, it has a massive fireplace to keep you cozy during the cool evenings. *$$$$*

2 NAIROBI AND THE NGONG HILLS

It was the distilled air of the Ngong Hills that made author Karen Blixen feel that "here I am, where I ought to be." Many newcomers feel the same affinity with this landscape. Nearby you'll find the bustling capital of Nairobi. The starting point for safaris since the days of Teddy Roosevelt and Ernest Hemingway, Nairobi is still the first stop for many travelers headed to the wildlife parks of East Africa.

JUST OVER A CENTURY AGO, Nairobi was little more than a water depot for the notorious "Lunatic Express." Every railhead presented a new nightmare for its British builders. Work was halted by hungry lions (a saga portrayed in the film *The Ghost and the Darkness*) as well as by masses of caterpillars that crawled on the tracks, spoiling traction and spinning wheels. Nearsighted rhinos charged the noisy engines. Africans fashioned jewelry from the copper telegraph wires, leading to a head-on collision between two engines after the communication wires were cut. The budget ballooned to £9,500 a mile, an enormous amount of money in 1900.

By Delta Willis

Nairobi, which means "cool water" in the language of the Maasai, wouldn't remain a backwater for long. In her 1942 memoir, *West with the Night,* aviatrix Beryl Markham wrote that less than three decades after it was founded, the city "had sprung from a collection of corrugated iron shacks serving the spindly Uganda Railway to a sprawling welter of British, Boers, Indians, Somalis, Abyssinians, natives from all over Africa and a dozen other places." Its grand hotels and imposing public buildings, she wrote, were "imposing evidence that modern times and methods have at last caught up with East Africa."

Today Nairobi's skyline surprises first-time visitors, whose visions of the country are often shaped by wildlife documentaries on the Discovery Channel or news reports about poverty on CNN. Since it was founded little more than a century ago, Nairobi has grown into one of the continent's largest capitals. Some early architecture survives here and there, but this city of 2 million people is dominated by modern office towers.

This is not to say the city has lost all its charm—the venerable Norfolk Hotel recalls the elegance of an age long since past, and the big black taxis from London lend a sense of style. Sometimes you can even describe the city as beautiful. After a good rain the city seems to have more green than New York or London. Brilliant bougainvillea line the highway from the airport, flame trees shout with color, and, in October, the horizon turns lavender with the blossoms of jacaranda.

But Nairobi has more than its share of problems. This city that grew too fast has paralyzing traffic jams, with many unsafe or overloaded vehicles on the road, and no hint of emission control. Crime is on the rise, and stories about muggings and car jackings have led to the capital's moniker "Nairobbery." In addition, there is a growing disparity between rich and poor. Private estates on the edge of Nairobi resemble those of Beverly Hills or Boca Raton, with elaborate wrought-iron fences surrounding opulent mansions with stables, tennis courts, and swimming pools. The upper crust is known as the *wabenzi,* with "wa" a generic prefix for a people or tribe and "benzi" referring to the ubiquitous Mercedes Benz cars lining the driveways. Not far away you can glimpse vast mazes of tin shacks, many with no electricity or running water.

These problems have pushed many travelers to the sanctuary of the suburbs. The Ngong Hills, consisting of "four noble peaks rising like immovable darker blue waves against the sky," mark the southwestern boundaries of Nairobi, embracing the townships of Langata and Karen. The latter is named after Baroness Karen Blixen, who wrote under the pen name Isak Dinesen about her life on a coffee farm here. Purple at dusk, the Ngong Hills are a restful symbol of *salaam,* Swahili for "peace." Here people take a deep breath, toast the setting sun, and discuss the remains of the day.

Exclusive guest homes such as the Giraffe Manor and Ngong House provide a sense of peace in the suburban bush. Some of the better boutiques selling everything from antiques to art are found in Karen and Langata. Alan Donovan, owner of the prestigious African Heritage Gallery in Nairobi, has also opened shops here. The suburb of Langata lies on the edge of the Nairobi National Park, a great introduction to the magnificent wildlife of Kenya. No wonder many visitors return here year after year. They discover how Blixen felt when she wrote in one of her letters: "Wherever I may be in future, I will always wonder whether there is rain on the Ngongs."

Pleasures and Pastimes

Archaeology

East Africa is often called the "cradle of humankind" because of the early human fossils and stone tools found here, many of them unearthed by the Leakey family and the team known as the Hominid Gang. The National Museum in Nairobi has interesting exhibits on human evolution as well as images of rock art paintings from Tanzania, which were traced and reproduced by Mary Leakey. Her daughter-in-law Meave Leakey and other scientists sometime lecture about their research at the nearby Louis Leakey Prehistory Institute. You can arrange excursions to Olorgesailie, a site 60 km (37 mi) south of Nairobi, in the eastern branch of the Great Rift Valley. Exhibits of hand axes and other tools provide an impressive glimpse into the Stone Age.

Dining

Prepare yourself for some of the most delectable flavors ever to strike your palate, from the pungent passion fruit, papaya, and mango served at your breakfast table to the robust Tusker beer that quenches your thirst after a long day on safari. Nairobi restaurants offer a bit of everything, from superb nouvelle cuisine at the Ibis Grill to game meat at the Carnivore (one of the few places where you can take a bite out of a crocodile). If you fancy fish, try the fabulous tilapia and perch from Lake Victoria. Fresh lobster and other seafood are made all the better by being cooked in coconut milk or seasoned with local spices, including tamarind. Indian *samosas,* spicy envelopes of *papadum* pastry with ground meat or vegetable fillings, and *chapati,* a thin skillet bread, are just a few examples of the great ethnic mix you'll find in Nairobi. Indian food is outstanding here—some think it's superior to that found in India because of the high quality of the ingredients in Kenya. Ginger is used to flavor soup, tea, coffee, and the refreshing bottled soda called Tangawizi. It is the second-best drink in town, the first being fresh-squeezed lime juice.

Tips are often included in the bill, so ask the waiter before adding 10%–12%. Credit cards are accepted in most establishments. Lunch is generally from 12:30 to 2:30, dinner from 7 to 10:30.

CATEGORY	COST*
$$$$	over Ksh 1,170
$$$	Ksh 780–Ksh 1,170
$$	Ksh 390–Ksh 780
$	under Ksh 390

Per person, for a main course at dinner.

Lodging

The two landmark lodgings in the capital, the Norfolk Hotel and the Stanley Hotel, have thrown their doors open to visitors for a century. Both have been beautifully renovated and now have everything from health clubs to business centers. New luxury hotels, such as the Nairobi Grand Regency, are giving them a run for their money.

Although corporate travelers may need to stay in Nairobi, those wishing to get away from the hustle and bustle can head to the Ngong Hills. The Giraffe Manor, Macushla House, and Ngong House offer more peaceful surroundings.

CATEGORY	COST*
$$$$	over Ksh 15,600
$$$	Ksh 7,800–Ksh 15,600
$$	Ksh 3,900–KSh 7,800
$	under Ksh 3,900

All prices are for a standard double room, excluding tax.

Shopping
Genuine tribal crafts can be found only in a few places in Nairobi, such as the African Heritage Gallery. City Market and the Maasai Market have woven baskets called *kiondos*. Most are made from sisal and are colored with natural or artificial dyes. *Kanga,* the local cotton printed with bright African designs, and *kikoi,* the sarong with fringed edges, make ideal gifts. Nairobi has a wealth of unusual jewelry; you'll get the best introduction at the African Bead Gallery, near the Carnivore restaurant. Look for the beautiful antique trading beads from all over Africa.

Wildlife
Even if you plan to visit several other game reserves while in Kenya, don't eschew Nairobi National Park because of its proximity to the city. The reserve is home to a growing herd of endangered black rhinos, and spotting a leopard draped over a tree limb is not so unlikely. Close-up views of the world's tallest mammals are found at the Giraffe Center in Langata. At the Daphne Sheldrick Animal Orphanage, baby elephants and rhinos get tender care.

EXPLORING NAIROBI AND THE NGONG HILLS

Nairobi National Park is to the south of the city, with Jomo Kenyatta International Airport and Wilson Airport on the park periphery. Karen and Langata are to the southwest of the city center, and the Ngong Hills, on the edge the Great Rift Valley, are beyond. Muthaiga, Gigiri, and Limuru are to the north.

Although the fastest way of traveling around the city center is on foot, you should be on guard when walking in Nairobi. Much safer is taking a taxi or hiring a car and driver.

Great Itineraries
IF YOU HAVE 2 DAYS
Begin your exploration of Nairobi at the **National Museum** ⑩. You can easily spend a half day at this sprawling museum, especially if you slither into the adjacent **Nairobi Snake Park** ⑪. For lunch consider the Ibis Grill. In the afternoon head to the cavernous **City Market** ①, where you can bargain for carved *kiisi* stones. For the best prices on the cotton sarongs known as kikois and kangas, explore the shops on nearby Bi-ashara Street, still featuring the colonial facades that characterized early Nairobi. Take a look at the rusty steam engines at the **Railway Museum** ⑨, then take the elevator to the top of **Kenyatta International Conference Centre** ⑦ for a bird's-eye view of the city. Return to your hotel to dress for dinner at Alan Bobbe's Bistro.

On your second day visit the **Giraffe Centre** ⑫ in Langata where you can see eye to eye with a Rothschild giraffe. Although the facility was designed to introduce Kenyan children to wildlife they might not otherwise see, it is a delightful place for visitors of all ages. Afterward head for the **Sheldrick Animal Orphanage** ⑬, just inside the gates of Nairobi National Park, to see the parade of infant elephants and rhinos that occurs weekdays before noon. Just up Dagoretti Road from the Karen Roundabout is the **African Butterfly Research Institute** ⑭. It's a real treat for children, but with such informed guides adults are equally entertained. Take a game drive in **Nairobi National Park** ⑰, followed by an early dinner at the Carnivore.

IF YOU HAVE 3 DAYS

Follow the above itinerary for the first two days. On day three visit the **Karen Blixen Museum** ⑮, once home to the eponymous author. The back lawn has a magnificent view of the Ngong Hills. The nearby Karen Blixen Coffee Garden is a good place to stop for lunch. In the afternoon arrange a visit at the **Kiambethu Tea Farm.** You can sip the local brew, hear about the farm's history, and stroll in the gardens where black-and-white colobus monkeys play. A mile from the farm is the gravesite of Louis Leakey. If you have an interest in archaeology, consider a drive down to **Olorgesalie** to see the ancient stone tools found in this former lake bed of the Great Rift Valley.

IF YOU HAVE 5 DAYS

With a little more time you can explore the game reserves southeast of Nairobi. Most people visit **Amboseli National Park,** one of the country's most popular reserves. Here you'll have amazing views of Mt. Kilimanjaro. If you want to escape the crowds, head to **Tsavo National Park,** which attracts only a fraction of the visitors. The park is so vast that you can drive for miles without seeing another soul.

Nairobi

Central Nairobi is a triangle bordered by the Nairobi River, Uhuru Highway, and the railway. Kenyatta Avenue and Moi Avenue divide this 4 square km (2½ square mi) area into three main districts: Southwest, Northwest, and East. Southwest Nairobi gives the city its imposing profile, boasting governmental buildings, office towers, and luxury hotels. It is dominated by the city's tallest landmark, the 28-story Kenyatta International Conference Centre. In Northwest you'll find more modest shops, restaurants, and hotels, while the East encompasses poorer neighborhoods. This is where you find the capital's cheap restaurants and hotels, bus stations and matatu terminals, and markets intended for locals.

Numbers in the text correspond to numbers in the margin and on the Nairobi map.

A Good Tour

To experience the hustle and bustle of the city, start at the **City Market** ① , at the corner of Market and Muindi Mbingu streets. In the center of the cavernous building you'll find bundles of fresh flowers and piles of ripe fruit. Dress conservatively if you intend to enter the **Jamia Mosque** ②, near the market on Banda Street. The elaborately carved minarets remind you of the city's Muslim history.

Where Banda Street meets Wanbera Street, huge lions flank the stone steps leading to the neoclassical **McMillan Library** ③. Besides the books you'll find furniture that once belonged to Karen Blixen, author of *Out of Africa*. Follow Wabera Street to Kenyatta Avenue, originally designed so that a cart drawn by 16 oxen could turn with ease. At the corner

14

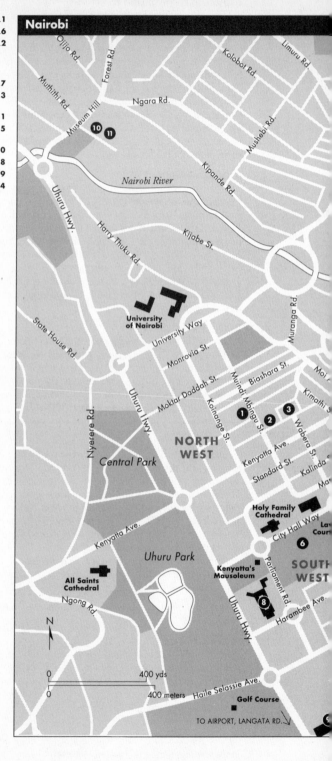

Nairobi

Ojijo Rd.
Forest Rd.
Kolobot Rd.
Limuru Rd.
Muthithi Rd.
Museum Hill
Ngara Rd.
Mushebi Rd.
10 11
Kipande Rd.
Uhuru Hwy.
Nairobi River
Harry Thuku Rd.
Kijabe St.
Muranga Rd.

University
of Nairobi
State House Rd.
University Way
Monrovia St.
Moktar Daddah St.
Biashara St.
Moi
Mundi Mbingu St.
Kimothi St.
Uhuru Hwy.
Nyerere Rd.
Koinange St.
Kenyatta Ave.
Wabera St.
Standard St.
Kalinda
NORTH
WEST
Central Park
Ma

Holy Family
Cathedral
City Hall Way
Lav
Court
6
Kenyatta Ave.
Uhuru Park
SOUTH
WEST
All Saints
Cathedral
Kenyatta's
Mausoleum
Parliament Rd.
Ngong Rd.
Uhuru Hwy.
8
Harambee Ave.

N

0   400 yds
0   400 meters
Haile Selassie Ave.
Golf Course
TO AIRPORT, LANGATA RD.

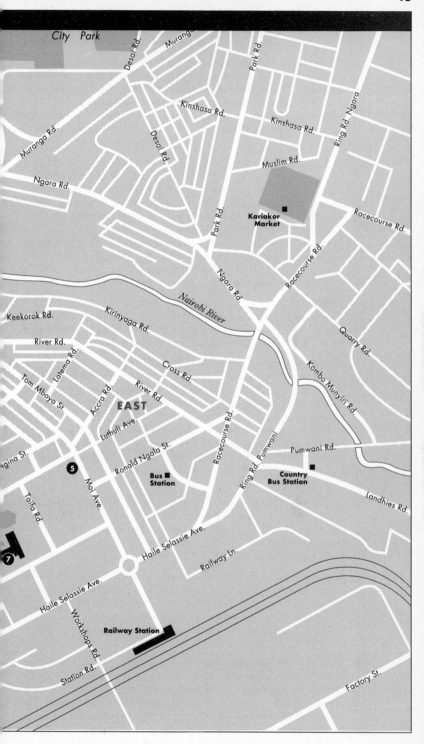

City Park

Desai Rd.

Muranga

Park Rd.

Kinshasa Rd.

Kinshasa Rd.

Ring Rd. Ngara

Muranga Rd.

Desai Rd.

Muslim Rd.

Ngara Rd.

Racecourse Rd.

Park Rd.

Kariakor
Market

Ngara Rd.

Racecourse Rd.

Nairobi River

Keekorok Rd.

Kirinyaga Rd.

Quarry Rd.

River Rd.

Cross Rd.

Kombo Munyiri Rd.

Latema Rd.

Accra Rd.

River Rd.

Tom Mboya St.

EAST

gina St.

Luthuli Ave.

5

Ronald Ngala St.

Racecourse Rd.

Pumwani Rd.

Country
Bus Station

Taita Rd.

Moi Ave.

Bus
Station

Ring Rd. Pumwani

Landhies Rd.

7

Haile Selassie Ave.

Railway Ln.

Haile Selassie Ave.

Workshops Rd.

Railway Station

Station Rd.

Factory St.

of Kimathi Street is the **Stanley Hotel** ④. For years adventurous types traded lies about their safaris at the Long Bar, now long gone. A few blocks south stands the colonnaded **National Archives** ⑤.

Head west on Harambee (Swahili for "pull together") until you reach Parliament Road. Take a right on Parliament Road to reach **City Square** ⑥. Dominating the plaza is one of the city's most imposing landmarks, the 28-story **Kenyatta International Conference Centre** ⑦. The view from the top is great on a clear day. On the opposite side of the square is the **Parliament** ⑧.

The next stop is a long walk, so you may want to consider catching a taxi, especially if there has been a recent rain. If you're game, head south on Moi Street. On the way you will pass the site of the former U.S. Embassy, which stood at the corner of Moi Avenue and Haile Selassie Avenue until it was destroyed by a terrorist bombing on August 7, 1998. A memorial garden park is now on the site. Just beyond is the dignified colonial edifice of the 1929 Railway Headquarters. A 10-minute walk west of the station is the **Railway Museum** ⑨. Look for the models of World War I steamships as well as the old steam engines on display. From here take a taxi north to the fascinating exhibits of the venerable **National Museum** ⑩. Nearby is the **Nairobi Snake Park** ⑪.

TIMING

This walk will take the better part of a day. If you begin early at City Market, you should reach the Railway Museum by noon. The National Museum can easily entertain you for the afternoon.

Sights to See

❶ **City Market.** Designed in 1930 as an aircraft hanger, this vast space is a jumble of color, noise, and activity. Head to the balcony to view the flower, fruit, and vegetable stands on the main level. Outside the market entrance is Biashara Street, where you'll find all sorts of tailors, haberdashers, and seamstresses. Look for kikois and kangas, colorful sarongs good for wearing over a bathing suit or throwing over a picnic table. Priced at $20 at many hotels, on Biashara Street they run as low as $6. ⊠ *Muindi Mbingu St.,* ☎ *no phone.* 🎫 *Free.* ☻ *Mon–Sat. 8–4.*

❻ **City Square.** A large statue of Jomo Kenyatta, the country's first president, sits in the center of this wide flagstone courtyard. During conferences when the flags are flying, fountains are gushing, and the tribal dancers are performing, this is one of Nairobi's most colorful scenes. ⊠ *Muindi Mbingu St.,* ☎ *no phone.* 🎫 *Free.*

❷ **Jamia Mosque.** Built in 1925, this mosque near Central Market is known for its elaborate white-and-green facade. The ornate touches on its cupolas and minarets contrast with the simple and spacious interior. On holy days the outside courtyard fills with Muslims, all facing the holy city of Mecca. Five clocks show the times for the five daily prayers. ⊠ *Banda and Muindi Mbingu Sts.*

❼ **Kenyatta International Conference Centre.** One of the most recognizable structures in the country, the 28-story office tower resembles a Maasai hut, symbolizing the conflux of the traditional and modern worlds. Take the elevator to the top, and you may be lucky enough to catch a glimpse of both Mt. Kenya and Mt. Kilimanjaro. There is no set admission, but it is common practice to tip the guard who directs you to the top about Ksh 100. ⊠ *Harambee Ave.,* ☎ *no phone.* 🎫 *Free.* ☻ *Weekdays 9:30–12:30 and 2–4:30.*

❸ **McMillan Library.** Like the New York Public Library, this building has two lions guarding the entrance. Dating from 1928, this impressive neoclassical structure was a gift of the widow of Sir Northrup McMillan, an American expatriate knighted for his service in World War II. The reference library also contains furniture from the home of Karen Blixen, author of *Out of Africa.* ✉ *Banda and Wabera Sts.,* ☎ *02/212–179.* 🎟 *Free.* ⊙ *Mon.–Sat. 10:30–5:30.*

⓫ **Nairobi Snake Park.** Near the National Museum you can get alarmingly close to some of the most poisonous snakes in Africa—carpet vipers, puff adders, and black mambas. You can also grin at a young crocodile, which might just grin back. An aquarium displays marine and freshwater fish. ✉ *Museum Hill, off Uhuru Hwy.,* ☎ *02/742–131.* 🆆🅴🅱 *www. museums.or.ke.* 🎟 *Ksh 200.* ⊙ *Daily 9–6.*

❺ **National Archives.** Originally the Bank of India, this archive holds interesting displays of musical instruments and weapons. On the first floor are photos of Presidents Moi and Kenyatta and an exhibition on the Mau Mau detention camps. ✉ *City Hall Way and Moi Ave.,* ☎ *02/ 225–959.* 🎟 *Free.* ⊙ *Weekdays 8:30–5, Sat. 8:30–1.*

★ ❿ **National Museum.** One of Nairobi's most popular attractions, the museum has extensive collections in ornithology, paleontology, and ethnography. Some of the discoveries of Meave and Richard Leakey are housed here in the Hominid Vault, and there are reproductions of the rock art uncovered by Mary Leakey. There are also excellent paintings by Joy Adamson, better known as the author of *Born Free.*

Past the columned facade of the main building you'll come to a courtyard where you will see a life-size statue of Ahmed, famous for his 300-pound tusks. The pachyderm was protected by presidential decree until his death in 1974. Modern buildings in the back house the Louis Leakey Prehistory Institute. You can join a free bird walk on Wednesday morning, leaving at 8:30 from the museum parking lot. ✉ *Museum Hill, off Uhuru Hwy.,* ☎ *02/742–131.* 🆆🅴🅱 *www.museums.or.ke.* 🎟 *Ksh 200.* ⊙ *Daily 9–6.*

❽ **Parliament.** Should you want to watch a budding democracy in action, obtain a permit to sit in the public gallery of the Kenya Parliament. Tours of the building can be arranged with the sergeant at arms. Although the exterior of the structure holds no surprises, inside there is a tapestry of the country's colonial history. Consisting of 49 colorful panels, it was a gift of the East African Women's League. ✉ *Parliament Rd. and Harambee Ave.,* ☎ *02/221–291.* 🎟 *Free.* ⊙ *Tues. 9:30– 12:30, Wed.–Thurs. 2:30–6:30.*

☚ ❾ **Railway Museum.** Established to preserve relics and records of East Africa railways and harbors, this museum is great fun for children of all ages. You can see the rhino catcher that Teddy Roosevelt rode during his 1908 safari and climb into the carriage where Charles Ryall, a British railroad builder, was dragged out a window by a hungry lion. There are great photos and posters, plus silver service from the more elegant days of the overnight train to Mombasa. ✉ *Station Rd. near Uhuru Hwy.,* ☎ *02/221–211.* 🎟 *Ksh 200.* ⊙ *Daily 8:30–5.*

NEED A BREAK? Nairobi's first outdoor eatery, the **Thorn Tree Café** (✉ Kenyatta Ave. and Kimathi St., ☎ 02/333–233) is a well-known meeting place. Here you can sit for hours with a glass of Kenya's excellent Tusker beer watching the people walk past. The fare has always included decent hamburgers and now has been expanded to feature pizzas, pastas, and pastries. Before Kenya had a postal system, travelers to and from the bush pinned notes on the trunk of the famous acacia tree in the central courtyard. Today there is a message board covered with personal messages.

4 **Stanley Hotel.** The oldest hotel in Nairobi, the Stanley has not always stood on its present site. It opened in 1899 on Tom Mboya Street, where it housed the workers building the Lunatic Line. When the hotel moved to its new location in 1913, it became known as the New Stanley (only recently has it reverted back to the original name). Ernest Hemingway lodged here in 1933 and again in 1953. ✉ *Kenyatta Ave. and Kimathi St.,* ☎ *02/228–830,* WEB *www.sarovahotels.com.*

The Ngong Hills

The Ngong Hills stand 25 km (15 mi) southeast of Nairobi, on the very edge of the Great Rift Valley. Rising to 2,460 m (8,071 ft), they form a natural divide between small-scale farming developments on the Nairobi side and the arid floor of the Rift Valley, where Maasai graze their herds.

A walk along the grassy crest of the hills rewards you with views of both the city, to the east, and the dry countryside, to the west. The rough, steep road leading from Ngong Village to the summit requires a four-wheel-drive vehicle during the wet season. It is easy walking along the ridge, but be on guard for the buffaloes sometimes found grazing here. Robberies have become common despite police patrols. It's best to travel with a guide or in a large group.

Numbers in the text correspond to numbers in the margin and on the Nairobi and Environs map.

A Good Tour

Drive south of Nairobi on the recently completed double-lane highway that leads past Wilson Airport. Turn left onto Langata South Road, then left onto Koitobos Road. When you reach GoGo Falls Lane, a sign leads you to the **Giraffe Centre** ⑫. Don't dawdle, as you'll want to reach the **Sheldrick Animal Orphanage** ⑬, just inside the Banda Gate of Nairobi National Park, by 11 AM to see the daily parade of infant elephants and rhinos.

On Dagoretti Road you'll find the **African Butterfly Research Institute** ⑭, where you can walk among thousands of the brightly colored creatures. On Ngong Road is the **Karen Blixen Museum** ⑮, the former home of the author of *Out of Africa*. The back lawn has a magnificent view of the Ngong Hills she wrote about so longingly. Stop at the nearby café for a cup of the coffee Blixen tried so hard to cultivate.

For an introduction to the many styles of African dance, head to the **Bomas of Kenya**. ⑯ Around 4 PM enter **Nairobi National Park** ⑰. You may be surprised to see so many species—hippos, antelopes, zebras, and rare black rhinos—so close to the city. You must be out of the park by 7. Stop at the African Heritage Gallery, which features a gallery devoted to the beads used in African jewelry, before stopping for dinner at the Carnivore.

TIMING
This tour takes most of the day. If you want to see Nairobi National Park without encountering dozens of minivans filled with picture-snapping tourists, head there when it opens, at 6 AM.

Sights to See

⑭ **African Butterfly Research Institute.** This complex, on Dagoretti Road just beyond the Karen Roundabout, features a 450-square-m greenhouse where you can walk among thousands of butterflies native to the region. The adjacent Caterpillar Café is a good place to stop for a snack. ✉ *256 Dagoretti Rd., Karen,* ☎ *02/884–972.* ⊙ *Daily 10–5.*

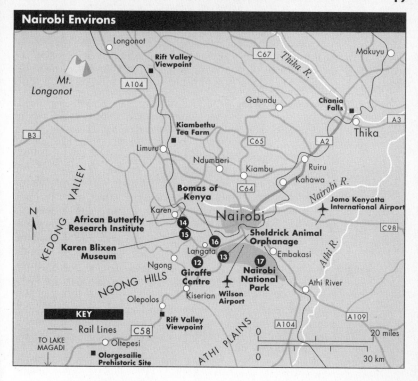

Nairobi Environs

⓰ **Bomas of Kenya.** Get a glimpse of the lifestyles of the various tribal peoples in Kenya at this collection of traditional *bomas,* or homesteads. This cultural center features a lively performance by the Harambee Dancers—more entertaining than authentic. ☒ *Langata Rd., past main entrance to Nairobi National Park, Langata,* ☎ *02/891–801.* ☒ *Ksh 350.* ☉ *Performances at 2:30 and 4.*

🖐 ⓬ **Giraffe Centre.** Run by the African Fund for Endangered Wildlife, the Giraffe Centre provides a chance to see eye to eye with Africa's tallest mammal. The center is dedicated to educating schoolchildren on the need for wildlife preservation, but adults are also enchanted by the chance to get close to the herd of Rothschild giraffes, all relocated from troubled areas. More than 160 species of birds have been identified in the 147-acre sanctuary, and you can spot many of them if you take a guided nature walk. You'll also see warthogs, bushbuck, and dik-diks, the tiny antelopes so named because of their distinctive warning cry. The center has a teahouse and gift shop stocked with giraffe mementos. ☒ *Go Go Falls La., near Hardy Estate Shopping Center, Langata,* ☎ *02/891–658,* WEB *www.giraffecentre.org.* ☒ *Ksh 500.* ☉ *Daily 9–5:30.*

⓯ **Karen Blixen Museum.** *Out of Africa* author Karen Blixen lived in this estate from 1913 to 1931. This is where she threw a grand dinner party for the Prince of Wales and where she carried on a torrid relationship with aviator Denys Finch Hatton. The museum contains a few of her belongings and some of the farm machinery she used to cultivate the land for coffee and tea. There's also some of her furniture, but most of it is found in the McMillan Library in Nairobi. There is a magnificent view of the surrounding hills from her lawn, which is dominated by euphorbia, the many-armed plant widely known as the candelabra cactus. On the way to the museum you may notice a signpost reading NDEGE. On this road, whose Swahili name means "bird," Finch Hatton once landed his plane for his visits with Blixen. After his plane crashed in Voi, he was buried nearby in the Ngong Hills. Guides will take you on a tour of the garden and the house, but there is little reference to the literary works by Blixen, who wrote under the pen name Isak Dinesen. ⊠ *Karen Rd., Karen,* ☏ *02/882–779,* WEB *www.museums.or.ke/ regkbm.html.* ⊠ *Ksh 200.* ☉ *Daily 9–6.*

Kiambethu Tea Farm. In the heart of Kenya's tea-growing region, Kiambethu Tea Farm is 35 km (22 mi) northeast of Nairobi. When you reach the town of Tigoni, turn right at the Limuru Girls School, which tea farmer Lewis G. Mitchell established to educate his four daughters. For years Evelyn Mitchell welcomed visitors and regaled them with stories about her family's experiences in Africa. She was pleased to point out that when Kiambethu opened in 1910, it was the first commercial tea farm in Kenya. She died in 1998, but her daughter Fiona will brew you a fresh pot of tea, take you on a short walk around the forest to see colobus monkeys, and provide insights on the history of tea in the region. ⊠ *Banana Rd., Tigoni,* ☏ *0154/40756,* FAX *0154/76230.* ⊠ *Ksh 250.* ☉ *Daily 11–2:30.*

★ ⑰ **Nairobi National Park.** The most striking thing about Nairobi National Park is not a mountain or a lake, but that it exists at all. This sliver of unspoiled Africa survives on the edge of a city of more than 2 million people. Where else can you get a photo of animals in their natural habitat with skyscrapers in the background? As you travel into the city from Jomo Kenyatta International Airport, you're likely to see gazelles grazing near the highway.

The park, covering 114 square km (44 square mi), is characterized by open plains that slope gently from west to east. Rocky ridges are covered with richer vegetation than the surrounding plains. Seasonal streams run southeast into the Mbagathi Athi River, which is lined with yellow fever trees and acacia trees. In the west it runs through a deep gorge where outcroppings are the favored habitat of leopards.

Fences separate the park from the nearby communities of Langata and Karen, but they do not always prevent the occasional leopard or lion from making a meal out of a dog or horse. This is because of an open corridor to the south that allows wildebeest and other animals to move to other areas in search of food; researchers believe the annual migration in this area was once as spectacular as that in the Serengeti.

Despite the urban pressures, the park contains a good variety of wildlife. Zebras, elands, impalas, and both Grant's and Thomson's gazelles are well represented. Warthogs and ostriches are common on the open plains. Larger game includes Maasai giraffes, which browse in the woodland, and a herd of 50 black rhinos, sometimes found in the light bush around the forest area. Hippos can be spied in the larger pools of the Mbagathi Athi River as well as from a nature trail in the eastern section of the park. In the extreme western border of the park, a low ridge covered by a stand of hardwood trees is home to herds of bushbucks and impalas as well as some of the park's olive baboons. Impala Point, at the edge of the ridge, makes a good vantage point to scan the plains with binoculars for concentrations of game.

Predators include about 30 resident lions; cheetahs can be found stalking game on the plains, but their hunting routines were seriously harmed a few years ago when commuters sped through the park, to avoid traffic jams on Langata Road. A new four-lane highway on Langata Road, plus stricter access, has diminished the problem. Rangers keep a careful note of the movements of the larger animals, so it is worth asking at the gate where to look for lions or rhinos.

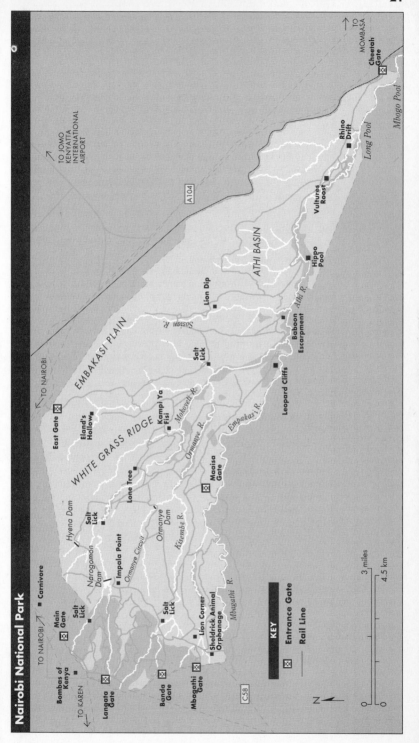

Nairobi National Park

TO MOMBASA

Cheetah
Gate

Mbogo Pool

Rhino
Drift

Long Pool

Vultures
Roost

Hippo
Pool

ATHI BASIN

Baboon
Escarpment

Athi R.

Lion Dip

Sosian R.

Salt
Lick

EMBAKASI PLAIN

Leopard Cliffs

A104

TO JOMO
KENYATTA
INTERNATIONAL
AIRPORT

Embakasi R.

Mokoyeti R.

Kampi Ya
Fisi

Eland's
Hollow

WHITE GRASS RIDGE

East Gate

Ormanye R.

Maaisa
Gate

Lone Tree

Salt
Lick

Hyena Dam

Ormanye
Dam

Kisembe R.

TO NAIROBI

Narogomon Dam

Impala Point

Omanye Circuit

Salt
Lick

Mbagathi R.

Lion Corner

Sheldrick Animal
Orphanage

Main
Gate

Carnivore

Salt
Lick

TO NAIROBI

Bombas of
Kenya

TO KAREN

Langata
Gate

Banda Gate

Mbagathi
Gate

C58

KEY

⊠ Entrance Gate

— Rail Line

N

0   3 miles

0   4.5 km

More than 400 species of birds have been spotted in the park. Around the dams used to create marshes you will find Egyptian geese, crowned cranes, yellow and saddle-billed storks, herons, African spoonbills, sacred ibis, hammerkops, Kittlitz's sand plovers, and marabou storks. In the plains look for secretary birds, vultures, helmeted guinea fowls, bustards, yellow-throated sand grouse, larks, pipits, and Jackson's widow birds, which display during the long rains in May and June. The forests hold cuckoo shrikes, sunbirds, waxbills, flycatchers, and warblers.

The park's network of paved and all-weather dirt roads can be negotiated by cars and vans, and junctions are generally signposted and clearly marked on the official map of the park. Open-roof hatches are not permitted in the park. Do not leave your vehicle except where permitted, as unsuspecting tourists have been mauled by lions and attacked by rhinos. ⊠ *Kenya Wildlife Service, Box 40241, Nairobi,* ☎ *02/501–081,* ℻ *02/505–866,* WEB *www.kenya-wildlife-service.org.* ☞ *$20.*

Olorgesailie. Set in the eastern branch of the Great Rift Valley, Olorgesailie is one of Kenya's best-known archaeological sites. Discovered in 1919 by geologist J. W. Gregory, the area was excavated by Louis and Mary Leakey in the 1940s. They discovered tools thought to have been made by resident of the region more than a half million years ago. A small museum shows some of the axes and other tools found nearby.

The journey here is unforgettable. As you drive south on Magadi Road, you'll find that past the town of Kiserian the route climbs over the southern end of the Ngong Hills, affording fine views of the entire valley. Volcanic hills rise out of the plains as the road drops into dry country where the Maasai people graze their herds. ⊠ *65 km (40 mi) south of Nairobi,* ☎ *02/742–131,* WEB *www.museums.or.ke.* ☞ *Ksh 200.* ⊙ *Daily 9–6.*

☝ ⑬ **Sheldrick Animal Orphanage.** This extraordinary enterprise—named for David Sheldrick, who for 30 years ran Tsavo East National Park—was founded to nurture orphaned animals. So far, more than 30 mature elephants have been returned to the wild. The orphanage is run by his widow, Daphne, a no-nonsense conservationist who was the first to successfully raise baby elephants yet to be weaned. The secret of her success was not only finding a special milk formula but by re-creating the extended family structure required by the very social elephants. You can watch the staff delivering the TLC needed for these very traumatized animals to recover, which includes taking them for walks and sleeping alongside them at night. On most days small groups are allowed to see the orphans between 11 and noon, but be sure to call first. In addition to baby elephants, you may see young rhinos and zebras. ⊠ *Banda Gate of Nairobi National Park,* ☎ *02/891–996,* WEB *www. sheldrickwildlifetrust.org.* ☞ *Ksh 200.* ⊙ *Daily 11–noon.*

DINING

A staple of Kenyan food is *ugali,* as in "the good, the bad, and the ugali." This stiff cornmeal porridge, which may have inspired the favorite in the U.S. South called grits, is often served with *sukuma wiki,* a delicious concoction of kale or other greens. Beyond African food, Nairobi offers an astonishing array of cuisines, with exceptional Indian, French and Italian food, plus several *nyama* (meat) restaurants cashing in on the success of the Carnivore.

The dress code for better restaurants in Nairobi is generally "smart casual," which discourages dressing as if you came to mow the lawn. Jackets for men are suggested for places like Alan Bobbe's Bistro and the

Ibis Grill. (A clean, pressed safari jacket will do if you dress it up with a bow tie.) Unless noted, reservations are not necessary.

Nairobi

$$$$
★ ✗ **Ibis Grill.** Run by Eamon Mullan, one of the country's finest chefs, this restaurant in the Norfolk Hotel reflects his talent for producing contemporary cuisine with a Kenyan twist. Specialties change daily, but you can't go wrong starting with the "taste of three soups," which recently included ostrich consommé, seafood chowder scented with Pernod, and creamy asparagus soup with a dumpling filled with spicy cream cheese. For your entrée move on to grilled giant prawns with mango-mint relish and garlic dip or mignons of ostrich fillet with black pudding served with a juniper berry glaze. The atmosphere is cool and sophisticated, with pink-linen tablecloths and heavy silverware. French doors open onto a lovely courtyard. ⊠ *Norfolk Hotel, Harry Thuku Rd.,* ☎ *02/335–422. Reservations essential. Jacket required. AE, DC, MC, V.*

$$$–$$$$
★ ✗ **Alan Bobbe's Bistro.** During the filming of *Out of Africa,* Robert Redford was a regular at this tiny, mirror-lined bistro. Seafood is a specialty, and the crab claws and grilled lobster are exceptional. The entrance is discreetly hidden off Koinange Street, but that doesn't stop the crowds from packing the place, especially on weekends. Monsieur Bobbe favors those who dress as dashingly as he does. If you brought a jacket, this is the place to wear it. ⊠ *Cianda House, Koinange St.,* ☎ *02/336–952. Reservations essential. Jacket required. AE, DC, V.*

$$$–$$$$ ✗ **Mandhari.** Taking its name from the Swahili word for "landscape," this elegant restaurant has an entire wall devoted to a *mandhari* carved of kisii stone. The attention to detail does not stop there, as the columns are trimmed in cedar and hand-polished tiles. As in the rest of the Nairobi Serena Hotel, there is abundant natural light during the day and a spectacular view of the city at night. This place is known for its spicy curry dishes, but there are also favorites such chicken Cordon Bleu. From the Mt. Kenya area comes a delectable smoked trout that tastes like salmon. ⊠ *Nairobi Serena Hotel, Kenyatta Ave.,* ☎ *02/725–111. Reservations required. AE, DC, MC, V.*

$$$–$$$$
★ ✗ **Tamarind.** Hands down the finest seafood restaurant in town, Tamarind is famous for its deep-fried crab claws, ginger crab, and *piri piri* (spicy, buttery prawns grilled over charcoal). Everything is flown up daily from the coast, including the Malindi sole and the Kilifi oysters, tiny but very flavorful and served either raw or as classic oysters Rockefeller. Try the delicious *kokonda,* based on a famous dish from Fiji—raw fish and shrimp are marinated in lime juice, coconut cream, fennel, mustard seed, and local chili peppers. The setting is quite lovely, with stained glass by renowned Kenya artist Nani Croze. ⊠ *National Bank of Kenya, Harambee Ave.,* ☎ *02/338–959,* WEB *www.tamarind.co.ke. Reservations essential. AE, DC, MC, V.*

$$–$$$ ✗ **Haandi.** Your first clue that this Indian restaurant is something special is the name, which comes from a narrow-mouthed cooking pot that traps in the flavors of foods. Try the *paneer pudina pakora,* which are fingers of homemade cottage cheese rolled in crushed mint and dried mango powder and then deep-fried and served with homemade chutney. Another favorite is *keema mattar adraki,* lamb cooked in yogurt, almonds, and onions. You can't go wrong with the traditional curries, the house specialty. Before coming to Nairobi in 1986, chef Pradeep Mullick honed his skills in Delhi, one of India's culinary capitals. It was in Mombasa, however, that he established his flair for using Kenyan spices. ⊠ *2nd floor, the Mall at Westlands Center,* ☎ *02/448–294. Reservations essential. V.*

24

Nairobi Dining and Lodging

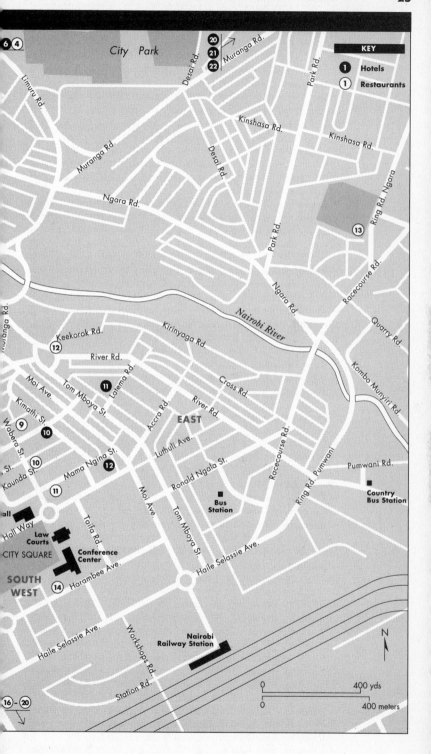

City Park

KEY

❶ Hotels

① Restaurants

Limuru Rd.

Desai Rd.

Muranga Rd.

Park Rd.

Kinshasa Rd.

Kinshasa Rd.

Muranga Rd.

Desai Rd.

Ngara Rd.

Park Rd.

Ngara Rd.

⓭

Ring Rd. Ngara

Racecourse Rd.

Quarry Rd.

Nairobi River

Keekorok Rd.

Kirinyaga Rd.

Kombo Munyiri Rd.

⓬

River Rd.

Latema Rd.

Cross Rd.

Accra Rd.

River Rd.

Moi Ave.

Tom Mboya St.

⓫

EAST

Kimathi St.

⑨

⑩

Racecourse Rd.

Ring Rd. Pumwani

Pumwani Rd.

Wabera St.

St.

⑩

Mama Ngina St.

⓬

Luthuli Ave.

Ronald Ngala St.

Country Bus Station

Kaunda St.

⑪

Bus Station

all

Hall Way

Law Courts

Taifa Rd.

Conference Center

Moi Ave.

Tom Mboya St.

Haile Selassie Ave.

CITY SQUARE

SOUTH WEST

⑭

Harambee Ave.

Haile Selassie Ave.

Workshop's Rd.

Nairobi Railway Station

Station Rd.

N

0   400 yds

0   400 meters

❻ ❹

⓴

㉑

㉒

Muranga Rd.

⑯ – ⓴

$$–$$$ ✕ **La Galleria.** One of several restaurants in the International Casino, La Galleria serves hearty Italian fare in a large, airy room filled with a changing collection of paintings by Davina Dobie. The seafood is particularly good, as is the wide selection of pastas. ⊠ *International Casino, near Museum Hill,* ☏ *02/742–600. Reservations required. AE, DC, MC, V.*

$$–$$$ ✕ **Lord Erroll.** Named after a member of the aristocracy who met a bullet one dark night in 1941, this elegant establishment has quickly earned a reputation for fabulous food. Wood paneling, brass fixtures, and vintage photographs reproduce the era when this area was the domain of British expatriates. Tables overlook a beautiful garden with tinkling waterfalls. A 15-minute drive from the center of the city, Lord Erroll is packed on "spouse night," when two eat for the price of one. Also popular is a Sunday barbecue. ⊠ *89 Runda Rd.,* ☏ *02/521–308. AE, MC, V. Closed Mon.*

$$ ✕ **Toona Tree.** A soaring mahogany tree is the centerpiece of this de-
★ lightful open-air restaurant. In the International Casino, Toona Tree offers a change of scenery for a leisurely, less expensive meal (pizza and pastas), snack, or drink. There is music three nights a week. ⊠ *Museum Hill,* ☏ *02/742–600. AE, DC, V.*

$–$$ ✕ **African Heritage Café.** The café at the African Heritage Gallery serves up fairly authentic African food, including *sukuma wiki* (a mixture of different greens) and *matoke* (steamed bananas). Ethiopian fare is often featured in the Friday-evening buffets, when the place comes alive with African music. The decor employs items from the gallery, and artists sometimes wander through to display their wares. ⊠ *Banda St.,* ☏ *02/337–507. Reservations essential. V.*

$–$$ ✕ **Daas Ethiopian.** Traditional East African food, including *njera* (a spongy bread) and *doro wat* (chicken in a spicy sauce) washed down with *tej* (honey wine), makes this an exotic culinary experience. Whatever you order, it's cooked right at your table on a *jiko* (stove). The decor includes artifacts from Ethiopia and wonderful large baskets. There's live music every evening except Monday. ⊠ *Nairobi Kirichwa Rd. off Ngong Rd.,* ☏ *02/727–353. No credit cards.*

$–$$ ✕ **Mayur.** A wonderful eatery in the small Supreme Hotel, Mayur has
★ a handful of tables upstairs and a bakery below. In business for a couple of decades, Mayur serves up excellent vegetarian dishes for under $3. The all-you-can-eat lunch buffet is one of the best deals in town. ⊠ *Keekorok Rd. and Ngariama La.,* ☏ *02/225–241. No credit cards.*

$–$$ ✕ **Minar.** Excellent Indian food is the attraction of this extremely popular chain, now with three locations. Try the tender chicken kebabs, which are marinated in yogurt and spices before being baked in a traditional tandoori oven. The subtly flavored curries, accompanied by *nan* (puffy bread), also make a good meal, especially when you end with the delicious *kulfi,* an ice cream spiced with saffron. ⊠ *Banda St.,* ☏ *02/229–999;* ⊠ *Hurlingham Centre,* ☏ *02/577–876;* ⊠ *Barclays Plaza on Loita St.,* ☏ *02/748–340. Reservations essential. AE, DC, V.*

$–$$ ✕ **Red Bull.** One of Nairobi's best budget restaurants, the Red Bull is a lively little place packed with business and professional people, as well as a healthy mix of travelers. Because of the Germanic tastes of the original owners, the food is hearty and filling. Try the impala or the fish flavored with a hint of coconut. ⊠ *Silopark House, Mama Ngina St.,* ☏ *02/335–717. Reservations essential. AE, DC, MC, V.*

$–$$ ✕ **Trattoria.** Although the atmosphere is chaotic and the service is indifferent at best, this place is one of the town's most popular people-watching venues. The four tables on Wabera Street have the best views of passersby. Stop by for a quick cappuccino, or settle in for a major Italian meal. Oven-baked pizzas are popular, and the ice cream is perhaps the best in Nairobi. ⊠ *Wabera St. at Kaunda St.,* ☏ *02/240–205. Reservations essential. DC, MC, V.*

$ Kariakor Market. Devour goat and other delicacies alongside the locals at this bustling outdoor market on Racecourse Road. As you enter, turn right and look for the NYAMA CHOMA sign. It's nothing fancy and certainly not for everyone, but where else can you get a filling lunch for about $1? As a bonus you get to eat with your hands. ⊠ *Racecourse Rd.,* ☎ *no phone. No credit cards.*

Ngong Hills

$$$$ ✕ Carnivore. One of the most famous restaurants in Kenya, Carnivore
★ is known for serving wild game—buffalo, giraffe, gazelle, impala, wildebeest, zebra, or even crocodile—grilled over a vast charcoal fire. Waiters carry the sizzling meat to your table on long skewers and carve whatever you wish onto the cast-iron platters that serve as plates. Various sauces, such as a garlic fruit salsa, tempt the taste buds. As strange as it may seem, there are also many excellent choices for vegetarians. The house drink is called *dawa,* a Swahili word for "medicine," and the secret blend of vodka, honey, and lime is prepared by a smiling man in a poncho of colorful kikoi cloth. Sunday night is Africa night, with live music. ⊠ *Langata Rd., between Nairobi and Langata,* ☎ *02/602–764,* WEB *www.tamarind.co.ke. Reservations essential. AE, DC, MC, V.*

$$–$$$ ✕ Horseman. Herbs fresh from the backyard garden of this restaurant's innovative Austrian owner enhances the food. The service, overseen by Rolf Schmid himself, is attentive and cheerful. Saddle of impala, fish soup flavored with coconut, and any of the quail dishes are all well worth trying. Grab a table in the equestrian-theme main dining room, where brass horse hooks hold back the drapes, or outside in the garden. The restaurant, housed in a Tudor-style building in Karen, has a post outside for tethering your polo pony. ⊠ *Ngong Rd. and Langata Rd., Karen,* ☎ *02/882–782. Reservations essential. DC, MC, V.*

$$ ✕ Karen Blixen Coffee Garden. This lovely outdoor café has tables on a terrace and around the garden that are each decorated with a single rose. Try the creamy carrot-and-ginger soup, then move on to the pepper steak. This is a great place to stop for afternoon tea. If you want something a little stronger, inside the billiard room is a long wooden bar. The Tudor-style house next door is being remodeled into a gift shop. ⊠ *Karen Rd., near Karen Blixen Museum,* ☎ *02/882–779. AE, DC, MC, V.*

$–$$ ✕ Caterpillar Café. In the beautiful gardens of the African Butterfly
★ Research Institute, the Caterpillar Café serves a variety of fish dishes, including a delicious seafood salad that is full of shrimp and crab. For dessert look for the homemade cakes and ice cream. ⊠ *256 Dagoretti Rd., Karen,* ☎ *02/884–972. No credit cards.*

$–$$ ✕ Ranger's. With spacious verandas where you can watch the rhinos, warthogs, and bushbuck that gather at the nearby watering hole, this is a great place to stop for a drink. The Safari Walk, which opened in 2001, allows you to stroll on an elevated boardwalk. Inside the safari-theme restaurant you'll find sofas covered in animal-print fabrics, wooden tables and chairs made by locals, and a fireplace to keep out the chill. The menu includes lamb, chicken, and beef cooked on a charcoal grill (the restaurant does not serve wild game). Rangers will cook up a "bush breakfast" for your game drive in Nairobi National Park. ⊠ *Main Gate, Nairobi National Park, off Langata Rd., Langata,* ☎ *02/352–335. No credit cards.*

LODGING

Most of Nairobi's larger hotels have their own water supplies and many secured their own generators after the brownouts the city experienced during the long drought of 2000. If you are visiting during a water shortage, you may want to inquire beforehand if your hotel has backup facilities.

Nairobi

$$$$ 🏨 **Grand Regency.** Overlooking Central Park, the Grand Regency would be right at home in New York City (no wonder its shopping arcade is called "5th Avenue"). Designed with the corporate traveler in mind, the hotel has everything from meeting rooms to secretarial services. The rooms are well appointed, and the baths are equipped with bidets. Head to the sunny atrium for a dip in the indoor pool, or swim laps in the heated pool outside. In between massages at the health club, relax in the sauna or hot tub. ✉ *Loita and Market Sts.,* ☎ *02/211–199,* FAX *02/217–120,* WEB *www.srs-worldhotels.com. 194 rooms, 32 suites. 2 restaurants, bar, room service, in-rooms safes, sauna, 2 pools, exercise room, travel services, business services, conference center, meeting rooms. AE, DC, MC, V.*

$$$$ 🏨 **Nairobi Serena.** Nature isn't far away at this centrally located hotel—
★ bountiful plants cascade from balconies, water trickles in little streams, and a magnificent traveler's palm stands sentry near the pool. The gardens outside blooms with acacia and jacaranda in October. The terrace café, bordered with tall reeds, is resonant with a chorus of resident bullfrogs. The feeling of being pampered overtakes you as soon as you arrive—a doorman wearing white gloves greets you with a smile, and the service only gets better from there. Richly colored fabrics from the region are featured in the well-appointed rooms, which have a view of the city or the garden. African art is showcased in the Mandhari restaurant. A new bar has decor inspired by the Aksum kingdom of ancient Ethiopia. ✉ *Nyene Rd. and Kenyatta Ave.,* ☎ *02/725–111,* FAX *02/725–184. 200 rooms. Restaurant, bar, in-room safes, minibars, pool, hair salon, shops, business center, meeting rooms, parking. AE, DC, MC, V.*

$$$$ 🏨 **Norfolk Hotel.** The elegant Norfolk Hotel refuses to be upstaged by
★ the flashy newcomers. It first opened its doors in 1904, and a complete renovation in 2000 has kept it up to date. Now it has a health club with the latest equipment and a business center with everything from meeting rooms to secretarial services. The renovation expanded the hotel, which now has a spacious lobby (with a chandelier made of antlers) and a new wing of luxurious suites. Even the old swimming pool has a new shine. But the hotel hasn't lost touch with its past—the rickshaw in the hotel's logo remains in the courtyard, and the old cottages at the back of the courtyard retain the character of early Nairobi. The Ibis Grill, which features award-winning international cuisine, has a spacious veranda that makes you feel like you're out in the countryside. ✉ *Harry Thuku Rd.,* ☎ *02/216–940,* FAX *02/216–796,* WEB *www.lonrhohotels.com. 167 rooms. 3 restaurants, bar, pool, health club, business services, meeting rooms. AE, DC, MC, V.*

$$$$ 🏨 **Stanley Hotel.** This venerable hotel is still one of the best lodgings in town. The Thorn Tree Café is a great place to people-watch. On the second floor, the Zen restaurant offers a mix of Mediterranean dishes infused with flavors from the Pacific Rim. The adjacent Exchange Bar is where the Nairobi Stock Exchange operated for 37 years, and the investors who still gather here to hear financial news are kept cool by overhead palm-leaf fans. (The band that plays here in the evening is called Mergers & Acquisitions.) Health-conscious travelers can work out in the state-of-the-art health club, then grab a bite in the new natural-food café, which sits beside the heated terrace pool. The room windows have double-thick glass to keep out the noise of the city. ✉ *Kenyatta Ave. and Kimathi St.,* ☎ *02/228–830,* FAX *02/229–388,* WEB *www.sarovahotels.com. 260 rooms. Restaurants, 2 bars, room service, pool, hair salon, health club, business center, meeting rooms. AE, DC, MC, V.*

$$$$ 🏨 **Windsor Golf & Country Club.** This Victorian-style lodging is set on grounds so expansive that fishing aficionados are invited to angle on

HOW TO
USE THIS GUIDE

Great trips begin with great planning, and this guide makes planning easy. It's packed with everything you need—insider advice on hotels and restaurants, cool tools, practical tips, essential maps, and much more.

COOL TOOLS

Fodor's Choice Top picks are marked throughout with a star.

Great Itineraries These tours, planned by Fodor's experts, give you the skinny on what you can see and do in the time you have.

Smart Travel Tips A to Z This special section is packed with important contacts and advice on everything from how to get around to what to pack.

Good Walks You won't miss a thing if you follow the numbered bullets on our maps.

Need a Break? Looking for a quick bite to eat or a spot to rest? These sure bets are along the way.

Off the Beaten Path Some lesser-known sights are worth a detour. We've marked those you should make time for.

POST-IT® FLAGS
Dog-ear no more!

"Post-it" is a registered trademark of 3M.

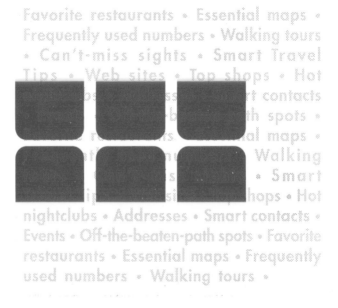

Favorite restaurants • Essential maps • Frequently used numbers • Walking tours • Can't-miss sights • Smart Travel Tips • Web sites • Top shops • Hot [...] contacts [...] spots • [...] maps • [...] Walking [...] • Smart [...] hops • Hot nightclubs • Addresses • Smart contacts • Events • Off-the-beaten-path spots • Favorite restaurants • Essential maps • Frequently used numbers • Walking tours •

ICONS AND SYMBOLS

Watch for these symbols throughout:

★	Our special recommendations
✕	Restaurant
⌂	Lodging establishment
✕⌂	Lodging establishment whose restaurant warrants a special trip
☺	Good for kids
☞	Sends you to another section of the guide for more information
✉	Address
☎	Telephone number
FAX	Fax number
WEB	Web site
🎟	Admission price
☉	Opening hours
$-$$$$	Lodging and dining price categories, keyed to strategically sited price charts. Check the index for locations.
① ❶	Numbers in white and black circles on the maps, in the margins, and within tours correspond to one another.

ON THE WEB

Continue your planning with these useful tools found at **www.fodors.com**, the Web's best source for travel information.

"Rich with resources." —*New York Times*

"Navigation is a cinch." —*Forbes* "Best of the Web" list

"Put together by people bursting with know-how."
—*Sunday Times* (London)

Create a Miniguide Pinpoint hotels, restaurants, and attractions that have what you want at the price you want to pay.

Rants and Raves Find out what readers say about Fodor's picks—or write your own reviews of hotels and restaurants you've just visited.

Travel Talk Post your questions and get answers from fellow travelers, or share your own experiences.

On-Line Booking Find the best prices on airline tickets, rental cars, cruises, or vacations, and book them on the spot.

About our Books Learn about other Fodor's guides to your destination and many others.

Expert Advice and Trip Ideas From what to tip to how to take great photos, from the national parks to Nepal, Fodors.com has suggestions that'll make your trip a breeze. Log on and get informed and inspired.

Smart Resources Check the weather in your destination or convert your currency. Learn the local language or link to the latest event listings. Or consult hundreds of detailed maps—all in one place.

one of three lakes. The big attraction here is an 18-hole golf course. There are magnificent views of the links from the soaring windows of the grand hotel, where a huge fireplace warms the gargantuan ballroom. The rooms are furnished in a style that is reminiscent of a British club. A butler on each floor assists you with car rentals, travel reservations, and the like. Cottages on the grounds, edging toward the last hole, are more private, with a living room separating two bedrooms. Built in 1992, this beauty is already a bit rough around the edges. ⊠ *Garden Estate Rd.,* ☎ *02/862–300,* FAX *02/802–322. 115 rooms, 15 cottages. 2 restaurants, bar, lounge, pool, 18-hole golf course, tennis, horseback riding. AE, DC, MC, V.*

$$$–$$$$ 🏨 **Holiday Inn Mayfair Court.** Dating from the 1940s, this longtime favorite retains its colonial charm, with wood paneling and marble floors, plus lots of gleaming brass. Surrounded by manicured gardens, the hotel gives you the choice of two pools. Breakfast is served in the Oasis Restaurant, and Mischief's Bar is known for its live rock music. If you get the urge to play a little roulette, the Mayfair Casino & Club is in another building nearby. The hotel is one of the few in Nairobi to have wheelchair access. ⊠ *Parklands Rd.,* ☎ *02/740–920,* FAX *02/748–823.* WEB *www.holiday-inn.com/nairobikenya. 171 rooms. Restaurant, bar, no-smoking rooms, hair salon, pool, health club, shops, casino, business services, convention center, meeting rooms. AE, DC, MC, V.*

$$$–$$$$ 🏨 **Hotel Inter-Continental.** Dancing the night away as the lights of Nairobi twinkle below—that's the memory of this hotel that many people cherish. The fine rooftop restaurant, Le Chateau, has wide windows with panoramic views of the city. For a more intimate meal try cozy Le Mistral, a Mediterranean restaurant on the ground level. Only a few minutes from the city center, this hotel has long been a favorite of international travelers but has slipped a bit in recent years. ⊠ *City Hall Way and Uhuru Hwy.,* ☎ *02/261–000,* FAX *02/214–617. 440 rooms. 2 restaurants, bar, room service, in-room data ports, in-room safes, pool, barbershop, hair salon, health club, shops, business services, convention center, meeting rooms, travel services, casino. AE, DC, MC, V.*

$$$–$$$$ ✕🏨 **Nairobi Safari Club.** Like its cousin on the slopes of Mt. Kenya, this hotel requires membership, meaning only guests can enjoy the bar or restaurant. The 11-story tower sits on a base of locally mined brown marble. Suites, which feature a sitting room with a writing desk, have small balconies with excellent views of the city. Kirinyiga, the restaurant on the top floor, serves delicious international cuisine. The Safari Terrace bar re-creates the atmosphere of an exclusive men's club with wood paneling and leather armchairs. There is a jazz brunch on Sunday. ⊠ *University Way,* ☎ *02/251–333,* FAX *02/224–625,* WEB *www.nairobisafariclub. com. 146 rooms. 2 restaurants, bar, room service, pool, sauna, exercise room, travel services, business services. AE, DC, MC, V.*

$$$ ✕🏨 **Hilton International.** Visible for blocks, the cylindrical tower of the Hilton International is a longtime landmark in the city center. Just because it's part of a chain doesn't mean it lacks character—the lobby is mellowed by a sculpture of *makonde* wood and a huge wildlife mural by local artist Joni Waites. The hotel dates from the '60s, but you'll discover all the modern amenities, such as a health club and satellite television. Most rooms have expansive views of the city, while executive suites have French doors that open onto the terrace surrounding the pool. Baths have plenty of hot water from the hotel's private well. The Jockey Pub is a popular watering hole, and there is a rather elegant lounge reserved for guests. ⊠ *Watali St. and Mama Ngina St.,* ☎ *02/250–000,* FAX *02/250–099,* WEB *www.hilton.com. 328 rooms. 4 restaurants, bar, room service, pool, health club, business services, convention center, meeting rooms. AE, DC, MC, V.*

$$$ 🏨 **Safari Park Hotel.** With 60 acres of gardens, the Safari Park Hotel is a great place for bird-watching—look for dozens of species amid the great explosions of colorful bougainvillea. Relax by one of the two pools, including one reputed to be the largest in Africa. Footbridges across ponds and streams lead you to a cluster of shops selling jewelry, clothes, and crafts. Lamu-style furniture graces the spacious rooms, each with a private balcony. Baths all have tubs with gold fittings, twin basins, and fluffy terry-cloth robes. There are six restaurants, including the Nyama Choma, which features a floor show with leggy dancers and acrobats. The Jambo Conference Center holds groups as large as 1,000. ✉ *Thika Rd.,* ☎ *02/802–493,* 📠 *02/802–477. 200 rooms. 6 restaurants, 2 bars, room service, health club, casino, business services, conference center, meeting rooms. AE, DC, MC, V.*

$$ 🏨 **Fairview Hotel.** A relaxed atmosphere sets this lodging, once a pri-
★   vate home, apart from the others in the Nairobi area. On Nairobi Hill, its 5 acres of manicured gardens make the chaos of the city seem far away. Birdsong greets diners at the Terrace Restaurant. The rooms are pleasant, with parquet floors and plenty of sunshine. All the rooms in the main house are different, so ask to see a few before deciding. There are also nine apartments that are perfect for longer stays. Just because it feels as if you are in the country doesn't mean the Fairview lacks amenities—there are a pool, health club, and new conference center. ✉ *Bishops Rd.,* ☎ *02/723–211,* 📠 *02/721–320.* 🌐 *www. fairviewkenya.com. 100 rooms, 9 apartments. Restaurant, bar, room service, pool, health club, playground, business services, convention center, meeting rooms. MC, V.*

$$ 🏨 **Hotel Boulevard.** Close to the National Museum, this hotel north of the city center is a great bargain. The rooms are very plainly furnished, but each has a balcony. Street noise is a problem, so bring earplugs or request a room facing the garden. Rates include breakfast. ✉ *Harry Thuku Rd.,* ☎ *02/227–567,* 📠 *02/334–071. 70 rooms. Restaurant, bar, coffee shop, room service, pool, tennis court, meeting rooms. AE, DC, V.*

$$ 🏨 **Kentmere Club.** Set in the Tigoni Highlands about 18 km (11 mi) north of Nairobi, this British-style manor is surrounded by coffee and tea plantations. Driving here is quite pleasant, as the well-maintained road winds through the picturesque countryside. There are only 16 rooms, each with fireplace and private veranda. The traditional British restaurant serves excellent food, or maybe it simply tastes wonderful because the wait is so long. All vegetables, fruits, eggs, and dairy products are from neighboring farms. The town of Limuru, a gathering point for Africans en route to the weekly market, has a refreshing feeling of being off the beaten path. ✉ *Latema Rd., Limuru,* ☎ *154/241–053. Restaurant, bar. AE, DC, MC, V.*

$$ 🏨 **The Landmark.** Previously known as the Jacaranda Hotel, this family hotel is near all the shopping centers in Westlands. There's a new restaurant on the premises, as well as a playground and plenty of other distractions for the kids. ✉ *Chiromo Rd.,* ☎ *02/448–713,* 📠 *02/545–948. 130 rooms. Restaurant, bar, room service, pool, tennis, volleyball, playground, airport shuttle. AE, DC, V.*

$$ 🏨 **Six-Eighty Hotel.** A hangout for Peace Corps volunteers, this centrally located hotel has clean, comfortable rooms. The Japanese restaurant, Akaska, attracts lunching office workers. The bar has been renovated and now includes a casino. ✉ *Muindi Mbingu St.,* ☎ *02/ 332–680. 380 rooms. Restaurant, bar, room service, shops, casino. AE, DC, MC, V.*

$$ 🏨 **Utalii House.** The Swahili word *utalii* means "tourism," and the stu-
★   dents on the staff here are learning all about that important industry. None of the smiles you encounter here are tired, which may be why airline crews come here to rest theirs. Housed in a square brick build-

ing about 7 km (4 mi) north of town, the hotel has an attractive garden and a pool where you can relax after a long day on safari. Each of the newly decorated rooms has its own balcony. Request one facing the garden to be out of earshot of the passing traffic. ⊠ *Thika Rd.,* ☎ *02/802–540,* FAX *02/803–094. 50 rooms. Bar, breakfast room, pool, tennis courts, airport shuttle. AE, DC, MC, V.*

$ 🍴 **Iqbal Hotel.** For decades travelers on a tight budget have chosen the Iqbal. Rooms are secure and clean, but all have shared baths that are down the hall (you must bring your own toilet tissue and towels). You'll get a hot-water shower only if you're an early bird. There is a restaurant that serves good, cheap fare. ⊠ *Latema Rd.,* ☎ *02/220–914. 13 rooms without bath. Restaurant. No credit cards.*

$ 🍴 **Mrs. Roche's.** A little far from the center of town, this guest house set in a garden is popular with backpackers and other budget-minded travelers. There are dormitory-style rooms, or you can pitch your tent outside—either way, it's less than $2. Shared baths are clean, as are the showers. It's very busy during the high season, so arrive early in the day. ⊠ *Limuru Rd.,* ☎ *no phone. 8 rooms without bath. Campground. No credit cards.*

Ngong Hills

$$$$ 🍴 **Giraffe Manor.** Housed in a distinguished old mansion featured in
★ the film *White Mischief,* Giraffe Manor was built in 1932 for coffee king David Duncan, a Scot who needed a place for his wife to play bridge while he went on safari. It was later the home of Jock and Betty Leslie-Melville, founders of the African Fund for Endangered Wildlife, who sheltered endangered Rothschild giraffes on the 147-acre nature sanctuary. No longer frightened of humans, the long-neck beasts stick their heads in the windows of second-story rooms for photo-ops. Delicious dinners in the wood-paneled dining room featuring what seem like the largest goblets in the world. The host is usually Betty's son, Rick Anderson, and his Tanzania-born wife, Bryony. Because there are only five rooms, reservations must be made well in advance. ⊠ *GoGo Falls La., Langata,* ☎ *02/891–078,* FAX *02/890–949,* WEB *www.giraffemanor.com. 5 rooms. Dining room. AE, DC, MC, V.*

$$$$ 🍴 **Ngong House.** If you ever wanted to stay in a tree house, this is your
★ chance. The five wooden bungalows on stilts are the folly of Paul Verleysen, a Belgian diplomat who oversees the place with his son Christof. One room has a bed designed to resemble an Arab dhow, while another has a canoe transformed into a bathtub. Sunlight streams through stained glass by local artist Nani Croze in some, while others let you relax in sleepers salvaged from the famed Lunatic Express. Baths are large, with lovely details such as hand-painted basins. Days are spent on game drives in nearby Nairobi National Park. Meals, all included in the price, are served outdoors under a *rondavel* (a round hut with a thatched roof). Watch the sunset from your private veranda or the porch of the main house—either way there's a matchless view of the Ngong Hills. ⊠ *Ndovu Rd., Langata,* ☎ *02/891–856,* FAX *02/890–674,* WEB *www.ngonghouse.com. 6 rooms. Restaurant, bar, room service, pool, shops. AE, DC, MC, V. Closed Apr.–May and Nov.*

$$$ 🍴 **Macushla House.** Macushla means "my beloved" in Gaelic, and this peaceful bed-and-breakfast is clearly the pride and joy of owner Carrie Henkel. Near the Giraffe Centre in Langata, this private home has two wings of rooms with beamed ceilings, very original art on the walls, and colorful kilims on polished floors. Two sitting areas, each with a fireplace, embrace the bar. Doors open out onto the terrace, where snacks are served by the pool at tables shaded by colorful umbrellas. The hotel is popular with families, and Kenyans sometimes come to the restau-

rant for the Italian cuisine. ⊠ *Nguruwe Rd., Langata,* ☎ *02/891–987,* FAX *02/891–971. 6 rooms. Restaurant, bar, pool, bar. V.*

$ 🖭 **Whistling Thorns.** An hour's drive south of Nairobi, this lodging is a good choice if you want to be close to the Ngong Hills. Rooms are in precious cottages decorated in shades of pink. There's a cozy dining area inside the main house where lunch and dinner are served. Horseback-riding trips can be arranged, along with bike and walking safaris. There's plenty of game nearby, from ostriches to zebras. ⊠ *Kiserian–Isinya Pipeline Rd., between Kiserian and Isinya,* ☎ *02/350–720,* WEB *www.africaonline.co.ke/campingsafaris. 6 rooms. Restaurant, pool. AE, DC, MC, V.*

NIGHTLIFE AND THE ARTS

The Arts

For information on Nairobi's cultural scene, see *Go Places,* a free monthly publication available at hotels and shops. Another good bet is *Sanaa,* a magazine that lists many cultural events around the city.

Film

The *Nairobi Daily Nation* newspaper lists current offerings at all the city's cinemas. Recent American, British, and Indian films are usually available. You should always stand for Kenya's national anthem, played before each film.

The **Kenya** (⊠ Moi Ave., ☎ 02/226–982) has two screens. Just west of the Kenya is the **Nairobi** (⊠ Uchumi House, 2nd floor on Aga Kahn Walk, near City Hall Way, ☎ 02/226–603), which has one screen. Both show recent releases. The **Twentieth Century** (⊠ between Standard and Mama Ngina, ☎ 02/338–070) has the most reasonable ticket prices, but you'll have to endure endless commercials before the movie starts. The newest venue, the **Fox Cineplex** (⊠ Sarit Center, Westlands, ☎ 226–981) is also the most modern, with comfortable seating and Dolby Digital sound.

Nairobi also has a pair of drive-in theaters. The **Belle-Vue Drive-In** (⊠ Uhuru Hwy., ☎ 02/802–293) is on the road to the airport. The **Fox Drive-In** (⊠ Thika Rd., ☎ 02/802–293) shows two features for less than $1 per carload.

Galleries
Gallery Watatu (⊠ Lonhro Bldg., Standard St., ☎ 02/228–737) holds exhibits of African-themed works by various artists. Although owner Ruth Schaffner passed away, the gallery continues to promote gifted artists. Look for the work of Davina Dobie, Shine Tani, Jonathan Kingdon, and Michael Adams. It's open daily from 9 to 6.

The **Gallery of Contemporary East African Art** (⊠ Museum Hill, ☎ 02/742–131) was established by the National Museum Society as a place for East African artists to display and sell paintings and sculptures. There are a large gallery for group exhibits and a small gallery for solo shows. A Studio Center encourages younger talent. The gallery is open daily from 9 to 6.

Theater
Opposite the Norfolk Hotel, the **National Theatre** (⊠ Harry Thuku Rd., ☎ 02/220–536) stages plays, musicals, and, from time to time, concerts. Built in 1952, the stone in its foyer and the rosemary bush outside its door are both from Shakespeare's birthplace, Stratford-upon-Avon. The **Phoenix Players** (⊠ Professional Center, Parliament Rd.) are a small but active group that produce high-quality dramas. The **Mzizi Cultural Center** (⊠ Sonalux House, Moi Ave., ☎ 02/245–364) hosts

theatrical performances, poetry readings, and concerts on a daily basis. The center also produces *Sanaa,* which lists many cultural events around Nairobi.

The **American Cultural Center** (✉ National Bank Bldg., Harambee Ave., ☎ 02/337–877) organizes films, performances, and lectures by visiting scholars. Most events are free, but you must be a member. If you are hungry for news from home, you can read major American newspapers. The **French Cultural Center** (✉ Maison Française, Loita St., ☎ 02/336–263) hosts art exhibits and speakers from France. The **British Council** (✉ ICEA Bldg., Kenyatta Ave., ☎ 02/334–855) organizes concerts and other events for expatriates.

Nightlife

Nairobi has considerable options after the sun goes down, from laidback bars to steamy discos. If you decide to check out the scene in Nairobi, use considerable caution. Have your hotel call a taxi if you're going out after dark.

Bars and Clubs

Bars at the city's hotels require "smart casual" dress, which means leave the T-shirts and shorts at your hotel. Chinos are preferred over jeans, and a sweater or jacket is expected for men.

At Wilson Airport, the **Aviators Pub** (✉ Langata Rd., ☎ 02/520–766) is a good place to meet local pilots. West of the city center is the notorious **Buffalo Bill's** (✉ Heron Court Hotel, Milimani Rd., ☎ 02/712–944), a raucous venue for singles. Be careful with whom you strike up a conversation, as many of the women here are prostitutes.

In the International Casino, **Galileo's** (✉ Westlands Rd., ☎ 02/744–477) is a private club, but you can probably swing a temporary membership. There's usually a live band. At the Mayfair Court Hotel, **Mischief's** (✉ Parklands Rd., ☎ 02/746–708) is known for its live music. At the Carnivore, the **Simba Saloon** (✉ Langata Rd., between Nairobi and Langata, ☎ 02/602–764) is a popular spot for singles. There's live music ranging from rock to reggae from Wednesday through Sunday.

Casinos

The glitzy **International Casino** (✉ Westlands Rd., Museum Hill, ☎ 02/742–600), the most popular gambling joint in town, offers roulette, blackjack, and an army of one-armed bandits. Men who aren't wearing jackets might be turned away, so be sure to dress appropriately. It's open until 3 AM on weekdays, 3:30 AM on weekends. In the Safari Park Hotel, **Casino de Paradise** (✉ Thika Rd., ☎ 02/802–477 is one of the swankiest in town.

OUTDOOR ACTIVITIES AND SPORTS

Participant Sports

Before you exert yourself, remember that Nairobi is at an altitude of 1,661 m (5,449 ft). The thinner air makes it difficult to exercise, especially if you've just arrived. Take it easy the first few days. The sun is bright, so don't forget the sunscreen.

Jogging

There are several jogging tracks around Nairobi, many of them in the city's beautiful parks. Check out the ones downtown in Central Park and Uhuri Park, or north of downtown in City Park. A group called the **Hash House Harriers** meets outside St. Francis Church in Karen on

Wednesday at 5:30 and Saturday at 4:30. To meet the members, call Raju Singh (☎ 02/446–266 or 02/565–871) to find out about the Monday-evening jogs. The group gets together for dinner afterward.

Sailing

The Nairobi Dam, off Langata Road, is where people congregate for sailing and windsurfing. To connect with the locals, contact the **Nairobi Sailing Club** (✉ Langata Rd., ☎ 02/501–250).

Tennis and Squash

Tennis courts are available at many of the city's hotels, such as the Nairobi Safari Club and the Boulevard Hotel. Several athletic clubs in the area also offer a chance for you to polish up your backhand.

Karen Club (✉ Karen Rd., Karen, ☎ 02/288–280), just across the road from the Karen Blixen Museum, attracts well-to-do locals. Founded more than a century ago, the **Nairobi Club** (✉ Ngong Rd., ☎ 02/223–603) is headquarters of the Kenya Lawn Tennis Association. **Parklands Sports Club** (✉ Ojijo Rd., ☎ 02/742–829) is home to numerous tennis tournaments.

Whitewater Rafting

Rafting trips can be arranged on several different rivers surrounding Nairobi, such as the Ewaso-Ng'iro and the Mathoya. **Savage Wilderness Safaris** (✉ Thigiri Rd., ☎ 02/521–590, WEB www.whitewaterkenya.com), formed in 1987 by a group of expats, pioneered rafting in Kenya. Trips with the organization last from two to five days.

Spectator Sports

Auto Racing

Enthusiasts call the **Kenya Safari Rally** (☎ 02/723–144, WEB www.safarirally.co.ke) the "last great road rally." The grueling three-day circuit starts in the center of the city and winds its way up into the mountains. It's not an easy drive—when it's dry the roads are choked with dust, but a little rain can turn the course into thick, black mud. For more than 40 years the race has attracted the best drivers from around the world. In 2000 Ian Duncan was crowned national champion for a record fifth time, driving his "kitchen-prepared" Toyota Land Cruiser. For years the three-day event was held on Easter, but in 2001 the date was changed to late July.

The **Rhino Charge Race** (✉ Box 39806, ☎ 02/748–307 or 02/750–485, WEB www.chelipeacock.com) is held each year to raise money to protect endangered black rhinos and elephants in the Aberdares.

Horse Racing

The **Ngong Race Course** (✉ Nairobi Ngong Rd., ☎ 02/566–108) was the setting for Beryl Markham's stories about training horses. The author of *West With the Night* lived nearby at a cottage at the Jockey Club until her death in 1986. Her ashes were scattered at the Cemetery Corner near the track. The Sunday meets are a splendid place to see the many different echelons of Nairobi culture. Races are held on Sunday, except in August and September, and on public holidays. In January crowds turn out for races such as the Kenya Guineas and Fillies Guineas. The Kenya Derby and Building Security Stakes are big draws in April, as is the Kenya Oaks in May. In June the Champagne Stakes is where you'll see some of the top horses compete.

Polo

This fast-paced sport is played on Saturday at 3 and Sunday at 10 in Jamhuri Park, on Ngong Road at Dagoretti Corner. For information call the **Nairobi Polo Club** (☎ 02/882–109).

Soccer

Nairobi's most popular sport draws crowds of 60,000 that root for the national team, the Harambee Stars. Matches at held the new **Moi International Stadium** (✉ Thika Rd., ☎ 02/803–295).

SHOPPING

Most shops are open from 8 to 6, sometimes with a break for lunch. Bargaining is acceptable in all places where prices are not marked, and occasionally where they are. Prices can often be negotiated to less than half of what the seller originally asked.

Markets

Whatever you need, chances are you'll find it at the bustling **City Market** (✉ Muindi Mbingu St., ☎ no phone). This is an excellent place to buy souvenirs. If you bargain, you can get good prices on soapstone sculptures, wooden utensils, and colorful fabrics. For a good selection of woven baskets, head east of the city to the crowded **Kariokor Market** (✉ Racecourse Rd., ☎ no phone), a motley collection of stalls where the scent of spices hangs heavy in the air. The market is also a source of cheap goods for locals, including the primitive rubber sandals known as "thousand-milers," so named because they are made from old tires.

Utamaduni (✉ E. Bogani Rd. off Langata Rd. S, Langata, ☎ 02/890–464), a small complex featuring local artists at work, devotes a percentage of profits to the conservation efforts of the Kenya Wildlife Service. There are several floors of shops selling items such as jewelry, masks, and beaded belts. If you get hungry, there's also a small café.

Shopping Malls

The two-story shopping mall called the **Sarit Centre** (✉ Westlands Rd., ☎ 02/747–408) has shops selling a variety of items, but it excels in fabrics. The hub of the Westlands shopping district, it's along the Uhuru Highway northwest of the National Museum. In the suburb of Hurlington there is the newer **YaYa Centre** (✉ Argwings Kodhek Rd., ☎ 02/567–641), where you'll find lovely restaurants such as Minar.

Specialty Stores

African Art

You never know what you'll find at the **Blue Rhino.** Besides exhibits of works by local artists, you may run across antique kilims, carved cedar chests, coconut-fiber lamp shades, and handcrafted furniture from the upcountry, including pieces constructed of wooden dhows. There are address books so beautifully illustrated that you may eschew your Palm Pilot. More than a gift shop, this lively space features a lovely rooftop restaurant with a view of the garden. Blue Rhino is near the ABC Plaza in Westlands. It's open from Monday through Saturday 10–6 and Sunday 10–2. ✉ *James Gichuru Rd. at Kabasiran Ave.,* ☎ *02/448–448,* WEB *www.bluerhinogifts.com.*

Founded in 1979 by artist Nani Croze, **Kitengela Glass Studios** has produced wonderful pieces of stained glass found all over Kenya, including windows at the Tamarind restaurant, in Nairobi, and the Ngong House, in Langata. Croze's son Anselm expanded the studio to include blown glass, and her daughter Katrineka explores molten glass, heated to temperatures of 1,050°C, to make unique hand-spun beads used in jewelry and curtains. Near the southern edge of Nairobi National Park in the suburb of Kitengela, the studio itself sparkles with recycled glass. It's a refreshing surprise at the end of a long dusty road. ✉ *Kitengela,* ☎ *02/711–121.*

Run by Denis Mathews, son of the famed artist Terry Mathews, **Matbronze** features wonderful works in bronze. You can tour the foundry and see depictions of wildlife, including delicate pieces such as a kingfisher perched on a branch. It's in Langata near the Karen Blixen Museum. ✉ *Kifaru La., Langata,* ☎ *02/891–251.*

Full of exquisite Africana, the **Urban Leopard** is owned by American Sandy Price, who has an eye for lovely things. Look for her own original wall hangings of mud cloth, plus beaded baskets and old-fashioned gourds with a new look. The shop is in the Westlands next to the Book Room Café. ✉ *General Mathenge Dr.,* ☎ *02/749–462.*

Antiques
It's not all from Africa, but the pieces you'll discover at the **Jahazi Trading Company** eventually wind up in the best lodges and camps in Kenya. Carved cedar chests, colorful kilims, hand-dyed textiles, and architectural pieces are found at the shop. It's open by appointment only. ✉ *Dagoretti Rd., Karen,* ☎ *02/883–091,* WEB *www.jahazi.com.*

Beads
Run by Lady Sue Wood, wife of Flying Doctors founder Sir Michael Wood, **Kazuri Beads** produces the beads you'll find at higher prices everywhere else. It's fascinating to watch the tiny beads being made. Each has to be carefully shaped, polished, fired, and painted, then fired again. The result is *kazuri,* Swahili for "small and beautiful." Begun in 1975 as a way to assist poor and undereducated women, the shop initially had fewer than 10 employees. Word of the unique jewelry spread, and today more than 80 women work in the factory. ✉ *Mbagathi Ridge, Karen,* ☎ *02/882–362.* ☉ *Mon.–Sat. 8–4:30, Sun. 11–4:30.*

Books
One of the capital's busiest bookstores, the **Nation** boasts a good selection of local maps, travel guides, and other reading material. The shop, inside the Stanley Hotel, also has its own entrance on Kenyatta Avenue. ✉ *Kenyatta Ave. and Kimathi St.,* ☎ *02/333–507,* ☉ *Mon.– Sat. 8–6, Sun. 9–1.*

The **Text Book Centre** carries textbooks and other scholastic items, as well as excellent books about Africa. ✉ *Kijabe St.,* ☎ *02/330–340.* ☉ *Mon.–Sat. 9–5.*

Book Point has a large selection of Africana and popular fiction. ✉ *Loans House, Moi Ave.,* ☎ *02/220–221.* ☉ *Weekdays 8–1 and 2–5.*

Crafts
The shop that "transformed souvenir trinkets to objet d'art," the **African Heritage Gallery** opened on Banda Street in 1970. Several workshops are now required to fill orders, and hundreds of artists produce more than 1 million designs. African Heritage pieces have been exhibited at the Los Angeles Museum of Natural History, the American Museum of Natural History in New York, and the Corcoran Gallery in Washington, D.C. The newest shop, near the Carnivore, opened in December 2000. It's hard to miss, as the building's design was inspired by the mud mosques in Timbuktu. The adjacent African Bead Museum chronicles the history of beads in Africa for the past 12,000 years. ✉ *Banda St. between Koinange and Mbingu,* ☎ *02/251–414;* ✉ *Libra House, Mombasa Rd., near Carnivore, between Nairobi and Langata,* ☎ *02/530–056,* WEB *www.africanheritage.net.* ☉ *Mon.–Sat. 10–6, Sun. 11–4.*

Fabrics

Beach 'n' Bush produces handsome canvas bags that rival those found in New York's Crouch & Fitzgerald. Look for camera bags, rucksacks, and duffel bags, as well as tents, hammocks, and some rather snazzy versions of the classic canvas safari chair. ⊠ *Ngong Rd., near Ngong Racetrack,* ☎ *02/567–568.* ⊙ *Weekdays 8–5:30, Sat. 8:30–1.*

A lovely but expensive shop among the Karen *dukas* (Swahili for "shops"), **Siafu** offers hand-painted wooden trays, batik scarves, beaded sandals, and yards of beautiful fabrics. ⊠ *Karen Shopping Center, Ngong Rd., Karen.* ⊙ *Weekdays 10–6, Sat. 10–6.*

At the **Spinner's Web,** you'll find handwoven carpets, handsome wall hangings, and other items produced by more than 182 workshops around the country. Look for sweaters knitted from hand-spun and natural-dyed local wools and multicolor sisal hats. ⊠ *Viking House, Waiyaki Way,* ☎ *02/441–485.* ⊙ *Weekdays 9–6, Sat. 9–5.*

Gems

Semiprecious stones can be found at **Kimathi Jewellers.** ⊠ *Norwich Union House, Kimathi St.,* ☎ *02/224–754.* ⊙ *Mon.–Sat. 9–5.*

Leather

Adelphi Leather Shop specializes in exclusive handcrafted articles using leather manufactured in Kenya. Products include handbags, briefcases, travel bags, wallets, and belts. ⊠ *Jubilee Insurance Exchange Bldg., Kaunda St.,* ☎ *02/228–925.* ⊙ *Weekdays 10–6, Sat. 10–6.*

SIDETRIPS FROM NAIROBI

Several game reserves are within easy driving distance of Nairobi. One of the most popular is Amboseli National Park, a stop along many tours through Kenya. Far less crowded is Tsavo National Park, home to great herds of elephants.

Amboseli National Park

241 km (150 mi) south of Nairobi.

Among the most popular destinations in Kenya, Amboseli National Park attracts more tourists than any other reserve except Maasai Mara. People trek to this reserve near Mt. Kilimanjaro to watch the huge herds of elephants. They have become accustomed to humans, so you can sit and study their fascinating behavior for hours.

But Amboseli, less than a fourth of the size of the Mara, has difficulty handling all the traffic. Off-road driving has transformed fragile grassland into desert. The soil is easily damaged by vehicles, and parts of Amboseli are so crisscrossed by tire tracks that they resemble the sand dunes of the California coast. Leaving the roads is illegal, but guides sometimes ignore the rules to get their clients closer to the animals.

The park's popularity has also taken its toll on the wildlife. It is not uncommon to see a dozen minivans circled around a lone cheetah that is clearly agitated by all the attention. The spotted cats altered their stalking schedule to avoid tourists, but hunting at midday isn't as efficient. Sadly, the very people who come to Amboseli to admire the cheetahs have helped drive them from the park.

Despite new laws designed to protect the park and its wildlife, Amboseli has not fully recovered. Its existence depends on tourism, but it may be tourists who end up destroying this unique part of Kenya's wilderness. Individuals can make a difference, however. Urge your driver to stick to the designated tracks and patronize those lodges that genuinely care about conservation.

A century ago this was part of the Southern Game Reserve, which covered 17,216 square km (10,700 square mi). This reserve sheltered one of the biggest populations of rhinos, elephants, and hippos in Kenya. Massive herds of wildebeest, buffaloes, zebras, impalas, and Grant's and Thomson's gazelles provided supper to lions, cheetahs, and leopards. In an effort to preserve this wealth of wildlife, the colonial government set aside 3,260 square km (1,259 square mi) for Amboseli National Reserve in 1948.

But the region was also important to the Maasai people, who grazed their cattle here. In an attempt to reconcile the competing needs for natural resources, Kenya embarked on an experiment in 1961. Maasai Amboseli Game Reserve was created and placed under the control of the Kajiado District Council, run by Maasai elders. But when grazing continued to destroy the fragile ecosystem, a plan was devised to create a core area where cattle would be banned. President Jomo Kenyatta decreed that 392 square km (150 square mi) would be off-limits to the Maasai. In 1977 the area was designated as Amboseli National Park, a move that was hailed as a great victory for wildlife conservation.

The plan was simple: water would be pumped to the outlying areas that the Maasai would be allowed to use as pasture. Unfortunately, pumps sometimes break down. During the severe droughts of the late 1970s and early 1980s, cattle could be seen among herds of wildebeest and zebras that had descended on the wetlands of Amboseli. The Maasai saw no problem with this arrangement. Their ancestors, after all, had shared this source of water with the wildlife for centuries. When the government tried to move the cattle out, some Maasai *morani* (warriors) waged an effective protest by spearing to death several rhinos and elephants. They didn't even bother to remove the horns or ivory; the motive was political, not profit. The two sides have reached a truce in recent years, although it's a fragile one.

The park is named Amboseli for the whirls of white, fine alkaline grit that dance like dervishes across this landscape. In Maa, the language of the Maasai, *empusel* means "dust." When explorer Joseph Thomson (after whom the Thomson's gazelle is named) came through in 1883, he was surprised to see game despite "the desolate and barren aspect of the country." The average annual rainfall is only about 12 inches, which means that for much of the year the reserve resembles a desert. When clouds deliver any moisture, they tend to do so over nearby Mt. Kilimanjaro.

Because of the lack of precipitation, Lake Amboseli is usually a dry plain that gleams with evaporated salts. The lake can flood during the rainy season, so beware of what might look like a solid surface but is merely a thin crust. After a downpour you could find yourself up to your axles in mud, as many a visitor has learned while seeking relief from the washboard roads.

You'll never forget the sight of a herd of elephants lumbering past Mt. Kilimanjaro when the snows are painted pink by the rising sun. The 5,894-m (19,340-ft) peak offers one of the more spectacular backdrops to wildlife photography in Africa. Don't wait too long to snap that photo, as the mountain will hide behind a veil of clouds from the middle of the morning until about an hour before sundown. The best photographs are taken before you have breakfast or after you settle down for a late-afternoon "sundowner." Take it from the edge of the big swamp, which provides some perspective because of the nearby trees.

Otherwise images of Mt. Kilimanjaro cannot come close to your first-hand impression.

The picturesque swamp is called Engongo Narok, which means "black and benevolent." Never has any piece of nature been so beautifully named. Here waters from melting snows trickle down from Mt. Kilimanjaro, eventually percolating out of black lava fissures. This water from the mountain grants verdant life to the notoriously dusty landscape. Here you'll find more than 420 species of birds. Buffaloes and giraffes wander by with yellow-and red-billed oxpeckers hitching a ride, picking off ticks and other parasites. Cattle egrets are often seen standing expectantly around the feet of elephants, waiting to pounce on insects stirred up by heavy footsteps. Keep an eye out for the Taveta golden weaver—it's seen only in the Amboseli region. Elegant crowned cranes are common, and huge flocks of sandgrouse invade watering holes during the dry season. Migrant waders are found around the wetlands between August and April.

The southeastern part of the park, mostly scrub, is not thick with game. But don't eschew open spaces; it makes it easier to track lions and other predators. Leopards thrive in the forested area in the southwest around the Kitirua Gate. From Observation Hill you can look down over the plains and spot the rare black rhinos, and sometimes see elephants down on their front knees in the thick grass, munching away.

Western Amboseli is made up mainly of dry flats covered with tufts of salt-tolerant grasses and shrubs. You can snap some good photos of ostriches against the mirage that develops in the shimmering heat. Kori bustards find this desert a good hunting ground for reptiles and insects. The northern and eastern parts of the park are mainly acacia thornbush where antelopes—massive elands and the diminutive dik diks are among the 13 species found here—are surveyed by the big cats. Don't overlook the smaller animals, however. Amboseli is home to the termite-eating aardwolf, the honey badger, and the ant bear. If you stay in a lodge or tented camp outside the reserve you can go on night game drives in search of nocturnal creatures, including African hares and bush babies, and learn how to distinguish the glowing eyes of carnivores from those of herbivores.

East of the park, a Maasai community has set up the Kimana Wildlife Sanctuary, where you can find elephants, leopards, lions and other animals. There is a lodge and tented camps, with revenue going back to the community. A similar conservation area has been established 17 km (11 mi) north of the park. Eselenkei is only half the size of Amboseli, but you won't see as many minivans because the number of visitors is limited to 60 per day.

June is one of the best times to see Amboseli, shortly after the heavy rains. You'll avoid the busiest months of July and August, when the park is most crowded. June is considered a shoulder season by many tour operators, so ask about a discount on safari packages. Otherwise, you may want to consider a visit during the short rains of October and November. ⊠ *Kenya Wildlife Service, Box 40241, Nairobi,* ☎ *02/501–081,* ⅋ *02/501–752.* ⊠ *$27.*

Lodging

$$$$ ⊡ **Amboseli Serena Lodge.** Built in the style of traditional Maasai dwellings, this comfortable lodge faces Engongo Narok. There is a fairly good view of the wetlands, which are often visited by elephants. Excellent bird-watching can be had in the lush and tropical gardens near the pool. The rooms are terribly small, but to compensate they are decorated with Maasai crafts; a gourd, for example, serves as a lamp shade,

Amboseli National Park

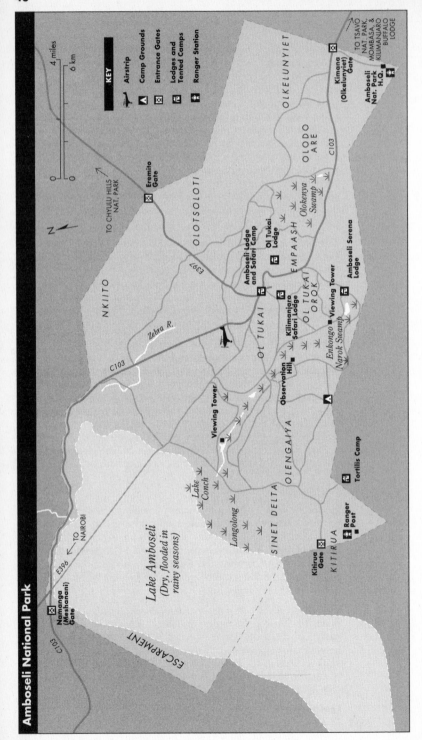

KEY

- Airstrip
- Camp Grounds
- Entrance Gates
- Lodges and Tented Camps
- Ranger Station

4 miles

6 km

N

TO CHYULU HILLS
NAT. PARK

Eremito Gate

OLOTSOLOTI

NKIITO

Zebra R.

C103

TO
NAIROBI

E396

Namanga
(Meshanani)
Gate

C103

ESCARPMENT

Lake Amboseli
(Dry, flooded in
rainy seasons)

Lake
Conch

Longolong

SINET DELTA

OLENGAIYA

Viewing Tower

Observation
Hill

OL TUKAI

Amboseli Lodge
and Safari Camp

Ol Tukai
Lodge

Kilimanjaro
Safari Lodge

OLTUKAI
OROK

EMPAASH

Olokenya
Swamp

Olokenya
Swamp

OLODO
ARE

C103

OLKELUNYIET

TO TSAVO
NAT. PARK,
MOMBASA, &
KILIMANJARO
BUFFALO
LODGE

Kimana
(Olkelunyiet)
Gate

Amboseli
Nat. Park
H.Q.

Amboseli Serena
Lodge

Enkongo
Narok Swamp

Viewing Tower

Tortilis Camp

Ranger
Post

Kitirua Gate

KITIRUA

E397

E397

and a shower curtain is held aloft on a Maasai spear. If you want to see the watering hole in the middle of the night, reserve rooms 45 or 51. If you want a view of Mt. Kilimanjaro, try 23 or 24. Cultural lectures are sometimes part of the afternoon fare, and dancers perform in the evening. ✉ *Amboseli National Park,* ☎ *02/725–111,* 🖷 *02/725–184,* 🕸 *www.serenahotels.com. 96 rooms. Restaurant, bar, pool, shop, library, meeting rooms. AE, DC, MC, V.*

$$$$ 🏕 **Tortilis Camp.** This luxurious camp, named after the elegant trees ★   that grace the area, is the nicest place to stay near the reserve. Located near the Kitirua Gate, the cluster of tents has a view of the plains, which are often dotted with wildlife. From the flagstone-floored lounge, sunsets paint a pink glow on the snows of Mt. Kilimanjaro. The spacious tents, each with a private veranda, have a thick thatch roof to keep you cool at midday. Creature comforts abound—solar panels provide electricity for lights and heat your hot water. A pool awaits after a long day in the bush. Because the camp is outside the park, you can take a walking safari led by a Maasai guide or go on a night game drives. The cuisine is Italian, made with herbs and vegetables grown near the camp. Some of your fee benefits the local Maasai community. Book through Cheli & Peacock. ✉ *Near the Kitirua Gate,* ☎ *02/748–307,* 🖷 *02/750–225,* 🕸 *www.chelipeacock.com. 17 tents. Dining room, bar, pool, shop, private airstrip. AE, MC, V.*

$$$$ 🏨 **Ol Tukai Lodge.** The first structures at Ol Tukai were bandas built by Paramount Pictures in 1948 for the filming of *The Snows of Kilimanjaro.* These cottages were demolished, but in their place is a modern hotel loaded with amenities. An electric fence surrounds the lodge, but zebra and gnu come close, and vervet monkeys are kept at bay by a hotel attendant who wields a mean slingshot. Yellow-barked acacia trees surround the beautiful wooden lodge. The decor is safari chic, with touches like chandeliers constructed of spears. Book through Block Hotels. ✉ *Amboseli National Park,* ☎ *02/535–412,* 🖷 *02/545–954,* 🕸 *www.blockhotelske.com. 80 rooms. Restaurant, bar, pool, shop, meeting rooms. AE, DC, MC, V.*

$$$$ 🏨 **Kilimanjaro Buffalo Lodge.** Located near a Maasai village, this traditionally designed lodge has cottages covered with *makuti* (dried palm leaves). The Hemingway Tower Bar overlooks a watering hole visited by game at night. The lodge offers excursions to Amboseli, but you can also use it as a base for exploring nearby Tsavo National Park. There are camel rides, guided nature walks, and charter flights over Mt. Kilimanjaro. The lodge can sometimes feel crowded, as there can be as many 200 guests here at any time. *15 km (9 mi) east of Amboseli National Park,* ☎ *02/227–136,* 🖷 *02/219–982. 100 rooms. Restaurant, bar, minibars, private airstrip. AE, DC, V.*

$$$$ 🏨 **Kilimanjaro Safari Lodge.** Originally a tented camp, this cluster of thatch-roofed chalets sits in a grove of acacia trees. Said to be on the site of a Hemingway encampment, the camp lacks the charm that fact might imply. The lodge shares an entrance with the Amboseli Lodge, and both are thick with tour groups. This lodge alone can house up to 200 guests at a time. If you book here, make sure to ask for one that faces Mt. Kilimanjaro. ✉ *Amboseli National Park,* ☎ *02/227–136,* 🖷 *02/219–982. 100 rooms. Restaurant, bar, pool, shop. AE, DC, V.*

Tsavo National Park

By far the largest reserve in Kenya, Tsavo National Park covers an area about the size of Wales. Because of its sheer size—an impressive 20,808 square km (8,034 square mi)—Tsavo is a great place to take in the vast landscape completely undisturbed. The park sees relatively few visi-

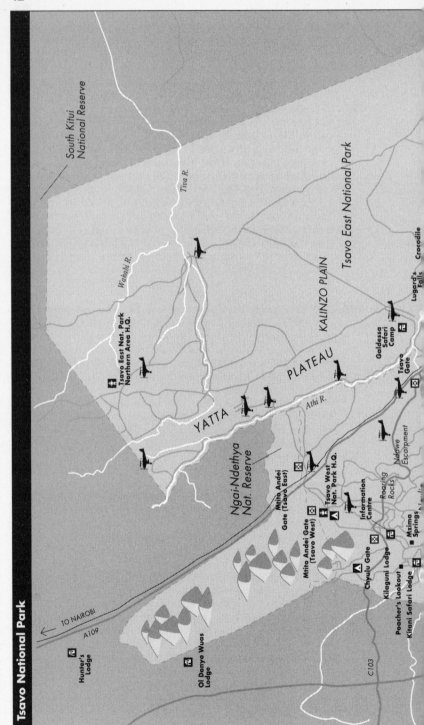

South Kitui
National Reserve

Tiva R.

Wakubi R.

Tsavo East Nat. Park
Northern Area H.Q.

Tsavo East National Park

KALINZO PLAIN

PLATEAU

Galdessa Safari
Camp

Lugard's
Falls

Crocodile

YATTA

Athi R.

Tsavo
Gate

Ngai-Ndethya
Nat. Reserve

Ndawe
Escarpment

Mtito Andei
Gate (Tsavo East)

Tsavo West
Nat. Park H.Q.

Information
Centre

Roaring
Rocks

Mtito Andei
Gate (Tsavo West)

Mzima
Springs

TO NAIROBI

A109

Hunter's
Lodge

Ol Donyo Wuas
Lodge

Chyulu Gate

Kilaguni Lodge

Poacher's Lookout

Kitani Safari Lodge

C103

43

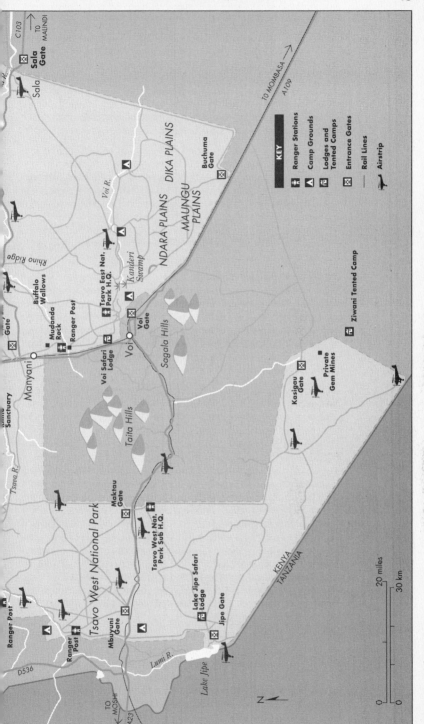

KEY

- Ranger Stations
- Camp Grounds
- Lodges and Tented Camps
- Entrance Gates
- Rail Lines
- Airstrip

TO MALINDI

Sala Gate

Sala

C103

TO MOMBASA

A109

DIKA PLAINS

Buchuma Gate

NDARA PLAINS

MAUNGU PLAINS

Voi R.

Rhino Ridge

Buffalo Wallows

Ranger Post

Mudanda Rock

Tsavo East Nat. Park H.Q.

Kanderi Swamp

Voi Gate

Voi

Sagala Hills

Voi Safari Lodge

Manyani

Sanctuary

Tsavo R.

Taita Hills

Ziwani Tented Camp

Kasigau Gate

Private Gem Mines

KENYA

TANZANIA

Maktau Gate

Tsavo West National Park

Tsavo West Nat. Park Sub H.Q.

Lake Jipe Safari Lodge

Jipe Gate

Mbuyuni Gate

Ranger Post

D536

Ranger Post

TO MOSHI

A23

Lumi R.

Lake Jipe

N

0   20 miles
0   30 km

tors, so you can easily escape the tour groups that are ubiquitous in Amboseli.

Established in 1948, Tsavo was split in two a year later to make governing the sprawling reserve more manageable. In theory they are parts of the same park, but in practice they operate autonomously, with separate headquarters, staff, and entrance fees. Tsavo's two sections, split by the Mombasa highway, stretch for more than 241 km (150 mi). Tsavo West extends southward to the Tanzanian border, while Tsavo East reaches north to the Galana River.

A wide variety of wildlife is found in Tsavo, including elephants that appear red from a dusting in the ocher soil. But the elephants here survived poachers, so they are wary of humans. It was in Tsavo that elephant expert Iain Douglas-Hamilton easily arranged for a charge in the IMAX film *Africa's Elephant Kingdom*. The great herds of rhinos that once roamed the park have been decimated, killed for their horns. Fetching a high price for their alleged aphrodisiac properties, the horns have about as much value as biting your fingernails, since they are made of the same substance.

Tsavo East National Park

Tsavo East is mainly dry thornbush country crisscrossed by streams during the rainy seasons. The vegetation has had three decades to recover from the drought of the early 1970s, when elephants desperate for food pushed over the trees to get at the leaves and branches. After the rains, the tall green grass and flowering shrubs turn this into a lush landscape. Fantastic baobab trees, sitting atop their impossibly thick trunks, dot the plains.

There are two main circuits in Tsavo East, centering on the park headquarters near the Voi Gate. The first takes you north to Mudanda Rock, a mile-long outcropping of stratified stone. A watering hole forms from the runoff, attracting elephants, buffaloes, and other game during the dry season. The spectacle of dense game can be viewed from a terrace ledge halfway up the rock, reached by steps leading up the side opposite the watering hole. This route then takes you northwest to the Galana River, where in the dry season you can spot much game. Soon you'll reach the turnoff to Lugard's Falls, where you can stroll down to the river to view broad rapids skidding over gigantic flat rocks. A short walk downstream brings you to the falls themselves, a violent gush of white water squeezed within a narrow fissure in solid rock. Below the falls are the calmer pools of Crocodile Point, where you may catch a glimpse of the reclusive creatures. The return trip takes you past Rhino Ridge, now a misnomer. The second route from the Voi Gate heads west along the seasonal Voi River, where there is a permanent reservoir of about 200 acres. The Kanderi wetlands are a good spot for birding. You'll return through light bush.

Most of the game species are present, including large herds of buffaloes. In Tsavo East dry country animals such as the fringe-eared oryx, gerenuk, and magnificent lesser kudu can be seen. Lions and cheetahs are numerous, but difficult to spot because of the high grass. You will see wildlife on a game drive, but not in such profusion as in Amboseli or Maasai Mara. The best place to see game, especially in the dry season, is around the watering holes of the lodges and tented camps. ⊠ *Kenya Wildlife Service, Box 40241, Nairobi,* ☎ *02/501–081,* FAX *02/501–752.* 🖙 *$23.*

$$$$ 🏨 **Galdessa Safari Camp.** This elegant camp is built on a bend in the Galana River, not far from Lugard's Falls. Decorated with flair, it is featured in the book *Safari Style*. Tents have wooden floors and thatch-covered roofs to keep you cool during midday. All have baths with flush toilets, and the three largest have private sitting rooms. Owner Pierre Andre Mourgue d'Algue helped reintroduce black rhinos into Tsavo East, and nearly 50 of the creatures can be spotted nearby. Solar power means no noisy generator, and your laundry is done by hand. You can charter a flight to the airstrip at Lugard's Falls. ⊠ *Tsavo East National Park,* ☎ *02/890–635,* FAX *02/891–307,* WEB *www.galdessa.com. Dining room, bar, hiking. 8 tents. AE, DC, MC, V.*

$$$$ 🏕 **Patrick's Camp.** This traditional tented camp can be found in Tsavo
★ East only in November and December, as Patrick Reynolds wants to ensure that it has a minimal impact on the environment. There are plenty of opportunities for hikes around the area, as walking safaris are his forte. Special bush picnics are organized for safari walks. Book through Bush Homes of East Africa. ⊠ *Tsavo East National Park,* ☎ *02/571–647,* FAX *02/571–665,* WEB *www.bush-homes.co.ke. 5 tents. Dining room. AE, DC, MC, V.*

$$$ 🏕 **Voi Safari Lodge.** Brilliantly situated high on Woressa Hill, Voi Safari Lodge overlooks three watering holes in the Ndara Plains. You can see game from your rooms and just about anywhere in the lodge, including the swimming pool. A popular lunch stop for people driving between Mombasa and Nairobi, the lodge has a gas station. Book through Africa Tours and Hotels. ⊠ *Tsavo East National Park,* ☎ *02/336–858,* FAX *02/218–109. Dining room, bar, pool, private airstrip. 16 tents. AE, DC, MC, V.*

Tsavo West National Park

Tsavo West has denser vegetation and a more varied landscape than Tsavo East, largely because of the presence of the Chyulu Hills. The 80-km (50-mi) range was virtually unexplored until 1938, when botanist Peter Bally (of the Swiss shoe family) and his wife Joy surveyed this region for the National Museum in Nairobi. She was an accomplished artist, and the beautiful watercolors she painted while on this journey are still on display at the museum. She is better remembered by her second married name, Joy Adamson.

There is a heavenly quality to these largely uninhabited hills, which are fed by the clouds at dawn. Because the rains that fall here filter down through the porous volcanic soils, you must bring plenty of water when exploring this region. Many trees have adapted by absorbing more water through their leaves than through their roots. The runoff eventually accumulates in underground rivers, which flow to Mzima Springs.

Only the southeast tip of the Chyulu Hills sits inside the national park. The rest belongs to the Maasai. A rough road traverses the length of the hills, offering stupendous views of Mt. Kilimanjaro as it winds from one side to the other. Around the base of the hills, which peak at 2,170 m (7,130 ft), hundreds of smooth volcanic cones dot the landscape. The Chyulu Hills are one of the youngest ranges in the world; one peak called Shaitani (meaning "devil" in Swahili) came into being only 200 years ago. The road leading through the Chyulu Gate passes over this jagged black mass of raw rock. A few hardy trees have begun to grow here. From barren lava flows you see grasses taking hold in the rock crevices, then green hills, and then dense cedar forests carpeted in orchids and ferns.

A central stop in Tsavo West is Kilaguni Lodge, the country's oldest park lodge. To the east are tracks that wind through the hills. A stop at Roaring Rocks is worthwhile for the view from the top of the 91-m (300-ft) cliff. Klipspringers can be spotted on the rock outcroppings of the Ngulia Mountains. South of Kilaguni Lodge are tracks lead to Poacher's Lookout, where the top of a grassy volcanic hill affords excellent views of Mt. Kilimanjaro. Also south of Kilaguni Lodge is Mzima Springs, where lush vegetation full of vervet monkeys and baboons surrounds large pools of sparkling spring water that surfaces at the rate of 50 million gallons a day. The water has traveled a long way to get here; it began as rain that fell on the Chyulu Hills some 48 km (30 mi) to the south. Much of the water is piped to Mombasa, where at one time it was the principal supply. From an underwater observation chamber sunk into the upper pool you can watch hippos and crocodiles. A well-worn nature trail encircles the springs.

If you are intrepid, consider a trip to Lake Jipe, a small, shallow lake sitting astride the Tanzanian border that has excellent views of the Pare Mountains. At the Lake Jipe Safari Lodge you can sail on an ancient dhow as you spot birds around the reed-covered lake. Your guide will take care to steer clear of the hippos that make their homes here.

Birds are profuse, especially around the lakes and rivers, with more than 400 different species making an appearance. Tsavo is on a migration corridor from the coast, and visitors from the north fly over the park in November and December. Ornithologists have tracked birds from as far north as Russia. Several species of starlings and weaverbirds abound, along with hornbills, which are always ready to take tea with guests at the Kilaguni Lodge. European and lilac-breasted rollers are common, and there is a good variety of raptors, including snake-eating secretary birds. Water birds such as herons and yellow-billed storks are easy to find. ⊠ *Kenya Wildlife Service, Box 40241, Nairobi,* ☎ *02/501–081,* ℻ *02/501–752.* ☞ *$23.*

LODGING

$$$$ 🏨 **Finch Hatton's Camp.** While the wildlife is scarce, so are the crowds
★ in this area of Tsavo West once favored by British bush pilot Denys Finch Hatton. His aristocratic style, remembered in the film *Out of Africa,* inspired the elegance of this tented camp. The main lounge has a crackling fireplace, leather couches, and writing desks lit by brass lamps. Crystal glassware makes dinners in the bush sparkle. Built near a spring, the camp's public areas are linked by elevated wooden walkways and bridges. A spacious lounge overlooks pools of hippos, while rooms look out over the plains. Morning brings good views of Mt. Kilimanjaro. ⊠ *Tsavo West National Park,* ☎ *02/604–321,* ℻ *092/604– 323. 35 tents. Bar, dining room, minibars, pool, shop. AE, MC, V.*

$$$$ 🏨 **Ol Donyo Wuas.** Profiled in Peter Mathiessen's book *Sand Rivers,*
★ Richard Bonham was the first conservationist in the Chyulu Hills to work with local Maasai people on finding ways to protect the area's wildlife. The result was Ol Donyo Wuas, situated on 300,000 acres in the Chyulu Hills. With a name that means "spotted hills," Ol Donyo Wuas sits in a region dotted with whistling thorn trees. You have some magnificent views of Mt. Kilimanjaro as at nearby Amboseli National Park, but rather than encountering herds of minivans you can canter alongside giraffes and zebras on horseback. Spacious rooms opening onto magnificent vistas were featured on the cover of *Safari Style.* Even the baths are cavernous. ⊠ *Tsavo West National Park,* ☎ *02/882–521,* ℻ *02/882–728,* 🌐 *www.richardbonhamsafaris.com. Dining room, bar, horseback riding, private airstrip. 6 cottages. AE, DC, MC, V.*

$$$ 🏨 **Kilaguni Lodge.** Big, busy, and full to overflowing in the high season, this well-situated lodge has its own watering hole and salt lick for attracting game, as well as good views of the Chyulu Hills and Mt. Kilimanjaro. Although it opened its doors in 1962, the lodge is still one of the best in the region. Private bandas have been added to supplement the 50 standard rooms. Game drives are available with lodge

vehicles. ✉ *Tsavo West National Park,* ☎ *02/336–858,* FAX *02/218–109. Dining room, bar, pool, meeting rooms, private airstrip. 50 rooms, 16 tents. AE, DC, MC, V.*

$$$ 🏨 **Lake Jipe Safari Lodge.** Located a short drive from the shores of Lake Jipe, the lodge has spectacular views of Mt. Kilimanjaro and the Pare Mountains. Spacious *rondavels* (round huts) surround a complex featuring a sunken lounge, dining room, and three bars. You have to venture to the pool to see the lake. Take along insect repellent or the mosquitoes will limit your fun in the sun. ✉ *Tsavo West National Park,* ☎ *02/227–623,* FAX *02/227–623. Dining room, 3 bars, pool, boating. 16 tents. AE, DC, MC, V.*

$$$ 🏨 **Ziwani Tented Camp.** Located near the Tanzanian border, Ziwani is just outside the boundary of Tsavo West. The original 16 tents are rather close together, but four others across the Sante River have more privacy. A small dam has created an oasis for birds, and you are lulled to sleep at night by the sound of trickling water. Each tent is shaded by a thatched roof. There is no electricity, so meals are prepared on charcoal grills and breads are baked in metal trunks. Because it is located outside the park, you can indulge in nighttime game drives and walking safaris. An airstrip is near the camp, but many visitors drive here from the coast. Book through Prestige Hotels. ✉ *South of Tsavo West National Park,* ☎ *02/338–084,* FAX *02/217–278,* WEB *www.africaonline.co.ke. Dining room, bar, private airstrip. 16 tents. AE, DC, MC, V.*

$ 🏨 **Hunter's Lodge.** Established by game warden John Hunter, this is where many travelers take a break on the main highway between Nairobi and Mombasa. It is near a pond shaded by yellow-barked acacia that contains black bass and tilapia. A peacock patrols nearby. The lodge is not luxurious, but it is a good place to stop for lunch and watch the Kamba woodcarvers. ✉ *Mombasa Rd.,* ☎ *02/221–439,* FAX *02/332–170. Dining room, bar. 20 rooms. AE, DC, MC, V.*

NAIROBI AND THE NGONG HILLS A TO Z

To research prices, get advice from other travelers, and book travel arrangements, visit www.fodors.com.

AIR TRAVEL TO AND FROM NAIROBI

Jomo Kenyatta International Airport, named after the country's first president, lies 13 km (8 mi) southeast of Nairobi. More than 30 international carriers fly into the airport. Numerous flights from Europe land in Kenya each day, giving you plenty of options. British Airways and Swissair offer direct flights into Nairobi. KLM and Kenya Airways offer daily service from Amsterdam and London. Gulf Air and Emirates offer reasonably priced service from Europe with stopovers in the Middle East. If you are flying from the United States, you will need to catch a connecting flight in Europe. Northwest Airlines offer a connecting service with KLM, American Airlines connects with British Airways, and Virgin Atlantic connects with Kenya Airways.

A few carriers, most notably Kenya Airways, also use the international terminal for domestic flights. Kenya Airways flies to Kisumu, Malindi, and Mombasa. Regional Air Services, a sister airline to Airkenya, is based at Jomo Kenyatta Airport and has jet services to Harare, Lusaka, and Khartoum.

Wilson Airport is the departure point for both regularly scheduled and chartered flights within Kenya. Flights leave frequently for Mombasa, Malindi, Lamu, and other destinations. Of all the domestic airlines,

Airkenya is by far the most reliable. Tropic Air offers flights to the Mt. Kenya area.

Airkenya has daily flights from Wilson Airport to the airstrip near Ol Tukai Lodge in Amboseli National Park. There are no scheduled flights to Tsavo National Park, but you can charter a flight to any of the more than 30 airstrips within the reserve.

➤ DOMESTIC CARRIERS: **Airkenya** (☎ 02/605–745, WEB www.airkenya.com). **Boskovic Air Charters** (☎ 02/501–210). **Eagle Aviation** (☎ 02/822–924). **Tropic Air** (☎ 0176/32890).

➤ INTERNATIONAL CARRIERS: **Kenya Airways** (☎ 02/210–771, WEB www.kenya-airways.com). **Regional Air Services** (☎ 02/311–623).

AIRPORTS AND TRANSFERS

If your visit to Kenya is through a tour operator, you will probably be met in the arrival area by a driver holding a placard bearing your name. Tour operators do not always dispatch a driver if you arrive at a different time from the rest of the group, so call to confirm.

Many hotels offer a shuttle service to and from the airports, so inquire when you make a reservation. Kenya Airways runs an hourly shuttle bus with drop-offs at any centrally located hotel for Ksh 1,000.

After leaving customs you will be approached by taxi drivers. Be sure to agree on a price before getting in, as many taxis have broken meters. The fare into the city center should be around Ksh 1,070, while fares to Langata should be Ksh 2,000. Kenatco is a reliable firm with fixed rates.

➤ TAXI COMPANIES: **Kenatco** (✉ Uchumi House, Aga Khan Walk, ☎ 02/225–123). **Kenya Airways** (✉ Barclays Plaza, Loita St., ☎ 02/229–291).

BIKE TRAVEL

Nairobi's deep potholes and unpredictable drivers make biking dangerous. Roads outside town are not any safer, as there are often no shoulders. That said, you'll notice that residents ride bikes in the city, and mountain bikes are the rage in the bush. Bike safaris can be arranged through such operators as Cheli & Peacock.

➤ BIKE SAFARIS: **Cheli & Peacock** (✉ Lengai Bldg., Wilson Airport, ☎ 02/748–307, WEB www.chelipeacock.com).

BUS TRAVEL TO AND FROM NAIROBI

For travel to neighboring Tanzania, use reputable companies such as Davanu Shuttle and Riverside Shuttle, which offer daily service to Arusha. Buses leave Nairobi and Arusha at 8 and 2. The five-hour journey costs $20–$25.

For travel within Kenya, Connection offers service to Mombasa. The eight-hour ride costs $15. Another good bus company is Akamba, which runs buses to Mombasa and many destinations in Kenya.

➤ BUS COMPANIES: **Akamba** (✉ Kitui Rd. off Kampala Rd., ☎ 02/555–690). **Connection** (✉ Jubilee House, Wabera St., ☎ 02/223–304). **Davanu Shuttle** (✉ University Way, ☎ 02/222–002). **Riverside Shuttle** (✉ Koinange St., ☎ 02/219–020).

BUS TRAVEL WITHIN NAIROBI

KBS, the municipal bus service, is extremely unreliable. Buses are especially packed during the morning (7:30–8:30) and evening (5–6) rush hours. The main city bus terminal is at Ronald Ngala and Mfangano streets.

Many independent travelers are robbed around the bus terminal and on Bus 34, which runs to and from the airport. Be on guard for pickpockets. There is an armed guard on the bus, so speak up if you have been ripped off. Just be sure of your claims. If you might have misplaced your wallet, it's probably better just to exclaim, "Where's my wallet?" Never accept drinks or food from strangers, as they may have been drugged.

MATATUS

These minibuses are easily identified by their colorful paint jobs, loud music, and turn-boys (porters), who help with bags and press people inside. Matatus are also known for the sheer number of passengers packed inside and, often, the ramshackle state of the vehicles. Their name comes from *senti tatu,* Swahili for "30 shillings," the original fare. Matatus are not recommended because of their terrible safety record; reforms were suggested in 2001, but enforcement will be another matter.

TUK TUKS

To get around quickly, try the tiny three-wheeled vehicles introduced here in 1997. Because they are barely larger than a motorcycle, tuk tuks can maneuver around traffic jams. Locals hire them to get to the shopping malls. Their fares are about half that of local taxis—about Ksh 100. Look for the tuk tuk stand near the Stanley Hotel.

CAR RENTAL

If you have reserved a rental car, you can arrange to have it delivered to the airport. Be sure to tip the driver between Ksh 200 and Ksh 400. Cars with or without drivers are available, at increasingly high prices. During the busy tourist seasons of July–September and December–February, it's best to reserve far in advance. You will get a better deal if you secure a weekly rate. During the low season rates are often negotiable.

For a typical small car expect to pay between Ksh 2,200 and Ksh 3,375 per day, plus an additional Ksh 60 per kilometer. A four-wheel-drive vehicle can cost between Ksh 4,350 and Ksh 7,800. If you do not have a major credit card, a hefty cash deposit is necessary. A driver's license is valid for three months in Kenya. Most agencies require you to be at least 23 to rent a car.

➤ CONTACTS: **Avis** (✉ Kenyatta International Airport, ☎ 02/336–794). **Budget** (✉ Parliament La. and Hailie Selassie Ave., ☎ 02/337–154). **Central Car Hire** (✉ Standard St.,, ☎ 02/222–888). **Concorde Car Hire** (✉ Ring Rd., ☎ 02/448–953 or 02/448–954). **Hertz** (✉ Muindi Mbingu St., ☎ 02/531–322). **Let's Go Travel** (✉ Waiyaki Way, ☎ 02/447–151 or ☎ 02/441–705).

CAR TRAVEL

The modern highway into downtown Nairobi, its median planted with colorful bougainvillea, is an excellent place to practice driving on the left. Yield to traffic on your right at the roundabouts. Because Kenyan drivers are so unpredictable, always proceed *pole pole,* which means slowly and with caution. If you break down along the road, the local custom is to indicate this by leaving branches on the road about 20–30 m (65–100 ft) behind your vehicle.

The twisting streets in the city can be confusing. The *Nairobi A–Z Street Guide* has good detailed maps of the city as well as the suburbs of Karen and Langata.

PARKING

Finding a parking space in Nairobi is a challenge, to say the least. Enterprising freelance parking attendants will wave you into a spot, then offer to "look after" your car. Sometimes a few will get together to lift another car out of its parking space so that you can have it. Of course, all this is for a fee. They will be there when you return, expecting a tip of about Ksh 50. Safer are lots at hotels such as the Inter-Continental, the Norfolk Hotel, and the Safari Park Hotel. Never leave anything valuable inside, even in the trunk.

DISABILITIES AND ACCESSIBILITY
Very few hotels have wheelchair ramps, with the Hilton International and Stanley hotels the exception. Both airports have toilet facilities for those in wheelchairs. For advice on getting around Nairobi, contact the Association for the Physically Disabled.
➤ INFORMATION: **Association for the Physically Disabled** (⊠ Box 46747, ☎ 02/224–443).

EMBASSIES
A new U.S. embassy is being built in Nairobi's industrial area and is scheduled to be completed sometime in 2005.
➤ EMBASSIES: **Australia** (⊠ ICIPE House, Riverside Dr., ☎ 02/445–034). **Canada** (⊠ Comcraft House, Haile Selassie Ave., ☎ 02/214–804). **Ireland** (⊠ Waumini House, Chiromo Rd., ☎ 02/444–367). **United Kingdom** (⊠ Upper Hill Rd., ☎ 02/719–082). **United States** (⊠ Mombasa Rd., ☎ 02/537–800).

EMERGENCIES
If you are robbed, report it to the police. Make sure to secure an incident number, the name of the officer, and the address and phone number of the police station. Don't expect your visit to the police station to be brief.
➤ EMERGENCY SERVICES: **Ambulance** (☎ 02/221–181). **Fire** (☎ 02/222–182).

HOSPITALS AND PHARMACIES
Two good private hospitals, Aga Khan Hospital and Nairobi Hospital, have intensive-care facilities and screened blood for transfusions. Gertrude's Garden specializes in children's illnesses.

The major pharmacies run a late-night *rota* (rotation) that is posted on their doors. Pharmacies at the major hospitals are open 24 hours.
➤ HOSPITALS: **Aga Khan Hospital** (⊠ Parklands Ave., ☎ 02/740–000). **Nairobi Hospital** (⊠ Argwings Kodhek Rd., ☎ 02/721–160). **Gertrude's Garden** (⊠ Muthaiga Rd., ☎ 02/763–474)

MAIL AND SHIPPING
Packages posted in Kenya must be wrapped in brown paper and tied with string. Do not bother to wrap packages until you get to the post office because officials may ask you to unwrap them for inspection.

The main post office is in downtown Nairobi on Haile Selassie Avenue. It's open weekdays 8–12:30 and 2–5, Saturday 8–12:30. TNT Express Worldwide and DHL have excellent express shipping services. Both have offices in downtown Nairobi.
➤ OVERNIGHT SERVICES: **DHL** (⊠ Kijabe St., ☎ 02/223–063). **TNT Express Worldwide** (⊠ Kiambere Rd., ☎ 02/723–554).
➤ POST OFFICES: **Downtown** (⊠ Haile Selassie Ave., ☎ 02/228–441).

MEDIA
Nairobi is the media center of East Africa, with stringers for the main wire services, major newspapers, and cable and network news stations based here.

NEWSPAPERS AND MAGAZINES

The *Nairobi Daily Nation* is exceptional, with good news coverage, excellent editorials, and listings of local arts events. The *Standard* has tabloid-style coverage, and the *Kenya Times* is owned by the government. You will be able to find international editions of *Time* and *Newsweek* at major hotels, as well as the *International Herald Tribune*. The *East African* covers Tanzania and Uganda as well as Kenya.

RADIO AND TELEVISION

A great source for world news is the BBC, broadcast every hour on the hour. CNN and Reuters News are featured on many hotel TVs. The KBC (Kenya Broadcasting Corporation) has local programs in English and Swahili, as well as foreign programs in English.

MONEY MATTERS

Barclays Bank has more than 60 locations within Kenya, most with automatic teller machines. In addition to bank cards, these ATMs accept Visa and MasterCard. If you use an ATM at a Barclays branch, you will find addresses for all its ATMs on the back of your receipt.
➤ BANKS: **Barclays Bank** (⊠ Haile Selassie Ave., ⊠ Moi Ave., ⊠ Jomo Kenyatta International Airport).

CREDIT CARDS

As the commercial with the rhino boasts, Visa is indeed accepted nearly every place that takes credit cards. If you have a Visa symbol on your ATM card, you may be able to use it to pay at establishments that accept Visa. Other widely accepted cards include Diner's Club and MasterCard. American Express does not seem to enjoy the popularity in East Africa that it does in other parts of the world. Many shops or airlines will advise you that using a credit card will add a percentage to your cost, then ask if you would rather pay in cash.

CURRENCY EXCHANGE

You can obtain Kenya shillings when you arrive at the airport. There are banks both inside the baggage area and outside in the arrivals area, as well as an ATM machine. You can also obtain local currency at your hotel, but the rates are usually not as good.

It is illegal to take Kenyan shillings out of the country. If you have small bills remaining at the end of your journey, exchange them at the airport. At Jomo Kenyatta International the bureau de change in the shopping arcade beyond customs has shorter lines.

SAFETY

Although the fastest way of traveling around Nairobi is on foot, always be on your guard. Avoid flashy jewelry and watches, and keep cameras and camcorders out of sight. Walk in a group during the day, and do not venture out on foot at night. On city streets do not dress like a tourist—avoid Bermuda shorts, T-shirts, and big white running shoes, and save that new safari suit and canvas hat for a safari. Imitate local expats by wearing long skirts or khaki slacks and leather shoes. Blend in with a few key forceful words of Swahili. *Hapana,* for "no," is handy. Smile and keep moving.

Avoid Uhuru Park and Central Park after dark, and be sure to take a taxi in the area around the National Museum and the International Casino.

LOCAL SCAMS

Be suspicious of hard luck stories ("Someone stole my bus ticket") or appeals to finance a scholarship. Don't be fooled if a taxi driver announces upon arrival that the fee you negotiated was per person or that he doesn't have change for your large bills. Be polite but firm if you are stopped by police officers charging you with an "instant fine" for a minor infraction. If you request to go to the police station, the charges are often dismissed.

TELEPHONES

Public pay phones have a digital screen to assist you with dialing. Coin phones are painted red, while card phones are blue. Phone cards of different denominations can be bought at any branch of the post office.

DIRECTORY AND OPERATOR ASSISTANCE

The Kenya phone books are updated annually and include E-mail addresses. There are usually phone books in hotel rooms, or you can dial 991 for directory assistance. This service is only available from 8 AM to midnight.

INTERNATIONAL CALLS

When in Kenya, dial 0191 to place an international call. International calls are fairly easy to make from Nairobi and Mombasa; elsewhere, you may need to use an international operator. To reach one, dial 0196.

LOCAL AND LONG-DISTANCE CALLS

The country code for Kenya is 254, and the city code for Nairobi is 02. The "0" in the city code is used only for calls placed from other areas within the country. While in Nairobi, you need only dial the six-digit number. To call Nairobi from another city in Kenya, add the city code. To place a call to Nairobi from another country, dial the international access code of 011, then the country of 254, then the city code of 2, then the number.

TIPPING

Tips are often included in the bills at restaurants; inquire if yours does not say. Most safari guides and drivers depend on tips; the normal rate for excellent service is Ksh 400 per day. Many tour operators include tips for hotel staff in their packages; if not, porters can be tipped Ksh 50 or Ksh 100. If you stay in a private home, it is customary to tip the house servants who have cleaned your room, pressed your laundry, or performed other services about Ksh 75 per day.

TOUR OPERATORS

Abercrombie & Kent, an international company that opened in Nairobi in 1962, offers everything from exclusive private safaris to affordable group tours. In Nairobi the company is on Standard Street, just around the corner from the Stanley Hotel.

Micato Safaris, a family-owned company, makes you feel as if you are personal guests. The Pinto family has been planning safaris for travelers since 1967 and has offices in New York as well as Nairobi. They organize safaris, but they are also known for cruises of the Indian Ocean. Because they do not accept walk-in clients, you may want to contact their New York office before your trip.

J. H. Safaris arranges day tours of Nairobi, safaris in nearby reserves, and excursions to Tanzania, Uganda, Rwanda, Ethiopia, and the Seychelles. Let's Go Travel provides comprehensive information about traveling in Kenya. Current listings of hotel and car-rental rates are available free, as are schedules for domestic flights. Other reliable travel agencies include Express Kenya and United Touring International.

➤ TOUR OPERATOR INFORMATION: **Abercrombie & Kent** (⊠ Windsor House, 1 University Way, ☏ 02/228–700, ⓦⓔⓑ www. abercrombiekent.com). **Express Kenya** (⊠ Standard St., ☏ 02/334–722). **J. H. Safaris** (⊠ Windsor House, 1 University Way, ☏ 02/

334–112). **Let's Go Travel** (✉ Caxton House, Standard St., ☎ 02/
340–331, WEB www.letsgosafari.com). **Micato Safaris** (✉ View Park
Towers, Uhuru Hwy., ☎ 02/220–743; ✉ 15 W. 26th St., New York,
NY, ☎ 212/545–7111, WEB www.africansafari.org/micato). **United
Touring International** (✉ Muindi Mbingu St., ☎ 02/331–960, WEB
utcn@attmail.com).

TRAIN TRAVEL
A decade ago traveling by train was an elegant experience, but now
the windows and doors on the overnight train are locked to keep
thieves from jumping on board at the stops. Even the first-class berths
cannot always be locked from the outside, so take your valuables with
you to dinner. Some tour operators do not recommend train travel because of the safety issues, but many independent travelers consider the
journey a highlight of their trip. There are a few hints of the glamour
of days gone by. On the Mombasa Express passengers are treated to
a four-course dinner served with linens, china, and silver.

Regular trains run from Nairobi to Mombasa, Kisumu, and Kampala.
At the beginning of your journey, request bed linens from the conductor
if you did not bring your own. The sleeping berths in the first-class
coaches are fairly clean, with washbasins and cooling fans. Second-class
accommodations have four beds, but the washbasins are unreliable,
as the cars were built in England in the 1920s. Third-class coaches have
only seats and can be very crowded. Men and women are separated
in first- and second-class berths unless an entire compartment is booked.

FARES AND SCHEDULES
The Mombasa Express departs each evening from Nairobi at 7 and
arrives at 8:17 the next morning. First-class tickets are $50; second-
class tickets, $35; third-class tickets, $9. The train to Kisumu leaves
Nairobi at 6 PM and arrives at 7:10 AM. Ticket prices are $35, $24,
and $7 for first-, second-, and third class, respectively. The train to Kam-
pala departs at 10 AM on Tuesday. Tickets are $80, $64, and $19.50
for first-, second-, and third class, respectively.

RESERVATIONS
You should book the night train to Mombasa at least one week in advance to secure a first-class berth. Round-trip tickets are valid for
three months. You must cancel any reservations 24 hours before departure to secure a refund.
➤ TRAIN INFORMATION: **Nairobi Station** (✉ Station Rd., ☎ 02/221–211).

VISITOR INFORMATION
A Tourist Information Center near the Hilton International is open from
Monday through Saturday 8:30–12:30 and 2–5. The Kenya Tourist
Board is not as efficient as its South African counterpart, but it is slowly
improving. The office is open weekdays 8:30–12:30 and 2–5.
➤ TOURIST OFFICES: **Kenya Tourist Board** (✉ Kenya Towers, 7th floor,
Upper Hill, off Ragati Rd., ☎ 02/724–042, WEB www.kenyatourism.org).
Tourist Information Center (✉ Moi Ave. and Mama Ngina, ☎ 02/221–
855).

3 WESTERN KENYA

Away from most of the well-known sights, Western Kenya offers an entirely different African experience. Those who need their fix of lions and elephants should head for the magnificent Maasai Mara National Reserve, but Western Kenya is more about the spectacular flamingoes of the brackish lakes, the butterflies that flutter about Mt. Elgon and the Kakamega Forest, and the soaring escarpments of the Kerio Valley and the Cherengani Hills. You'll not soon forget the sight of Lake Victoria, Africa's greatest inland sea.

by Melissa
Shales

ONE OF THE MOST DRAMATIC GEOLOGICAL FORMATIONS in the world, the Great Rift Valley stretches for more than 6,000 km (3,600 mi) through the heart of Africa. It is at its deepest and most spectacular just west of Nairobi, where a truly grand canyon effectively separates Western Kenya from the rest of the country. Here the steep valley walls, the cones of extinct volcanoes such as Mt. Longonot, and a necklace of fresh and soda lakes—Naivasha, Elementeita, Nakuru, Bogoria, and Baringo—create spectacular vistas.

Despite its obvious attractions, Western Kenya is largely unexplored. Except for visiting Lake Naivasha and Lake Nakuru, which are an easy day trip from Nairobi, the region is not often included on a first-time visitor's itinerary, though it offers that tantalizing sense of being off the beaten path in unspoiled Africa, especially for the independent traveler with a vehicle.

The region consists of arid badlands dotted with hot springs that may vaporize into clouds or rush together into a warm waterfall, as well as vast peaks like Mt. Elgon, where generations of elephants have gathered for a midnight snack in Kitum Cave, scraping salt off the cave walls with their tusks. Evidence of volcanic activity is everywhere, especially in the dramatic craters of Mt. Suswa and Mt. Elgon. With habitats ranging from windswept plains to Kenya's last surviving patch of true tropical rain forest, the Kakamega Forest, the bird life in this region is extraordinarily rich. A quick walk on any given day will yield dozens of species. Take time, care, and a good pair of binoculars, and you will spots literally hundreds. No wonder birders from around the world flock here.

In the midst of this vast region are thriving communities where you'll encounter people whose traditions are stronger than those along the more popular tourist routes. The most prominent is Kisumu, the country's third-largest city. It borders Africa's biggest body of water, Lake Victoria, where the triangular-sailed boats of the Luo people set out each day. They share the lake with colonies of hippos, crocodiles, and rare roan antelopes with scimitar-shape horns and long tufted ears. The diminutive potto, a small, furry primate known as a bush baby, can be spotted in the trees at night.

The Rift Valley has some excellent accommodations, such as a very romantic lodge on Lake Baringo and the cluster of luxurious safari camps surrounding Maasai Mara National Reserve. There are also opportunities for fascinating homestays in various parts of the region, where your hosts are residents who offer a fund of local knowledge and immense hospitality. There are also some places where *bandas* afford little more than a thatched roof over your head.

Stand on a precipice many hundreds of feet high and look out over a flat plain scattered with almost perfect volcanic cones. In the foreground, the deep blue-greens of the woodland slopes are broken by sharp spikes of purple, red, and yellow flowering trees. In the distance rolling hills fade to a lilac haze beneath a cobalt sky. This is just one of the many spectacular scenes that Western Kenya has to offer. Gaze across the Great Rift Valley to vast rolling plantations of emerald green tea bushes, dry yellow seas of sugar cane, and terraced villages of mud huts with intricately woven fields. The landscape of Western Kenya is infinitely varied, a tangle of winding roads and mountain passes, almost always beautiful and ever fascinating.

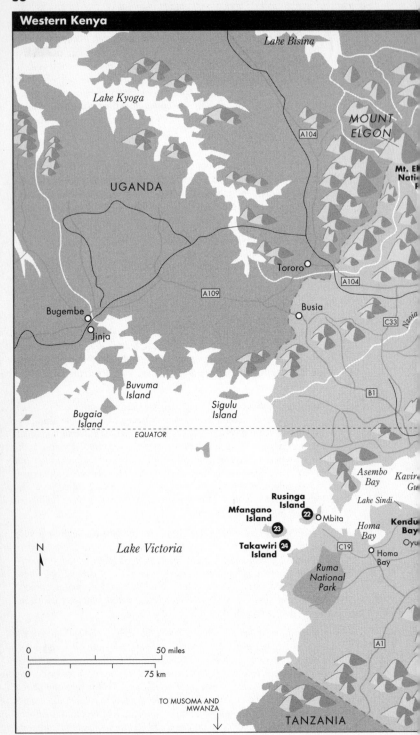

Lake Bisina

Lake Kyoga

MOUNT ELGON

Mt. El
Natio
P

A104

UGANDA

Tororo

A104

A109

Busia

C33

Nzoia

Bugembe

Jinja

Buvuma
Island

Sigulu
Island

Bugaia
Island

B1

EQUATOR

Asembo
Bay

Kavir
Gu

Lake Sindi

Rusinga
Island

Mfangano
Island

22 Mbita

23

Homa
Bay

Kendu
Bay

Oyu

Lake Victoria

Takawiri 24
Island

C19

Homa
Bay

N

Ruma
National
Park

A1

0   50 miles

0   75 km

TO MUSOMA AND
MWANZA

TANZANIA

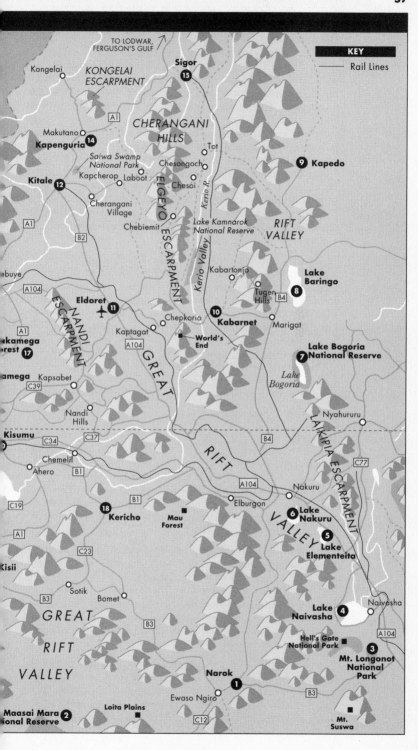

KEY
—— Rail Lines

TO LODWAR,
FERGUSON'S GULF

Kongelai

KONGELAI
ESCARPMENT

Sigor **15**

CHERANGANI
HILLS

Tot

Makutano

Kapenguria **14**

Saiwa Swamp
National Park

Chesongoch

Chesoi

Kapcherop   Laboot

Kapedo **9**

Kitale **12**

Cherangani
Village

Chebiemit

Lake Kamnarok
National Reserve

RIFT
VALLEY

ebuye

Kabartonjo

Lake
Baringo **8**

Eldoret **11**

Chepkorio

Tugen
Hills

B4

kamega
rest **17**

Kaptagat

Kabarnet **10**

Marigat

A104

World's
End

Lake Bogoria
National Reserve **7**

amega   Kapsabet

Lake
Bogoria

Nandi
Hills

Nyahururu

Kisumu

C34   C37

Chemelil

Ahero

Nakuru

C77

B4

A104

C19

Elburgon

Lake
Nakuru **6**

Kericho **18**

Mau
Forest

Lake
Elementeita **5**

Kisii

C23

Sotik   Bomet

GREAT

B3

Lake
Naivasha **4**

Naivasha

Hell's Gate
National Park

A104

RIFT

Mt. Longonot
National Park **3**

VALLEY

Narok **1**

Ewaso Ngiro

B3

Maasai Mara
ional Reserve **2**

Loita Plains

C12

Mt.
Suswa

Kongelai ESCARPMENT

ELGEYO ESCARPMENT

Kerio R.

Kerio Valley

RIFT VALLEY

GREAT

NANDI ESCARPMENT

LAIKIPIA ESCARPMENT

B2

A1

A1

A1

A104

C39

B1

B1

B3

A1

B4

Pleasures and Pastimes

Dining

It's unlikely that gourmet cuisine will be one of your main reasons for visiting Western Kenya. The good news is that you can eat reasonably well. The only true local regional specialty is fish, mainly perch and tilapia fresh from Lake Victoria, served as anything from fish-and-chips to fish curry. There is also a smattering of traditional African food—cornmeal porridge, meat stews, and barbecues. But most of the food in this former British colony is old-fashioned meat dishes with two vegetables on the side, french fries with everything. Most of the better restaurants are in the hotels. You will eat well in the game lodges and homestays in the Naivasha area, although the buffet will inevitably sink under a load of taste-free, bright-pink, wobbly desserts. The food in many of the smaller towns often consists of curly sandwiches, cold french fries, and watery ketchup. The beer is good, the wine reasonable if uninspired. Local spirits are a fraction of the price of the international brands, and sodas are plentiful and cold.

Breakfast is usually served from around 7 to 9, unless you are doing a game drive. In that case breakfast will be served on your return at around 10. Lunch is usually between noon and 1:30. Dinner is served from 7 to 9 PM. If you are staying in a game lodge, tips are normally left in the staff box at the end of the stay; if you are dining elsewhere, leave a tip of around 10%.

CATEGORY	COST*
$$$$	over Ksh 1,170
$$$	Ksh 780–Ksh 1,170
$$	Ksh 390–Ksh 780
$	under Ksh 390

Per person for a main course at dinner.

Lodging

The first thing to remember is that a hotel is not always a hotel—most of the HOTEL signs you see are actually for very basic local restaurants. The Great Rift Valley is full of good lodges that are relatively expensive but provide excellent service in delightful settings. The area immediately around Maasai Mara National Reserve is loaded with small, luxurious private camps—some with chalets, others using tents. Rates include all meals and activities.

The rest of Western Kenya has few good places to stay. Most of the accommodations are in concrete-block government-run hotels. There is a handful of friendly homestays, where you sleep in a private home and share meals at the dinner table. The atmosphere is definitely more bed-and-breakfast than hotel, but the food is good, the people friendly, and you'll learn a good deal about the country. Your hosts will organize guided birding and walks, help you plan your trip, and provide picnics and even transport.

The other option is private clubs. Technically, you have to be a member or have reciprocal membership with an overseas club, but many are now welcoming tourists and offer day memberships on the nod. Accommodations here are generally comfortable but spartan. Simple meals are served in the clubhouse. Membership will include use of the golf course and other sporting facilities.

Reservations are rarely needed in Western Kenya. Except for Maasai Mara, so few people visit the region that you are unlikely to have difficulty finding accommodations at any time.

CATEGORY	COST*
$$$$	over Ksh 15,600
$$$	Ksh 7,800–Ksh 15,600
$$	Ksh 3,900–Ksh 7,800
$	under Ksh 3,900

*All prices are for a standard double room, excluding tax.

Markets

In Narok, en route to Maasai Mara National Reserve, you may meet persistent gangs of street vendors who know exactly how to force hapless tourists into submission. Elsewhere, Western Kenya is mercifully free of high-pressure sales techniques. Nakuru has a huge market, with a good selection of souvenirs, while Naivasha is home to one of the largest souvenir shops in Kenya, with a positive army of polished wooden figurines. The only other serious shopping centers are the villages of Kisii and Tabaka, where you'll find soapstone carvings. The colorful fruit and vegetable markets in other towns are strictly local affairs—wonderfully atmospheric but not really yielding anything much worth buying.

Wildlife

Maasai Mara National Reserve, one of the greatest wildlife spectaculars in the world, falls geographically in Western Kenya. An extension of Tanzania's vast Serengeti, the reserve is an area of golden grasslands where great herds of antelope and wildebeest graze nervously under the predatory eyes of lions and hyenas. Although Maasai Mara is unmissable, Western Kenya has much more to offer. Lake Nakuru National Park, in the Great Rift Valley, is home to one of Africa's great visual feasts. Giant flocks of salmon-pink flamingoes gather each year at Lake Nakuru and neighboring Lake Elementeita. Farther west, the Kakamega Forest is Kenya's last surviving patch of true tropical rain forest, home to hundreds of exotic species of plants. In the far northwest, the richly forested slopes of Mt. Elgon support a massive bird population as well as hard-to-spot forest elephants, buffaloes, and even black rhinos. Saiwa Swamp National Park, in the north, was set up to protect the tiny sitatunga antelope. Roma National Park, in the far south, is designed to preserve the roan antelope.

Exploring Western Kenya

Like all highways in Kenya, the state of those in the west depends on a seemingly random repair schedule. The roads are generally better than those around Nairobi, but heavy rains and large numbers of tour buses mean that those that are excellent one month can crumble the next. Always assume that they will be heavily potholed, and you may be pleasantly surprised.

The major roads from Nairobi allow you to reach Western Kenya in five or six hours if you drive as if you're in the Kenya Safari Rally. The main road up the Great Rift Valley is excellent as far as Naivasha, appalling from Naivasha to Nakuru, then improves again north of Nakuru. The road south from Kisumu around the edge of Lake Victoria is diabolical and only just passable without a four-wheel-drive vehicle. The best option is simply to slow down, enjoy the spectacular scenery, and take a few detours that may well become the highlight of your safari.

It is always sensible to travel with a blanket and a cooler packed with food and plenty of drinking water. The distribution of gas stations is good along the main roads and as far north as Lodwar and Ferguson's Gulf. Safety is not an issue in most of the region, but you should not drive north of Ferguson's Gulf unescorted. Think twice before driving at night. The heavy traffic on the winding mountain roads can be treacherous.

Numbers in the text correspond to numbers in the margin and on the Western Kenya map.

Great Itineraries

IF YOU HAVE 3 DAYS

With only a few days to spend in Western Kenya, head to ⬚ **Maasai Mara National Reserve** ②. There's more than enough to do in and around this sprawling reserve.

IF YOU HAVE 6 DAYS

With a little more time in the region you can see much more. Start in ⬚ **Maasai Mara National Reserve** ②, where you can easily spend three days. On your fourth day head to ⬚ **Lake Naivasha** ④, stopping to explore **Mt. Longonot National Park** ③. The next day head north to ⬚ **Lake Nakuru** ⑥, stopping en route at **Lake Elementeita** ⑤. Make sure you arrive at Lake Nakuru in time for the evening game drive. After a morning game drive, head north to **Lake Bogoria National Reserve** ⑦ to see the hot springs before returning to Nairobi.

IF YOU HAVE 9 DAYS

On your first day, head to ⬚ **Lake Nakuru** ⑥, making sure to stop en route at **Lake Naivasha** ④. The next morning, after a game drive, drive through **Eldoret** ⑪ to ⬚ **Kitale** ⑫, where you can spend the day bird-watching at Saiwa Swamp National Park or **Mt. Elgon National Park** ⑬. On your third day drive south to the ⬚ **Kakamega Forest** ⑰ for an afternoon walk through Kenya's last remaining sliver of tropical forest. Get up at dawn so you can spot some of the reserve's early birds, then drive to ⬚ **Kisumu** ⑳ in time to catch the sunset over Lake Victoria. Take a morning boat ride on Lake Victoria on your fifth day before heading inland to stay overnight at Kweisos House in ⬚ **Kericho** ⑱. On your sixth day, take a leisurely drive through the region's beautiful tea plantations before heading to the ⬚ **Maasai Mara National Reserve** ② for your last three days.

When to Tour

The equator runs through Africa just north of Lake Victoria, so the climate of Western Kenya is controlled far more by altitude and rain than by any distinct seasons. It is always reasonably warm to hot near sea level and a bit cooler as you climb into the highlands.

The best time to visit this region is from January through March. The rainy seasons are officially from April through June and from mid-July to mid-December, but in practice they can often run together. The only exception to the rule is if you are planning to visit the Maasai Mara, which is at its best from July through October, when the migrating herds are in the area.

MAASAI MARA AND ENVIRONS

In southwest Kenya the flatlands covered with vast fields of sugarcane eventually gives way to the golden plains that are home to Kenya's most famous and colorful tribe, the Maasai. The Maasai arrived in the area from southern Sudan around 1,000 years ago and still lead a traditional life as seminomadic cattle herders, living in dung-and-mud *manyattas* (villages) as they have for centuries. Clad in brilliant red, the *morani* (warriors) are a marvelous sight as they stride across Maasai Mara National Reserve carrying their heavy spears.

Narok

❶ *160 km (96 mi) west of Nairobi.*

Narok is the main trading center of the Maasai people in southwestern Kenya. It is also a town of service stations because virtually everyone passing through the town headed to the Maasai Mara stops for gas. The small shops clustered around these stations have become the town's major (and only) tourist attraction. There are literally dozens of shops selling thousands of artifacts: necklaces, bracelets, spears, knives, shields, animal carvings, masks, and weavings are but a few of the items for which you may barter. The shopkeepers are used to hard-driving tourists, so you may not get quite the bargain you expect.

As you approach Narok you pass the northern rim of **Mt. Suswa,** a volcano that makes a pleasant excursion well away from the usual tourist route. The outer crater is easily accessible by four-wheel-drive vehicles. The inner crater, surrounded by a dry moat that measures 305 m (1,000 ft) across at its narrowest point, is more difficult to reach. The forbidding area, where you'll find a cedar forest, was not explored until 1980, when it was surveyed by an international expedition of young people called Operation Drake. The only source of water in the central plateau comes from volcanic steam vents, which issue jets of hot vapor. Check on the security situation before setting out, and make sure you are down the mountain in plenty of time to continue your journey in daylight.

The road beyond Narok continues southwest to Ewaso Ngiro, 18 km (11 mi) away. Shortly after this village there is a left fork, C12, which takes you across the **Loita Plains.** You can spot much wildlife here, as the area is adjacent to Maasai Mara. From the road you usually see large herds of wildebeest, zebras, giraffes, and Thomson's and Grant's gazelles, as well as lesser numbers of buffaloes, spotted hyenas, topis, warthogs, and impalas. The open grasslands are a particularly good place to spot birds of prey, as six species of vultures, as well as martial eagles, bateleurs, and secretary birds, make their homes here. In the riverine forests look for Livingstone's turacos, Narina's trogons, and double-toothed barbets.

Maasai Mara National Reserve

★ **❷** *105 km (65 mi) west of Narok, 249 km (154 mi) west of Nairobi.*

The landscape of the Maasai Mara National Reserve is classic Africa, with golden savannas dotted with acacia trees. The word *mara* means "mottled" in Maa, the language of the Maasai people. It can also refer to specks on the horizon, and that is exactly how you feel in this seemingly endless space. Maasai Mara is the northern extension of Serengeti National Park in Tanzania, and together they consist of 24,860 square km (9,600 square mi) of gently rolling grasslands. There is no fence separating the two parks, only the geopolitical border that the animals ignore.

The Mara, as it is often called, sits at an altitude of 1,650 m (5,412 ft), about the same as Nairobi. This makes the weather here more temperate than in many of the country's other reserves. The open plains are cut by dark green forests of acacias that thrive along the reserve's two main rivers, the Mara and Talek. The eastern section of the reserve is more heavily forested, making game more difficult to spot. The western border is formed by the Oloololo Escarpment, where you can focus your binoculars on the largest concentrations of animals.

Maasai Mara is the most popular game reserve in East Africa, and with good reason. One of the greatest wildlife spectacles in the world takes place here from July through October, when wildebeest, antelopes, and zebras move north from the Serengeti to Maasai Mara in search of fresh grass. The sheer number of animals is astounding—in 2001, 1.5 million white-bearded gnus migrated north, followed by 200,000 zebras, 18,000 elands, 500,000 Thomson's gazelles, and hundreds of prowling lions and hyenas. For many the most exciting part of the migration is the frantic stampede as the herds struggle to cross the Mara River.

You won't be alone as you watch the spectacle. The first lodge, Keekorok, was built in Maasai Mara in 1963. Four decades later, after the success of the film *Out of Africa,* the number of permanent accommodations has reached 25, and that doesn't count tented camps outside the reserve or the temporary camps set up inside the reserve. If you want to see the migration of wildebeests rather than tourists, head to the reserve's southern boundaries in September, after the crowds have diminished.

Tours

Every lodge and tented camp has its own vehicles for taking visitors on game drives. The price for most lodges includes two game drives per day. Kichwa Tembo and Bateleur Camp have newer four-by-four vehicles with graduated seats and semiopen sides. Cottar's 1920s Safari Camp has a classic wood-sided safari cruiser that not only collects you at the airstrip but also takes you on elegant excursions into the plains.

In the 1970s the wildebeest migration was recorded by filmmaker Alan Root, who shot the spectacle from the gondola of a hot-air balloon. After *Year of the Wildebeest* was released in 1975, Alan and Joan Root launched their company Balloon Safaris. Now at least a half dozen companies cater to tourists, taking off from Governor's Camp, Sarova Camp, and Fig Tree Campsite. Fans say it's a great way to see the reserve, with the occasional noisy burns of propane flushing leopards from their hiding places. To critics, it has turned Maasai Mara into a Disneyland. There have even been threats of restrictions because every landing requires off-road driving to retrieve the passengers from wherever the winds have taken them. Yet the colorful balloons continue to dot the horizon. For many visitors floating over the plains is a highlight of their trip.

Wildlife

Many species of plains animals reside in the rolling grasslands throughout the year, including buffaloes, wildebeest, hartebeest, impalas, zebras, and gazelles. Common to Maasai Mara, but found in only a few other places in Kenya, are topis, reddish-brown antelopes that are often spotted standing on top of termite mounds. They aren't posing for photos—they are actually scanning the horizon for predators. There may be remnants of a small herd of roan antelopes in the western section of the reserve, although naturalists fear they may no longer be found in the reserve. They certainly are no longer found at Roan Hill near Keekerok Lodge. Herds of up to 20 stately giraffes are seen in all parts of the reserve.

With all of these animals around, it is not surprising that Maasai Mara has Kenya's largest population of big cats. Lions are easy to spot, especially the lionesses hunting for their pride. Cheetahs are also numerous, although this predator is elusive. Elephants are a common sight in the northern reaches of the reserve near Kichwa Tembo and Governor's Camp. The reserve's tiny population of rhinos can be located by look-

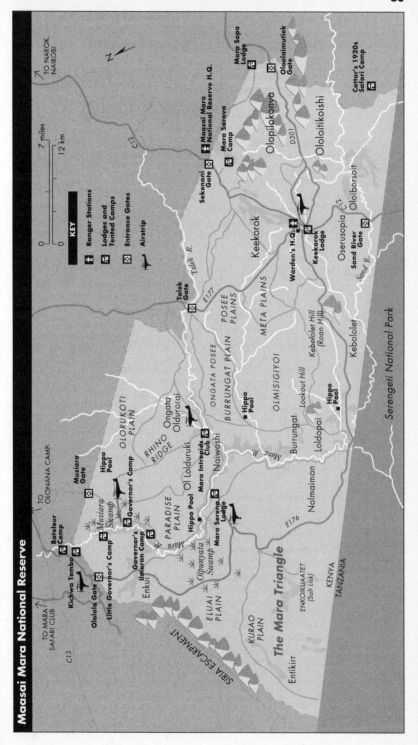

Maasai Mara National Reserve

KEY

🏠 Ranger Stations
⛺ Lodges and Tented Camps
☒ Entrance Gates
✈ Airstrip

TO NAROK, NAIROBI

TO MARA SAFARI CLUB

TO OLONANA CAMP.

7 miles
12 km

Bateleur Camp
Kichwa Tembo
Olololo Gate
Little Governor's Camp
Governor's Camp
Governor's Il moran Camp
Musiara Gate
Hippo Pool
Mara Intrepids Club
Ol Tolduruki
Naiwoshi
Hippo Pool
Mara Serena Lodge
Olpunyata Swamp
Musiara Swamp
Mara R.
PARADISE PLAIN
RHINO RIDGE
OLORUKOTI PLAIN
OLORUKOTI PLAIN
Ongata Olduroroi
Ongata Posee Plain
BURRUNGAT PLAIN
POSEE PLAINS
Talek Gate
Talek R.
E177
E176
SIRIA ESCARPMENT
ELUAI PLAIN
KURAO PLAIN
Entikirr
ENKOIKUAATET (Salt lick)
Nolmaiman
Loldopai
Burrungat
Lookout Hill
Kebololet Hill (Roan Hill)
Kebololet
OLMISIGIYOI
META PLAINS
Hippo Pool
Hippo Pool
Keekorok
Warden's H.Q.
Keekorok Lodge
Oserusopia
Oloiborsoit
Sand River Gate
Sand R.
Oseruspia C2
Ololoitikoishi
Olopilokonya
Oloolaimutiek Gate
Mara Sopa Lodge
Mara Sarova Camp
Maasai Mara National Reserve H.Q.
Sekenani Gate
Cottar's 1920s Safari Camp
C12
C12
C13
D301
The Mara Triangle
KENYA
TANZANIA
Serengeti National Park

ing for a large cluster of vehicles. If you find yourself in this situation, it's best to move on and give the animals room.

In all, some 95 species of mammals have been noted in Maasai Mara. It is the vast array of birds—more than 485 species—that is particularly astounding. On the plains a variety of bustards can be seen strutting along with secretary birds and giant ground hornbills. The forests have their own species, including the beautiful Ross's turaco, recognized by the flash of its scarlet wings as it flies through the trees. Beautiful Eurasian bee-eaters were spotted in 2001 near the Oloololo Escarpment. ✉ *Kenya Wildlife Service, Box 40241, Nairobi,* ☎ *02/501–081,* ℻ *02/ 505–866,* ⓦ *www.kenya-wildlife-service.org.* 🎫 *$27.*

Lodging

$$$$ 🏨 **Bateleur Camp.** One of most luxurious lodgings in the Maasai Mara
★ area, Bateleur Camp is nestled in a secluded forest. There are only nine tents here, reflecting the growing trend away from bigger and bigger camps. Bold mahogany beds, writing desks, and polished wood floors distinguish the accommodations from others in the area. Each tent, far enough from the others to ensure your privacy, has a private veranda with stuffed leather chairs and a good view of the reserve. The appointments in the private baths, as well as the elegant light fixtures, could qualify for any top hotel in London. Chef George announces menus with a smile nearly as wide as his white hat. Breakfast pastries are enhanced by his passion-fruit curd, and lunches can feature fresh tilapia from Lake Victoria. At dinner you may be served fresh lobster. ✉ *Outside Oloololo Gate,* ☎ *02/750–780,* ℻ *02/750–512,* ⓦ *www.ccafrica. com. 9 tents. Dining room, bar, lounge, pool, shop, private airstrip. AE, DC, MC, V.*

$$$$ 🏨 **Cottar's 1920s Safari Camp.** On the edge of Maasai Mara, this lux-
★ urious camp summons up the romance once associated with safaris. It can accommodate only eight guests, who can explore the private 22,000-acre reserve on walking safaris and night game drives with the most interesting guides in East Africa. You can learn about wildlife behavior from Johnny Moller, who choreographed the lion charge in the film *Out of Africa.* The spacious tents of white canvas are luxuriously furnished with antiques from the 1920s and have baths with vintage tubs and private verandas. If you fly into the Keekorok strip, the staff will meet you in a vintage safari car. ✉ *East of Maasai Mara,* ☎ *02/ 884–508,* ℻ *02/882–234,* ⓦ *www.cottars.com. 4 tents. Dining room. AE, DC, MC, V.*

$$$$ 🏨 **Governor's Camp.** Located where Teddy Roosevelt camped when he visited Maasai Mara, this popular retreat is in a wooded area along the Mara River (tents 19, 22, and 23 have the best views of the hippos below). The canvas tents, all with private baths, are illuminated by the soft glow of kerosene lanterns. The massive dining tent, where you dine by candlelight, seats 100 guests. When the weather is good, meals are served on the riverbank. Maasai warriors often arrive during dinner to entertain you with traditional dances. The reception area is made of local stone, and the gallery is filled with bronze sculptures. ✉ *Near Musiara Gate,* ☎ *02/331–871,* ℻ *02/726–427,* ⓦ *www. governorscamp.com. Dining room, shop. 38 tents. AE, DC, MC, V.*

$$$$ 🏨 **Governor's Ilmoran Camp.** Elephants often wander through this small camp along the banks of the Mara River. Each tent has a veranda large enough to host a private dinner party. Furnishings are first rate, including beds that are handmade from wood taken from ancient olive trees. Baths have double showers filled to order with piping-hot water so you can wash away the dust after a day on safari. Meals are served outside under the giant trees. ✉ *Near Musiara Gate,*

☎ 02/331–871, FAX 02/726–427, WEB *www.governorscamp.com. Dining room. 10 tents. AE, DC, MC, V.*

$$$$ 🏕 **Kichwa Tembo.** Very innovative when it was built two decades ago, this camp now has more than three dozen tents that are spaced a bit too close together. Kichwa Tembo, whose name means "elephant skull," is run by the same people as Bateleur Camp. It has many of the same amenities, but at the end of the day you may wish you had taken the left fork in the road to its more exclusive sister. ✉ *Outside Oloololo Gate of Maasai Mara,* ☎ 02/750–780, FAX 02/750–512, WEB *www. ccafrica.com. 45 tents. Dining room, bar, pool, shop, private airstrip. AE, DC, MC, V.*

$$$$ 🏕 **Little Governor's Camp.** Wrapping around a watering hole, this
★ camp is a great place to spot wildlife ranging from elephants and hippos to giraffes and warthogs. Getting here is part of the fun, as you reach this camp by taking a boat across the Mara River. The steep climb up and down the riverbanks is difficult for some people, however. It's popular, so book far in advance. ✉ *Near Musiara Gate,* ☎ 02/331–871, FAX 02/726–427, WEB *www.governorscamp.com. Dining room. 17 tents. AE, DC, MC, V.*

$$$ 🏕 **Mara Intrepids Club.** This luxurious tented camp near the Talek River is reached by a suspension footbridge. The decor, inspired by the style of the Kenyan coast, has Lamu chests, richly colored carpets, and four-poster beds. Tents are nicely separated from each for privacy, but some clusters of three or four tents share a "club tent," where you'll find a bar, ice box, and dining table. You can order your meals to be served here, but so can your neighbors. Dinners at the main tent are served by waiters, a refreshing change from the buffets of other camps. An observation tower nearby is an excellent place for drinks at sundown. ✉ *Maasai Mara,* ☎ 02/338–084, FAX 02/217–278, WEB *www. africaonline.com. 27 tents. Restaurant, bar, pool, private airstrip. AE, DC, MC, V.*

$$$$ 🏕 **Mara Safari Club.** At the foot of the Aitong Hills, this lodge sits outside Maasai Mara in the Ol-Choro Oiroua Conservation Area. It's surrounded on three sides by the Mara River, so all the tents have views from private verandas. Facilities are quite modern, with electricity, flush toilets, and hot and cold running water. The main building, where you'll find the dining room as well as a bar and a lounge, juts out over the river. For a bit extra you can enjoy a "bush dinner" served on the game-viewing platform instead of the dining room. Evening activities include performances by Maasai dancers, slide shows about the region's history, and lectures on the Mara River's ecosystem. An airstrip is nearby. ✉ *North of Maasai Mara,* ☎ 02/216–940, FAX 02/216–796, WEB *www. lonrhohotels.com. 80 rooms. Restaurant, bar, lounge, minibars, pool, shop. AE, DC, MC, V.*

$$$ 🏕 **Keekorok Lodge.** In the southern end of Maasai Mara, this longtime favorite was the first lodge to be built in the reserve. Although rather tired looking, the facility is comfortable and well managed. There is a rather unsightly jumble of buildings leading to the complex, and the view onto a nearby rise is disappointing. There's an airstrip nearby, and balloon flights are available. ✉ *Maasai Mara,* ☎ 02/540–780, FAX 02/545–948, WEB *www.blockhotelske.com. 85 rooms. Dining room, lounge, pool, shop, private airstrip. AE, DC, MC, V.*

$$$ 🏕 **Mara Serena Lodge.** Occupying a hilltop with panoramic views of the Mara Triangle, this large lodge is set deep inside Maasai Mara. The architecture is inspired by the domed huts of the Maasai, but the rooms are terribly small. There is a pool with a great view of the valley below and a garden that attracts countless species of birds. Traditional dancing is performed every evening after dinner. An airstrip is nearby. ⊠ *Maasai Mara,* ☎ *02/725–111,* ℻ *02/725–184. 80 rooms. Restaurant, bar, pool, shop, laundry service. AE, DC, MC, V.*

$$$ 🏠 **Mara Sopa Camp.** On the edge of the Oloolaimutia Valley, this sprawling lodge is built in the traditional style of the Maasai people. The emphasis is on learning more about these fascinating people, so the lodge organizes trips to a nearby village. Each of the nicely decorated rooms has an elevated veranda with views across the valley. After a game drive relax in the free-form pool. ⊠ *East of Maasai Mara,* ☎ *02/336–088,* ℻ *02/223–843,* 🌐 *www.sopahotels.com. 90 rooms. Dining room, lounge, minibars, pool, shop. AE, DC, MC, V.*

$$$ 🏠 **Olonana Camp.** Named for one of the legendary leaders of the Maasai people, this camp gives you the opportunity to learn about their culture. It's run by the well-regarded firm of Abercrombie & Kent, so it's not surprising that the camp also has a touch of luxury. A dozen spacious tents, many of which overlook the hippos in the Mara River below, have spacious bedrooms with queen-size beds, dressing rooms with terry-cloth robes, and expansive verandas. ⊠ *North of Maasai Mara,* ☎ *02/535–219,* ℻ *02/556–664,* 🌐 *www.abercrombiekent.com. 12 tents. Dining room, lounge, pool, shop, airstrip. AE, DC, MC, V.*

THE GREAT RIFT VALLEY

Extending more than 6,000 km (3,600 mi), the Great Rift Valley formed around 20 million years ago when a huge mountain range was torn apart and the land between dropped to form a flat-sided valley up to 45 km (27 mi) in width. Although not unique to Kenya, this violent seismic scar is at its most dramatic here, where sheer walls rise as much as 2,000 m (6,060 ft) above the valley floor. It was during an 1893 expedition here, in an area not far from Baringo, that geologist J. W. Gregory determined that this valley was not cut by erosion, like the Grand Canyon, but by shifting faults. The eastern branch of the Great Rift Valley, named in honor of Gregory, extends through Olorgesailie and Olduvai.

Today, with rain wearing away at its slopes, the soaring heights of the Great Rift Valley can be difficult to comprehend. It is best seen from the air (the low-level flight from Nairobi to Maasai Mara offers superb views) or from a viewing point high on one of the steep-sided escarpments.

Although most of its volcanoes in the valley have been extinct for more than 2 million years, there is still considerable seismic activity. There are 30 active or sleeping volcanoes and numerous hot springs fueled by underground lava chambers. A series of once-vast lakes have now shrunk to a necklace of smaller reservoirs. Naivasha and Baringo are fed by rivers and springs and contain fresh water. Elementeita, Nakuru, and Bogoria, solely dependent on rainwater, have become soda lakes because of the sodium carbonate bubbling up through underground faults. They are perfect breeding grounds for algae and the flamingoes who feed on it.

The area is geologically fascinating, but its human history is no less compelling. Koobi Fora (near Lake Turkana) may grab the headlines, but the entire Great Rift Valley is lined by archaeological sites. Every scrap of current information makes it clear his area of East Africa was the birthplace of humankind. The walls of the valley can tell the story of humanity and are simply waiting for the archaeologists to dig them out.

Even modern history has its say. The area around Naivasha and Nakuru was the heart of colonial society during the early years of the 20th century. Happy Valley (of *White Mischief* fame) lay between the two towns in the foothills of the Aberdares. The Djinn Palace, on the shore of Lake Naivasha, still exists, but is in private hands and is not open to the public. The Delamere Estates are still much in evidence, while Lord Cole's house now serves as the Lake Elementeita Lodge. Those who have read the book and seen the movie can now see it for themselves.

Mt. Longonot National Park

❸ *63 km (39 mi) northwest of Nairobi.*

A dormant volcano soaring 2,885 m (9,466 ft), Mt. Longonot's name is derived from the Maasai word *o-loo-nong'ot,* meaning "mountain of the valleys." The view from the top, overlooking the cavernous crater and the Great Rift Valley, is spectacular.

As you draw closer, the mountain seems to get dramatically taller, rising in solitary splendor from the valley below. The route up from the National Park gate is just as steep as it appears. Allow about an hour to hike up the slope and two or three more hours to walk around the rim of the crater. All groups should be accompanied by a ranger from the Kenya Wildlife Services.

Take plenty of water, as there are no refreshments within the park. There is a wide variety of wildlife on the mountain, including larger and more aggressive species such as buffalo. The area is home to a staggering 475 species of birds. ⊠ *Kenya Wildlife Service, Box 40241, Nairobi,* ☎ *02/501–081,* FAX *02/505–866,* WEB *www.kenya-wildlife-service.org.* ⬜ *$15.*

The tiny **Italian Chapel,** on the main highway at the foot of the pass, was constructed by the same Italian prisoners of war who built the road over the mountains to Nairobi. It is dedicated to the memory of the many people who died during construction.

Dining and Lodging

$$$$ 🏠 **Longonot Game Ranch.** Perched on the lower slopes of Mt. Longonot, this remote ranch on an 80,000-acre estate has spectacular views of nearby Hell's Gate National Park. Formerly the home of writer Martha Gellhorn (one of Ernest Hemingway's wives), it has four rooms in the main ranch house, and two others in a separate cottage. All are attractively furnished, but life revolves around the comfortable lounge, dining room, and long veranda. Book through Safaris Unlimited. ⊠ *19 km (11 mi) from main road,* ☎ *02/891–168,* FAX *02/891–113,* WEB *www.safarisunlimited.com. Dining room, horseback riding. No credit cards.*

Lake Naivasha

❹ *83 km (51 mi) northwest of Nairobi.*

One of the largest of the lakes in the Great Rift Valley, Lake Naivasha is also one of the few that has fresh water. Extraordinarily, it is actually a two-story structure—the cave system beneath the lake holds a second, much larger store of water. The first European to explore the lake was German Gustav Fisher, who ventured here in 1883. Its name derives from the Maasai word *en-aipsha,* which simply means "the lake."

From 1937 to 1950 Lake Naivasha served as the region's airport. Today it provides the water for one of the most intensively farmed areas in Kenya. The introduction of foreign animals and plants such as the dreaded water hyacinth (now gradually being brought under control) and heavy use of polluting chemicals have disrupted the lake's ecosystem, something environmentalists are belatedly trying to right. This, together with a shore lined with holiday cottages (including some elegant colonial mansions, such as the Djinn Palace made famous in *White Mischief*) makes Lake Naivasha too "un-African" for some. But the lake still has many hippos along the largely undeveloped western shore and fish eagles perched in yellow-bark acacia trees. And there are fine views, especially the purple peaks of Mt. Longonot in the distance. If not ruggedly exciting, Lake Naivasha is a pleasant place in which to base yourself to explore the southern Rift Valley.

The rim of a submerged volcanic crater, the 300-acre **Crescent Island** is a sanctuary renowned for its birds that is also home to small herds of antelope, zebras, and giraffes. There are no predators here, so it is possible to walk freely among the wildlife (avoiding the inevitable snorting heaps of hippos). Most local hotels and lodges operate or will organize boat trips across for guests. ⊠ *Near southeastern shore of the lake.* ☉ *Sunrise–sunset.*

Formerly the home of conservationists Joy and George Adamson (authors of *Born Free*), **Elsamere** is now a small museum, with a fascinating collection of photographs of the couple and their famous lioness, Elsa. Tea is served on the lawn outside the rambling colonial-style bungalow, and you may also inquire about a room in one of the cottages. ⊠ *S. Lake Rd., 22 km (13 mi) from main road,* ☎ *0311/21055.* ☉ *Daily 3–5.*

Near the western edge of Lake Naivasha, **Crater Lake Game Sanctuary** is an idyllic little sanctuary surrounding a flooded volcanic caldera with breathtakingly vivid blue-green water. It has a wide variety of small game, including a large colony of black-and-white colobus monkeys who hang around in the tall trees along the shore. There are also around 150 species of birds in the area. Hikers should allow about two hours to circle the crater. ⊠ *S. Lake Rd., 60 km (36 mi) off main road.* 🎫 *$2.* ☉ *Daily 6–6.*

Resembling a smaller version of the Grand Canyon, **Hell's Gate National Park** is one of the few reserves in Kenya where you can get out of your vehicle and wander among the elands, zebras, and hartebeest. Clouds of steam still rise from the earth's depths—hence, the rather diabolical name. Dominated by unusual rock formations, the area's volcanic past is very much in evidence. Fischer's Tower is an 82-ft eroded volcanic outcrop named after the German explorer. It's a favorite haunt for the rock hyrax, the rabbitlike mammal thought to be related to elephants because of its foot-bone structure. Amateur geologists can find huge chunks of the black glassy obsidian, used by early humans to fashion tools.

This is great for bird-watching, as just before sundown you can see martins turn wing over wing to enter their cliffside homes. There also are grand birds of prey. There are two park entrances; the main Elsa Gate is reached by the turnoff near the YMCA on the Moi South Lake Road that runs along the southern shoreline of Lake Naivasha, and the Oikaria Gate is reached via the turnoff near Elsamere. ⊠ *Kenya Wildlife Service, Box 40241, Nairobi,* ☎ *02/501–081,* 🖷 *02/505–866,* 🌐 *www.kenya-wildlife-service.org.* 🎫 *$15.*

Dining and Lodging

$$$$ 🏨 **Olerai House.** An enchanting deep red farmhouse, Olerai House is
★   run by Iain and Oria Douglas-Hamilton, Africa's leading experts on elephants. You could not wish for a better introduction to Kenya than their boating trips and game walks. Oria is of French/Italian ancestry, a fact reflected in the wonderful menus that are several notches above most of what you will eat in Kenya. Each of the rooms is individually decorated using natural woods and cottons. The breezy lakeside setting, framed by jacarandas and acacias, has great views of the dazzling

sunsets. You can fly in from Nairobi to the private airstrip. ✉ *N. Lake Rd., near Crater Lake,* ☎ *02/334–868 or 02/242–572,* 🖷 *02/332–106 or 02/890–441,* 🌐 *www.olerai.com. 7 rooms. Dining room, pool, boating, private airstrip. No credit cards.*

$$$ 🏨 **Lake Naivasha Country Club.** Although supposedly open only to members, Lake Naivasha Country Club has long since given up that pretense. This resort hotel, housed is an old colonial building, is perfect for weekend getaways from the hustle and bustle of Nairobi. Wooden cottages are scattered around the carefully manicured lawns leading down to the water's edge. Meals are often served in the shade of acacia and pepper trees. ✉ *S. Lake Rd., 9 km (6 mi) from main road, Naivasha,* ☎ *0311/20925,* 🖷 *0311/2161,* 🌐 *www.blockhotelske.com. 52 rooms. Bar, restaurant, pool, massage, spa, boating, bicycles, billiards, playground. AE, DC, MC, V.*

$$ 🏨 **Elsamere.** The former home of Joy and George Adamson, Elsamere offers rooms in the main house and a collection of bright cottages with verandas strewn about the beautiful gardens. Dinner is often a lively affair, as many of the guests are visiting researchers who offer a whole new perspective on the country. Children under seven are not allowed. A full breakfast is included. ✉ *S. Lake Rd., 22 km (13 mi) from main road, Naivasha,* ☎ *0311/21055,* 🖷 *0311/21074. 9 rooms. Dining room, lake, boating. MC, V.*

$ 🏨 **La Belle Inn.** Houses in an attractive colonial building dating from 1922, this inn in the town of Naivasha is a popular pit stop for people traveling farther afield. The food is surprisingly good, with the main restaurant offering steaks and other substantial fare, while the café serves sandwiches and pastries. The rooms are simple and clean. ✉ *Moi Ave., Naivasha,* ☎ *0311/21007,* 🖷 *0311/21119. 11 rooms, 1 with bath. Restaurant, bar, café, business services. MC, V.*

$ ⛺ **Fisherman's Camp.** The finest of the campgrounds scattered along the lake, Fisherman's Camp is set among yellow-bark acacias. There are two camps—the rowdier Bottom Camp, near the shore, and the quieter Top Camp, a little farther up the hill. Accommodations range from basic bandas to dormitories that sleep up to four people, and you can rent a tent or pitch your own. Firewood and basic staples are for sale. ✉ *S. Lake Rd., 19 km (13 mi) from main road, Naivasha,* ☎ *0311/ 30088. 7 dormitories, 11 bandas. Bar, restaurant, boating, waterskiing, shop. No credit cards.*

Shopping

Campbell Clause Gallery (✉ S. Lake Rd., 3 km [2 mi] off main road, ☎ 0311/20681) has an excellent collection of local crafts and curios. **Elementeita Weavers** (✉ S. Lake Rd., 4 km [2 mi] off main road, ☎ 0311/30115) boasts a fine collection of tapestries, mats, and carpets. It's not cheap, but the work is beautiful. The shop is open daily 9–5. One of the largest souvenir shops in Kenya, **Naivasha Ebony Curio Shop** (✉ on Moi Ave. near A104, ☎ 0311/30164) is the barracks for eerie armies of polished hardwood figures that range from thimble- to lifesize. They are backed up by a cavalry of stone elephants and wildebeest and announced by batik pennants overhead. The quality is good, and the prices on the whole are reasonable. The shop will ship across the world.

Lake Elementeita

❺ *120 km (74 mi) northwest of Nairobi.*

Originally part of the same vast stretch of water as Lake Naivasha, Lake Elementeita is now a shallow soda lake south of Lake Nakuru. The area is slowly being transformed into a nature preserve as owners of the land around the lake consolidate their holdings. The private park currently covers more than 740 acres, but the owners hope to incorporate the entire shore, allowing tourists to wander among the area's 300 species of birds, including the flocks of flamingoes and pelicans that make their homes here. The **Rosalu Ostrich Farm** (✉ beside Lake Elementeita Lodge, ☎ 036/5029), offers guided tours of the area on foot and horseback.

Originally discovered in 1928 by Louis Leakey, the archaeological site of Kariandusi dates back hundreds of thousands of years. The **Kariandusi Museum** exhibits simple tools that belonged to *Homo habilis,* who lived between 1.5 and 2.5 million years ago, as well as the more sophisticated knives, scrapers, and axes that were the tools of *Homo erectus,* who dominated the region 400,000–500,000 years ago. As there is no evidence of habitation here, Leakey thought that Kariandusi was established to make tools. Enthusiastic and knowledgeable guides will take you to visit two excavation sites and around the small museum. ✉ *1.5 km (1 mi) off A104,* ☎ *no phone.* 🎫 *Ksh 200.* ☉ *Daily 9–6.*

Dining and Lodging

$$$ 🏨 **Lake Elementeita Lodge.** Called Kekopey Ranch by Lord Galbraith Cole when he built it in 1916, Lake Elementeita Lodge is a long, low building surrounded by a wide veranda with fine views of the lake. The simple but attractive rooms are in a series of small cottages scattered around lovingly tended gardens. There is a barbecue out on the deck near the pool most evenings. Owned by a community group, the lodge will one day be the centerpiece of a private game sanctuary. The staff will guide you on bird-watching walks. ✉ *Gilgil,* ☎ *037/850–863,* 🆑 *037/850–833,* 🌐 *www.lakenakurulodge.com. 33 rooms. Restaurant, bar, pool, horseback riding. MC, V.*

Lake Nakuru

❻ *156 km (97 mi) northwest of Nairobi.*

With a population of around 500,000, Nakuru is now the third-largest city in Kenya. Like Nairobi, it was founded with the arrival of the railroad a little over a century ago. It is now primarily an agricultural center, with the surrounding area producing corn, wheat, and potatoes.

Nakuru has a few attractions for those staying here overnight. There are a number of fine old colonial buildings, many of them now falling into disrepair and threatened with demolition to make way for "tower blocks." The street market is one of the most vibrant in all of Kenya.

★   A magical little nature preserve, **Lake Nakuru National Park** covers an area of 188 square km (73 square mi). At its center is Lake Nakuru, a shallow soda lake fed by the Njoro, Makalia, Lamuriak, Ngosur, and Nderit rivers. At the height of the rainy season it covers an area of about 40 square km (15½ square mi) but shrinks to a fraction of that during the dry season, leaving the vast flood plains open for spectacular game viewing.

This remarkably pretty park consists of grasslands studded with yellow-bark acacias against a backdrop of the Rift Valley escarpments. In these wooden hills you'll find the world's largest forest of euphorbias, the many-armed plant widely known as the candelabra cactus. Most people, however, come here for the wide variety of wildlife. There are now more than 75 rhinos here, making it is almost impossible to drive around the park without coming across at least a few. Rothschild giraffes, moved here after upsetting farmers in nearby Eldoret, have flourished. Between 300 and 400 buffaloes inhabit the park, and the most likely place to spot them is in the forested areas at dawn or dusk. The cliffs along the lake are ideal for the leopards and lions that make their home here. The only Big Five animal not present is the elephant, as the park is too small to cope with its destructive eating habits.

The lake itself was deemed "the greatest bird spectacle on earth" by the late ornithologist Roger Tory Peterson. The country's first bird sanctuary was created here in 1961 to protect the lake's estimated 450 species. The highlight without a doubt is the extraordinary flocks of lurid pink flamingoes that spend their days paddling in the shallow water, slurping up beakfuls of blue-green algae. A dramatic sight any time of the day, to watch them take to the air by the thousand in front of a setting sun is truly one of the most magnificent spectacles on the planet. There are also large flocks of white pelicans. ⊠ *Kenya Wildlife Service, Box 40241, Nairobi,* ☎ *02/501–081,* FAX *02/505–866,* WEB *www. kenya-wildlife-service.org.* ☞ *$15.*

The ancient peoples who chose to live on the rocky promontory called **Hyrax Hill** certainly had an eye for natural beauty. This archaeological site, on a hillside outside Nakuru, was discovered by Louis and Mary Leakey in 1926 and excavated at various times ever since. This is a relatively new site, with evidence of human habitation as long as 3,000 years ago. There are several excavations where you'll find the remains of huts and a burial ground. Ask one of the resident guides to walk you around, or you will probably miss most of the detail. The little museum does a good job explaining the importance of the site. ⊠ *Turn right off the A104 just before you reach Nakuru,* ☎ *no phone.* ☞ *Ksh 100.* ☉ *Daily 8–6.*

On the northern edge of Nakuru, a dramatic extinct volcano soaring to 2490 m (7545 ft) holds the **Menengai Crater.** You can drive right up to the rim of the largest caldera in the world, at a staggering 12 km (7 mi) across and 483 m (1463 ft) deep. The views, needless to say, are magnificent. ⊠ *8 km (5 mi) north of Nakuru,* ☎ *no phone.*

Dining and Lodging

$$$ ⬧ **Deloraine.** Built in 1920 by Lord Francis Scott, this lovely example ★ of colonial architecture is set on a private 5,000-acre farm. The main activity here is horseback safaris, but those who don't want to get on a horse have plenty to do, from croquet on the lawn to tennis on the excellent courts to wandering among the imposing stone arches in the garden. Only a dozen guests can stay at any one time, which means you'll feel like a part of the family. The estate, near the pretty village of Rongai, is on the western side of the Rift Valley. ⊠ *Rongai,* ☎ *02/ 571–647,* FAX *02/571–665,* WEB *www.unchartedoutposts.com. 6 rooms. Dining room, horseback riding, tennis. AE, DC, MC, V.*

$$$ ⬧ **Juani Farm.** A few kilometers west of Nakuru National Park, this charming colonial house is a nice alternative to nearby lodges. At Juani, whose name means "a place in the sun," you are treated to traditional English meals in the beautiful gardens. Each bedroom has a fireplace and private bath where the water is heated by firewood. Luxurious touches include hot-water bottles to warm your bed, fresh flowers on the bureau, and hand creams on the vanity. ⊠ *Molo,* ☎ *02/749– 062,* FAX *02/741–636. 3 rooms. Dining room. AE, DC, MC, V.*

$$$ ⬧ **Lake Nakuru Lodge.** The community group that operates the Lake Elementeita Lodge also runs this comfortable establishment high on the hillside near the Nderit Gate of Lake Nakuru National Park. It has fine views past the pretty gardens to the lake. The gray volcanic stone makes the buildings look a little forbidding from the outside, but the rooms inside are very comfortable. ⊠ *Lake Nakuru National Park,*

☎ *037/850–228*, FAX *037/850–518*, WEB *www.lakenakurulodge.com. 68 rooms, 8 suites. Restaurant, bar, pool, horseback riding. MC, V.*

$$$ 🏨 **Sarova Lion Hill.** This low-slung lodge near the eastern shore of Lake Nakuru consists of glass-fronted cottages with small verandas set along winding paths up the hillside. The lodge grounds are fenced, so you can walk around freely. Dine in the Flamingo Restaurant, which overlooks the lovely pool, or enjoy the sunset from the Rift Valley Bar. ⊠ *Lake Nakuru National Park*, ☎ *037/85455*, FAX *037/210–836*, WEB *www.sarovahotels.com. 67 rooms, 4 suites. Restaurant, bar, 2 pools, sauna, shop. AE, MC, V.*

$ 🏨 **Waterbuck Hotel.** A good deal for independent travelers, this hotel in the town of Nakuru is clean and modern. Rooms have private baths and balconies. The breakfast is well above average, and the copious buffet lunch is very reasonable. ⊠ *Government Ave. at West Rd., Nakuru*, ☎ *037/215–672. 68 rooms. Restaurant, bar. AE, DC, MC, V.*

Shopping

Nakuru has no formal souvenir shops, but it does have one of the largest and most vibrant street markets in Kenya running right through the center of town. Be prepared to haggle and fend off overly persistent vendors. As in all crowded areas, keep a firm hold on your valuables.

Lake Bogoria National Reserve

❼ *80 km (50 mi) north of Lake Nakuru.*

This slender lake is found in a valley west of the Siracho Escarpment. About halfway down the lake on the western side is a series of hot springs and geysers that blast steam into the sky, the most dynamic of their kind in East Africa. The acacia trees around the lake are the habitat of hornbills, mousebirds, barbets, weavers, and shrikes. The basalt cliffs west of the lake hold some of the most spectacular birds, such as Verreaux's eagle.

The alkalinity of the lake water provides a perfect environment for the blue-green algae on which lesser flamingos thrive. Flocks of up to 2 million of the beautiful birds have been recorded here. The reserve was established to protect not the flamingos but the lesser kudus that wander down from the Laikipia Plateau in the evenings to lick salt at the lake's eastern edge. Nonetheless it is more often than not a bird-watcher's paradise. ⊠ *Kenya Wildlife Service, Box 40241, Nairobi*, ☎ *02/501–081*, FAX *02/505–866*, WEB *www.kenya-wildlife-service.org.* 🎫 *$15.*

Lodging

$$$ 🏨 **Lake Bogoria Lodge.** This secluded lodge, north of Lake Bogoria Na-
★   tional Reserve, is a real find. Accommodations are in cottages set in a flower garden. The place is rather charming, and certainly makes access to the reserve easier. There are two pools, one fed by natural hot springs. ⊠ *2½ km (1½ mi) from north entrance of reserve*, ☎ *02/336–858*, FAX *02/218–109. 48 rooms. Dining room, pool. AE, DC, MC, V.*

$ ⛺ **Fig Tree Campsite.** This campground near the southern shore of Lake Bogoria is the best in the reserve. Baboons can be a problem, so make sure not to leave valuables unattended. A freshwater stream runs through the campsite. ⊠ *Lake Bogoria National Reserve*, ☎ *02/501–081*, FAX *02/501–752.* WEB *www.kenya-wildlife-service.org. MC, V.*

Lake Baringo

❽ *30 km (19 mi) north of Lake Bogoria.*

The largest freshwater lake in Kenya's Rift Valley, Lake Baringo sits at a height of 975 m (3,185 ft). It's hard to imagine a more beautiful setting—the steep-walled Laikipia escarpment runs to the east of the lake, while in the west are the much smaller, yet still impressive, Tugen Hills. Both show clear evidence of shifting faults. It was while working near Lake Baringo in 1893 that geologist J. W. Gregory discovered how the Great Rift Valley was formed.

Although erosion has caused it to become a perpetual muddy brown, Lake Baringo is still a beautiful sight. It continues to be a mecca for birdlife, with more than 470 species recorded. Sailing along the shore and around the central islands gives you a good opportunity to see pelicans, yellow-billed storks, spoonbills, pintail ducks, coots, sandpipers, and cormorants. Hemprich's hornbills are often spotted on the lake's islands—one of the rarer finds in Kenya. You'll also see hippos and crocodiles. The Baringo Fishermen's Cooperative Society (☎ 0328/51408), searching for new ways for locals to make a living, offers a variety of boat trips around the lake and tours of villages.

Three tribes live around Lake Baringo. The Pokots inhabit the north and east, making their living by tending livestock. To the south, fishing the lake, are the Njemps. These people speak a language similar to that of the Maasai, wear similar ocher clothing, and have many of the same initiation ceremonies. Like the Maasai they herd cows, sheep, and goats, but they also paddle small canoes made from the ambatch plant out into the lake to catch both tilapia and catfish. The third tribe, the Tugens, are part of the Kalenjin group; they live in the hills to the west that bear their name.

Dining and Lodging

$$$ ⊞ **Baringo Island Camp.** This camp on an island in the middle of Lake Baringo is reachable only by boat, and during the 20-minute journey here you'll doubtless pass a few curious hippos. One of the first permanent camps in Kenya, it has thatch-covered tents with shaded verandas, electricity, and private baths with running water. Perched on a hillside at the narrow southern end of the island, getting here requires climbing a considerable number of steps. One of the delights of the camp is visiting a Njemp village, where you can listen to evocative reed music and witness fishermen set out in boats made of branches from the ambatch trees. A big thrill is waterskiing in the lake—the crocs are well fed by abundant tilapia, or so say the locals. ⊠ *Ol Kokwe Island,* ☎ *02/340–331,* FAX *02/336–890,* WEB *www.letsgosafari.com. 23 tents. Restaurant, bar, pool. AE, DC, MC, V.*

$$ ⊞ **Lake Baringo Club.** Once called a country club, this rather basic hotel is still a dream for bird-watchers. The resident ornithologist will escort you on walks and assist with identifying dozens of species. All rooms have verandas looking out onto the robust bougainvillea and shaded tables and chairs in the gardens. Ask for one of the rooms in the new wing, as they have higher ceilings and brighter decor. Activities include visits to a nearby Njemp *manyatta* (homestead) and cruises to the mouth of the Molo River. ⊠ *West side of Lake Baringo,* ☎ *02/540–780,* FAX *02/545–948,* WEB *www.blockhotelske.com. 68 rooms. Restaurant, bar, pool, shop, meeting rooms. AE, DC, MC, V.*

$ ⚠ **Robert's Campsite.** Near the village of Kampi ya Samaki, this well-run camp lets you watch hippos walking past your tent on moonlighted nights. Showers, toilets, and drinking water are provided, but bring all other supplies. ⊠ *West side of Lake Baringo,* ☎ *no phone. 3 bandas, 2 houses, campsites. Shop. No credit cards.*

Kapedo

9 *70 km (43 mi) north of Baringo.*

Because of a local mission, this town has grown into a regional center for the Turkana people. Here, you can see something of their way of life without having to travel much farther north. Just outside town a hot springs emerges from barren ground and flows over a 9-m (30-ft) cliff. The water continues north as a broad warm river, eventually drying up in the Suguta Valley. Water is scarce in the surrounding country, so most animals are dependent on this river. By day you'll see pelicans, herons, and storks compete for small fish; in the evening baboons and lions come to drink.

This remote area on the edge of Kenya's northern desert is best seen as a day trip from Baringo. You'll need a four-wheel-drive vehicle to cope with the roads. Check the security situation with locals before setting out.

MT. ELGON AND ENVIRONS

Northwestern Kenya is one of the most beautiful, and most undiscovered, regions of the country. Very few tourists make it to this fertile region with its cascades of terraces and lush forested mountains. Those who do are usually attracted by the fabulous array of colorful birds near Mt. Elgon, the Kenyan half of a giant volcano that straddles the Ugandan border. Yet there is much more here for those looking for something off the beaten path.

One of the best reasons to venture in this direction is to meet the people who live here. There are no cities—the largest, a university town called Eldoret, has a population of less than 100,000. The small villages scattered across the mountains are home to the Luhya people, who settled in the area more than 600 years ago, and the Kalenjin people, who migrated here about 2,000 years ago.

Almost all the vast farms that filled the region in colonial times have been broken up into small *shambas*. The competition for this land has been fierce, causing increasing tension among ethnic groups. The cattle-farming Pokots, in particular, have a long-running dispute with the Turkanas, their desert-dwelling neighbors to the north, while to the north a political battle has erupted between the Tugens, to the west, and the Kikuyus, to the east. Some say that this is all a little too convenient, with trouble flaring before each election. President Daniel Moi is a Tugen, as are many members of his cabinet. The northwest has seen a great many benefits from the connection, including some of the best roads in the country.

Kabarnet

10 *60 km (37 mi) west of Baringo; 80 km (50 mi) east of Eldoret.*

Perched on the summit of the Tugen Hills, Kabarnet is the hometown of Kenyan President Daniel Moi. There is little to hold your interest here besides the spectacular location. Once at Kabarnet you must choose between turning left or right along the crest of the hills or going down the steep, twisting road that leads across the Kerio Valley and on to Eldoret. Whichever route you choose, the views are some of Kenya's finest.

The road north of Kabarnet passes through small farms and patches of montane forest to **Kabartonjo,** 19 km (12 mi) away. A wooded area about 3 km (2 mi) before you reach the village is particularly good for bird-watching. Beyond Kabartonjo the road is extremely rough, but it eventually joins the B4 a half hour's drive north of Lake Baringo.

Rising to 2,500 m (8,200 ft), the **Tugen Hills** are a small range of mountains between two forks of the Rift Valley. They can be a pleasant place to spend a day exploring away from the heat and humidity of the valley floor. There are spectacular views, both east to the lakes sparkling in the haze 1,525 m (5,001 ft) below and west across a 1,220-m (4,001-ft) drop to the Kerio Valley and the Elgeyo Escarpment beyond.

★ A spur of the Great Rift Valley, the **Kerio Valley** is, if possible, more dramatic than its big brother. The air is refreshingly cool at the top but becomes bakingly hot as you descend into the valley below. Much of the land, dotted with thorny acacias, prickly euphorbias, and castlelike termite mounds, has been desperately eroded by the many local goats. The people are friendly, and their lifestyle is largely untouched by the modern world. On the valley floor the road crosses a dramatically deep, narrow gorge carved out by the Kerio River that local warriors once had to leap over as a test of courage. The gorge is about 1½ km (1 mi) long, opening out into a broad, shallow river where numerous contented crocodiles bask in the sun.

In the Kerio Valley, about 25 km (14 mi) north of Kabarnet, is the **Lake Kamnarok National Reserve.** Here you'll find a good array of wildlife, including elephants, buffaloes, zebras, antelopes, and leopards. The Kenya Wildlife Service has plans to build roads, but as of now getting around the park requires a four-wheel-drive vehicle. ✉ *Kenya Wildlife Service, Box 40241, Nairobi,* ☎ *02/501–081,* ℻ *02/505–866,* 🌐 *www. kenya-wildlife-service.org.* 🎫 *$15.*

On the western side of the Kerio Valley, the road climbs up a series of agonizingly steep hairpin curves to the **Elgeyo Escarpment.** The views get better with every turn until your reach the little village of Iten, famous as the training ground of some of the world's best long-distance runners. Bolstered by the success of their fellow Kenyans, many other national squads are coming to this area for high-altitude training sessions.

To reach **World's End,** the highest point on the Elgeyo Escarpment, travel southeast for 32 km (20 mi) past the Kaptagat Forest, until you reach Chepkorio. Turn left along a narrow farm road (impassable in the rainy season) for 3 km (2 mi), then follow a track bringing you to the rim of the escarpment. World's End is a rocky outlook where you'll find a small chapel. The view from the peak of the 64-km (40-mi) width of the Great Rift Valley is unforgettable.

Dining and Lodging

$ 🏨 **Kabarnet Hotel.** High in the Tugen Hills, the Kabarnet Hotel has magnificent views from the terrace and from many of the rooms, but there's little else to recommend it. However, it is the only option in an area desperately short of decent accommodations. The threadbare rooms are reasonably clean, the service willing but chaotic. Avoid the restaurant, where the food runs to stale egg sandwiches and cold french fries. ✉ *1 km (½ mi) north of Kabarnet,* ☎ *0328/22150,* ℻ *0328/ 22374. 29 rooms. Bar, terrace, pool. V.*

Eldoret

🔟 *110 km (68 mi) west of Baringo; 311 km (193 mi) northwest of Nairobi.*

Originally known as simply as "64" because it was built on Farm 64 in an area settled by Afrikaans farmers, Eldoret later became the administrative center for the many Kalenjin tribes in the northwest. It has Kenya's third international airport but currently has no international flights. It is an attractive little town but can't compete with the scenic wonderland surrounding it.

Dining and Lodging

$$ ☶ **Hotel Sirikwa.** This concrete hotel in the center of town is popular among business travelers but also serves as a convenient stopover for travelers in the region. The hotel needs a makeover, but if you ignore the dated furnishings, the rooms are quite comfortable. The staff is efficient and friendly and offers services ranging from currency exchange to baby-sitting. The restaurant is probably the best in Eldoret, serving standard Kenyan fare. The pool is open to nonresidents for a daily fee of Ksh 100. ⊠ *Oloo Rd. and Elgeyo Rd., Eldoret,* ☎ *0321/63433, 02/224–273 for reservations,* ☒ *0321/61018. 105 rooms, 7 suites. Restaurant, bar, hair salon, pool, children's playground. AE, MC, V.*

Kitale

⓬ *69 km (43 mi) northwest of Eldoret.*

A busy little market town, Kitale is at the center of an agricultural area often described as "the granary of Kenya." The original settlement, called Quitale, was established long before the arrival of the Europeans as a stop along the slave route. The town began to flourish in 1925 with the arrival of the railway.

★ An annex of the Kenya National Museums, the **Kitale Museum** is seldom visited by tourists. This is a shame, as it is one of the best regional museums in the country. Note the colorful murals by American photographer Carol Beckwith at the entrance. Much of the collection was bequeathed by Lieutenant Colonel Hugh Stoneham, who established the Stoneham Museum in 1927. His private study is re-created here alongside his excellent collection of sadly underlabeled insects, butterflies, and moths. There are also small exhibits on geology, archaeology, and local culture, together with open-air exhibits including a display of traditional homes of the Bukusu, Luo, and Turkana peoples. The museum has its own 30-acre nature reserve, where the rare De Brazza's monkey can be spotted. You can request that one of the informative guides show you around. ⊠ *Eldoret Rd.,* ☎ *035/20670.* ☷ *Ksh 200.* ☉ *Daily 8–6.*

One of Kenya's smallest reserves, **Saiwa Swamp National Park** encompasses only 3 square km (1 square mi). It was established in 1974 to protect the rare sitatunga antelope, which has developed wide hooves that allow it to walk adeptly in the wetlands. Resembling a nyala in high heels, it is also a good swimmer. When in danger it dives underwater, leaving only its nose above the surface. Saiwa is also home to the endangered De Brazza's monkey, giant forest squirrels, black-and-white colobus monkeys, bushbucks, and grey duikers. The park has three nature trails leading to a trio of viewing platforms. The walkways are slippery when it rains, so wear shoes with treads. ⊠ *Kenya Wildlife Service, Box 40241, Nairobi,* ☎ *02/501–081,* ☒ *02/505–866,* ☒☒ *www.kenya-wildlife-service.org.* ☷ *$15.*

Dining and Lodging

$$ ☶ **Kitale Club.** One of the oldest clubs in Kenya, this time capsule of the colonial era was built on the site of the old slave quarters. The 18-hole golf course is the big draw, but there are also a pool, sauna, and tennis courts. Try to stay in the new wing, which has fireplaces in each room. The English-style dining room often serves up delicious Indian

food. The bar is an excellent place to meet locals. ⊠ *Eldoret Rd.,* ☎ *0325/20036. Bar, restaurant, pool, 18-hole golf course, tennis. AE, V.*

Mt. Elgon National Park

⑬ *60 km (37 mi) west of Kitale.*

Straddling the border of Uganda, Mt. Elgon is a remnant of what was once a huge volcano. Over the past 15 million years erosion has worn it down to a mere 4,321 m (14,178 ft). The highest summit is on the Ugandan side, but you can reach a summit on the Kenyan side that is only 20 m (65 ft) lower. From here you can see the Cherangani Hills to the east.

The park is famous for a system of caves once inhabited by the Maasai. Kitum Cave, measuring 50 m (165 ft) wide, is a destination for elephants in search of salt, which is contained in the rock walls. The massive creatures mine great quantities of it with their tusks, going farther and farther into the dark cave. Thousands of bats roost in the rear of the cave, and as you explore the labyrinth, hundreds of eyes gleam in the reflection of your flashlight.

Elephants are relatively numerous, although they are difficult to spot. Buffaloes, reedbucks, waterbucks, bushbucks, black-fronted duikers, bushpigs, and giant forest hogs are all present in substantial numbers but can easily be overlooked in the thick bamboo forest. Primates include black-and-white colobus monkeys, which jump from tree to tree with their long capes of fur streaming out behind. You may also see De Brazza's monkeys, known for their distinctive white beards.

The array of birds is unusually rich. There are many turacos (including the brilliant red and blue Ross's turacos), silvery-cheeked and red-billed hornbills, white-naped ravens, Kenya crested guinea fowls, white-headed wood hoopoes, and red-fronted parrots. ⊠ *Kenya Wildlife Service, Box 40241, Nairobi,* ☎ *02/501–081,* ℻ *02/505–866,* 🌐 *www.kenya-wildlife-service.org.* ⌬ *$15.*

Lodging

$$$$ 🏠 **Lokitela Farm.** Bird-watchers from around the world head to this
★ farm west of Kitale because 260 species have been sighted here in the heavily forested foothills of Mt. Elgon. You need wander no farther than the garden, ablaze with Nandi flame trees, to see a dozen or so. Your hosts, Tony and Adrianne Mills, can organize safaris to the Cherangani Hills, the Kakamega Forest, or Mt. Elgon. There are three guest bedrooms, each with a private bath. Meals are made with home-grown vegetables from the 874-acre farm. ⊠ *19 km (12 mi) west of Kitale,* ☎ *02/884–091,* ℻ *02/882–723,* 🌐 *www.bush-homes.co.ke. 3 rooms. Dining room, horseback riding. AE, V.*

$$ 🏠 **Kapuro Bandas.** In a glade near Mt. Elgon, these simple bandas are a good deal for budget travelers. Each banda is designed to accommodate eight guests. Run by the Kenya Wildlife Service, these units have kitchens and eating utensils, but no refrigerators. Barbecue facilities are outside. ⊠ *Kenya Wildlife Service, Box 40241, Nairobi,* ☎ *02/501–081,* ℻ *02/505–866,* 🌐 *www.kenya-wildlife-service.org.*

Kapenguria

⑭ *34 km (21 mi) north of Kitale.*

Those interested in Kenyan history should stop briefly in this little town to visit the **Kapenguria Museum.** It's housed in the former district commissioner's office where Jomo Kenyatta, later elected president of the country, was imprisoned for nationalist activities during the colonial era. He and five others were tried and sentenced in the nearby school, rather than in Nairobi, in an effort to keep protesters away from the high-profile trial. The displays center around the cells where the six men were imprisoned. There are also exhibits on the daily lives of the Pokot and Sengwer peoples. ⊠ *Kapenguria,* ☎ *no phone.* 🎫 *Ksh 200.* ⏲ *Daily 8:30–6.*

Kapenguria is in the **Cherangani Hills,** an impressive mountain range that stretches for more than 80 km (50 mi). The highest peak, Naku-gen, rises to 3,370 m (11,025 ft). The easiest route is to head east from Kitale, passing through the village of Cherangani. The road once crossed over the mountains to the Kerio Valley, but at at press time the route was blocked by landslides. The road is good as far as Makutano, but beyond that you will need a four-wheel-drive vehicle. You can also get out and start hiking. Take a good map or hire a local guide, and follow the usual safety precautions for high-altitude trekking. Rain, wind, and clouds can descend with little or no warning at any time of year. Check with locals before traveling in this area, as there have been long-running ethnic disputes and it may not be safe.

The **Kongelai Escarpment,** northwest of Kapenguria, is a delightful place to spend a day. The area is famous for its wide array of birds. The road descends through several densely forested valleys, the habitat of the white-crested turaco. Farmlands give way to fields where shepherds tend sheep and goats. The sun is strong at the bottom of the escarp-ment, but many fine fig trees bordering the lugga on the right of the road offer excellent shade for a picnic. Driving farther north toward the village of Kongelai, the climate changes again, becoming more arid. Acacia bushes dominate the landscape and nomadic herdsmen tend not only sheep and goats but also camels. Although four-wheel-drive ve-hicles are not necessary for this safari, make sure to take a sturdy, re-liable car. Check the security situation before setting out.

North of Kapenguria, the road crosses the breathtaking terrain of **Marich Pass,** with the Cherangani Hills rising steeply on the east. Keep an eye open for the complex system of ancient irrigation canals said to have been created by the little-known Sirikwa people. The canals, still used by the local Marakwet people, run for nearly 40 km (24 mi), channelling water from the hills into the nearby plains. The Sirikwas were ingenious builders, living in large holes that they dug in the ground. These holes can still be seen all over the Tugen Hills and the Cheranganis, but the tribe itself dispersed in the early 20th century.

Lodging

$ 🏨 **Sirikwa Safaris Guest House.** More commonly known as the Barn-
★   ley House, this delightful inn run by mother and daughter Jane and Julia Barnley is a true home away from home. Built in 1951, it is beau-tifully situated in the foothills of the Cherangani Hills. Both women are passionate about the area and can arrange for expert birding and hiking guides. Choose from among two cozy rooms with fireplaces in the house and three well-appointed tents in the lush garden. All have shared bathrooms. Julia is an enthusiastic cook, producing enormous quantities of delicious, locally grown food.⊠ *24 km (15 mi) north of Kitale,* ☎ *0702/767–055,* 📠 *0325/20061. 2 double rooms, 3 tents. No credit cards.*

Sigor

⓯   *40 km (25 mi) north of Kitale.*

About 8 km (5 mi) off the main road you'll find the little market town of Sigor. The weekly market in Sigor is on Thursday, but the Saturday market in nearby Lomut is even bigger and better. This is a great place to meet the Pokots, a colorful people who live north and east of the Cherangani Hills. The Pokots mostly herd livestock, although some grow millet and other crops. Despite their similarity to the Turkanas, the Pokots are a Kalenjin tribe. Like other Kalenjins, they practice circumcision as part of their initiation ceremonies. Perhaps because of close contact with their Turkana neighbors, the Pokots have a similar style of dress; however, their language and customs are quite different.

LAKE VICTORIA

As you approach Lake Victoria, Kenya's landscape changes dramatically. In the north you'll encounter the Nandi Hills, farmed by the Kipsigi people. Much of this fertile land is at a fairly high altitude; good rains allow the Kipsigis to grow corn, potatoes, and beans, as well as the white-blossomed pyrethrum, the base for many insecticides. In the far west lies Lake Victoria, the largest lake in Africa and the source of the Nile. At 69,483 square km (26,821 square mi), the lake is bigger than Ireland. Kenya's tiny share of this vast expanse is little more than one huge bay, the Kavirondo Gulf, cut off from the rest of the lake by the narrow Rusinga Channel.

Until very recently, Lake Victoria seemed to be under a death sentence, clogged by the beautiful but deadly water hyacinth. This ornamental plant, imported from Southeast Asia, has run riot across the waterways of Africa, often growing so thick that shipping is brought to a standstill. In the last few years, however, after trying a multitude of solutions, the cure seems to have been found: two species of weevil that devour the weed. The results have been miraculous. It hasn't helped trade, however. Where shipping trade between Uganda, Tanzania, and Kenya once flourished, there are now only a few dhows and endlessly delayed plans to reintroduce the lake steamer (the last one sank in the 1980s).

The shores of Lake Victoria are home to the Luo people, Kenya's second-largest tribe, which arrived in the area from southern Sudan about 600 years ago. They are expert fishermen; morning is the best time to see them returning home in their brightly painted boats. Away from the lake, the Luos herd cattle and grow corn and beans. The Luo women are known throughout Kenya for their expertly crafted clay pots.

Kakamega

16 *120 km (74 mi) southwest of Eldoret.*

Kakamega, which began as an isolated trading post in 1896, is home to the Luhyas, the umbrella name for the more than 18 Bantu tribes that farm this area northeast of Lake Victoria. Many families can trace their genealogy back for more than 20 generations. Legend has it that the Luhyas migrated from Egypt and Sudan about 250 years ago—earlier than the Luo people, who settled farther south. Like the Luos, Luhyas have a complex series of initiation ceremonies for young men. Most of the tribes practice circumcision, and some also remove two teeth from the lower jaw. They are primarily farmers, growing corn, tea, and coffee.

The sprawling, open-air **Kakamega Market** is a good place to wander for an hour or so. The squawking chickens, jumble of household goods, stacks of clay pots, and piles of brightly colored clothes are typical of what many imagine an African market to be.

Dining and Lodging

$$ ▥ **Kakamega Golf Hotel.** Golfers will love this hotel, which has a 9-hole course with beautiful wide fairways. Dating from 1931, the course has some unusual hazards, such as the marabou storks that occasionally steal away with unattended balls. This three-story hotel is the most comfortable lodging in Kakamega. Surrounded by slightly faded flower gardens, it is frequently booked by bird-watchers on their way to Kakamega Forest. ✉ *Khasakala Rd.,* ☎ *0331/30150, 02/330–820 for reservations,* FAX *0331/30155, 02/227–815 for reservations. 61 rooms. Restaurant, bar, pool, 9-hole golf course, dance club, business services. MC, V.*

Kakamega Forest

★ ⑰ *18 km (11 mi) northwest of Kakamega.*

A remnant of the rain forest that once covered much of the continent, the Kakamega Forest is a haven for many animals found nowhere else in Kenya. It is of particular interest to ornithologists, who travel here from all over the world. Almost 60 species of birds are found only in the reserve, including magnificent great blue turacos, black-billed turacos, huge black- and white-casqued hornbills, blue-headed bee-eaters, brown-eared woodpeckers, shrike flycatchers, red-headed malimbes, bar-tailed trogons, metallic sunbirds, and many others, such as barbets, wattle-eyes, and weavers.

A walk in the forest is also a rewarding experience for the nonbirder. Huge trees, tangled vines, and dense undergrowth are a thousand shades of green. Blue, red-tailed, and colobus monkeys can be seen feeding in the trees. Rarely seen animals, including the bush-tailed porcupine, giant water shrew, and hammer-headed fruit bat, with a wing span of a meter or more, can often be spotted. The forest is also home to flying squirrels that can glide for 90 m (295 ft). Morning, when most animals are active, is the best time to visit the forest. If you are adventurous and lucky, a night walk with a guide from the forest station can turn up such nocturnal creatures as the *potto* (bush baby). ✉ *Kenya Wildlife Service, Box 40241, Nairobi,* ☎ *02/501–081,* FAX *02/505–866,* WEB *www.kenya-wildlife-service.org.* ⌑ *$15.*

Dining and Lodging

$$ 🏨 **Rondo Retreat.** This rustic retreat inside Kakamega Forest has a handful of charming cottages surrounded by lush gardens. Rooms are elegantly furnished with four-poster beds. Managed by the Trinity Fellowship, it does not serve alcoholic beverages. ✉ *3 km (2 mi) east of Isecheno Forest Station,* ☎ *0331/30268. 4 rooms. Dining room. No credit cards.*

$ 🏨 **Isecheno Guest House.** Within the Kakamega Forest, this pleasant house perched on stilts has four rooms, each with two single beds and a bath. There are wonderful views of the trees from the veranda. There is no electricity, and bed linens are not provided. There is a small café nearby. ✉ *Near Isecheno Forest Station,* ☎ *no phone. 4 rooms. No credit cards.*

$ 🛖 **Udo's Bandas and Campsite.** In the northern sector of the Kakamega Forest, these are basic thatch rooms with no running water or electricity. You should bring your own bedding, as well as food and water. ✉ *Near Kenya Wildlife Service ranger station,* ☎ *0331/20425. No credit cards.*

Kericho

⑱ *105 km (65 mi) north of Narok; 110 km (68 mi) west of Nakuru.*

You may be surprised to find so many flowers in Kericho, the administrative center of the Kipsigi people. The large amount of rain that keeps the gardens lush also sustains the vast tea plantations that surround the town. This is the tea-growing center of Kenya, which is the third-largest producer in the world (after India and Sri Lanka). Tea is Kenya's largest cash crop, accounting for up to 30% of the country's exports.

The tea estates are best visited in the morning, when the weather is clear and pickers are at work, their brightly colored headscarves and aprons a vivid contrast to the rich green bushes. A skilled picker can gather upwards of 70 kilograms (150 pounds) a day, carefully selecting only the tips (two new leaves and a bud). Each bush can be harvested every 17 days. The large plantations are impressive for their size, but most of the country's crop is actually produced on smaller holdings. (To request a guided tour of the largest farm, contact P. G. Scott, operations director, Eastern Produce Ltd., ✉ Box 22, Nandi Hills, ☎ 0326/43333).

A wide assortment of indigenous trees flourish at the well-maintained **Kericho Arboretum** (✉ 7 km (4 mi) east of Kericho on Rte. B1, ☎ 0326/20377). Next to the lake created by the Chagaik Dam, the arboretum makes an excellent site for a picnic lunch.

One of the largest undisturbed montane forests in Kenya, the **Mau Forest** lies to the east of Kericho. Although much of the wooden area is inaccessible, a walk to the Kiptiget River is a rewarding way to spend a half day. Elephants, buffaloes, and bushbucks make their home in the forest, but they are seldom seen. You will spot a varied assortment of birds and a multitude of stunning butterflies.

To the north of Kericho, Route B1 descends to Chemelil, home to huge sugarcane plantations, before climbing the spectacular **Nyando Escarpment.** Here you'll be treated to splendid views of the valley below. The surrounding hills hold the small farms of the Luhya people, their traditional homes scattered among hillsides strewn with large chunks of granite. This region is reputed to be the lair of the Nandi Bear, Kenya's own version of Bigfoot. Gorilla country is nearby, which may account for this legend.

Dining and Lodging

$$ 🏨 **Kericho Tea Hotel.** Set amid attractive gardens, this tile-roofed hotel was constructed in 1953 for executives of the Brooke Bond Tea Company. The peaceful location near a tea estate, where pickers are often hard at work, is its main asset. The cottages are a better bet than the main hotel, but the rooms are overpriced, given the tired state of the furnishings and facilities. ✉ *Moi Hwy.,* ☎ *0361/30004,* ⊠ *0361/20576. 45 rooms, 8 cottages. Pool, tennis. AE, DC, V.*

$ 🏨 **Kweisos House.** A delightful estate dating from the colonial era,
★ Kweisos House is on a 3,000-acre farm. Its name means "place of palms," but the main house and two smaller cottages are surrounded by mature gardens. As well as watching the farmers tend to tea and other crops, you can wander through wilderness areas that are home to monkeys and other small animals and a lake where you can fish for tilapia and bass. The friendly staff takes care of all your needs. You can have them prepare all your meals, or buy fresh produce and organize your own menu. The owners are delighted to take you horseback riding, bird-watching, or fishing and to share the swimming pool and tennis courts at their farmhouse, about 6 km (4 mi) away. A little over an hour's drive from Lake Victoria, this is an ideal base from which to explore the southwest. It is within easy driving distance of Kerio Valley and Kakamega Forest. ✉ *Koru,* ☎ *0341/51064,* ⊠ *0341/51419. 5 rooms. Dining room, games room. No credit cards.*

$ 🏨 **Nandi Bears Golf Club.** Life is laid-back at this friendly old lodging set on an attractive 9-hole golf course. You won't find many frills, but you will be given a warm welcome as you enter the colonial-era club house. The comfortable if basic accommodations are in small cottages in the garden, where you will enjoy the fresh air and wonderful views of the Nandi Hills. Simple meals are available in the bar. ✉ *Nandi Hills,* ☎ *0326/43238,* FAX *0341/51419. 3 cottages. Bar, snack bar, golf. No credit cards.*

Kisii

🅢 *110 km (66 mi) south of Kericho.*

Most famous for the soapstone carvings that come in shades of pink, yellow, and white, the small town of Kisii is the trading center for the Bantu Gusii tribe. The carvings can be purchased in many parts of Kenya, but here you can choose among hundreds of pieces before deciding. Several stalls are set up along the main street, but it is far more exciting to watch the artisans at work. The best way to do this is to drive 17 km (10 mi) south to the village of Tabaka, site of the soapstone quarries and home to most of the workshops. Because these carvings are produced in private residences, you must move from house to house. Do not feel as if you are imposing, for the carvers are more than happy to show you their work.

Kisumu

🅤 *83 km (50 mi) northwest of Kericho.*

On the eastern shore of Lake Victoria, Kisumu is the third-largest city in Kenya. The western terminus of the famous Lunatic Line, the town was originally named Port Florence, after the wife of the East African Railway's general manager. For many years the hot and humid city was a busy commercial center, transferring goods arriving by rail or ship. In recent years, however, the city has suffered from a dramatic drop in trade. Despite this, Kisumu is still an attractive place. Remember, though, that this one of the poorest areas of the country. Be careful of your possessions, as poverty has led to a high incidence of petty crime.

A pleasing place to stop, the **Kisumu Museum** has the usual array of stuffed animals (including a very graphic tableau of a lion savaging a wildebeest) as well as displays on the Luo, Maasai, and Kalenjin peoples. Outside exhibits include a small snake house, tortoise pen, crocodile pond, and aquarium displaying the catch of the day. ✉ *Nairobi Rd., 4 km (2 mi) from town center,* ☎ *035/40803.* 🎫 *Ksh 200.* ☉ *Daily 8:30–6.*

A tiny wildlife reserve, **Kisumu Impala Sanctuary** is home to a herd of impalas, as well as a few vervet monkeys, striped ground squirrels, leopards, hyenas, and baboons. Its large fig trees attract large numbers of birds, including the African hobby and the Eastern gray plantain-eater. Large flocks of bishops and weaverbirds wear their best plumage from April through November. There's also a small, desolate animal orphanage. Don't take valuables or walk in the area on your own. ✉ *Near Sunset Hotel.* 🎫 *Free.* ☉ *6–6.*

About 3 km (2 mi) south of Kisumu, **Hippo Point** is the traditional place to watch the sunset. From the jetty you can gaze out at the small colony of hippos. At press time, the old campsite was being refurbished, and the foundation of a new fish restaurant was being laid.

Lake Victoria is frequently gray and hazy, but it also has enormous charm. Book a boat through your hotel, or head down to Hippo Point and ask for Titus, a local guide who is very knowledgeable about the lake. He will arrange anything from a short excursion in a rowboat to a full day's fishing trip. Start early in the day to avoid the worst of the midday heat. You'll see fishermen as they struggle to bring in their unwieldy nets, as well as colonies of cormorants and herons perched like statues on the shore. The **Ndere Island National Reserve,** a small island not far from shore, can be reached by speedboat from Hippo Point. Along the shore are hippos and crocodiles, but with a little caution it is possible to wander around the island in search of impalas and rare sitatungas. ⊠ *Kenya Wildlife Service, Box 40241, Nairobi,* ☎ *02/501–081,* FAX *02/505–866,* WEB *www.kenya-wildlife-service.org.*

The many bird sanctuaries near Kisumu make good side trips. The most interesting site is the **Kisumu Heronry.** An "extraordinary spectacle," to quote Sir Fredrick Jackson, who visited it in 1901, the reserve is still one of Kenya's greatest birding destinations. African spoonbills, sacred ibis, yellow-billed storks, cormorants, and open-billed storks can all be seen nesting in the same tree. Black-headed herons, great white egrets, cattle egrets, and yellow-billed egrets are also present, though the number of birds varies from year to year. The nesting period coincides with the long rains, beginning in March or April and continuing through July. During the rest of the year there are few birds. Because the reserve is rather difficult to find, ask directions from locals. ⊠ *11 km (7 mi) east of Kisumu on Rte. B1,* ☎ *no phone.*

About 16 km (10 mi) east of Kisumu, a right turn takes you down a rough road to a market, and a second right leads to the **Sacred Ibis Colony.** Several hundred pairs of this bird usually make their home here, with up to 30 nests in the same tree. The black-headed birds are very tame and seem happy to pose for you. ⊠ *16 km (10 mi) east of Kisumu on B1,* ☎ *no phone.*

Dining and Lodging

$ ⊞ **Imperial Hotel.** A wood-paneled lobby leads to what is undoubtedly the best hotel in Kisumu. Rooms, all of which are air-conditioned, are quite comfortable. There is an impressive menu in the Florence Restaurant, including a good array of local fish. The gleaming white structure suffers from its position in the center of town, as only rooms on the upper floors have views of the lake. ⊠ *Jomo Kenyatta Ave.,* ☎ *035/20002 or 035/22661,* FAX *035/22687,* WEB *www.imperialkisumu.com. 70 rooms, 4 suites. Restaurant, coffee shop, snack bar, minibars, pool, laundry service, business service. AE, DC, V.*

$ ⊞ **Sunset Hotel.** It could do with a face-lift, but this modern hotel about 2 km (1 mi) from the center of Kisumu is comfortable and has excellent views of Lake Victoria. The rooms, many with air-conditioning, all have balconies that let you enjoy the sunset. There are a pleasant terrace bar and an inviting pool. The food is a bit lackluster, but you can get fine fresh fish, caught right in the lake. ⊠ *Aput La.,* ☎ *035/41100 or 035/42445,* FAX *035/22745. 50 rooms, 2 suites. Restaurant, bar, pool. AE, DC, V.*

Shopping

There is a good collection of souvenir stalls opposite the Hotel Royale, on Jomo Kenyatta Avenue. **Kisumu Market** (⊠ Otieno Oyoo St.) is one of the best in Western Kenya. Although most items are not intended for tourists, you may find good baskets and *kikois* (woven fabrics). On Sunday the huge open-air **Kibuye Market** (⊠ Jomo Kenyatta Ave.) is even more vibrant.

Kendu Bay

㉑ *75 km (47 mi) from Kisumu.*

Many small fishing communities, including Kendu Bay, are found along the shores of Lake Victoria. The clusters of brightly painted boats with upturned prows make a striking sight. Fishermen set out at dawn, returning with the breeze around midday. Negotiate a fee, and many will be happy to take you along. Remember that the boats are not built for comfort—there are no toilets, for example. Bring your own food and drinking water.

The shore of the lake, especially the papyrus beds adjacent to Kendu Bay, is a great place to spot some of East Africa's spectacular water birds, including fish eagles, hammerkops, yellow-billed storks, cormorants, and ibis, as well as a range of other species. Several local species are found here, including yellow-backed weavers, swamp flycatchers, papyrus canaries, and stunning black-headed gonoleks, which have brilliant red breasts.

Contained inside a volcanic crater framed by wooded hills, **Lake Simbi** is another area known to ornithologists. The strange green color comes from a wealth of blue-green algae, the lesser flamingo's favorite food. This lake is now home to thousands of these beautiful birds. Local legend holds that the lake is on the site of a village that was cursed after refusing to give shelter to an old woman during a storm. To get here, drive 4 km (2 mi) west on Route C19. Turn left down Route D219 toward Pala, and after 3 km (2 mi) turn left again at the Lake Simbi marker. ⊠ *9 km (5 mi) west of Kendu Bay.*

Covering 194 square km (75 square mi) of the Lambwe Valley, **Ruma National Park** is famous for its population of rare animals, including roan antelopes (only a small breeding herd stands between the species and extinction), Rothschild's giraffes, Jackson's hartebeest, Bohor reedbucks, and oribis. Other animals found in this stretch of grassland include buffaloes, leopards, hyenas, and a variety of antelopes and gazelles. Colorful birds are abundant, including several unusual species such as rufous-bellied herons, bare-faced go-away birds, Senegal coucals, black-headed gonalekas, silverbirds, Mariqua sunbirds, coppery sunbirds, red-chested sunbirds, and zebra finches.

There has been a concerted effort to get rid of the large number of tsetse flies that plague visitors, but there are still a few, along with plenty of mosquitoes; take along a good insect repellent, and don't wear black or blue, the colors that attract tsetse flies. There are only basic campsites in the park, so you'll need to take all your own supplies. ⊠ *Kenya Wildlife Service, Box 40241, Nairobi,* ☎ *02/501–081,* 𝖥𝖠𝖷 *02/505–866,* 𝖶𝖤𝖡 *www.kenya-wildlife-service.org.* 🎫 *$15.*

The important archaeological site of **Thimlich Ohinga,** similar in construction to the stone enclosures of Zimbabwe, is also believed to date from the 15th century. This is the finest of many such enclosures scattered across the area. A stone retaining wall 150 m (492 ft) in diameter surrounds five smaller enclosures. There is evidence of iron working. To get here from Homa Bay, follow Route C20 for 15 km (9 mi) to Rod Kopany. Head south toward Miranga and then follow the signs. ⊠ *60 km (36 mi) south of Homa Bay.*

Rusinga Island

㉒ *40 km (25 mi) west of Homa Bay.*

This ragged, somewhat barren island near the northeastern shore of Lake Victoria is reached by a causeway from the mainland. The island is best known for its amazing fossils and rock paintings. The alkaline qualities of the volcanic soil helps preserve bones, and sometimes even flesh and patterns of feathers. The most important discovery was the remains of an *Proconsul africanus,* an ape that lived in the area 17 million years ago, uncovered by Louis and Mary Leakey in the late 1940s. The ape, now thought to be a significant step in the course of human evolution, can be seen in Nairobi at the National Museum.

The island is also a major fishing center. Hundreds of colorful boats belonging to the Luo people can be spotted near the shore. You can watch the locals hauling in their catch, or try your luck at catching an enormous Nile perch—the record setter weighed in at more than 500 pounds. Fish of well over 100 pounds are caught regularly. You can also go in search of the wildlife, including giant monitor lizards and spotted-necked otters.

Those interested in Kenyan history should make the trip to see the **Mausoleum of Tom Mboya,** the black nationalist and civil rights leader who was murdered in Nairobi in 1969. It is on the northwest side of the island, about 7 km (4 mi) from the causeway.

Dining and Lodging

$$$$ 🖬 **Rusinga Island Lodge.** This little cluster of thatched cottages, each
★   with a dazzling view of Lake Victoria, is designed for those who want to try a little fishing, birding, or simply relaxing. You certainly won't be roughing it, as the accommodations are well-appointed. The easiest way to get here is by plane, and many visitors take a 45-minute by charter plane here from Maasai Mara National Reserve. ⊠ *Northwest side of Rusinga Island,* ☎ *02/574–689 or 02/567–251,* ℻ *02/564–945 or 02/577–851,* 🖺 *www.kenya-direct.com/rusinga. 5 cottages, 3 tents. Dining room, boating, waterskiing, fishing, private airstrip. AE, DC, V. Closed May.*

Mfangano Island

㉓ *8 km (5 mi) west of Rusinga Island.*

More remote and inaccessible than its neighbor to the east, this small island sees very few visitors. It's a great place for spotting wildlife, as plenty of hippos and monitor lizards make their homes along the shores. For the energetic, a climb up 1,694-m (5,133-ft) Mt. Kwititu offers wonderful views. There are are a number of interesting abstract rock paintings along the way (get one of the locals to guide you). Other rock paintings, of insects, can be seen in the nearby Odengere Hills. Boat head here from Kisumu or from Rusinga Island.

Dining and Lodging

$$$$ 🖬 **Mfangano Island Camp.** Shaded by giant fig trees, this luxurious camp is set along the shores of Lake Victoria. Accommodations are in clay cottages with banana-leaf roofs, typical of the structures built by the Luo people. All have modern baths and private verandas. The fish served at meals come straight from the lake, and the vegetables are grown in the camp's own gardens. Many of the lodge's guests fly here for a day of relaxing by the shore or for a couple days of stress-free fishing. ⊠ *North side of Mfangano Island,* ☎ *02/331871 or 02/336169,* ℻ *02/726427,* 🖺 *www.governorscamp.com. 6 cottages. Dining room lounge, boating, fishing, private airstrip. MC, V.*

Takawiri Island

㉔ *2 km (1 mi) east of Mfangano Island.*

Smaller by far than Rusinga or Mfangano, tiny Takawiri Island has the same mix of wildlife. It is the proud possessor of the only white-sand beach in the area. To get here, take a boat from either Kisumu or Rusinga Island.

Dining and Lodging

$$$$ 🏠 **Takawiri Island Resort.** This charming lodge, at the western end of Takawiri Island, isn't as well known as those on Rusinga or Mfangano, but it also isn't as pricey. It's a relaxing place for those who want to fish or hire a boat to explore the coastline. Accommodations are in stone-and-thatch cottages that have lake views from the balconies. The resort prides itself on its eco-friendly solar power. Visitors rave about the inexplicable but delightful lack of mosquitoes. ✉ *Western side of Takawiri Island,* ☎ *035/40924 or 035/45088,* ✆ *035/41030 or 035/ 44644. 8 rooms. Dining room. No credit cards.*

WESTERN KENYA A TO Z

To research prices, get advice from other travelers, and book travel arrangements, visit www.fodors.com.

AIR TRAVEL TO AND FROM WESTERN KENYA

Eldoret and Kisumu both have good airports, with regular services to Nairobi operated by Flamingo Air, the domestic branch of Kenya Airways. There are numerous small airstrips near game reserves for those who charter private planes. Some of the most luxurious lodges also have their own airstrips. Airkenya flies twice daily to Maasai Mara, with departures at 10 and at 11 from Wilson Airport in Nairobi. Boskovic Air Charters and Eagle Aviation also offer charter flights to the region.

Eldoret International Airport is 15 km (9 mi) south of Eldoret. Kisumu Airport is 8 km (5 mi) south of Kisumu.

➤ AIRLINES: **Airkenya** (☎ 02/605–745, 🌐 www.airkenya.com). **Boskovic Air Charters** (☎ 02/501–210). **Eagle Aviation** (☎ 02/822–924). **Kenya Airways** (☎ 0321/23236 in Eldoret, 035/44055 in Kisumu).
➤ AIRPORTS: **Eldoret International Airport** (☎ 0321/63377). **Kisumu Airport** (☎ 035/23236).

BUS TRAVEL TO AND FROM WESTERN KENYA

Regular bus service runs between Nairobi and all the main towns in Western Kenya. Service is fast and cheap, but also uncomfortable and potentially dangerous. The major companies, Akamba and Eldoret Express, have offices near the main bus stations in most towns. Buses get particularly crowded on weekends and during public holidays. There are often no set departure times—just show up and wait for the next bus.

For traveling shorter distances, *matatus* (shared taxis) are a better solution. They are plentiful, cheap, and a bit rickety, but they usually get you there in one piece.

CAR RENTAL

The international car-rental companies all operate out of Nairobi. There are a few local companies in the larger towns of Western Kenya, but their range of vehicles is limited, and the quality is sometime suspect. One reputable Kenyan company is Glory Car Hire, which has offices in Eldoret and Kisumu.
➤ LOCAL AGENCIES: **Glory Car Hire** (✉ Box 6584, Eldoret, ☎ 0321/ 32301; ✉ Oginga Odinga Rd., Kisumu, ☎ 035/41525).

CAR TRAVEL

Traveling by car is easy in Western Kenya, although you may need to invest in a four-wheel-drive vehicle if you want to go off the beaten track. Many secondary roads are poorly paved, and heavy rains can make dirt roads impassable. Bring along food, water, and a blanket in case you have car trouble. Many roads are remote, so you may have quite a wait before help arrives.

The area is generally safe, although it is probably not sensible to travel off the main roads at night. Keep a sharp eye out for large animals and children, as both wander freely onto the roads. Consult locals before heading north of Lake Baringo or to the Saiwa Swamp.

EMERGENCIES
A part of Moi University, Eldoret Hospital is Kenya's major teaching hospital. In Kitale, Mt. Elgon Hospital is smaller but is well-staffed by foreign aid workers. Run by the Aga Khan Foundation, Aga Khan Hospital, in Kisumu, is a well-equipped hospital.
➤ EMERGENCY NUMBERS: **Emergencies** (☎ 999).
➤ HOSPITALS: **Aga Khan Hospital** (✉ Otiena Oyoo St., Kisumu, ☎ 035/43516). **Eldoret Hospital** (✉ Makasembo Rd., ☎ 0321/62000). **Mt. Elgon Hospital** (✉ Hospital Rd., Kitale, ☎ 0325/20025).

HEALTH
Use common sense about food hygiene and you should have no problems in Western Kenya. The water in the larger towns is perfectly healthy to drink. In smaller villages and in remote lodges, stick to bottled water.

Remember that malaria is still found in this region, so consult your doctor about antimalarial prophylactics well before you leave on your trip. When in the bush, always slather yourself with insect repellent. If walking in the bush, always wear stout shoes with a good grip and ankle support, long trousers that can be tucked into your socks, and a hat. Watch out for snakes, scorpions, and other lurking nasties. Don't swim in lakes and rivers because of the danger of bilharzia, a disease caused by parasitic worms.

INTERNET
Internet cafés have sprung up in most towns, but they tend to come and go. Ask at your hotel about the nearest connection. There is functioning Internet access in this part of Kenya, but it is slow.

MAIL AND SHIPPING
There are post offices in all towns in Western Kenya. The postal system is slow and can be unreliable, so use overnight services for important packages.
➤ POST OFFICES: **Eldoret** (✉ Uganda Rd. at Dharma Rd.). **Kericho** (✉ Moi Hwy. near Kenyatta Rd.). **Kisumu** (✉ Oginga Odinga St. near New Station Rd.). **Nakuru** (✉ Moi Rd. and Kenyatta Ave.). **Naivasha** (✉ Moi Rd. and Postal La.).

MONEY MATTERS
There are banks with ATMs in all of Western Kenya's main towns—Eldoret, Kitale, Kisumu, Kericho, Naivasha, and Nakuru. However, not all accept foreign cards. Barclays and Standard Chartered are the most common banks. In smaller towns you may find it hard to change money because few hotels will exchange foreign currency or accept credit cards. Make sure you have plenty of small change, as no one ever seems able to accept a note.
➤ BANKS: **Barclays** (✉ Uganda Rd. at Kenyatta St., Eldoret; ✉ Moi Hwy. at Kenyatta Rd., Kericho; ✉ Kenyatta St. and Askari Rd., Kitale; ✉ Kampala St. at Oginga Odinga Rd., Kisumu; ✉ Moi Ave. and Station La., Naivasha; ✉ Kenyatta Ave. and Bank La., Nakuru). **Standard Chartered** (✉ Uganda Rd. at Kenyatta St., Eldoret; ✉ Moi Highway at Kenyatta Rd., Kericho; ✉ Kenyatta St. and Askari Rd., Kitale;

✉ Mosque Rd. at Oginga Odinga St., Kisumu; ✉ Kenyatta Ave. and Moi Rd., Nakuru).

SAFETY
Be on the safe side—don't wear expensive jewelry or watches, carry cash in a pocket rather than a wallet, and hold purses and camera bags close to your body. If you're driving, always lock your car, don't leave valuables lying around on the seat, and pay someone a few shillings to guard the vehicle while you are away from it. Don't get out of the car inside the game parks except in areas where it is specifically permitted, such as Saiwa Swamp. Take local advice before heading north into the Cherangani Hills, where local ethnic disputes have been known to erupt.

TELEPHONES
Local phone service is improving, and you will find public phones operated by coins or cards in most towns. All calls are expensive, especially those to other countries. To save money, ask your long distance provider for an access number before leaving home.

Mobile phones are ubiquitous in the urban areas and operate in some surprisingly remote locations. A cell phone from the United States will not work, but you can rent one at the airport when you arrive.

TOUR COMPANIES
Most tour operators in Kenya are based in Nairobi or Mombasa, although they will usually organize tailor-made tours almost anywhere in the country. Few stray into Western Kenya beyond the Great Rift Valley and Maasai Mara.

Kwa Kila Hali Safaris, based in Eldoret, is an excellent small operator specializing in Western Kenya. Run by Annette Ruthman and Ina Kalliske, the company offers personalized service, enormous expertise, and a true passion for this little-known area of the country. One of the largest tour operators in Kenya, Wildlife Safaris puts together personalized itineraries ranging from day trips to two-week adventures.

Balloon Safaris was the first company to let you float high above Maasai Mara in a hot-air balloon. There are now at least a half dozen others. The gondolas are always full between July and October, when the annual wildebeest migration entices herds of humans.
➤ TOUR COMPANIES: **Balloon Safaris** (✉ Keekorok Lodge, ☎ 02/ 540–780, 🌐 www.africaonline.co.ke/balloonsafaris). **Kwa Kila Hali Safaris** (✉ Box 6793, Eldoret, ☎ 📠 0321/22154, 🌐 www. kwakilahalisafaris.com). **Wildlife Safari** (✉ Box 56803, Nairobi, ☎ 02/340–319, 📠 02/338–972, 🌐 www.africa-wildlife-safari.com).

TRAIN TRAVEL
A dramatic section of Kenya's famous Lunatic Line crosses Western Kenya, running from Nairobi to Kisumu via Nakuru. The highlight is a dramatic but agonizingly slow climb down the eastern wall of the Great Rift Valley. Sadly, the only train with any type of passenger accommodation travels at night. Even worse, the only seats available are in highly uncomfortable third-class coaches. Train service once ran to Eldoret and Kitale, but no longer.
➤ TRAIN INFORMATION: **Kenya Railways** (✉ Box 30121, Nairobi, ☎ 02/221–211, 📠 02/340–049).

VISITOR INFORMATION
There are no tourist offices in the region. Ask for information at hotels or at the offices of local tour operators.

4 NORTHERN KENYA

Mt. Kenya, the country's largest peak, can be seen for hundreds of miles. For many people climbing the "gigantic cone of misty purple" is the highlight of their excursion to East Africa. But Northern Kenya has much more to offer, from the rain forests of the Aberdare Range to the grassy plains of Meru National Park. In the extreme north lies Lake Turkana, shimmering like silk in the afternoon sun.

by Tara
Fitzgerald and
Mary Anne
Fitzgerald

A **GRACEFUL SPIRE OF ROCK AND ICE,** hard and clear against the light of blue sky," is how explorer Eric Shipton described Mt. Kenya in his 1947 book, *Upon That Mountain*. Shipton is one of many people to become captivated by Mt. Kenya—from the Kikuyu people, who consider it to be sacred, to Felice Benuzzi and two fellow Italian prisoners of war, who escaped to it, to the many visitors who flock to its slopes today.

For many visitors Mt. Kenya is one of the first sights they see as they fly into Nairobi. Although it provides an impressive vista from the air, exploring the mountain and its surrounding region proves an even more worthwhile experience from the ground. To watch the sun rise over Mt. Kenya, Africa's second-highest mountain, is a spectacular introduction to the country. The highland areas around Mt. Kenya, which includes the Aberdare Range and the Laikipia Plateau, offer a variety of experiences from hiking in the mountains to fishing in the clear streams.

About 150 km (93 mi) northeast of Nairobi, the region can be reached by a three-hour drive through the cultivated *shambas* (small holdings) of the Kikuyu farmers. The contrast of the lush coffee and banana plantations against the rich, red earth provides an impressive backdrop as the road wends its way through the Coles Plains. To the west is the Aberdare Range, a spectacular series of mountain peaks that shelters one of the country's most untouched forest reserves.

North of Mt. Kenya are several less-visited game reserves, including Meru National Park and the triumvirate of Samburu National Reserve, Buffalo Springs National Reserve, and Shaba National Reserve. These parks contain species not seen in southern Kenya, including the thinly striped Grevy's zebra, the blue-shanked Somali ostrich, and the Beisa oryx. Farther still is the jewel of Northern Kenya, the shimmering Lake Turkana. Along its eastern shore is Sibiloi National Park, set up to protect the rich fossils found around Koobi Fora and Ileret.

Pleasures and Pastimes

Hiking and Climbing
Many first-time visitors are surprised to find that Mt. Kenya's slopes are easily accessible. You don't need to be an experienced climber to enjoy a trek up one of the 14 marked paths. No ropes or other climbing equipment are needed until you reach the higher altitudes. Tour companies offer a variety of excursions up the mountain, ranging from daylong hikes into the forests to full-scale assaults on the peaks of Batian and Nelion. There is also some great hiking in the Aberdares, and several of the higher peaks are relatively easy to climb.

Dining
Most visitors to Northern Kenya head to the national parks, where gourmet meals are served by the lodges and camps where they are staying. Restaurants, therefore, are in short supply, but some very good ones can be found in the hotels of some of the larger towns.

CATEGORY	COST*
$$$$	over Ksh 1,170
$$$	Ksh 780–Ksh 1,170
$$	Ksh 390–Ksh 780
$	under Ksh 390

*per person, for a main course at dinner

Fishing

Both Mt. Kenya and the Aberdare Range have a number of streams running from their peaks that are the perfect environment for both brown and rainbow trout. These fish, introduced to the region early in the 20th century, draw anglers from around the world. There are also a number of lakes in the area where you can cast your line, and few are as lovely as Lake Alice, on the slopes of Mt. Kenya.

Lake Turkana is known for its trophy fish. Nile perch weighing hundreds of pounds were fairly common in the past, but catches that large are rare these days. Sport fishermen prefer the ferocious tiger fish (named for its toothy jaws), which puts up a better fight than the sluggish perch. There is even a small puffer fish, normally found near coral reefs, considered evidence that the lake was once linked to the sea.

Lodging

Accommodations vary greatly in this part of Kenya. You will find charming colonial-era clubs with views of the mountains, game lodges set deep in the forests, and even single cottages far off the beaten track. Many larger establishments offer a wide variety of activities—from game drives and fishing trips to exhibits of local crafts and demonstrations of traditional dancing—for guests.

CATEGORY	COST*
$$$$	over Ksh 15,600
$$$	Ksh 7,800–Ksh 15,600
$$	Ksh 3,900–KSh 7,800
$	under Ksh 3,900

All prices are for a standard double room, excluding tax.

Wildlife

With a wide variety of terrains, Northern Kenya gives you the opportunity to view different types of wildlife. You can spend a night at a watering hole where you may see a leopard from unusually close quarters. Walking through the forest you might spot a rare black-and-white colobus monkey or even chance upon a herd of elephants moving through the brush. You can take a game drive and see the zebras and giraffes that migrate across the open plains. This is also a great area for birding, as on a typical outing you will spot dozens of species. The highlands of the Aberdares are home to the green ibis, mustached green tinker, fine-banded woodpecker, and more than a dozen species of the brilliantly colored sunbird. The savannas around Meru yield the yellow-bellied eremomela, rosy-patched shrike, and eastern violet-backed pytilia.

Exploring Northern Kenya

North of Nairobi, the plains of Northern Kenya are easy to reach by car. The view of Mt. Kenya makes this one of the country's most pleasant routes. You can also fly, as the towns of Nyeri and Nanyuki have airports close to many of the region's major sights. You can also charter a flight to take you to airstrips at some of the national parks and private game reserves. Should your destination be Lake Turkana or Sibiloi National Park, flying is a must.

Numbers in the text correspond to numbers in the margin and on the Mt. Kenya and the Aberdares map and the Central Highlands and Lake Turkana map.

Great Itineraries

IF YOU HAVE 3 DAYS

Heading from Nairobi, drive north to ☒ **Mt. Kenya National Park** ⑦, where you can stay at the Mountain Lodge. Ringed by rain forest, it comes alive at night, when buffaloes, rhinos, and waterbucks visit the watering hole. On your second day take a guided hike up the slopes of Mt. Kenya National Park. On the third day head for **Lewa Downs** ⑩, where you can see the black rhinos at the Ngare Sergoit Rhino Sanctuary before undertaking the three-hour return journey to Nairobi.

IF YOU HAVE 5 DAYS

From Nairobi head north to ⬚ **Mt. Kenya National Park** ⑦, arriving in time for a splendid buffet lunch at the Mt. Kenya Safari Club. Enjoy the view as you take your afternoon tea on the terrace, or stroll through the lovely gardens. For a night to remember, organize a bush dinner on the banks of the Likii River. Spend the next day or two hiking around the snowy peaks. On your fourth day head to ⬚ **Nyeri** ①, stopping for lunch at the Outspan Golf & Country Club before heading to **Aberdare National Park** ②, staying at one of the lodges inside the reserve. Then trek through the rain forest, keeping a sharp eye out for elephants, before returning to Nairobi.

IF YOU HAVE 7 DAYS

From Nairobi head north to ⬚ **Mt. Kenya National Park** ⑦, which you can explore for two or three days. If you really want to get away from it all, stay a night or two at the Rutundu Log Cabins. On your fourth day head to ⬚ **Meru National Park** ⑧, overnighting at the luxurious Elsa's Kopje. Explore the swamps in the northern parts of the reserve, home to more than 4,000 buffaloes. On your fifth day drive north to ⬚ **Samburu National Reserve** and neighboring **Buffalo Springs National Reserve** ⑪. Lions and cheetahs can sometimes be spotted, and the elusive leopard makes a frequent appearance at the game lodges. Visit nearby **Shaba National Reserve** ⑫ before you head back to Nairobi.

When to Tour Northern Kenya

Northern Kenya is spectacular at any time of year, although you should avoid the rainy seasons, when the roads in the national parks are particularly treacherous. Wet weather comes twice a year—the long rains in April and May and the short rains in October. The best season for climbing Mt. Kenya is from December through March, when the cloudless skies allow you to catch the most spectacular views of the peaks. Throughout the year the evenings are chilly, so make sure to bring along warm clothing.

THE ABERDARES

As the road from Nairobi climbs into the central highlands, the Aberdare Range rises to the west. There are no alpine peaks here such as the spire of Mt. Kenya, which stands in splendid solitude some 130 km (80 mi) to the east; nevertheless, here you'll find a superb scene of rolling moors cut by deep valleys where bubbling streams transform into a series of cascading waterfalls. Coming out of the lush rain forests, you pass through a surrealistic forest of giant lobelia and yellow-flowered groundsel. Redwing starlings are plentiful, and luminescent sunbirds shimmer as they hover around the giant plants.

Named in 1883 for the president of the Royal Geographic Society, Lord Aberdare, this range is known locally as Nyandarua, a Kikuyu word meaning "drying hide." Some say the peaks resemble an animal skin hung out to dry. The western slopes, forming part of the border of the Great Rift Valley, drop sharply to the plains around Lake Naivasha. The gentler eastern slopes trail off into to the highland farming country. The mountains are covered with a thick forest of hardwoods, which hide a number of streams that are the source of the main catchment for Nairobi's water supply.

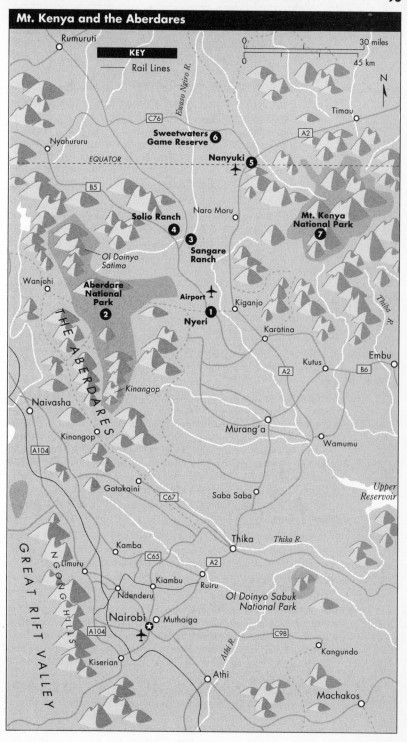

Mt. Kenya and the Aberdares

KEY
— Rail Lines

0 ___ 30 miles
0 ___ 45 km
N

Rumuruti

Ewaso Ngiro R.

C76

Timau

A2

Sweetwaters Game Reserve **6**

Nyahururu

EQUATOR

Nanyuki **5**

B5

Naro Moru

Solio Ranch **4**

3 Sangare Ranch

Mt. Kenya National Park **7**

Ol Doinyo Satima

Wanjohi

Aberdare National Park **2**

Airport

Kiganjo

Thiba R.

Nyeri **1**

Karatina

THE ABERDARES

Kutus

A2

Embu

B6

Naivasha

Kinangop

Murang'a

Wamumu

A104

Kinangop

Upper Reservoir

Gatakaini

C67

Saba Saba

GREAT RIFT VALLEY

Kamba

C65

Thika

Thika R.

Limuru

A2

NGONG HILLS

Kiambu

Ruiru

Ndenderu

Ol Doinyo Sabuk National Park

Nairobi

Muthaiga

A104

C98

Kangundo

Kiserian

Athi R.

Athi

Machakos

Toward the north of the Aberdares stands 3,999-m (13,120-ft) Ol Doinyo Satima, the highest point in the range. Jagged volcanic cones near this peak are aptly named the Dragon's Teeth. Turning toward the south you can see 3,906-m (12,815-ft) Kinangop, the most impressive summit in the range. The big ridges of Kinangop are in marked contrast to the rolling moors of the northern Aberdares.

The Aberdares have a great variety and quantity of wildlife, but because of the dense growth you may see very little. Elephants, buffaloes, elands, and giant forest hogs, as well as lions and leopards, prowl the forests. Look up and you'll see some black-and-white colobus monkeys as they jump from tree to tree with their long fur streaming out behind. These animals have been sought after because of their beautiful fur: once found throughout Kenya, they are now found only in isolated patches.

Notable birdlife includes the crowned eagle (known to eat monkeys), the silvery-cheeked hornbill, and Hartlaub's turaco. The red feather of the latter bird is very rare in this region. Jackson's francolins are found in the higher altitudes, while scaly francolins replace it in the valleys.

Nyeri

❶ *20 km (12 mi) north of Karatina.*

Nyeri is the principle town of the Kikuyu, Kenya's largest tribe. At the base of the Aberdares, the bustling community is the commercial center for this farming region. Nearby you'll see many shambas growing coffee and other crops.

Robert Baden-Powell once wrote, "The nearer to Nyeri, the nearer to bliss." Baden-Powell, who distinguished himself in the Boer War, became the youngest general in the British army. It was as the founder of the Boy Scouts, however, that Baden-Powell is remembered. In Nyeri, on the grounds of the Outspan Hotel, you'll find **Paxtu,** a little cottage where he spent the last years of his life. It now serves as a small museum. Baden-Powell died here in 1941, and his obituary summed up his place in history: "No chief, no prince, no king, no saint was ever mourned by so great a company of boys and girls, of men and women in every land."

Near St. Peter's Church is the cemetery where you'll find **Baden-Powell's Grave.** In a private message to Boy Scouts around the world, he had chiseled into the headstone a trail marker that means "I have gone home."

Dining and Lodging

$$$$ ✕▥ **Aberdare Country Club.** Nestled on the slopes of Mweiga Hill, this colonial-era farmhouse with a lovely red-tile roof is a great starting point for those headed to Aberdare National Park. Peacocks strut around gardens bursting with color, particularly in December when the purple jacarandas are in full bloom. Most rooms have fireplaces, and all have balconies with stunning views of the plains—a fabulous way to wake up in the morning. You can relax by the pool, play a set of tennis, or golf on the 9-hole course (avoid hitting the resident warthogs). Game-viewing opportunities range from walking and riding safaris in the adjacent 1,300-acre wildlife sanctuary to game drives in the nearby parks. Bush lunches are available for those who fancy a touch of elegance. Book through Lonrho Africa Hotels. ⊠ *North of Nyeri,* ☎ *02/ 216–940 in Nairobi, 941/951–1155 in the U.S.,* ℻ *02/216–496 in Nairobi, 941/951–7744 in the U.S.,* ⺼ *www.lonrhohotels.com. 48*

rooms. *Restaurant, bar, pool, 9-hole golf course, tennis courts, convention center. AE, MC, V.*

$$$ ✕⌂ **Outspan Golf & Country Club.** Built in 1928, this gracious hotel has unparalleled views of Mt. Kenya jutting up between the trees. The name, suggested by a friend of the original owners, comes from the fact that the oxen that brought the materials to build the structure had to be outspanned, or unyoked, at the end of the day. The spacious rooms, decorated with leather chairs and other well-worn furnishings, open onto the well-maintained gardens. Best of all are the colonial-style baths. At the end of the day it's a pleasure to luxuriate in a hot bath before heading down for cocktails by the fireplace in the bar, followed by a meal in the wood-paneled dining room. You can use the adjacent Nyeri Golf Club for a challenging round of golf. You can also enjoy nature walks along the river or relax in the pool. Book through Block Hotels. ⊠ *West of Nyeri,* ☎ *02/535–412,* 𝔽𝔸𝕏 *02/545–954,* 𝕎𝔼𝔹 *www.blockhotelske.com. 45 rooms. Restaurant, bar, minibars, pool, golf course, tennis courts, meeting rooms. AE, MC, V.*

$ ⌂ **Green Hills Hotel.** South of Nyeri, this modern hotel is popular among Kenyans. After a day exploring the Aberdares you can lie in the sun beside the pool or head to the spa to relax in the sauna. Golfers will be happy to learn that it's beside a beautiful course. ⊠ *Mumbi Rd., Nyeri,* ☎ *0171/30604. 124 rooms. 2 restaurants, bar, pool, sauna, spa, playground. AE, DC, MC, V.*

Aberdare National Park

❷ *10 km (6 mi) west of Nyeri, 165 km (102 mi) northwest of Nairobi.*

Covering an area of 590 square km (228 square mi), Aberdare National Park consists primarily of misty highlands covered with heather. Here you may catch sight of a black leopard hunting a duiker through the open moors. Peaks drop dramatically into sheltered valleys where you'll find some of the country's most spectacular waterfalls. Among those worth visiting are Gura and Karuru falls, which lie on opposite sides of a deep valley. Gura cascades down without interruption, while Karuru falls in three steps. To the north is Chania Falls, a spectacular spray where Winston Churchill camped while here on safari.

The eastern spur of the park that drops down toward Nyeri is primarily rain forest, and this is where you'll find most of the wildlife. This was once part of an elephant migration route before the Laikipia Plateau became so populated by humans. Local ranchers have been contributing parts of their land to private reserves in the hope that these creatures will continue this annual ritual. There are still elephants found here, as well as the country's second-largest herd of black rhinos. The park is the best place to see the rare giant forest hog and the most elusive of the antelopes, the bongo.

You need not head out into the forest to see a dizzying array of wildlife. At some game lodges you are likely to see the resident spotted genets looking for handouts. Olive baboons are sometimes troublesome, as they will enter your room through an open window and snatch your tea cakes off your plate. If you are staying here on your own, be careful not to leave food or garbage within reach of other primates. ⊠ *Kenya Wildlife Service, Box 40241, Nairobi,* ☎ *02/501–081,* 𝔽𝔸𝕏 *02/501–752.* 🎫 *$27.*

Dining and Lodging

$$$$ ⌂ **The Ark.** Hidden in the heart of Aberdare National Park is the Ark, a lodge built from cedar and brown olive in the shape of a boat. The small cabins are comfortable and cozy, with thick blankets to keep you

Aberdare National Park

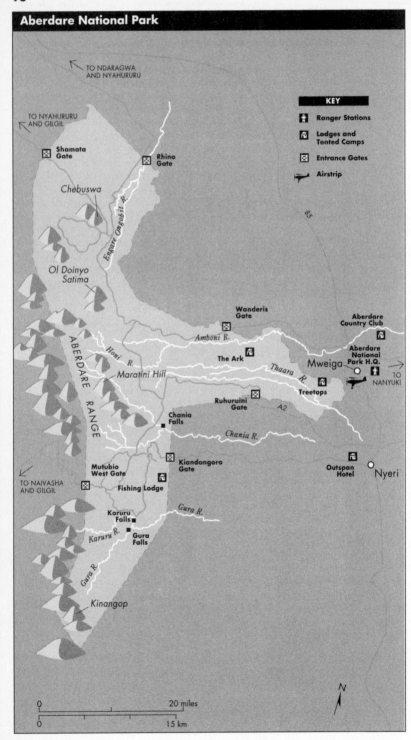

TO NDARAGWA
AND NYAHURURU

TO NYAHURURU
AND GILGIL

KEY

Ranger Stations

Lodges and
Tented Camps

Entrance Gates

Airstrip

Shamata
Gate

Rhino
Gate

Chebuswa

Engare Ongobit R.

*Ol Doinyo
Satima*

Wanderis
Gate

Aberdare
Country Club

Amboni R.

ABERDARE

RANGE

Honi R.

The Ark

Aberdare
National
Park H.Q.

Mweiga

Maratini Hill

Thaara R.

TO
NANYUKI

Treetops

Ruhuruini
Gate

A2

Chania
Falls

Chania R.

TO NAIVASHA
AND GILGIL

Kiandongoro
Gate

Outspan
Hotel

Nyeri

Mutubio
West Gate

Fishing Lodge

Karuru
Falls

Gura R.

Karuru R.

Gura
Falls

Gura R.

Kinangop

0   20 miles

0   15 km

N

warm on chilly evenings. Buzzers alert you throughout the night to the arrival of any animals. Three decks provide excellent vantage points for viewing the wildlife that visits the watering hole and salt lick below. Should you wish to see eye to eye with a bushbuck, a ground-level bunker takes you closer to the animals than you can imagine. A stay at the Ark generally starts with lunch at the Aberdare Country Club before you are driven to the lodge itself. Meals are served in the refectory-style dining room. After dinner everyone settles down in the leather armchairs surrounding the huge fireplace for the nightly parade of animals. Children under seven are not allowed, except on designated "children's nights." Book through Lonrho Hotels. ⊠ *Aberdare National Park,* ☎ *02/216–940 in Nairobi, 941/951–1155 in the U.S.,* FAX *02/216–496 in Nairobi, 941/951–7744 in the U.S.,* WEB *www.lonrhohotels.com. 48 rooms. Dining room, bar. AE, MC, V.*

$$$$ 🏠 **Fishing Lodge.** In the southern foothills of the Aberdares, this charming lodge run by the Kenya Wildlife Service consists of two comfortably furnished bandas. Both are decorated in a rustic style using locally produced fabrics for the curtains. A large living room with an enormous fireplace gives each cottage a cozy atmosphere during the chilly evenings. Both sleep seven, with beds divided among three rooms. Bedding and towels are provided, as are dishes, eating utensils, and a gas stove. There's no refrigerator, and you should bring your own supply of drinking water. ⊠ *Kiandongoro Gate of Aberdare National Park,* ☎ *02/501–081,* FAX *02/501–752,* WEB *www.kws.org. 6 rooms. Dining room. No credit cards.*

$$$$ 🏠 **Treetops.** One of the world's most famous game lodges, Treetops became known around the world in 1952 when Britain's Princess Elizabeth, vacationing here with her husband, received the news that she had just become queen. The lodge is built on stilts so that the rooms are level with the beautiful cape chestnut trees that abound in this part of the Aberdares. Guests usually lunch at the Outspan Golf & Country Club in Nyeri, then are escorted to the lodge itself. Dinner is served at long tables, which stimulates conversation among the guests. Afterward some guests retire to the small and somewhat faded rooms, awaiting a buzzer that means animals have arrived at the illuminated watering hole. Others simply wait on the four decks. Bush babies, which are long-eared primates, are frequent visitors, often climbing up onto the railings. Elephants, rhinos, and buffaloes, best seen from the two ground-level blinds, wallow in the salt lick. Children under five are not allowed at the lodge. Book through Block Hotels. ⊠ *Aberdare National Park,* ☎ *02/535–412,* FAX *02/545–954,* WEB *www.blockhotelske.com. 45 rooms. Restaurant, bar. AE, MC, V.*

Sangare Ranch

❸   *14 km (9 mi) north of Nyeri.*

One of the most beautiful private farms in Kenya, Sangare Ranch consists of 6,500 acres in the foothills of the Aberdares. From the wooded ravines at the lower elevations you drive up to open plains where you can spot snorting buffaloes. Owner Mike Prettejohn is part of Elephant Corridor Project, a group of ranchers donating land so that elephants can once again move freely between Mt. Kenya and the Aberdare Range. Sangare currently protects a herd of 70 of the gentle giants.

Dining and Lodging

$$$$ 🏠 **Sangare Tented Camp.** On a small lake bordered by yellow-barked ★   acacia trees, Sangare Tented Camp is one of the area's most charming lodges. There are a half dozen tents along the shore, each with a private bath. A rustic cedar cottage with a fireplace is where guests share

meals and tales of the day's adventures. Everything is very informal—the owners will meet you at the airport or tell you where to find the key. Night hikes are one of the draws here, with bats, bush babies, and the beautiful maned rat on the itinerary. By day you can hike along nature trails through the riverine forests in search of black-and-white colobus monkeys or fish for trout along the streams that crisscross the plains. Book through Savannah Camps. ⊠ *North of Nyeri,* ☎ *02/331–684,* FAX *02/216–528,* WEB *www.savannahcamps.com. 2 cottages, 6 tents. Dining room, private airstrip. AE, DC, MC, V.*

Solio Ranch

❹ *40 km (25 mi) north of Nyeri.*

This beautiful 18,000-acre reserve was Kenya's first privately funded rhino sanctuary. With its rolling plains and bountiful marshes, the game ranch proved to be the perfect environment for the endangered creatures. More than 140 white and black rhinos can now be seen here. The stud for much of the increasing rhino population is a mature male raised at the Sheldrick Animal Orphanage, near Nairobi. He is apparently so attractive that rhinos are being exported from Solio Ranch to Aberdare National Park and other suitable habitats.

A large variety of predators make their home here, including lions, leopards, and cheetahs. You'll also spot two northern species: the besia oryx and the reticulated giraffe.

Dining and Lodging

$$$$ 🏕 **Patrick's Camp.** A safari guide with more than 20 years of experi-
  ★   ence in Africa, Patrick Reynolds pitches a traditional tented camp in Solio Ranch from December through March. Part of your cost goes toward the continued protection of the reserve's rhinos. Because this camp is seasonal, there is minimal impact on the environment. Close proximity to Aberdare National Park means you can enjoy game drives in the rain forest and in the open plains. One of the best features of the camp is the daily walking safaris, with spirited narration by Reynolds. Special bush picnics are organized for these walks. ⊠ *North of Nyeri,* ☎ *02/571–647,* FAX *02/571–665,* WEB *www.bush-homes.co.ke. 5 tents. Dining room. AE, DC, MC, V.*

MT. KENYA

On a clear morning Mt. Kenya can be seen from Nairobi—little wonder, as this behemoth rises 3,048 m (9,997 ft) above the surrounding highlands. Mt. Kenya is actually a volcano that became extinct more than 3 million years ago. Instead of the smooth contours of many other volcanic mountains, it has jagged peaks: 5,199-m (17,057-ft) Batian and 5,189-m (17,024-ft) Nelion. These rocky points are separated by the icy Gates of the Mists.

The name *kenya* is a corruption of the Kikuyu word *kirinyaga,* which means "mountain of brightness." The brightness is, of course, the snow that contrasts so sharply with the volcanic rock. Kikuyu legend has it that the god Ngai lives in the mountains peaks. It was to the summit that he summoned Gikuyu, the first Kikuyu man, and commanded him to build a home in a grove of fig trees in the heart of the fertile land on the mountain's slopes. Gikuyu descended the mountain to find that Ngai had provided for him a wife named Mumbi. The couple produced nine daughters, and it was their families that founded today's nine Kikuyu clans.

Nanyuki

⑤ *190 km (118 mi) north of Nairobi.*

Founded in 1907 by the British, this little town still retains a bit of its colonial charm. Strolling down its tree-lined main street is a pleasant diversion. Originally a trading post, the town now caters to tourists heading up Mt. Kenya. Here you'll find banks where you can exchange currency and markets where you can stock up on supplies for your ascent.

Dining and Lodging

$$$$ 🏨 **Mount Kenya Safari Club.** After being purchased by film star William Holden and a few friends in 1959, Mount Kenya Safari Club became one of the world's most exclusive destinations. The guest list reads like a who's who of the rich and famous. With Mt. Kenya as a backdrop (sometimes literally, as many films have been shot here), the hotel exudes a stately elegance. Luxuriously furnished rooms all have wood-burning fireplaces, especially cozy in the cool mountain evenings. Most have private verandas overlooking the mountain. Dining at the club is an elegant affair. Lunch is an extravagant buffet indoors, while afternoon tea is served on the terrace overlooking the mountain. Sumptuous seven-course dinners are served in the Mawingo Restaurant (of course, you must dress for dinner). Alternatively, you can enjoy a bush dinner on the banks of the Likii River, where you will be welcomed by Chukka drummers. ⊠ *East of Nanyuki,* ☎ *02/216–940 in Nairobi, 941/951–1155 in the U.S.,* FAX *02/216–496 in Nairobi, 941/951–7744 in the U.S.,* WEB *www.lonrhohotels.com. 114 rooms. 2 restaurants, 2 bars, pool, hair salon, 9-hole golf course, tennis courts, shops, chapel, convention center, meeting rooms. AE, MC, V.*

$$ 🏨 **Kentrout Guest Cottages.** Just outside the town of Timau, this place offers simple but comfortable accommodations in three stone cottages. The adjacent restaurant, a longtime favorite, serves up grilled trout. There's a trout farm where you can select your fish for lunch. ⊠ *Timau,* ☎ *02/228–391,* WEB *www.letsgosafari.com. 5 rooms. Hiking. No credit cards.*

$$ 🏨 **Sportsman's Arms.** On the outskirts of Nanyuki, this hotel is set in a pretty garden with a view of Mt. Kenya. The accommodations are simple but comfortable and clean. It's a great place for families and independent travelers who need a bath. ⊠ *Nanyuki,* ☎ *0176/32347,* FAX *0176/22895,* WEB *www.sportsmansarms.com. 15 rooms. Restaurant, 3 bars, pool, sauna, tennis courts, health club, disco, meeting rooms. AE, MC, V.*

Sweetwaters Game Reserve

⑥ *15 km (9 mi) west of Nanyuki.*

A 24,000-acre private ranch, Sweetwaters Game Reserve enjoys magnificent views across the plains to the snowcapped peaks of Mt. Kenya. ℭ Here you'll find **Morani's Boma,** home of a black rhino named Morani who was brought to the reserve after poachers killed his mother. He now lives a contented existence—with his own guard. A visit to Morani is a special treat, especially for children.

The **Sweetwaters Chimpanzee Sanctuary,** a 200-acre habitat on the Sweetwaters Game Reserve, is the only one of its kind in Kenya. You can observe the chimpanzees as you travel by boat down the Ewaso Nyiro River. The riverine forest and savannah grasslands that make up the sanctuary are home to 26 chimpanzees, including two born on the island. Most of the chimps came from the Jane Goodall Institute in Burundi.

Dining and Lodging

$$$$ ⚑ **Sweetwaters Tented Camp.** Overlooking a watering hole that is illuminated at night, this cluster of thatch-covered tents is a great place to see wildlife. A few are raised on stilts for better views. In the evening you hear lectures on local conservation efforts. Optional activities include safaris on horses or even camels. ⊠ *Sweetwaters Game Reserve,* ☎ *02/216–940 in Nairobi, 941/951–1155 in the U.S.,* FAX *02/216–496 in Nairobi, 941/951–7744 in the U.S.,* WEB *www.lonrhohotels.com. 25 tents. Restaurant, bar, pool. AE, DC, MC, V.*

$$$$ ⚑ **Ol Pejeta Ranch House.** This rustic hunting lodge, complete with mounted trophies and ivory tusks, can accommodate a maximum of a dozen guests in the wood-beamed main house. The lavishly decorated rooms have more than the usual amenities—one even has a terrace overlooking a private pool. For recreation there are tennis courts, a pool, a sauna, a steam room, a hot tub, and a well-equipped health club. Lounge in the sumptuous chairs on the veranda and enjoy a cocktail as you watch game coming to drink at the nearby watering hole. If you want more seclusion, the nearby Buffalo Cottage has two rooms around a shared sitting room with a central fireplace. ⊠ *Sweetwaters Game Reserve,* ☎ *02/216–940 in Nairobi, 941/951–1155 in the U.S.,* FAX *02/216–496 in Nairobi, 941/951–7744 in the U.S.,* WEB *www. lonrhohotels.com. 8 rooms. Dining room, bar, 2 pools, hot tub, sauna, steam room, tennis courts, health club. AE, DC, MC, V.*

Mt. Kenya National Park

★ ❼ *13 km (8 mi) east of Nanyuki.*

Sir Halford Mackinder was the first person to climb Mt. Kenya, reaching the summit of Batian on September 13, 1899. After several failed attempts, Mackinder and his Italian guides, Cesar Ollier and Joseph Brocherel, finally found a route to the top. The summit of Nelion remained untrodden until 1929, when Eric Shipton and Percy Wyn Harris climbed up by what is now the Normal Route. The pair then crossed the Gates of the Mists, the icy ridge between the twin peaks, to make the second ascent of Batian.

In 1943 three Italian prisoners of war being held in Nanyuki spent many of their hours behind barbed wire gazing up at the mountain. They dreamed of the audacious: to escape, climb the mountain, and return to the prison camp. How they made mountaineering equipment from bed springs and sacking, how they escaped, and how they left the Italian flag on Point Lenana is superbly related in Felice Benuzzi's memoir *No Picnic on Mount Kenya.*

The lower slopes of the mountain are heavily cultivated, particularly on the southern and eastern sides, where heavy rains and rich volcanic soil support intensive farming. Higher up are dense rain forests of cedar, olive, and podo. Here you'll find an abundance of wildlife, including elephants, buffaloes, bushbucks, and giant forest hogs. The forests are home to endangered species such as the bongo and the suni (the smallest of the antelopes). Don't forget to look up to see the black-and-white colobus monkeys and Syke's monkeys. The rain forest eventually gives way to bamboo forests. Elephants are rarely seen here, but buffaloes are numerous.

Mt. Kenya National Park itself encompasses the mountain's upper reaches. At about 3,500 m (11,480 ft) you'll find moors covered in tussock grass and studded with many species of giant lobelia and groundsel, some growing to a height of 3–5 m (10–17 ft). The ground is covered in a rich profusion of everlasting helichrysum and alchemilla, interspersed with gladioli, delphiniums, and red-hot pokers. Lions inhabit the moors, although they are not common. Eland are often seen on the northern slopes, and zebras migrate up from the lower plains when grazing there is scarce. Leopard tracks have been found in the snows in the park's upper reaches, where the spotted cats find easy prey among rock hyraxes.

More than 150 species of birds have been recorded around Mt. Kenya. Among the most distinctive species are crowned eagles and mountain buzzards in the valleys, giant kingfishers and mountain wagtails along mountain streams, sape grass owls and long-eared owls in the moors, white-starred bush robins in the bamboo forests, and Verreaux's eagles in the highest altitudes. ⊠ *Kenya Wildlife Service, Box 40241, Nairobi,* ☎ *02/501–081,* ℻ *02/501–752.* ✒ *$15.*

Climbing

The slopes of Mt. Kenya offer a great variety of climbs. Scaling Batian or Nelion demands a high degree of mountaineering skill, but there are many enjoyable treks that do not require experience. You can even reach a summit—4,986-m (16,354-ft) Point Lenana can be reached by anyone in relatively good shape.

There are three main routes for climbing Mt. Kenya: the Naro Moru, the Sirimon, and the Chogoria. The main obstacle on any of these routes isn't the ascent, it's the altitude. Even people who are very fit can fall ill if they don't allow their bodies to acclimatize. Altitude sickness—which causes shortness of breath, nausea, and splitting headaches—may result. If you feel these symptoms coming on, take a break before ascending any higher. If symptoms persist, return to lower elevations. Even more dangerous is pulmonary edema, a serious illness that causes water to collect in the lungs.

Serious climbing is best attempted during Kenya's two dry seasons: from late December to mid-March and from July through September. Climbs can be made during the rainy seasons, but there is more snow and ice, and the summits are more likely to be obscured by clouds.

THE NARO MORU ROUTE

Begin your climb at the meteorological station on the west side of Mt. Kenya at 3,000 m (9,750 ft). To help get acclimatized, consider spending the night near the station. The ascent begins up a winding dirt track through a rosewood forest to the "vertical bog," a sodden hill covered with tussocks. You will want to wear an old pair of running shoes or waterproof boots for this two-hour upward slog. The track is well marked with red and white poles every few hundred meters. After about three hours you'll reach the last ridge, where you can gaze up at the U-shape Teleki Valley.

It is then, rising eerily above you, that the mountain's impressive peaks appear for the first time. With stops to appreciate the majestic countryside, you'll reach Mackinder's Camp, at about 4,200 m (13,650 ft), after another two hours. This is as far as you should travel the first day. The camp provides spare accommodations in small pup tents on raised wooden platforms. A stone building serves as a kitchen and dining room. Be careful about leaving things unattended, as hyraxes might run off with your supplies. At night expect the weather to get extremely cold.

Most people start for Point Lenana on the second day, but it's a better idea to stay here another night to get used to the altitude. To see

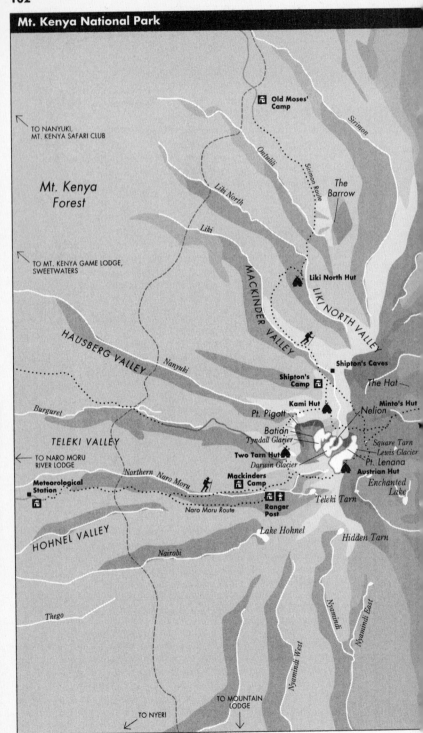

TO NANYUKI,
MT. KENYA SAFARI CLUB

Mt. Kenya
Forest

TO MT. KENYA GAME LODGE,
SWEETWATERS

Old Moses'
Camp

Sirimon

The
Barrow

Ontulili

Liki North

Liki

Simon Route

Liki North Hut

MACKINDER VALLEY

LIKI NORTH VALLEY

HAUSBERG VALLEY

Nanyuki

Shipton's Caves

The Hat

Burguret

Shipton's
Camp

Kami Hut

Pt. Pigott

Minto's Hut

Nelion

TELEKI VALLEY

Batian

Square Tarn

Lewis Glacier

TO NARO MORU
RIVER LODGE

Tyndall Glacier

Two Tarn Hut

Pt. Lenana

Darwin Glacier

Austrian Hut

Northern Naro Moru

Mackinders
Camp

Enchanted
Lake

Meteorological
Station

Naro Moru Route

Ranger
Post

Teleki Tarn

HOHNEL VALLEY

Lake Hohnel

Hidden Tarn

Nairobi

Nyamindi

Thego

Nyamindi West

Nyamindi East

TO MOUNTAIN
LODGE

TO NYERI

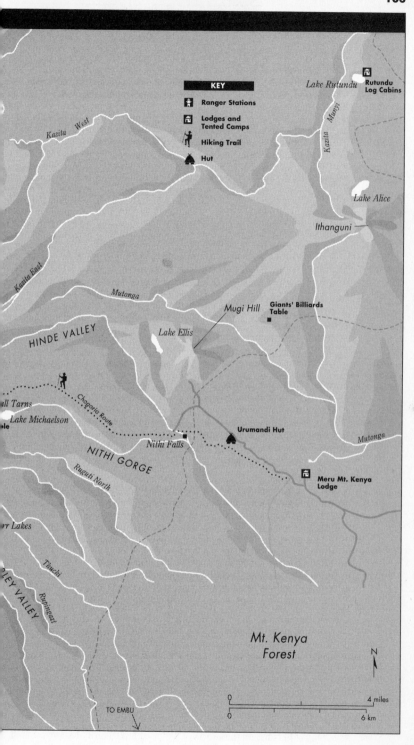

KEY

🏠 Ranger Stations

🏕 Lodges and
   Tented Camps

🚶 Hiking Trail

⛺ Hut

Lake Rutundu

🏕 Rutundu
Log Cabins

Kazita West

Kazita Mureyi

Lake Alice

Ithanguni

Kazita East

Mutonga

HINDE VALLEY

Mugi Hill

■ Giants' Billiards
  Table

Lake Ellis

🚶

all Tarns

Chogoria Route

Lake Michaelson

⛺ Urumandi Hut

Mutonga

Nithi Falls ■

NITHI GORGE

🏕 Meru Mt. Kenya
Lodge

Ruguti North

rr Lakes

Mt. Kenya
Forest

Thuchi

EY VALLEY

Ruguti North

Rupingazi

N

0   4 miles

0   6 km

TO EMBU

the sunrise on the third-highest peak on Mt. Kenya, you must begin the three-hour trek at around 3 AM. This rude awakening makes it easier to walk over a boggy area at the head of the valley, as it's still frozen solid at that hour. You cross an icy expanse, then scramble up some steep, sandy slopes in a two-steps-forward-one-step-backward manner. At last the path reaches the ridge, and a short walk takes you to the Austrian Hut, the highest lodging on the mountain, capable of accommodating about 30 people.

About 200 m (650 ft) away is the Curling Pond, named in honor of an early explorer who amazed his guides by playing a game of curling (similar to boccie) on its frozen surface. Some 200 m (650 ft) of ascent remain to the summit. Point Lenana is a great location for viewing the Aberdares and, on a rare day, the dome of Mt. Kilimanjaro. You can return to the meteorological station the same day.

THE SIRIMON ROUTE

Offering spectacular views to the north, the Sirimon Route is less crowded than the other routes. It's also drier, making the ascent easier. This route starts from the northern side of the mountain at the end of a dirt road that turns off Route A2 before you reach Timau. Leave your vehicle at a campsite beside the stream that crosses the road. A path leads toward a prominent hill called the Barrow, and you turn right on reaching a large pile of stones. The track winds around Liki North Valley, then climbs steeply up the west side of the valley to the ridge overlooking Mackinder's Valley. Follow the valley side for 3 km (2 mi), then cross up out of the valley to Kami Hut, beside a little lake just north of Batian and Nelion.

THE CHOGORIA ROUTE

Taking you up the eastern side of the mountain, the Chogoria Route climbs through beautiful forests and rolling moorlands crisscrossed by streams. It's also the longest trail—so make sure to wear comfortable shoes. Leave your car at Nithi Falls, a few kilometers past Urumandi Hut. A well-defined path follows the ridge westward from the falls, and after about four hours of walking you reach Minto's Hut, set amid the five sparkling lakes called the Hall Tarns. A bit of scrambling up rocky slopes is required to get this far, but nothing very difficult. A five-minute walk south of Minto's Hut brings you to the Temple, where you can look down to Lake Michaelson and into the Nithi Gorge, a classic U-shape glacial valley. Point Lenana is about a two-hour walk past this point, so you might want to spend the night in Minto's Hut.

Dining and Lodging

$$$$ ⚏ **Mountain Lodge.** In the heart of a dense rain forest, this lodge is built
★   along the length of a watering hole, offering an excellent vantage point for watching the visiting buffaloes, rhinos, and waterbuck. All the rooms have private balconies, allowing you to watch the nighttime spectacle in your pajamas. You can always watch from the veranda or, for a really close encounter, descend to the underground bunker, where you are so close you can hear an elephant's stomach rumble. The more adventurous can arrange a nature walk that gives insight into the flora and fauna of Mt. Kenya. Like many lodges in this area, the chef takes advantage of the fresh trout from nearby streams. ⊠ *Near Karatina,* ☎ *02/711–077. 42 rooms. Restaurant, bar. AE, DC, MC, V.*

$$$$ ⚏ **Rutundu Log Cabins.** On the northern slopes of Mt. Kenya, this pair
★   of log cabins sits on the shores of secluded Lake Rutundu. Surrounded by alpine country, they are close to a unique variety of bird species. Not only is this place a nature lover's paradise, but it is also an ideal spot for anglers. Lake Rutundu and Lake Alice, a two-hour walk up the mountain, are both stocked with rainbow trout. The cabins are rus-

tic, but this isn't quite roughing it. Each has a wood-burning fireplace and a fully functional bath. A staff is on hand to cook, clean, and help with the laundry. Book through Let's Go Travel. ⊠ *Lake Rutundu,* ☎ *02/447–151,* FAX *02/447–270,* WEB *www.letsgosafari.com. 2 cabins. AE, MC, V.*

$$$ 🏨 **Naro Moru River Lodge.** On the edge of the Tigithi River, this inn attracts plenty of anglers for the large number of brown and rainbow trout. The main attraction, however, is clear when you walk into the bar festooned with flags from the many teams that successfully climbed Mt. Kenya. The store is stocked with all the equipment you might require. All types of ascents can be arranged here, from daylong strolls along the gentler slopes to weeklong expeditions to scale the peaks. There are a variety of accommodations, from campsites to rooms with views of the mountain and fireplaces to keep you toasty. ⊠ *Naro Moru,* ☎ *0176/62212,* FAX *0176/62211,* WEB *www.alliancehotels.com. 2 restaurants, bar, pool, sauna, tennis courts, horseback riding, squash, meeting rooms. AE, MC, V.*

$$ 🏨 **Sirimon Bandas.** Run by the Kenya Wildlife Service, these cheap and cheerful cottages feel like home with their matching rugs, cushions, and curtains. Works by local artists adorn the walls. Each cottage has two rooms, one with a double bed and one with two single beds. The main house has a kitchen, dining room, and spacious veranda. Game drives can be arranged with the park rangers who are based nearby. Stargazing here is incomparable—you feel as though you could reach and touch them. ⊠ *North of Nanyuki,* ☎ *02/501–081,* FAX *02/501–752,* WEB *www.kws.org. 2 cottages. Kitchenettes, hiking. No credit cards.*

$$ 🏨 **Warden's Cottage.** The old warden's cottage, near the main gate at Naro Moru, has been refurbished. Its two basic bedrooms are decorated with local artwork. Linens and towels are provided, and the kitchen is equipped with cutlery, plates, and gas cookers. The delightful staff brings firewood to keep you warm during the cool mountain evenings. ⊠ *Near Naro Moru Gate,* ☎ *02/501–081,* FAX *02/501–752,* WEB *www.kws.org. 1 cottage. Kitchenette, hiking. No credit cards.*

Outdoor Activities and Sports

To discuss climbing Mt. Kenya, contact Iain Allen of **Tropical Ice.** This experienced climber, profiled in Rick Ridgeway's book *The Shadow of Kilimanjaro,* can arrange treks up Mt. Kenya. ⊠ *Karen,* ☎ *02/884–652,* WEB *www.tropical-ice.com.*

THE CENTRAL HIGHLANDS

A triumvirate of national parks—Samburu National Reserve, Buffalo Springs National Reserve, and Shaba National Reserve—are huddled together where the foothills of Mt. Kenya give way to the sun-baked hills of northern Kenya. You may hear the region referred to as the Northern Frontier District; it's a designation that is no longer used, but it's good to think there are frontiers left in the world. Samburu and Buffalo Springs are found to the west of the Great North Road, while Samburu lies to the east.

The country here is mostly semiarid plains covered in thornbush. Cutting through the landscape is a thick band of rich woodlands along the Uaso Nyiro River. There are also some rocky hills along the northern borders, and farther north is the rugged granite peak of Mt. Ololokwe. For such a small area, the reserves sustain a surprising variety of game. Along the river you can find elephants, buffaloes, and waterbuck, along with many troops of baboons munching away on palm nuts.

The Central Highlands and Lake Turkana

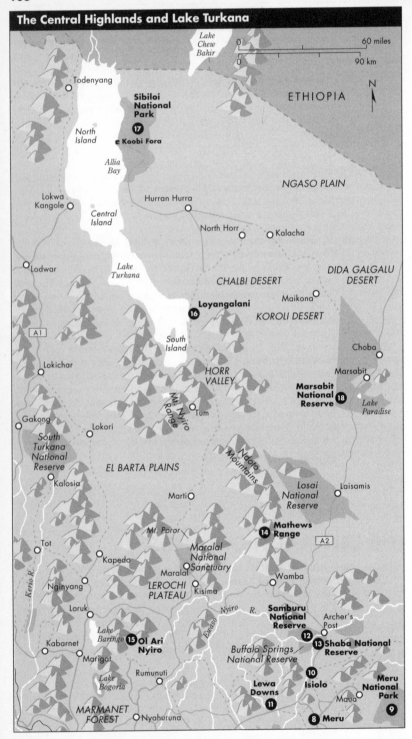

Lake Chew Bahir

0   60 miles
0   90 km

N

Todenyang

Sibiloi National Park ⑰

North Island

● Koobi Fora

ETHIOPIA

Allia Bay

NGASO PLAIN

Lokwa Kangole ○

Central Island

Hurran Hurra ○

North Horr ○   ○ Kalacha

Lodwar ○

Lake Turkana

CHALBI DESERT

DIDA GALGALU DESERT

Maikona ●

Loyangalani ⑯

KOROLI DESERT

A1

South Island

HORR VALLEY

Choba ●

Marsabit ●

Marsabit National Reserve ⑱

Lake Paradise

Lokichar ○

Mt. Nyiro Range

Tum ●

Gakong ○

Lokori ○

South Turkana National Reserve

EL BARTA PLAINS

Ndoto Mountains

Losai National Reserve

Laisamis ○

Kalosia ○

Marti ○

Mt. Poror

Mathews Range ⑭

A2

Tot ○

Kapedo ○

Maralal National Sanctuary

Maralal

Wamba ●

Kerio R.

Nginyang ○

LEROCHI PLATEAU

Kisima ●

Nyiro R.

Samburu National Reserve ⑫

Archer's Post ●

Shaba National Reserve ⑬

Loruk ○

Lake Baringo

Ol Ari Nyiro ⑮

Ewaso Nyiro R.

Buffalo Springs National Reserve

⑩

Isiolo

Meru National Park ⑨

Kabarnet ○

Marigat ○

Rumunuti ○

Lake Bogoria

Lewa Downs ⑪

Maua ●

MARMANET FOREST

Nyahurura ○

⑧ Meru

To the southeast is another reserve, Meru National Park. The Rojewero River, which flows down from the nearby Nyambeni Hills, runs through the center of the park. The main concentrations of game, including most of the park's 4,000 buffaloes, are found in the swamps north of the river. They are also a favorite haunt of the elephants, which cross over the plain to take mud baths. The thornbush territory in the southern region is a good place to spot long-necked gerenuks, which stand on their hind legs to reach tastier leaves, and timid lesser kudus, crowned with magnificent horns.

All four of these parks are associated with Joy and George Adamson, the couple portrayed in the film *Born Free*. They were instrumental in the creation of Samburu, Buffalo Springs, and Shaba. The need for reserves is evident from the tragedies that befell the Adamsons after they released their lioness, Elsa, in Meru. She was murdered in Shaba while working with leopards in 1980, and he was killed near Meru by poachers in 1989. Richard Harris powerfully portrayed him in the movie *To Walk with Lions*.

Other reserves, many of them run by private groups, are farther west. Here you'll find Ol Ari Nyiro, with the most black rhinos outside the national parks, and the Namunyak Wildlife Conservation Trust, where local communities protect the elephant population from poachers.

Meru

8 *56 km (35 mi) southeast of Isiolo.*

This small town, an important commercial center in the region, serves as a gateway for Meru National Park. Many travelers stop here to stock up on supplies before heading out into the wilderness. One good reason to stay in Meru for an afternoon is the **Meru National Museum** (✉ off main road, ☎ 0164/20482; ☉ Mon.–Sat. 9:30–6, Sun. 11–6). This little museum provides an excellent introduction to the lives of the Meru people. The display includes a typical Meru house and an explanation about *miraa*, the locally grown stimulant that is highly prized in Somalia. There are also stone artifacts from a prehistoric site near Lewa.

Lodging

$ ⚜ **Pig & Whistle.** This colonial-style inn is by far the best lodging in Meru. The best accommodations are in the stone cottages in the back. The wooden main building has a restaurant and bar. Breakfast is included in the rate. ✉ *Mwendandu Rd.,* ☎ *0164/31411. 12 rooms. Restaurant, bar. AE, V.*

Meru National Park

9 *35 km (22 mi) east of Meru.*

One of the most unspoiled of Kenya's major parks, Meru National Park is bounded by the Tana River on the south and by the Rojewero River on the east. Here you'll find thick stands of acacia and fig trees. To the north are the swamps favored by the park's large herd of buffaloes, while in the east are the open plains dotted with doum palms. You'll find plenty of game here, including the Somali ostrich, the Beisa oryx, and the occasional Grevy's zebra.

Meru was once known for its semitame group of white rhinos—the only ones in Kenya—but the herd fell to poachers in 1988. Other animals, such as buffaloes, were also nearly wiped out. The Kenya Wildlife Service fought back, and currently the problem seems under control. Many animals, including some leopards, have been reintroduced to the park.

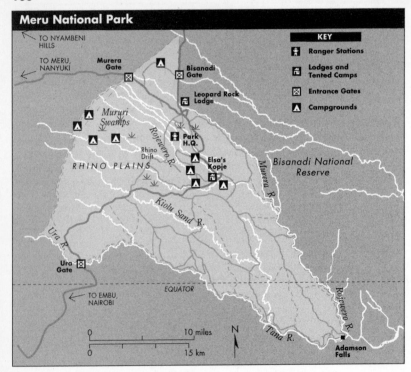

Meru National Park

KEY

⛺ Ranger Stations
🏕 Lodges and Tented Camps
⊠ Entrance Gates
🏕 Campgrounds

TO NYAMBENI HILLS
TO MERU, NANYUKI
Murera Gate
Bisanadi Gate
Leopard Rock Lodge
Mururi Swamps
Rojuero R.
Rhino Drift
Park H.Q.
Elsa's Kopje
RHINO PLAINS
Murera R.
Bisanadi National Reserve
Kiolu Sand R.
Ura R.
Ura Gate
EQUATOR
TO EMBU, NAIROBI
Rojuero R.
Tana R.
Adamson Falls

0 ——— 10 miles
0 ——— 15 km
N

More than 300 species of birds have been sighted in Meru, but one of the most fascinating is the palm nut vulture, which gnaws the sweet outer layer of the doum palm nut. The palm swift builds a tiny nest on the underside of a palm frond. When a chick hatches, it must hold on upside down until it can fly. The rare tufted guinea fowl, along with the more common helmeted and vulturine species of guinea fowl, are all found in the park.

A good network of tracks traverses the park. Roads are generally well maintained and pose little problem for a sturdy passenger car in the dry season, but in the wet season four-wheel-drive vehicles are recommended for negotiating the numerous river crossings. In the northwest the roads follow a series of loops parallel to the course of the rivers, while the plains are crisscrossed with a network of good tracks. South of the Rojewero River a few tracks stretch to the southeastern corner of the park—although it is a long, dusty haul 24 km (15 mi) each way, the thick thornbush scenery makes it well worth the effort. The white-throated bee-eater is often seen perched on the very end of a branch of a thorn tree. ⊠ *Kenya Wildlife Service, Box 40241, Nairobi,* ☎ *02/ 501–081,* 𝖥𝖠𝖷 *02/501–752.* 🖾 *$20.*

Lodging

$$$$ 🏕 **Elsa's Kopje.** Named for Elsa, the lioness whose life is recounted in the film *Born Free*, this new lodge is in the heart of Meru. It's near Mughwango Hill, the first camp established by conservationist George Adamson, who devoted his life to studying lions. The stone cottages, built into a rock outcropping called a *kopje*, all have panoramic views of the breathtaking terrain. Guides take you fishing along the Tana River or on game drives through the countryside. When you return, take a dip in the pool. ⊠ *Meru National Park,* ☎ *02/604–053,* 𝖥𝖠𝖷 *02/604–*

050, WEB *www.chelipeacock.com. 8 rooms. Dining rooms, pool, shop, private airstrip. AE, MC, V.*

$$$ 🏨 **Leopard Rock Lodge.** On the banks of the Murera River, this cluster of cottages surrounded by acacia trees lies just outside the park's Bisanadi Gate. The rooms all have electricity and and baths with hot water. There is a kitchen with a refrigerator where you can prepare you own meals. Bring your own food, as the store here is often closed. Nearby is a trail to a rock where more lions than leopards are seen, but that may reflect the nocturnal nature of the elusive spotted cats. ⊠ *Meru National Park,* ☎ *02/246–982,* FAX *02/212–389. 10 cottages. Pool, hiking. No credit cards.*

Isiolo

⑩ *84 km (52 mi) north of Nanyuki.*

Literally the end of the road, Isiolo is where the pavement stops. Beyond this small town the roads are much more difficult to navigate. Not only are they in a poor state of repair, they are also dangerous. Robberies are all too common. Check with locals before driving any farther than the nearby national parks.

Isiolo is a good place to stock up on supplies before heading north to Shaba, Samburu, or Buffalo Springs. There are also banks here, where you should exchange currency before going any farther.

Lewa Downs

⑪ *17 km (11 mi) north of Timau.*

Near Isiolo, the private 45,000-acre ranch of Lewa Downs is known for the Ngare Sergoit Rhino Sanctuary. The fenced reserve is home to more than 60 rhinos, about half of them the endangered black rhinos. There are other rare animals as well, including Grevy's zebra and the lovely sitatunga, an antelope with wide hooves adapted for swimming. You'll also spot the more than 250 elephants who lumber through the reserve. It's easy to get here, as Airkenya has regular flights to Lewa Downs from Nairobi. ⊠ *North of Timau,* ☎ *0164/31405,* WEB *www.lewa.org.* 🎫 *$35.*

Lodging

$$$$ 🏨 **Borana Lodge.** All over East Africa a fierce competition rages among
★ game lodges for the best bath with a view. Borana Lodge is famous for its tubs, but also for its luxurious accommodations. Polished cedar brightens the half-dozen bandas, each of which is configured to conform to the surrounding hillside. Despite being so close to the equator the evenings can be cool, so each room has its own fireplace. A gargantuan slab of rosewood is used for the table in the dining room. The lodge has 35,000 acres to explore by jeep or by foot. Book through Tandala, Ltd. ⊠ *Northeast of Nanyuki,* ☎ *02/567–251,* FAX *02/564–945. 6 bandas. Dining room, pool, hiking. AE, DC, MC, V.*

$$$$ 🏨 **Lerai Tented Camp.** In the Ngare Sergoi Rhino Sanctuary, these dozen tents are well spaced to provide more privacy. Each is built on a raised platform and shaded by papyrus thatch. And each has a writing table where you can chronicle your safari adventures. The central dining area, graced by a stone fireplace, is in a wooden cottage that was part of the sanctuary when it was launched in 1983. ⊠ *North of Timau,* ☎ *02/331–684,* FAX *02/216–528,* WEB *www.savannahcamps.com. 12 tents. Dining room, pool, hiking, horseback riding. AE, DC, MC, V.*

$$$$ 🏠 **Wilderness Trails.** These rustic cottages, the first to be constructed on Lewa Downs, each have two rooms sharing a sitting area and a veranda with a view of the reserve. Two newer cottages have only one room, affording more privacy. There are also rooms in the Segera Ranch House, an hour's drive. Book through Bush Homes of East Africa. ✉ *North of Timau,* ☎ *02/571–647,* FAX *02/571–665,* WEB *www. bush-homes.co.ke. 8 rooms. Dining room, hiking. AE, MC, V.*

$$ 🏠 **Il Ngwesi Lodge.** This 30,000-acre sanctuary is on the edge of the
★   Mukogodo Hills, giving you a commanding view across the northern plains. Built of local materials, the lodge's design calls to mind Barcelona's Antonio Gaudi with its fantastic curved lines. Thatch-roofed bandas have lots of windows to capitalize on the lush surroundings. This lodge prides itself on being ecologically friendly—water comes from a spring, and solar power provides the electricity. You must bring your own food and drink, although the staff will prepare your meals. Activities include exploring the area around the Ngare Ndare River by foot or by camel and visiting a Samburu village. Book through Let's Go Travel. ✉ *North of Timau,* ☎ *02/447–151,* FAX *02/447–270,* WEB *www.letsgosafari.com. 4 cottages. Dining, pool, hiking, horseback riding. AE, DC, MC, V.*

Samburu National Reserve and Buffalo Springs National Reserve

⑫   *17 km (11 mi) north of Isiolo.*

Separated by the Uaso Nyiro River, Samburu and Buffalo Springs are connected only by a bridge found near the park headquarters. But the reserves share more than a common border. This protected area is one of the best places in East Africa to photograph animals such as Grevy's zebras, Beisa oryx, and Somali ostriches. The reserves also abound with lions and cheetahs, although they are more elusive. Leopards are easy to spot at most lodges, where bait is set out in the afternoon; you can watch them having their dinner while you have yours.

Both Samburu and Buffalo Springs have well-marked tracks for game runs. In the dry season most animals congregate along the riverbanks. In Buffalo Springs are the Lower River and Upper River circuits, which cover a variety of habitats, from swamps to open plains to rolling hills. Buffalo Springs, a cluster of clear pools in the park's northeastern region, is also a good area to find wildlife. Besides attracting visitors who want to cool off, the springs draw a constant stream of birds. More than 300 species inhabit the area, among them the martial eagle and the pygmy falcon. There are also red-rumped buffalo weavers and red-billed hornbills. ✉ *Kenya Wildlife Service, Box 40241, Nairobi,* ☎ *02/ 501–081,* FAX *02/501–752.* 💰 *$15.*

Samburu is home to **Save the Elephants** (☎ 02/891–673, WEB www.savetheelephants.org). Founded in 1993 by Iain and Oria Douglas-Hamilton, the project seeks to find ways to allow elephants and humans to share the land. Researchers use special collars to record migration patterns. If you arrange to visit Elephant Watch Safari Camp, you can ask the researchers about their conservation efforts and perhaps track elephants with them.

Lodging

$$$$ 🏠 **Elephant Watch Safari Camp.** Perched on a sloping riverbank beneath great kigelia and acacia trees, this lodge is home to some of the largest bull elephants in Samburu. Greater kudus and impalas stop by to munch on seedpods, as do a multitude of birds. Gourmet dinners are often served under a starry sky. The desert-style tents are wide and breezy,

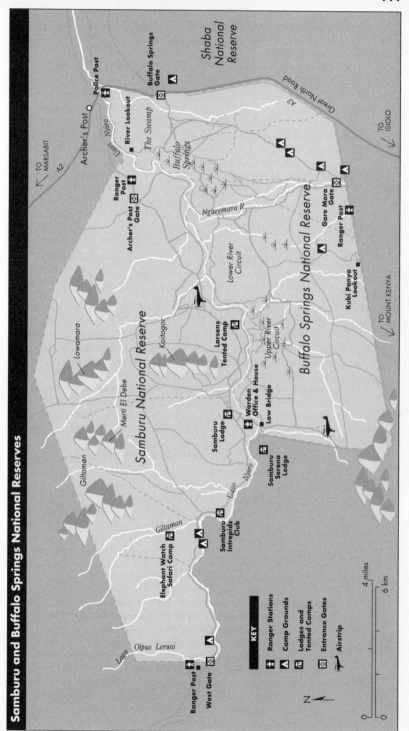

Samburu and Buffalo Springs National Reserves

KEY

Ranger Stations
Camp Grounds
Lodges and Tented Camps
Entrance Gates
Airstrip

with colorful cushions covered with Samburu beads adorning furniture made from fallen trees. About 7 km (4 mi) upriver from a research center for Save the Elephants, the focus of this lodge is learning about these giant creatures roaming through the reserve. You can study elephant behavior with some of the experts in the field. There are other activities, including birding expeditions along the river, visits with the Samburu people, and game drives to find reticulated giraffes. ⊠ *Samburu National Reserve,* ☎ *02/334–868,* FAX *02/243–976,* WEB *www.olerai.com. 4 tents. Dining room, bar, hiking, shop. AE, DC, MC, V.*

$$$ 🏕 **Larsens Tented Camp.** Set among the acacia trees and doum palms on the northern bank of the Uaso Nyiro River, this camp offers an excellent chance to see leopards and other big cats. There are other attractions as well, such as greater kudus, oryx, and even ostriches. Each double tent is situated to give the best possible view of the surrounding hills. Superb meals are served from a large barbecue area. Children under 10 are not allowed. Book through Block Hotels. ⊠ *Samburu National Reserve,* ☎ *02/535–412,* FAX *02/545–954,* WEB *www.blockhotelske.com. 17 tents. Dining room, lounge, shop. AE, DC, MC, V.*

$$$ 🏕 **Samburu Lodge.** This well-established lodge, popular with tour groups, is constructed of locally quarried stone and mountain cedar. Numerous hippos can be seen in the nearby river, and the best place for viewing crocodiles is from the famous Crocodile Bar. The sign reading DON'T FEED THE CROCODILES means you shouldn't venture onto the low stone wall for a closer look. Rooms are built along the river, and all have views from private verandas. An airstrip is close by. Book through Block Hotels. ⊠ *Samburu National Reserve,* ☎ *02/535–412,* FAX *02/ 545–954,* WEB *www.blockhotelske.com. 60 rooms. Dining room, bar, pool, shop. AE, DC, MC, V.*

$$$ 🏕 **Samburu Serena Lodge.** This peaceful lodge is on the south bank of the Uaso Nyiro River just outside Buffalo Springs. Artifacts from the Samburu people decorate the dining room and lounge, which open onto an extended upper terrace with river views. Below you'll find an invitingly grassy area and the best pool in the area. The original cottages with private terraces are small but pleasant and are preferred by frequent visitors. The new two-story wings have modestly decorated rooms that are much larger. Lunch here is always a treat, as beautiful genet cats appear on low branches looking for a handout. Hot-air balloons depart from the lodge. ⊠ *West of Buffalo Springs National Reserve,* ☎ *02/710–511,* FAX *02/718–100,* WEB *www.serenahotels.com. 62 rooms. Restaurant, bar, shop, pool. AE, DC, MC, V.*

Shaba National Reserve

⑬ *17 km (11 mi) north of Isiolo.*

Taking its name from the copper color of the igneous rock found in the area, Shaba National Reserve centers around Mt. Shaba, a dormant volcano with a summit of 1,622 m (5,322 ft). Surrounding the peak is open savanna and acacia woodland. Joy Adamson's camp was located in a grassy plain beyond the mountain, and a 12-m (40-ft) waterfall to the northeast on the Uaso Nyiro River is called Penny's Drop after a leopard that she was working with at the time of her death. The reserve is particularly beautiful after the rains, when the bouldered hillsides blossom with wildflowers and the plains are filled with tall green grass. Shaba has become increasingly attractive to people who want to get away from the more crowded parks and those who appreciate its parched grandeur. ⊠ *Kenya Wildlife Service, Box 40241, Nairobi,* ☎ *02/501–081,* FAX *02/501–752.* 🎫 *$15.*

Lodging

$$$ 🏨 **Sarova Shaba Lodge.** With dozens of thatch-roof cottages, this massive oasis is one of the few places to stay in Shaba. The gardens feature ponds and waterfalls. Each room has a view of the surrounding countryside. A private landing strip is nearby. ✉ *Shaba National Reserve,* ☎ *02/333–233,* 🖷 *02/211–472,* 🌐 *www.sarovahotels.com. 85 rooms. Dining room, pool, sauna, shop. AE, DC, MC, V.*

Mathews Range

⑭   *83 km (52 mi) north of Isiolo.*

This isolated stretch of mountains is about as far off the beaten track as you can get. The thick forests are home to a small herd of black rhinos, as well as a good number of elephants. Much of the land here is now protected by the Namunyak Wildlife Conservation Trust, a private wildlife sanctuary.

Lodging

$$$$ 🏨 **Kitich Camp.** On the western side of the Mathews Range, this fig tree shaded lodge is accessible only by plane. Five well-appointed tents overlook the lush forests that border the Ngeng River. Lions, leopards, and elephants are among the species found here, along with more than 100 species of birds. Book through Bush Homes of East Africa. ✉ *Mathews Range,* ☎ *02/571–647,* 🖷 *02/571–665,* 🌐 *www.bush-homes.co.ke. 5 tents. Dining room, hiking. AE, MC, V.*

$$$$ 🏨 **Sarara Camp.** Recalling Africa as it was a century ago, this lodge on the eastern side of the Mathews Range has spectacular views from its row of luxurious tents. From the natural-rock pool you can sometimes watch elephants stroll by. The camp is run by members of the Samburu community, who will take you on game drives. In the dry season you can visit the famous singing wells where the Sarara water their herds. ✉ *Mathews Range,* ☎ *02/607–197,* 🖷 *02/607–893,* 🌐 *www.lewa.org. 5 tents. Dining room, hiking. AE, MC, V.*

Ol Ari Nyiro

⑮   *64 km (40 mi) north of Nyahururu.*

This 100,000-acre sanctuary is home to the largest-known population of black rhinos outside the national parks, as well as elephants, buffalo, and even leopards. You travel through the park on foot, coming closer than you'd think possible to zebras, waterbuck, and impalas. Here you can also get a glimpse into the culture of the Pokot people. The sanctuary was the vision of Kuki Gallmann, whose life here was chronicled in the film *I Dreamed of Africa.* On the grounds of Ol Ari Nyiro is the **Laikipia Wilderness Education Centre,** which allows teenagers to learn a bit of Swahili as they search for wildlife in the vast Laikipia Plateau. ✉ *Ol Ari Nyiro,* ☎ *02/522–589,* 🖷 *02/522–589,* 🌐 *www.gallmannkenya.org.*

Lodging

$$$$ 🏨 **Makena's Hills.** Constructed in beige canvas to blend with the landscape, these Arab-style tents are decorated with luxurious touches such as Oriental carpets, Moroccan lamps, and hand-carved four-poster beds. Warmed by a fireplace, the central sitting room and dining room have grand views of the landscape. You have a choice of Italian or Indian cuisine made from organic ingredients grown nearby. ✉ *Ol Ari Nyiro,* ☎ *02/520–799,* 🖷 *02/521–220,* 🌐 *www.mukutan.com. 3 cottages. Dining room, hiking, private airstrip. AE, MC, V.*

$$$$ · ⊞ **Mukutan Retreat.** On the edge of the Great Rift Valley, the Muku-
★   tan Retreat has cottages so elegant they were featured in *Architectural
Digest.* Furniture from the coastal region of Lamu decorates the sitting rooms, while double fireplaces warm the spacious dressing rooms
as well as the bedrooms. A private veranda opens to the Mukutan Gorge.
One of the thatch-covered cottages has a tub with a view of this spectacular natural wonder. Power is collected by solar panels, but most
illumination is by candlelight. Because the retreat allows a maximum
of six guests, you have a great sense of privacy. ⊠ *Ol Ari Nyiro,*
☎ *02/520–799,* FAX *02/521–220,* WEB *www.mukutan.com. 3 cottages.
Dining room, hiking, private airstrip. AE, MC, V.*

LAKE TURKANA

Nothing can prepare you for the extraordinary sight of Lake Turkana,
a vast expanse that changes from shimmering silver to luminous blue
as clouds skim above the surface. And when the wind stirs the particles of algae beneath, the lake reveals how earned its nickname, the
Jade Sea. The southern end of the lake is set in a desert of gray stones
and boulders. Farther north, around Sibiloi National Park, the terrain
changes to open plains where you'll witness spectacular golden light
on the spear grass in the late afternoon and early morning.

There are several islands in the lake, and the three most prominent are
named North Lake, Central Lake, and South Lake. The latter two have
been made into national parks, protecting wetlands that are home to
dozens of species of birds. But Lake Turkana is most famous for its
rich treasure trove of paleontological fossils—ancestors of both man
and beast dating back a million years and more—that have been unearthed on the lake's shores. Koobi Fora is the most famous archaeological site, but there are others scattered around the lake as well.

By far the largest in the Great Rift Valley—more than 250 km (155 mi)
from tip to tip—Lake Turkana was created 7,000 years ago when geological shifts severed it from the Nile. As proof of the ancient link, Nile
perch are found here in abundance. Some weighing hundreds of pounds
have been caught in the past, but fish that large are rare these days. Fishermen prefer the tiger fish (named for its toothy jaws), which puts up
more of a fight than the sluggish perch. There is even a small puffer fish,
considered evidence the lake was at one time linked to the sea.

Once called Lake Rudolph in honor of Austria's Prince Rudolph, Lake
Turkana was renamed in 1975 after the principle indigenous tribe, the
nomadic Turkanas, who live on the lake's western and southern shores.
Turkanas net fish in the shallows or spear them by using a wooden shaft
with a detachable metal point secured by a rope tied to their waists.
They also venture onto the lake's treacherous waters on tiny rafts
made of four or five doum-palm logs lashed together.

Arid conditions make Lake Turkana difficult to explore. Midday temperatures average 40°C (104°F), while strong easterly winds can gust
up to 80 kph (50 mph). But for such a hostile environment, the area
supports a surprising variety of wildlife, including lions, cheetahs, and
rare striped hyenas. There are also sizable herds of the northern
species such as oryx, topi, and Grant's gazelle. The lake hosts extraordinary bird life, particularly around Sibiloi National Park, as well
as crocodiles (which don't attack humans) and hippos (which sometimes do).

Loiyangalani

16 *117 km (73 mi) north of Maralal.*

The only trading center for hundreds of miles, this small town straddling El Molo Bay attracts Samburu cattle herders, Rendille camel nomads, and Turkana fishermen. It's name means "place of trees," which is appropriate enough, as Loiyangalani is a shady oasis of doum palms around a hot springs. Stop by one of the local *hotelis* (eating houses) and join the locals in a cup of sweet, milky tea. Delicacies here include the *mandazi* (a crispy doughnut) and the *injera* (a spongy bread).

One of the Loiyangalani's main attractions is the tiny **El Molo settlement,** on El Molo Bay. This community moves from time to time, but it always remains on the shore north of Loiyangalani. Thought to be related to the tribes of South Africa's Kalahari Desert, the El Molo people are fishermen. To visit the village you must pay a small fee that goes into the village fund. After that you are welcome to wander around and take photos.

Steam hisses out of volcanic craters, giving **Central Island National Park** an eerie feeling. The island is home to more than 12,000 crocodiles—more than anywhere else in the world. These ancient reptiles have hardly changed over the past 2 million years. They bask on the beaches, fleeing if you get too close. It is a treat to walk out along the shore with a flashlight at night and see the many pairs of eyes watching you. Time your visit for April and May, when the baby crocodiles hatch.

A breeding ground for birds, **South Island National Park** is a short trip from Lake Turkana's eastern shore. Feral goats wander this ash-covered tip of an ancient volcano. There are no tours, but you can hire a boat from Loiyangalani.

Standing about 30 km (18 mi) to the east of Loiyangalani, **Mt. Kulal** is the source of the scorching winds that are so characteristic of Lake Turkana's eastern shore. Its slopes are strewn with jasper, blue agate, quartz, and amethyst, which you can find if you search carefully. You can also purchase them from locals in Loiyangalani. The mountain is a reserve where you'll find elephants, rhinos, cheetahs, lions, and leopards. You can arrange a day trip to the mountain from Loiyangalani.

Dining and Lodging

$$$ ⊡ **The Oasis Club.** Put on the map yet again in John LeCarre's novel *The Constant Gardener,* this lodge on the edge of Loiyangalani was for decades the only place to get a cold drink on the eastern side of Lake Turkana. The rooms are adequate if a bit rundown. At the restaurant you are likely to be served fresh tilapia or Nile perch from the lake, along with German fare. Two pools fed by natural springs are joined by a waterfall. This is a good place to book boat trips, fishing expeditions, or journeys to South Island National Park. The airstrip next to the lodge is one of the best ways to get to this isolated area. ⊠ *Loiyangalani,* ☎ *02/750–034,* ℻ *02/750–035. 24 bandas. Dining room, bar, pool, airstrip. AE, DC, MC, V.*

$$ **El Molo Camp.** On the southeastern edge of Lake Turkana, this lodging is a group of simple bandas. There are a restaurant and bar, as well a pool that is refreshing after a day exploring this dusty regions. Electricity is from a generator that is turned off at night. ⊠ *Loiyangalani,* ☎ *02/750–034,* ℻ *02/750–035. 24 bandas. Dining room, bar, pool, airstrip. AE, DC, MC, V.*

Sibiloi National Park

⑰ *98 km (61 mi) north of Loiyangalani.*

Unlike other reserves in Kenya, Sibiloi National Park was created to protect the fossils found northeast of Lake Turkana. In the badlands around Koobi Fora, teams of researchers from all over the world have uncovered thousands of ancient bones. It was here that mysterious hominid skulls dating from 2 million years old ago were found. The discoveries in this region, along with the many finds of Mary Leakey at Olduvai, have led to East Africa being called the Cradle of Humankind.

Sibiloi is blasted by hot and dry winds, but that isn't enough to keep away those hoping to get a glimpse into the past. Still here is the main research camp, built of flagstone taken from the shores of the lake. The long debate table in the central dining area, so often featured in *National Geographic*, can still be seen, but most research has now shifted to the western and southern shores of the lake.

The small but impressive **Koobi Fora Museum,** on a ridge overlooking the lake, contains replicas of some of the most interesting discoveries, as well as explanations of the region's geological and biological history. There is also a vast fossil of an elephant dating back 1.5 million years. More than 4,000 fossil artifacts were unearthed nearby, and you can visit the sites of the most important finds. You can see the shell of a giant tortoise dating back 3 million years, and a set of 1½-m (5-ft) jaws of a crocodile estimated to have been more than 14 m (45 ft) long.

The vegetation at Sibiloi is mostly thorn scrub, with an occasional *koobi*, the Oromo word for "hill." Strewn around the base of Sibiloi Hill are chunks of petrified wood dating back 7 million years, the last remnant of the juniper forest that grew here when the rains were more frequent. The area is sparsely inhabited by the Gabbra people, who raise their camels along the shore, and the Dassenech people, fishermen who occasionally travel here from Ethiopia. In many places stone cairns mark the graves of those who lived in the area 4,000 years ago. The Gabbra and Rendille peoples still bury their dead under smaller stone cairns, carrying on millennia-old traditions.

Sibiloi is a good place for bird-watching and has hosted distinguished birders such as Prince Philip of Great Britain and Prince Bernhard of the Netherlands. There are can be thousands of flamingos on Lake Turkana, as well as pelicans, gulls, ducks, and geese, along with such rarities as black-tailed godwits and spotted redshanks. Between March and early May the lake is invaded by vast numbers of European migratory birds, especially wagtails and marsh sandpipers. ⊠ *Kenya Wildlife Service, Box 40241, Nairobi,* ☎ *02/501–081,* FAX *02/501–752.* 🎟 *$15.*

Lodging

$ 🏠 **Koobi Fora Bandas.** These very simple thatch huts have sand floors, open windows, and lighting by kerosene lanterns. There's no running water, and the only rest room is an outhouse. The staff is very hospitable and will cook freshly caught tilapia from the lake. Book through National Museums of Kenya. ⊠ *Sibiloi National Park,* ☎ *02/882–779,* WEB *www.kenyamuseums.org, Dining room. No credit cards.*

Marsabit National Reserve

⑱ *242 km (150 mi) north of Isiolo.*

Rising out of the arid plains of Northern Kenya, Mt. Marsabit is the centerpiece of this isolated game reserve. All the native peoples in the area—the Rendilles, to the south and west, the Gabbras, to the north and west, and the Borans, Sakuyus, and Somalis, to the east—bring their animals to graze here. The crossing of these cultures has made this area something of a melting pot.

Forests around the mountain have been felled to make way for farms, but in the national reserve you'll find a thick tropical forest covered in a cap of drizzling mist every night. No wonder Marsabit means "place of cold." This 1,600-m (5,250-ft) massif provides the water that fills the spectacular volcanic craters on the lower slopes. The best known is Gof Sokorte Guda (also known as Lake Paradise), ringed with a bright green marshes that attracts buffaloes, baboons, and other wildlife. It also attracts varied bird life, especially coots. A local hunter relates this interesting recipe for coot: Boil the bird with a brick for six hours, and then throw away the bird and eat the brick!

Below Gof Sokorte Guda is a rocky pool named Boculi, a popular watering place for elephants. Two from this area, Mohammed and Ahmed, had tusks approaching 45 kilograms (100 pounds) each. Ahmed was protected by presidential decree and was guarded by rangers until his death in 1974. A life-size model of Ahmed now stands in the courtyard of the Kenya National Museum, in Nairobi. ✉ *Kenya Wildlife Service, Box 40241, Nairobi,* ☎ *02/501–081,* FAX *02/501–752.* ⌫ *$15.*

Lodging

$$$$ ☶ **Kalacha Camp.** At the edge of the Chalbi Desert, this rustic camp in the oasis of Kalacha Goda is a good stopover if you are driving from Marsabit to Lake Turkana. Kalacha is a community-based project benefiting the nomadic Gabbras. The sight of people watering their cattle at the nearby wells provides stunning photographic opportunities. This cluster of bandas, made of doum-palm leaves woven into matting, is utterly remote. The pool is half inside the banda used for a dining room so that you can escape the desert heat. Book through Tropic Air. ✉ *Kalacha Goda,* ☎ *0176/32890,* FAX *0176/32787,* WEB *www.tropicair-travel.com. 4 bandas. Dining room. No credit cards.*

$$ ☶ **Marsabit Lodge.** On the edge of a lake, this old lodge is the only accommodation in the park, so it can get away with being poorly managed and serving bad food. Its peaceful forested surroundings, however, make up for its defects. Elephants are often seen feeding in the swampy grass around Sokorte Dika. Each room has a large window with a view of the water hole. ✉ Marsabit National Reserve, ☎ 02/330–820, FAX 02/227–815. 27 rooms. Restaurant, bar. AE, DC, MC.

NORTHERN KENYA A TO Z

To research prices, get advice from other travelers, and book travel arrangements, visit www.fodors.com.

AIR TRAVEL TO AND FROM NORTHERN KENYA

Airkenya operates regular flights between Nairobi and Nyeri, Nanyuki, and Samburu National Reserve. Once in Nanyuki, you can charter planes through Tropic Air to bring you to private airstrips in the region.
➤ AIRLINES AND CONTACTS: **Airkenya** (☎ 02/605–745, WEB www.airkenya.com). **Tropic Air** (☎ 176/32890).

BIKE AND MOPED TRAVEL

Mountain biking is becoming more and more popular in East Africa. Naro Moru River Lodge rents mountain bikes for treks up Mt. Kenya.
➤ BIKE RENTALS: **Naro Moru River Lodge** (✉ Naro Moru, ☎ 0176/62212, FAX 0176/62211, WEB www.alliancehotels.com).

CAR RENTAL
There are no rental agencies in Northern Kenya. If you wish to rent a car, you will need to do so in Nairobi or one of the other larger cities.

CAR TRAVEL
Although flying is quicker, the best way to see this region is by car. You'll be amazed at the views as you drive between Mt. Kenya and the Aberdare Range. The road ends north of Isiolo—the paved part, anyway—so make sure you have a four-wheel-drive vehicle if you are headed north. A vehicle with high clearance is required because the road is rippled and potholed. There have been robberies in this stretch of the road, so always check with locals before you set out.

TELEPHONES
You are only likely to find public phones in larger towns such as Nanyuki or Nyeri. Hotels in the towns are likely to have telephones, but lodges in the national parks and private game reserves may not. Check before your trip.

VISITOR INFORMATION
There are no official tourist offices in Northern Kenya. You can get information about national parks at the ranger stations in each reserve.

5 THE KENYA COAST

Guided by a captain's sinewy foot on the rudder, the graceful dhow is a common sight in the shimmering waters off the Kenya Coast. These triangular-sailed boats symbolize a region where the culture of Arabia fused with that of Africa. Sultry languor prevails in places like Mombasa, Malindi, and Lamu, enticing you to trade your safari shorts for a soft sarong, then to shed that to slip into the warm sea.

by Delta Willis

NTRICATELY CARVED DOORWAYS studded with brass and white walls draped with bougainvillea distinguish the towns that dot Kenya's coastline. Arab traders who landed on these shores in the 9th century brought their own culture, so the streets are dominated by a different style of dress and architecture than what you see in other parts of Kenya. Men stroll the streets wearing traditional caps called *kofias* and billowing caftans known as *khanzus,* while women cover their faces with black veils called *bui-buis* that reveal only their sparkling eyes.

The creation of Swahili, a combination of Arabic and African Bantu, came about when Arab traders married African women. Swahili comes from the Arabic words *sahil,* meaning "coast," and *i,* meaning "of the." As seductive as the rhythm of the sea, Swahili is one of the most melodic tongues on earth. The coastal communities of Lamu, Malindi, and Mombasa are strongholds of the language that once dominated communities from Somalia to Mozambique.

Mombasa, the country's second-largest city, was once the gateway to East Africa. Karen Blixen described people arriving and departing by ship in the book *Out of Africa.* Mombasa's harbor still attracts a few large cruise ships, but nothing like the hundreds that sailed here before World War I. The long, lonely trip from Europe initiated the rhetorical: "Are you married, or do you live in Kenya?" It still works as a pickup line because it hardly matters what you say when you're flirting.

In Lamu, a Swahili proverb prevails: *Haraka haraka haina baraka* (Haste, haste, brings no blessing.) The best-preserved Swahili town in Kenya, Lamu has streets hardly wide enough for a donkey cart. Narrow, winding alleyways are lined with houses set tight against one another. It is said that the beautifully carved doors found here are built first, then the house constructed around them. By the same token, a mosque is built first, and the town follows. Due north—the direction of Mecca—is easy to discern because of the town's orientation.

Azure waters from Lamu to Wasini are protected by the 240-km (150-mi) coral reef that runs parallel to the coast. Broken only where rivers cut through it, the reef is home to hundreds of species of tropical fish. The beaches themselves, famous in the 1970s as a location for the *Sports Illustrated* swimsuit cover, have calm and clear waters that hover around 27°C (80°F). As Ernest Hemingway put it, "The endless sand, the reefs, the lot, are completely unmatched in the world."

Mombasa has an international airport, but many travelers deplane at Nairobi, then make their way to the coast. Others fly directly to Lamu. However you get here, don't miss putting your foot in this ivory white sand.

Pleasures and Pastimes

Architecture

Finely carved doors grace many an entrance in the city of Mombasa. Many lead to an interior courtyard surrounded by spacious, high-ceiling rooms. The region's architectural style is characterized by arcaded balconies and red-tile roofs. One of the great concepts of coastal interiors is the *baraza,* an open sitting area with cushions perfect for parties, intimate conversations, or simply admiring the view in solitude. Lamu furniture, with its deep brown color, provides a compelling contrast to the white walls. Local decorations can include fish traps made of palm rib or bamboo and—the latest thing—items made of wood from old dhows. This decor has become so fashionable, at least two coffee-table books focus on East African interiors.

Dining

The excellent cuisine reflects the region's rich history. Thanks to Italians, basil is everywhere, along with olive oil, garlic, and fresh lettuce. The Portuguese introduced tomatoes, corn, and cashews. It's all combined with pungent spices such as coriander and ginger and the rich coconut milk often used as a cooking broth.

The Indian Ocean delivers some of the world's best fishing, so marlin, sailfish, swordfish, kingfish, and many other types of fish are on every menu. Not surprisingly, sashimi made from yellowtail tuna is favored by connoisseurs (and was listed on menus here as "fish tartare" before the rest of the world discovered Japanese cuisine). Prawns can be gargantuan, and wild oysters are small and sweet. Diving for your own lobster is an adventure, but you will easily find young boys happy to deliver fresh seafood to your door. Sometimes they simply march from door to door laden with fresh pineapples, bananas, mangos, and papayas. You can even place your order for the next day.

CATEGORY	COST*
$$$$	over Ksh 1,170
$$$	Ksh 780–Ksh 1,170
$$	Ksh 390–Ksh 780
$	under Ksh 390

Per person for a main course at dinner.

History

The ancient cities along the coast dazzled Diogenes and Ptolemy, who ventured here in AD 110 and AD 130 and were awestruck by the huge cargoes of brass, copper, and ivory flowing out of the ports. Ships also carried human cargo, as this was a hub of the slave trade. About 80 km (50 mi) south of Mombasa is Shimoni, which means "place of the holes." Tunnels along the coast were used to hold slaves, and iron shackles are a grim reminder of this era.

Mosques are at the heart of every town in the region, and ruins of dozens of others dot the coastline. At Gedi, north of Mombasa, you'll find the remains of an ancient Islamic city. Just north of Lamu are the ruins of Shanga, a town with a well-preserved mosque at its center. Here you'll find the remaining coral walls of 160 houses, two palaces, three mosques, and hundreds of tombs.

Lodging

Accommodations along the Kenya Coast range from sprawling resorts with several restaurants to small beach houses with kitchens where you can prepare your own meals. To really get a sense of the region consider staying in a private home. Most accommodations along the coast can arrange snorkeling, windsurfing, waterskiing, and deep-sea fishing.

CATEGORY	COST*
$$$$	over Ksh 15,600
$$$	Ksh 7,800–Ksh 15,600
$$	Ksh 3,900–KSh 7,800
$	under Ksh 3,900

All prices are for a standard double room, excluding tax.

Water Sports

Near Lamu and Shimoni you can arrange to swim alongside wild dolphins. For snorkeling head to the beautiful Kisite-Mpunguti Marine

National Park, an area often compared to Australia's Great Barrier Reef. North of Mombasa is the town of Kilifi, famous for windsurfing. Not far away is Watamu, known for its annual fishing tournaments.

Exploring the Kenya Coast

Getting to the towns along the Kenya Coast is easier than ever. Nearly every traveler to the region once had to travel through Mombasa, but this is no longer the case. Expanded service means you can fly directly to once-isolated towns such as Malindi and Lamu. Travel by car around Mombasa is fairly safe, but the road to Lamu has been plagued by armed robberies. Avoid this route if at all possible.

Numbers in the text correspond to numbers in the margin and on the Kenya Coast map.

Great Itineraries

IF YOU HAVE 3 DAYS

Fly north on your first day to the ancient city of ⌂ **Lamu** ㉒. This will serve as your base for exploring the archipelago. On your second day spend the morning strolling the sands of Shela Beach, then sail across the channel in the afternoon to Manda Island to tour the ruins of Takwa. On your third day head north to Kiwayu Island and snorkel at Kiunga Marine National Reserve. Return to Lamu for a dinner cruise on a dhow.

IF YOU HAVE 5 DAYS

Start in ⌂ **Mombasa** ①–⑬, the city where most visitors to the Kenyan Coast pass through at one time or another. Explore the narrow streets of the Old City, where you'll find remnants of the city's colonial past. On your third day head south to ⌂ **Diani Beach** ⑭, a good base for exploring the coast. Some of the best snorkeling is off the coast of nearby **Shimoni** ⑯, especially at Kisite-Mpunguti Marine National. On your last day head to ⌂ **Shimba Hills National Reserve** ⑮ to see the country's last herd of rare sable antelopes. Stay overnight at one of the jungle lodges if you want to spot one of the elusive lions or leopards.

IF YOU HAVE 7 DAYS

After following the above itinerary, head north of Mombasa to ⌂ **Malindi** ㉑, a port town that has been an important stop on the trade routes for hundreds of years. Give yourself a few days to explore Arabuko-Sokoke Forest, the last remaining stretch of coastal woodlands, and the ancient city of Gedi.

When to Tour

The Arabs who landed here a millennium ago timed their voyages to coincide with the winds that still dictate the region's two rainy seasons. From October through March the *kaskazi* winds blow from the northeast, delivering rain in November. The calm after the storms brings the region's warmest weather in January and February. In April the stronger *kusi* winds blow from the southeast, delivering heavy rains in May and June.

There are no real seasons here because of the proximity to the equator. Lamu's popularity has increased exponentially, and reservations for the high season in December and January need to be made months in advance.

MOMBASA

The origin of the word *mombasa* remains a mystery, as does much of the city's early history. Little beyond the foundations of a few mosques remains of when Mombasa was an important seaport in the 11th cen-

The Kenya Coast

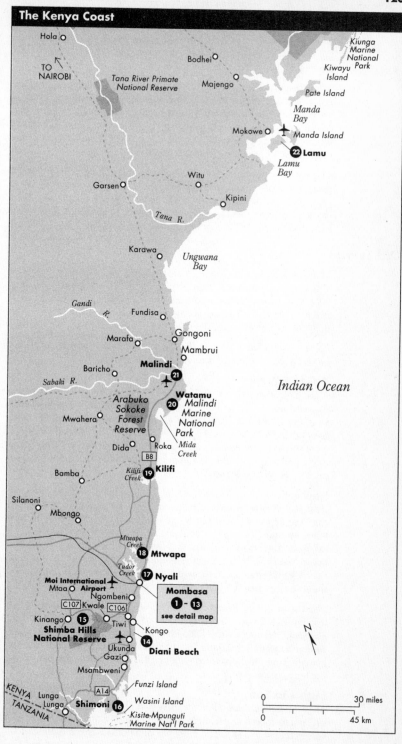

Hola

TO NAIROBI

Bodhei

Majengo

Tana River Primate National Reserve

Kiunga Marine National Park

Kiwayu Island

Pate Island

Mokowe

Manda Bay

Manda Island

✈

22 Lamu

Lamu Bay

Witu

Garsen

Kipini

Tana R.

Karawa

Ungwana Bay

Gandi R.

Fundisa

Gongoni

Marafa

Mambrui

Baricho

Malindi

Sabaki R.

✈ **21**

Indian Ocean

Arabuko Sokoke Forest Reserve

Watamu

20 *Malindi Marine National Park*

Mwahera

Dida

Roka

Mida Creek

B8

Kilifi Creek

19 **Kilifi**

Bamba

Silanoni

Mbongo

Mtwapa Creek

18 **Mtwapa**

Tudor Creek

17 **Nyali**

Moi International Airport ✈

Mtaa

Ngombeni

C107

Kwale

C106

Mombasa

1 - **13**

see detail map

Kinango

15

Shimba Hills National Reserve

Tiwi

Kongo

14 **Diani Beach**

Ukunda

Gazi

Msambweni

Funzi Island

KENYA

TANZANIA

Lunga Lunga

A14

Wasini Island

Shimoni **16**

Kisite-Mpunguti Marine Nat'l Park

N

0   30 miles

0   45 km

tury. What is known is that the earliest settlement was not in the part of the city called Old Town but on the promontory called Mzizima. Some of the earliest pottery found here was recovered from that area. On the beach below, bits of colorful glazed bowls from southern Iran have been discovered that date back more than 700 years.

Mombasa's position as the country's most important port was unquestionable after the Imperial British East Africa Company built the great Lunatic Railway from Mombasa to Nairobi in 1899. In the past century its position has not diminished. Today it's a major hub for the import of grain into East Africa. A new $100 million grain facility means huge cargo ships still sail through the harbor.

The sprawling city, Kenya's second largest, has long been a destination for tourists as well, many of them scattering to beaches to the north or south or to the game reserves to the west. Many people avoid this chaotic city altogether, as airlines now fly directly to other coastal towns such as Kiwayu, Malindi, and Lamu.

Old Town

Old Town looks like a maze, but it is small and easy to navigate. If you get lost, remember that all the major thoroughfares, such as Nkrumah Road, Makadara Road, and Ndia Kuu Road, all lead you toward Fort Jesus. You can always hire a guide outside Fort Jesus, but the walk can be accomplished without assistance.

Numbers in white bullets in the text correspond to numbers in black bullets in the margins and on the Mombasa map.

A Good Walk

A good place to start a tour of the Old City is at Treasury Square, surrounded by handsome buildings from the early 20th century. To the west along Nkrumah Road is the **Anglican Cathedral** ① and the **Shiva Temple** ②. To the east is the elegant facade of the **Old Law Court** ③. Continue east, and you'll reach the imposing **Fort Jesus** ④, one of the city's most recognizable landmarks. Nearby is the recently reconstructed **Ndia Kuu Mosque** ⑤.

Head north past the Mombasa Club to the conical minaret of the ancient **Mandhry Mosque** ⑥. Past the mosque the road takes a sharp left turn and deposits you in a little square. Just ahead is the **New Burhani Bohra Mosque** ⑦. From here you can gaze down at the port, where dhows sail from Abu Dhabi, Dubai, and Zanzibar. At the square is the famous **Leven House** ⑧. In front of the building a short tunnel cuts through the rock and emerges on the water's edge. The view of the harbor and the ships is worth the slight detour to get here.

Head west of Old Kilindini Road past the **Basheikh Mosque** ⑨. Follow Langoni Road when it branches to the right, and you'll find the **Municipal Market** ⑩. Cross Digo Road and head north to Biashara Street. *Biashara* means bazaar, and like the street of the same name in Nairobi, here are rows of shops filled with brightly colored *kangas* and *kikois*, the long cotton sarongs.

Sights to See

❶ **Anglican Cathedral.** Built in the early part of the last century, the cathedral is a memorial to Archbishop James Hannington, a missionary who was executed in 1885. The influence of Middle Eastern Islamic architecture is clear in the frieze, the dome, and the tall, narrow windows. The paneling behind the high altar is reminiscent of the cathedral in Stone Town. ⊠ *Nkrumah Rd. and Cathedral Rd.*

Mombasa

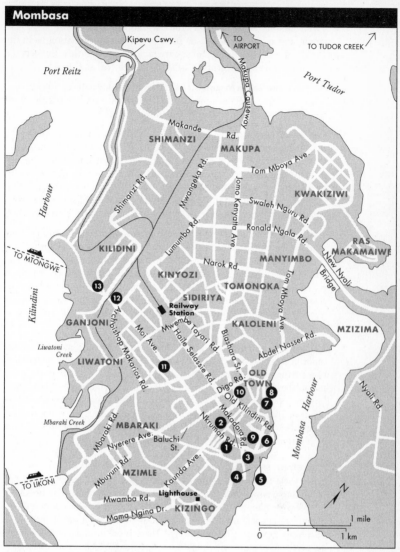

Anglican
Cathedral **1**

Basheikh Mosque . . .**9**

Dodwell House **13**

Fort Jesus **4**

Kenya Uganda
Railway Bridge . . .**12**

Leven House **8**

Mandhry
Mosque **6**

Municipal
Market **10**

Ndia Kuu
Mosque **5**

New Burhani Bohra
Mosque **7**

Old Law Court **3**

Shiva Temple **2**

Tusks **11**

❾ Basheikh Mosque. Like other Swahili towns, Mombasa probably had a Muslim community from the time it was founded. This mosque, painted cream and white, is said to be built on a foundation dating from the 11th century. The purposeful square facade of this mosque reflects the best in Islamic architecture. ⊠ *Old Kilindini Rd. at Kibokoni Rd.*

❼ New Burhani Bohra Mosque. The elaborate facade and soaring minaret of this mosque overlook the Old Harbor. Built in 1902, it's the third mosque to occupy this site. ⊠ *Buchuma Rd.*

★ **❹ Fort Jesus.** This massive edifice was built in the late 16th century by the Portuguese, who were keen to control trade in the region. At the seaward end a bastion carries the cannons that controlled the approach from the open sea. This bastion also shielded the nearby beach, so it was always possible, even when the fort was under siege, to bring in reinforcements. On the side facing the city, the old square bastions were modified after the fort was captured in the early 17th century.

When the Omanis took the fort at the end of the 17th century, they made some adjustments. The walls were raised to account for the improved trajectory of cannons mounted aboard attacking ships. By the end of the 18th century, turrets were erected. For water, the garrison relied on wells. There is a large pit cistern in the center of the compound, which some guides say was the bath of the harem—an intriguing notion. The captain's house retains some traces of the Portuguese—note the outline of the old colonnade.

The exhibits at the museum include an important display on ceramics of the coast, beautiful carved doors studded with brass, and the remains of a Portuguese gunner, *San Antonio de Tanna,* which sank outside the fort at the end of the 17th century. Objects from the ship—shoes, glass bottles, a powder shovel, and a cannon with its muzzle blown away—bring the period to life. There are also exhibits of finds from archaeological excavations at Gedi, Manda, Ungwana, and other sites. ⊠ *End of Nkrumah Rd.* 🖼 *Ksh 400.* ☉ *Daily 8:30–6.*

OFF THE
BEATEN PATH

FORT ST. JOSEPH – The Portuguese built several smaller forts in Mombasa, some still hidden among the mangroves. Fort St. Joseph, at the tip of the island's two channels for the Old and New harbors, can be found by following the path near the Mombasa Golf Club. Guardroom graffiti of the 1630s confirm that the soldiers took seriously the notion they were "His Majesty's most Christian Army." There is not a single literary infelicity, and only one arrow through a heart, among all the drawings of chapels, crosses, and soldiers in their helmets. ⊠ *Off Mama Ngina Dr.*

❽ Leven House. One the few buildings in Old Town that is documented to date to the early 19th century, Leven House seems to have been built for a wealthy trading family. It served as offices of the ill-fated British protectorate in the 1820s, then became the headquarters of the Imperial British East Africa Company. It housed the German diplomatic mission at the beginning of the 20th century, and the building's facade dates from this period. ⊠ *Ndiaa Kuu Rd.*

❻ Mandhry Mosque. With its white minaret, this mosque overlooks the old port. It dates from 1570. ⊠ *Bachawy Rd.*

❿ Municipal Market. Formerly called Mackinnon Vegetable Market in honor of a colonial administrator, this colorful market does indeed have fresh produce. You can also bargain for baskets, boxes, and carvings. ⊠ *Digo Rd. and Langoni Rd.*

❺ Ndia Kuu Mosque. Just a few yards from Fort Jesus, this 17th-century mosque lay for years under a rubbish heap. After being carefully excavated, the mosque was reconstructed and is now once again a house of worship. The mosque's history is obscure, and its architecture is unique on this coast. Make sure to see the two pilasters on the outer niche wall, perhaps an influence of northwestern India or Baluchi. ⊠ *Near Fort Jesus.*

❸ Old Law Court. Near Fort Jesus, the Old Law Court was erected during the early 1900s. Currently the offices of the National Museums of Kenya, it has an interior that you can see when there's an exhibit inside. ⊠ *Nkumah Rd. near Treasury Sq.*

❷ Shiva Temple. Catercorner to the Anglican Cathedral is this modern Hindu temple, constructed in 1998. With the tallest spire in Mombasa, it has a crown of gold. It's guarded by statues of lions. ⊠ *Nkumrah Rd. and Mwagogo Rd.*

Moi Avenue

The city's most popular shopping strip, Moi Avenue is Mombasa's equivalent of New York's 5th Avenue. Here you'll find prominent landmarks such as the Tusks, the symbol of the city.

A Good Walk

Start anywhere along Moi Avenue. Head west until you reach the two sets of **Tusks** ⑪, which extend across the roadway. Nearby you'll find Uhuru Gardens, a shady spot under the trees. Farther along Moi Avenue is the **Kenya Uganda Railway Bridge** ⑫, left over from the days when the railroad was the only way to travel around the country. Nearby is **Dodwell House** ⑬, one of the most beautiful buildings from the colonial era.

Sights to See

⑬ Dodwell House. You can locate this shipping house by its impressive Mangalore-tile roof, still in excellent condition. The interior is evocative of another era, with clerks busy at sturdy mvule-wood desks. Past the spacious entry hall's massive columns is a long wooden counter where countless passengers once bought tickets to Europe. Others stood a little breathless, savoring their first moments ashore after a long trip from London or Bombay. ⊠ *Moi Ave.*

⑫ Kenya Uganda Railway Bridge. This stone bridge at the end of Moi Avenue still carries the logo of the old Kenya Uganda Railway. The original railway station once stood on the other side of the bridge. ⊠ *Moi Ave.*

OFF THE BEATEN PATH

MBARAKI PILLAR – Built of coral rag with a coral plaster finish, this towering pillar overlooks the New Harbor. It was originally a tomb next to a mosque built in the 14th century to serve a small village along Mbaraki Creek. The mosque fell into disrepair after the community was abandoned in the 18th century, but it has now been reconstructed. Locals leave rosewater offerings and burn incense here to appease the spirits. ⊠ *Off Mbaraki Rd.*

⑪ Tusks. Dominating Moi Avenue are the famous elephant tusks that cross above the roadway. They were erected to commemorate the 1952 visit of Britain's Princess Elizabeth, now Queen Elizabeth II. ⊠ *Moi Ave. at Uhuru Gardens.*

Dining

$$$$ ✕ **Jahazi Sundowner Cruise.** The evening begins on a dhow that delivers you to Fort Jesus. Men carrying blazing torches greet you as you enter the edifice. After a performance about the history of the coast, you'll dine by candelabra as waiters in Portuguese attire serve a range of seafood dishes. Following the feast, you can choose to continue to the Bora Bora Nightclub for the midnight show. The show is largely for organized tour groups. ⊠ *Fort Jesus,* ☎ *011/472–213.* WEB *www. africaonline.co.ke/jahazi. AE, DC, MC, V.*

$$$ ✕ **Hunter's Bar.** One of Mombasa's best restaurants, Hunter's Bar serves a wide range of dishes but is best known for its mouthwatering steaks. With trophy animals mounted on the walls, the place resembles a hunting lodge. It's also a good place to stop for a cold beer. ⊠ *Ambala House, Nkrumah Rd.,* ☎ *011/471–771. DC, V. Closed Sun.*

$$–$$$ ✕ **Hard Rock Café.** Part of the world-famous chain, this loud burger joint is extremely popular. This isn't why you came all the way to Africa, but if you need a pop music fix, this Tusker's for you. ⊠ *Nkrumah Rd. and Digo Rd.,* ☎ *011/222–221. AE, DC, MC, V.*

$$ ✕ **Le Bistro.** Within sight of the Tusks, this place has a bit of everything, from seafood and steak to pizza and pasta. It's open late into the evening. ⊠ *Moi Ave. east of Kisumu Rd.,* ☎ *011/229–470. DC, V.*

$$ ✕ **Pistacchio.** People come here to sip a cappuccino at one of the outdoor tables and watch the passersby. The restaurant also serves ice cream and a bargain lunch buffet. ⊠ *Meru Rd. at Maungano St.,* ☎ *011/471– 771. DC, V.*

$–$$ ✕ **Blue Room.** Famous for its *bhajias* (deep-fried pastries filled with vegetables), this family-owned Indian restaurant has been in business for more than 50 years. It seats more than 140 people, making it one of the largest restaurants in the city. You'll also find a cybercafé where you can send an E-mail back home. ⊠ *Haile Selassie Rd. and Digo Rd.,* ☎ *011/224–021,* FAX *011/315–275. No credit cards.*

$–$$ ✕ **Singh.** For rich, delicious curries, try this family-style restaurant. The menu is limited, but all the freshly prepared Indian dishes are delicious. Wall calendars add a splash of color to the decor. ⊠ *Mwembe Tayari Rd.,* ☎ *011/493–283. No credit cards.*

$–$$ ✕ **Chinese Overseas.** Competent Cantonese fare is served in simple surroundings at this family-style restaurant run by a pleasant Chinese couple. The menu features sweet-and-sour jumbo prawns, ginger crab, and sizzling platters of meat and fish. It's just west of the Tusks on Moi Avenue. ⊠ *Moi Ave.,* ☎ *011/221–585. No credit cards.*

Lodging

$$$ ⊞ **Mombasa Club.** Founded in 1897, this private club on Mbarak Hi-
★ nawy Street was one of the city's most important social organizations at the turn of the last century. It may be possible to stay here if you belong to a reciprocating club or if all the rooms are not booked by members. There's loads of British charm, a pool that juts into the harbor, and a slew of interesting characters. ⊠ *Mbarak Hinawy St.,* ☎ *011/312–449,* FAX *011/311–810. Restaurant, bar, pool. No credit cards.*

$$ ⊞ **New Outrigger Hotel.** South of Mombasa in the suburb of Likoni, this hotel overlooks Kilindi Harbor. Rooms surround a pool and a tropical garden. Fishing excursions are available. ⊠ *Ras Liwatoni,* ☎ *011/220–822,* FAX *011/315–801. 50 rooms. Restaurant, bar, pool. AE, DC, V.*

$ ⊞ **Hermes.** With an unusual facade of curtained glass, this hotel is a good choice for budget travelers. The location, near the Judoni Mosque, puts you within walking distance of most major sights. The restaurant serves excellent shrimp and seafood dishes. ⊠ *Msanifu Kombo St. and*

Haile Selassie Rd., ☎ *011/313–599. 126 rooms. Restaurant, bar. No credit cards.*

$ 🏨 **Lotus.** Wood-shuttered windows overlook a central courtyard at this charming lodging. The clean, comfortable rooms are all air-conditioned. The hotel, near the Anglican Cathedral, is a short walk from the town center. ⊠ *Cathedral La. at Mvita Rd.,* ☎ *011/313–207,* 🖷 *011/220–673. 17 rooms. Restaurant, bar. No credit cards.*

$ 🏨 **New Palm Tree.** A potted palm on the small second-floor balcony leads you to this popular hotel. Rooms are quiet and have fans. The cavernous reception area leads to a bar and simple restaurant that serves grilled meats and adequate curries. ⊠ *Nkrumah Rd., Mombasa,* ☎ *11/311–756. 17 rooms. Restaurant, bar. AE, DC, V.*

$ 🏨 **Royal Court Hotel.** A huge samovar sits inside the lobby of this six-story hotel on Haile Selassie Road. Rooms are air-conditioned and have balconies overlooking the city. There's a great view from the rooftop restaurant, which serves good Indian fare. ⊠ *Haile Selassie Rd. at Shimoni St.,* ☎ *011/312–389,* 🖷 *011/312–398. 45 rooms. Restaurant, bar. AE, DC, V.*

Nightlife and the Arts

Bars and Pubs

It is rare to hear good live Swahili music, but try the rooftop bar at the **Excellent Hotel** (⊠ Haile Selassie Rd., ☎ 011/227–683). **Hotel Splendid** (⊠ Msanifu Kombo St., ☎ 011/220–967) often features African music.

The **Casablanca Bar** (⊠ Mnazi Moja Rd. at Wakatwa Rd., ☎ 011/461–2440), one of the city's most popular dance clubs, draws an exuberant crowd to its terrace. **Sky Bar** (⊠ Moi Ave., near the Tusks, ☎ 011/220–967), is a raucous dance club. The **New Florida** (⊠ Mama Ngina Dr., ☎ 011/311–127) has a dance floor that's always packed. When you need a breather, head to any of the three terraces overlooking the harbor.

Outdoor Activities and Sports

Fishing

Howard Lawrence-Brown Sea Fishing (⊠ Mombasa, ☎ 011/485–680) has several boats available for charter. On several recent trips they've returned with record-setting wahoos and black marlins. **Dick Chater** (⊠ Mombasa, ☎ 011/225–244) brings fishing aficionados out to the area's best fishing spots.

Golf

On the southeastern shore of Mombasa, the **Mombasa Golf Club** (⊠ Mama Ngina Dr., ☎ 011/222–620) is a 9-hole course surrounded by a sandy beach. If you get tired of the links, the club also has several billiard tables.

Sailing

The **Mombasa Sailing Club** (⊠ Mnazi Mosi Rd., ☎ 011/313–350) has a bar and boats available for temporary members; it's for experienced sailors only.

Shopping

Like its counterpart in Nairobi, **Biashara Street** is where you'll find all sorts of beautiful fabrics. You will get a good price here on colorful kikois, which make perfect shawls. **Moi Avenue,** near the Tusks, is more oriented toward tourists.

Established in 1969 for handicapped artists, **Bombolulu** operates four sheltered workshops for 160 employees. Products include jewelry, clothing, wood carvings, and leather items. The main workshop, 3 km (2 mi) north of Mombasa, has a restaurant called Ziga, a Swahili word that means "cooking pot." ✉ *Nyali,* ☎ *011/471–704.* WEB *www.africaonline. co.ke/bombolulu.* ☉ *Mon.–Sat. 8–5.*

Mombasa A to Z

To research prices, get advice from other travelers, and book travel arrangements, visit www.fodors.com.

AIR TRAVEL TO AND FROM MOMBASA

Kenya Airways has daily flights between Nairobi and Mombasa, as well as four flights a week between Mombasa and Zanzibar. Airkenya has daily flights between Nairobi and Mombasa and continuing flights to Malindi and Lamu.

Moi International Airport is 16 km (10 mi) west of Mombasa.
➤ AIRLINES: **Airkenya** (✉ Ambalal House, Nkrumah Rd., ☎ 011/ 229–777). **Kenya Airways** (✉ Electricity House, Nkrumah Rd., ☎ 011/ 210–771).

BIKE AND MOPED TRAVEL

Fredlink delivers bikes as far north as Malindi and as far south as Diani Beach for an extra charge of Ksh 600. It also rents scooters and motorbikes.
➤ BIKE RENTALS: **Fredlink** (✉ Shimanzi Rd., ☎ 011/230–484).

BUS TRAVEL TO AND FROM MOMBASA

Bus service to Mombasa from Nairobi is operated by the Connection. The eight-hour trip costs Ksh 1,170. Another good bus company is Akamba. In Mombasa and up and down the coast, transport is provided by *matatus* (minibuses named for the pennies that used to be the fare). Matatus are numerous and cheap, but have people jammed in the aisles and pop music blaring through loudspeakers. And the names of the matatus—such as Rambo Jet and Rocket Rover—are a clue these are not the safest way to travel.

For journeys to Dar Es Salaam, try Al-Yumeiny. The journey takes nearly 12 hours, and the Ksh 800 fare includes lunch.
➤ BUS COMPANIES: **Akamba** ✉ Jomo Kenyatta Ave., Mombasa, ☎ 011/ 316–770. **Al-Yumeiny** (✉ Kenyatta Ave., near Kobil Station, ☎ 011/ 490–281). **The Connection** (✉ Jubilee House, Wabera St., Nairobi, ☎ 02/223–304).

CAR RENTAL

Given the corrosive salt air and the state of the roads, you will find rental prices higher than in Nairobi. Expect to pay Ksh 3,375 per day. If you do not have a major credit card, a cash deposit is required. A driver's license from abroad is valid for three months in Kenya. At most agencies you need to be at least 23.
➤ CONTACTS: **Avis** (✉ Moi Ave., ☎ 011/223–048). **Coast Car Hire** (✉ Ambalal House, Nkrymah Rd., ☎ 011/311–752). **Hertz** (✉ Moi Ave., ☎ 011/316–333).

CAR TRAVEL

The highway from Nairobi to Mombasa is narrow and full of potholes, but the scenery is beautiful. The drive may take anywhere from four to six hours, so make sure you have enough gas. There are good service stations near Voi.

➤ CONTACTS: **Automobile Association of Kenya** (✉ Jomo Kenyatta Avenue, ☎ 011/492–431).

EMERGENCIES
➤ HOSPITALS: **Aga Khan Hospital** (✉ Vanga Rd., ☎ 011/312–953). **Pandya Memorial Hospital** (✉ Kimathi Ave., ☎ 011/314–140).
➤ HOT LINES: **Police** (☎ 011/222–121).

MAIL AND SHIPPING
The main post office on Digo Road is open weekdays 8–6 and Saturday 9–noon.
➤ POST OFFICES: **Mombasa** (✉ Digo Rd. and Makadara Rd.).

MONEY MATTERS
ATMS
Barclay's Bank has three ATMs in Mombasa: on Moi Avenue near the corner of Mnazi Moja Road; on Kenyatta Avenue near Digo Road, and on Nkrumah Road near Fort Jesus.

CURRENCY EXCHANGE
Forex Bureau have exchange shops on Digo Road near the Municipal Market and near the entrance of Fort Jesus.

SAFETY
The best way to see Mombasa town is on foot, but you should not walk around at night. If you take a taxi at night, make sure it delivers you all the way to the door of your destination. Purse snatchers are all too common. Beware of people who might approach you on Moi Avenue offering to become your guide. Tell them "*Hapana, asante sana*" ("No, thank you") and move on.

TAXIS
Taxis in Mombasa are inexpensive. The drivers are friendly and helpful and will wait or return to collect you if you ask. For journeys north to Malindi or other destinations, check out the shared taxis, which come in the form of Peugeot station wagons.

TELEPHONES
The city code for Mombasa is 011. If you are calling from outside Kenya, drop the "0" when dialing.

TOUR OPERATORS
Reputable tour companies based in Mombasa include Big Five, Pollmans Tours and Safaris, and Somak Tours.
➤ OPERATORS: **Big Five** (✉ Mikindani Rd., ☎ 011/311–426). **Pollmans Tours and Safaris** (✉ Taveta Rd. and Shimazi Rd., ☎ 011/229–082). **Somak Tours** (✉ Nyerere Ave., ☎ 011/313–871).

TRAIN TRAVEL
The Mombasa Express departs every evening from Mombasa at 7 PM, pulling into Nairobi at just past 8 the next morning. Once a rather elegant experience, it is no longer. But many independent travelers still consider the journey a highlight of their trip to Kenya.
➤ TRAIN INFORMATION: **Mombasa Railway Station** (✉ Haile Selassie Rd., ☎ 011/312–220).

VISITOR INFORMATION
Mombasa Tourist Information, near the Tusks, sells books on city sights such as Fort Jesus. The best map is *The Streets of Mombasa Island*, which sells for Ksh 200.
➤ CONTACTS: **Mombasa Tourist Information** (✉ Moi Ave., ☎ 011/311–231).

SOUTHERN BEACHES

Kenya's coast south of Mombasa contains some of the country's most beautiful beaches. The highway from Mombasa runs all the way to the Tanzania border, providing easy access to a string of resorts. Shimba Hills Reserve, a little-known but excellent game park, is now joined by the small Mwaluganje Elephant Sanctuary. Farther south there is Kisite-Mpunguti Marine Park, which rivals the beauty of the reef off Diani Beach. It also has the eerie caves of Shimoni, where slave shackles are still bolted to the stone.

Diani Beach

⑭ *30 km (19 mi) south of Mombasa.*

The 20-km (12-mi) stretch of sand that makes up Diani Beach is the most developed along the southern coast. One reason that Diani Beach is so popular is that the reef filters out the seaweed, so the sandy shores are truly pristine. If you stay in one of the private cottages, local fishermen will take your order and deliver lobsters and other delicacies of the deep to your door.

At the mouth of the Mwachema River is a well-preserved 16th-century **Mwana Mosque.** It's surrounded by baobab trees, which grow to great size here with no elephants to rout them. At the southern end of Diani is what remains of **Jadini Forest,** home to colobus monkeys, as well as butterflies and birds. It's a great place for a picnic.

The village of Ukunda is on the main road where a smaller road leads to Diani Beach.

Dining and Lodging

$$$$ ✕ **Ali Barbour's Cave.** You can dine in a naturally formed cave deep underground or on an outdoor terrace at this popular seafood restaurant. You can't go wrong with the crab salad marinated with lemon and chilies. There is a shuttle bus that will pick up people staying in the Diani Beach area. ⊠ *Between Diani Sea Lodge and Trade Winds,* ☎ *0127/2163. Reservations essential. AE, DC, MC, V.*

$$$ ✕ **African Pot.** Here you'll find excellent Swahili food, including the traditional *ugali* (the inspiration for grits), greens, and gumbo. Live African music is occasionally featured here. ⊠ *Near entrance to Coral Beach Cottages,* ☎ *no phone. No credit cards.*

$$–$$$ ✕ **Vulcano.** Delectable seafood, including crab, lobster, and yellowfin tuna, is on the menu at this top-notch Italian eatery. The best place to start is with the delicious calimari. ⊠ *Southern end of Diani Beach,* ☎ *0127/2004. Reservations essential. AE, DC, MC, V.*

$$$$ ⌂ **Diani House.** This colonial mansion on Diani Beach is surrounded by 12 acres of forested gardens. You are hosted by a local couple who will arrange excursions for you. Each double room is cooled by lazily turning ceiling fans and has a private bath and a veranda. All meals and safaris to nearby nature reserves are included in the rate. ⊠ *Diani Beach,* ☎ *0127/3487,* ℻ *0127/2412,* 🆆🅴🅱 *www.dianihouse.com. 4 rooms. Dining room. No credit cards.*

$$$ ⌂ **Jadini Beach Hotel.** Diani Beach's oldest accommodation, Jadini Beach Hotel keeps people coming back with its fine service and friendly atmosphere. The high-ceilinged rooms all have a balcony or terrace facing the ocean. The hotel's restaurants, including the popular Jambo Village, also have lovely views. ⊠ *Ukunda,* ☎ *0127/2622,* ℻ *0127/2269,* 🆆🅴🅱 *www.alliancehotels.com. 78 rooms. Restaurant, bar, pool, 3 tennis courts, squash, shop, dance club, airport shuttle. AE, DC, MC, V.*

$$$ ⊞ **Papillon Hotel.** Spectacular thatched-roof cottages are strewn around this 20-acre resort. Built in traditional Swahili style, the rooms have big windows and private balconies. Wander through gardens and around ponds, which are illuminated at night. Larger rooms are popular with families. ⊠ *Diani,* ☎ *0127/2627,* FAX *0127/2216. 150 rooms. Restaurant, bar, pool, snorkeling, horseback riding, playground. AE, DC, MC, V.*

$$$ ⊞ **Robinson Club Baobab.** Perched high on coral cliffs overlooking the Indian Ocean, this hotel has steep steps leading down to the beach. The all-inclusive resort is frequented by German tour groups. There are Swahili-language classes, but the sound system is unpleasant. ⊠ *Diani,* ☎ *0127/2623,* FAX *0217/2032. 150 rooms. Restaurant, bar, pool, hair salon, dive center. AE, DC, MC, V.*

$$ ⊞ **Nomad.** Set amid towering palms, these cottages on Diani Beach are popular with British travelers, so book early during the high season. Nomad began as a restaurant, and the famous curry buffet on Sunday morning is still one of the best reasons to drop by. ⊠ *Ukunda,* ☎ *0127/2155,* FAX *0127/2391. 25 rooms. AE, DC, MC, V.*

Outdoor Activities and Sports

Kisite Dhow Tours (⊠ Diani, ☎ 1261/2331) offers glass-bottom boat tours and snorkeling in Kisite-Mpunguti Marine National Park. Departures are at 9 AM daily.

Shopping

Moiz Boutique (⊠ Diani Beach Rd., ☎ no phone), in Diani Beach, sells jewelry, carvings, and other items. It's open from Monday through Saturday 9–1 and 3–7. In Ukunda the craftspeople at **Ukunda Carvers** (⊠ Ukunda, ☎ no phone) can be found working under a huge baobab tree where black-and-white colobus monkeys can sometimes be spotted. The quality of the carvings here is among the best on the coast.

Shimba Hills National Reserve

⓯   *30 km (19 mi) south of Mombasa.*

Although it encompasses only 1,922 square km (742 square mi), this reserve of forest-covered hills attracts many visitors because it is home to the country's only herd of sable antelopes, which are known for their scimitar-shape horns. You'll also find an almost equally rare population of roan antelopes.

The best places to spot game are on the flat grasslands near the spectacular Sheldrick's Falls and on Lango Plains near Giriama Point, where you can see all the way to the Indian Ocean. A few elephants roam the reserve, but they are timid and usually only spotted at night. Lions and leopards are also present but seldom seen. Bird life is profuse, including occasional clouds of carmine bee-eaters, palm-nut vultures, silvery-cheeked hornbills, and, of course, spur fowls (called *kwale* in Swahili, they lend the region its name). Butterflies are a particular attraction, as are ground orchids, gladioli, and other flowers growing wild that decorate the meadowland.

Camping is permitted within the park. About 3 km (2 mi) from the main gain to the reserve are campsites and bandas with communal showers and toilets. ⊠ *Box 40241, Nairobi,* ☎ *02/501–081,* FAX *02/505–866,* WEB *www.kenya-wildlife-service.org.* ⊡ *$20.*

Dining and Lodging

$$$$ ⊞ **Mukurumuji Tented Camp.** On the edge of Shimba Hills National Reserve, these tents make roughing it a pleasure, as they have comfortable twin beds, private verandas, and private baths. There are hot

showers that feel great after a day of hiking. Guided safari walks venture into the Sable Valley, and you can arrange day trips to Mwaluganje Elephant Sanctuary. The rate includes meals and excursions. ⊠ *Shimba Hills National Reserve,* ☎ *0127/3487,* ⅌ *0127/2412. 4 tents. Dining room. AE, DC, MC, V.*

$$$ 🏠 **Shimba Rainforest Lodge.** Surrounded by thick forest, this jungle lodge looks directly on a watering hole. A 60-m (197-ft) wooden walkway offers several vantage points for gazing down on sable antelopes and other animals stopping by for a drink. You can also view wildlife from the balcony of your room. The accommodations are small but are cheerfully decorated and kept cool by ceiling fans. When you arrive, a guide will take you on a short nature walk through the Mkomba Valley. The trail has several wood blinds to duck into in case elephants or buffaloes also decide to use the path. Guests who stay more than one night can also hike to Sheldrick's Falls, where you can swim in the clear pool at the bottom of the 23-m (75-ft) cascade. ⊠ *Shimba Hills National Reserve,* ☎ *02/540–780,* ⅌ *02/545–948,* 🕸 *www. blockhotelske.com. 40 rooms, 1 with bath. 3 bars, dining room, pool, shop. AE, DC, MC, V.*

Shimoni

⑯ *60 km (37 mi) south of Diani.*

On the tip of a peninsula known for its excellent deep-sea fishing you'll find the village of Shimoni, which means "place of the holes." Ocean currents dug out a maze of coral caves, one of them 11 km (7 mi) long. This catacomb was used as an underground tunnel for loading slaves onto dhows. You can see iron shackles that still remain on the cave walls.

On nearby **Wasini Island** you can take a walk to the ancient Arab settlement near the modern village. Here you'll find the ruins of 18th- and 19th-century houses and a Muslim pillar tomb inset with Chinese porcelain.

★ **Kisite-Mpunguti Marine National Park.** A few miles off the coast, this 28-square-km (11-square-mi) national park is known for its beautiful coral gardens. More than 40 varieties of coral have been identified, including staghorn, brain, mushroom, and pencil. More than 250 species of fish have been spotted feeding around the reef, including butterfly fish, parrot fish, and angelfish. Humpback dolphins are a common sight, as are big schools of bonitos and frigate mackerels. The entire protected area, just past Wasini Island, is in shallow water and can be easily reached by motor boat or dhow. ⊠ *4–8 km (2–5 mi) from Shimoni,* 🕸 *www. kws.org.* 🎫 *$5.*

Dining and Lodging

$$$$ 🏠 **Funzi Island Fishing Club.** This secluded fishing retreat accommodates only 14 people in tents clustered together on an atoll of mangrove trees. You reach the camp by canoe and are greeted with a glass of wine and music from an old gramophone. Facilities are primitive—traditional bucket showers and long-drop toilets. You may find it rather elegant, though, when you retire on one of the lovely Lamu beds. Fishing is not mandatory, and there is much to entertain bird-watchers. ⊠ *Funzi Island,* ☎ *0127/204–4546.* ⅌ *0127/2346. 7 tents. Dining room, boating. AE, DC, MC, V.*

$$$$ 🏠 **Pemba Channel Fishing Club.** With the best fishing this side of
★ Watamu, this resort overlooking Wasini Island attracts anglers from around the world. Here you'll find three fishing boats, each equipped for a trio of anglers. But it isn't merely for fishing fans. Each of the

colorfully decorated bandas has a private veranda. ✉ *Shimoni*, ☎ *011/ 313–749*, FAX *011/316–875*, WEB *www.kenyabeach.com/pembafishing. html. 14 rooms. Restaurant, pool, boating. AE, DC, MC, V.*

$ 🏠 **Mpunguti Lodge.** Basic bandas and a good restaurant are what you'll find at this lodging on Wasini Island. The reasonable rates include all meals. The staff can arrange snorkeling trips in the marine park. ✉ *Wasini Island*, ☎ *0127/2331. Restaurant. No credit cards.*

Outdoor Activities and Sports

CRUISES

Dolphin Dhow (✉ Shimoni, ☎ 0127/2094, WEB www.dolphindhow.com) offers daylong excursions in the *Pomboo* (Dolphin) and *Al-lkhlas* (Purity). They cruise down the Shimoni Channel, where humpback dolphins are often sighted. Spotted dolphins are more likely to interact with humans, so the boats head out to Kisite-Mpunguti Marine National Park.

FISHING

Run by the father-and-son team of Simon and Pat Hemphill, **Sea Adventures** (✉ Shimoni, ☎ 0127/52204) specializes in catching really big fish. There are trophy-size marlin in these waters, and the Hemphills know just where to find them.

SCUBA DIVING

Overlooking Wasini Island, **Shimoni Reef Lodge** (✉ Shimoni, ☎ 011/ 471–771) caters to scuba divers. All skill levels are welcome, including beginners.

Southern Beaches A to Z

To research prices, get advice from other travelers, and book travel arrangements, visit www.fodors.com.

AIR TRAVEL TO AND FROM THE SOUTHERN BEACHES
Most people fly into Mombasa's Moi International Airport and make their way down the coast by taxi, rental car, or hotel shuttle. There is an airstrip at Ukunda for charter flights.

BUS TRAVEL
From the southern side of the Likoni Ferry terminal there are KBS buses heading south every 20 minutes from 7 to 7, less frequently in the evening. It takes about a half hour to reach Diani Beach.
➤ BUS COMPANIES: **KBS** (✉ Jomo Kenyatta Ave., ☎ 011/224–851).

CAR TRAVEL
You must take the Likoni Ferry to travel south of Mombasa. Two ferries run simultaneously, departing about 20 minutes apart, with fewer departures late in the day and in the evening. Vehicles are charged by length, usually about Ksh 35 per car. Pedestrians ride free.

MONEY MATTERS
Barclay's Bank has an ATM in Ukunda, north of the junction headed for Diani Beach.

MAIL AND SHIPPING
The region's largest post office is south of the Ukunda Road junction headed for Diani Beach. It's open from Monday through Saturday 8–5.

SAFETY
If you take a taxi at night, make sure it delivers you all the way to your destination. Tourist Police officers patrol beaches, but don't tempt

fate by bringing jewelry, cameras, or cash. Women should not walk alone on the beach.

If you are walking from Tiwi to Diani, consult the tidal chart beforehand. A creek that you must swim across at high tide is known as "Panga Point," after the machete used as a weapon by muggers.

Drink plenty of bottled water and wear sunscreen. It's a good idea to wear a thick T-shirt to protect your back from sunburn when snorkeling.

TELEPHONES
The city code for Diani Beach and the surrounding communities is 0127. If you are calling from outside Kenya, drop the "0" in the city code.

TOURIST INFORMATION
➤ CONTACTS: **Ukuna Tourism** (✉ Private Safaris Bldg., Ukunda Rd.).

NORTHERN BEACHES

North of Mombasa is a long stretch of shoreline where you'll find many resorts, some of them gargantuan. You first come to Nyali, followed by Kenyatta, Bamburi, and Shanzu. There's more to do here than lie on the beach, however. A dense forest of casuarina trees is where you'll find the famous Bamburi Quarry Nature Reserve, well worth a visit.

Nyali

17 *2 km (1 mi) north of Mombasa.*

Crossing the Nyali Bridge from Mombasa you reach this beachfront community. In the days when the British were trying to thwart the slave trade, freed slaves settled around Nyali. Here you'll find a **bell tower** built by missionaries. The bell sounded an alarm whenever a slave ship was spotted on the horizon.

★ What once were bare stone quarries left by Bamburi Cement Works are now forests crisscrossed with trails at **Bamburi Quarry Nature Reserve.** The transformation was due to Dr. René Haller, who developed a remarkable reclamation effort that attracted the attention of ecologists around the world. To increase the mineral content in the soil, he imported soil-enriching millipedes. On the premises you'll find a crocodile farm and a domesticated herd of elands. An animal orphanage is home to "Sally the Hippo," made famous in a documentary by Alan and Joan Root called *Balloon Safari.* Feeding time is 4 PM. ✉ *North of Nyali,* ☎ *011/485–729.* ◻ *Ksh 350.* ⊙ *Daily 7–6.*

The largest crocodile farm in the country, **Mamba Crocodile Village** has guides that lead you on a brief tour and show videos documenting the conservation and commercial aspects of the operation. If you want to see more, you can arrange a safari on the Tana River to watch crocodile catching. You'll find a shop selling handbags and boots, as well as an excellent restaurant. ✉ *Across from Nyali Golf Club, Nyali,* ☎ *011/472–709.* ⊙ *Daily 8–6.*

Dining and Lodging
$$$$ ✕ **Tamarind.** Perched high above a waterway leading to the Indian
★ Ocean, this Moorish-style palace is the country's most beautiful restaurant. Through the high arches you are treated to an unparalleled view. Excellent food is served with enormous flair and a great sense of fun. Especially worthwhile are the trout in banana leaves, prawns in a spicy butter sauce, and oysters with soy sauce, garlic butter, and coconut. Try the seafood platter, which gives you the chance to taste a

bit of everything. The Tamarind is a 15-minute drive north of downtown Mombasa. ⊠ *Silo Rd., Nyali,* ☎ *011/474–600.* WEB *www. tamarind.co.ke. Reservations essential. AE, DC, MC, V.*

$$$$ ✕ **Tamarind Dhow.** The same fine food of the Tamarind restaurant is
★ offered on board a lunch or dinner cruise on the *Nawalilkher,* the largest dhow on the coast. When you step onboard, a traditionally dressed waiter offers you a *dawa* (medicinal) cocktail made from vodka, lime, honey, sugar, and crushed ice. Grilled lobster and steak are among the best choices; don't turn down the coffee, served from a traditional brass pot. ⊠ *Silo Rd., Nyali,* ☎ *011/471–948,* FAX *011/471–257,* WEB *www. tamarind.co.ke. Reservations essential. AE, DC, MC, V.*

$$$ ✕ **Harlequin.** One of the region's better restaurants, Harlequin is northeast of the city on Tudor Harbor. The seafood is remarkably fresh— you can even pick out your own crab from the pool. ⊠ *Nyali,* ☎ *011/ 472–373. DC, V. Closed Sun.*

$$–$$$ ✕ **Imani Dhow.** This ship that once sailed the waters near Zanzibar is now a restaurant that draws visitors from up and down the coast. The menu focuses on local seafood, including Kilifi oysters and Malindi sole. ⊠ *Bamburi Beach,* ☎ *011/485–212. AE, DC, V.*

$$$ ▥ **Mombasa Continental.** This sprawling hotel, one of the largest in the area, sits right on Shanzu Beach. The luxurious rooms have balconies that overlook the pool and the beautifully landscaped gardens. ⊠ *Shanzu Beach,* ☎ *011/485–811,* FAX *011/485–437. 192 rooms. Restaurant, bar, 2 pools, 2 tennis courts, health club squash, casino, nightclub, meeting rooms.*

$$$ ▥ **Serena Beach Hotel.** On a sliver of white sand, this resort resembles
★ an Arab village. Swahili-style furniture graces all the rooms, including the spacious ones facing the garden. The dhow-shape Jahazi Grill, flying an authentic triangular sail, serves up fresh seafood. The Nyota Terrace serves far more formal fare. The rate includes water sports such as snorkeling, sailing, and windsurfing. ⊠ *Shanzu Beach,* ☎ *011/485– 721,* FAX *011/485–453,* WEB *www.serenahotels.com. 166 rooms. Restaurant, bar, pool, hair salon, 2 tennis courts, squash. AE, DC, MC, V.*

$$$ ▥ **Severin Sea Lodge.** Set among towering palm trees, this expansive lodge has air-conditioned bungalows facing the beach. A seafood restaurant on the premises, the Imani Dhow, is extremely popular. Unfortunately, the beach is totally under water at high tide. ⊠ *Kenyatta Beach,* ☎ *011/485–212,* FAX *011/485–212,* WEB *www.severin-sea-lodge. com. 200 rooms. Restaurant, in-room safes, pool, tennis courts, meeting room. AE, DC, V.*

$$$ ▥ **Nyali Beach Hotel.** A vast colonial-style structure, the Nyali Beach Hotel is just a few miles north of Mombasa. Most rooms in the main building and the newer annex have balconies overlooking the tropical gardens. The Mvita Grill, in a thatch-roof building on the beach, offers excellent seafood. In the evening try your luck at the casino or listen to live music at the Blues Night Club. ⊠ *Nyali,* ☎ *011/471–551,* FAX *011/484–8080,* WEB *www.blockhotelske.com. 235 rooms. 5 restaurant, 5 bars, pool, 3 tennis courts, casino, shop. AE, DC, MC, V.*

$$$ ▥ **Whitesands Hotel.** One of the oldest accommodations on the coast, the Whitesands Hotel holds its own against the newcomers on Bamburi Beach. Rooms in the colonial-style main building look out over the freeform pool and colorful gardens. There are four gazebos where buffet-style meals are served, but lines can be long if the hotel is full. ⊠ *Bamburi Beach,* ☎ *011/485–926,* FAX *011/485–405. 340 rooms. 3 restaurants, 2 bars. AE, MC, V.*

$$ ▥ **Bamburi Beach Hotel.** Popular among tour groups, this well-managed hotel has 125 air-conditioned rooms with balconies facing the sea. There are plenty of activities, from snorkeling to windsurfing. The small beach is often crowded. ⊠ *Bamburi Beach,* ☎ *011/485–611,* FAX *011/*

485–900. 125 rooms. Restaurant, bar, pool, tennis court, gym, horse-back riding, meeting rooms. AE, DC, MC.

$$ ☒ **Mombasa Beach Hotel.** Perched on coral cliffs overlooking the ocean, this hotel has gardens full of bougainvillea. Relax by either of two pools, or head down to the beach for a ride in a glass-bottom boat. ☒ *Nyali,* ☎ *011/471–861. 156 rooms. Restaurant, bar, snack bar, pool, tennis court, meeting room. AE, DC, V.*

Mtwapa

⑱ *13 km (8 mi) north of Mombasa.*

In this village on the north bank of Mtwapa Creek, artisans carve beautiful statues out of ebony.

With a name that means "house of slaves," **Jumba la Mtwana** is the ruins of a 15th-century village. Covering several acres, you'll find eight houses, three mosques, and several tombs. You will notice that little has changed in domestic architecture during the past millennium, as modern versions of the houses are visible as you pass through the villages on the main road. Guided tours are available, and there is a pleasant picnic facility overlooking the sea. ☒ *North of Mtwapa Creek,* ☎ *011/485–543,* WEB *www.museums.or.ke.* ☒ *Ksh 200.* ☉ *Daily 9–6.*

Kenya Marineland has glass-sided tanks where you can watch as sharks are fed. ☒ *North of Mtwapa Creek,* ☎ *011/485–248.* ☒ *Ksh 200.* ☉ *Daily 9–6.*

Dining and Lodging

$$$–$$$$ ✗ **Le Pichet.** Enjoy the innovative seafood served up by Belgian chef
★   Willy Wainwiler in this huge restaurant overlooking Mtwapa Creek. From here you can arrange a dhow cruise from the jetty for a barbecue served on a sandy beach, followed by African dancing and music under the stars. ☒ *North of Mtwapa Creek,* ☎ *011/585–923. Reservations essential. AE, DC, V.*

$–$$ ✗ **Moorings.** On the water near the northern bank of Mtwapa Creek, this floating restaurant is frequented by sailors and anglers. When you're trying to locate this seafood restaurant, remember that the signpost is a surfboard. ☒ *Mtwapa Creek,* ☎ *011/485–427. DC, V.*

$ ✗☒ **Kanamai.** This rambling compound of cottages by a beautiful beach was once a youth hostel, and it retains its no-frills outlook. Meals are served in a dining hall. The staff is charming and helpful. ☒ *Kikambala,* ☎ *0125/32046. Dining room. No credit cards.*

Kilifi

⑲ *60 km (36 mi) north of Mombasa.*

The village of Kilifi, midway between Mombasa and Malindi, has a spectacular bridge crossing Kilifi Creek. From here you can see the yachts and villas belonging to the Europeans who vacation here. It's the least developed town in this region, at least as far as tourism is concerned.

The ruins of **Mnarani** are found along the banks of Kilifi Creek. The large mosque is the site's most impressive edifice. Just behind the mosque is a pillar tomb constructed from coral rag. Leaning at a precarious angle, it is covered with ornate carvings. A short walk through the forest path leads to another little mosque with another pillar still standing. ☒ *Kilifi Creek.* ☒ *Ksh 200.* ☉ *Daily 7–6.*

Dining and Lodging

$$$ ✗☒ **Seahorse Inn.** On the northern bank of Kilifi Creek, this lodge has thatch-roof bungalows shaded by palm trees. The Seahorse is

known for water sports and is a watering hole for sailors and contacts for deep-sea fishing. Locals enjoy the delicious seafood at the Boat Grill ($$). ⊠ *Kilifi,* ☏ *0125/22813. 40 bungalows. Restaurant, bar, sailing. AE, MC, V.*

$$$$ 🏠 **Al Qasr.** On the south bank of Kilifi Creek, this guest house is constructed in the traditional Moorish style. Generously proportioned rooms surround a central courtyard. Furnished with four-poster beds, the rooms look out onto the water through dramatic arches. Hosts Peter and Joanna Nicholas know the area and guide you on excursions to the Arabuko-Sokoke Forest. ⊠ *Kilifi Creek,* ☏ *02/571–647 in Nairobi, 404/888–0909 in the U.S.,* 𝙁𝘼𝙓 *02/571–665 in Nairobi, 404/888–0188 in the U.S,* 𝖶𝖤𝖡 *www.unchartedoutposts.com. 3 rooms. Dining room, pool, beach. AE, DC, MC, V. Closed Apr.–May.*

$$$$ 🏠 **Takaungu House.** Arab ruins beckoning to be explored are within
★ a stone's throw of this rambling house on a sandy beach south of Kilifi. Much of the pleasure of a stay at this peaceful place comes from the hosts, Kenya-born Charlotte and Philip Mason. The easygoing couple is likely to entice you into taking the helm of their 40-ft ketch *Moonspinner.* They'll also accompany you on picnics up Kilifi Creek and on hikes in the Arabuko–Sokoke Forest. Local fishermen deliver their fresh catches of crabs, oysters, and prawns in time for lunch on the courtyard. A small pool sits near the beach. ⊠ *Kilifi,* ☏ *02/571–647 in Nairobi, 404/888–0909 in the U.S.,* 𝙁𝘼𝙓 *02/571–665 in Nairobi, 404/888–0188 in the U.S,* 𝖶𝖤𝖡 *www.unchartedoutposts.com. 6 rooms. Dining room, pool, beach. AE, DC, MC, V. Closed Apr.–May.*

Watamu

⑳ *60 km (37 mi) from Kilifi.*

Once a fishing village, Watamu is now a bustling little town that attracts its share of travelers intent on seeing the sights both on land and in the sea.

The **Arabuko–Sokoke Forest,** covering an area of more than 400 square km (154 square mi), is the surviving fragment of indigenous coastal forest in Kenya. Coastal dry forest once extended from northern Mozambique to southern Somalia. Now, apart from a few small *kaya* forests, the Arabuko–Sokoke Forest is all that remains. More than 260 species of birds have been recorded in the forest including the rare Sokoke Scops owl, Sokoke pipit, East Coast akalat, spotted ground thrush, and Clarke's weaver. The forest walk is good for nonbirders, who may want to look for the resident herd of elephants. Hundreds of butterflies gather to drink from pools near the forest trail. ⊠ *8 km (5 mi) north of Watamu,* ☏ *0122/32462.* ⊘ *Daily 8–4.*

About 4 km (2 mi) from Watamu are the ruins of an ancient village of
★ **Gedi.** Although it may seem an unlikely location for a Swahili village because it's several kilometers from the sea, the 14th-century community was once on an inlet leading to the Galana River. The inlet changed course, leaving the community high and dry.

Surrounded by an imposing wall, Gedi was once home to more than 2,000 people. The large central mosque, one of seven on the site, indicates this was once a wealthy community. During the 16th century Gedi was deserted, perhaps as a result of an attack by the Oromo from the north. Gedi was soon reoccupied, but it never regained its economic footing. It was finally abandoned in the 17th century. The site has fascinated many archaeologists, and a museum on the premises holds artifacts found here.

Gedi is also a wildlife sanctuary, home to mammals such as the black-and-white colobus monkeys and a rich variety of birds including Harrier eagles, silver-cheeked hornbills, and Zanzibar shrikes. ⊠ *6 km (4 mi) north of Watamu,* ☎ *0122/32065,* WEB *www.museums.or.ke.* ⊠ *Ksh 200.* ⊗ *Daily 9–6.*

Set up in 1993 to prevent farmers around the Arabuko–Sokoke Forest from destroying more of the remaining trees, the **Kipepeo Project** gives them a sustainable income by collecting butterflies that are sold abroad. You are briefed about the project before entering the large flight cage, where you can photograph these lovely creatures as they feed on nectar or banana and palm wine. ⊠ *Arabuko–Sokoke Forest,* ☎ *0123/ 32380.* ⊗ *Daily 8–5.*

The **Watamu Marine Park,** just south of the village, is one of the best spots in the area for snorkeling and scuba diving. Coral reefs, only 50 m (164 ft) from the beach at low tide, hold an astounding variety of fish. Among the masses of reeds you may even spot an octopus, shy of humans. Mida Creek, situated within Watamu Marine Reserve, is an important feeding habitat for marine turtles. Green, hawksbill, and loggerhead turtles make their home here. ⊠ *Watamu.* ⊗ *Daily 8–5.*

Dining and Lodging

$$$$ 🏨 **Hemingway's.** A 750-pound blue marlin hangs over the bar, which should tell you the reason fishing enthusiasts head to this lodging on Turtle Bay. The hotel maintains its own deep-sea fishing fleet, taking guests out for full- or half-day excursions. There are also two pools and miles of private beach just outside your door. Rooms in the older wing are small but have the best views of the ocean. The excellent cuisine, heavy on the seafood, includes fresh vegetables from the fertile shores of Lake Naivasha. The dining room, under a thatch roof, has a dance floor. ⊠ *Watamu,* ☎ *0122/32624,* FAX *0122/32256. 90 rooms. Restaurant, bar, in-room safes, minibars, 2 pools, conference room. AE, MC, V.*

$$$ 🏨 **Ocean Sports Hotel.** Overlooking Turtle Bay, these comfortable bungalows sit amid gardens filled with fragrant frangipani trees. Meals are served in a large thatch-roof dining room. The Sunday brunch is famous; locals drive for great distances to have a meal at Ocean Sports, known colloquially as "Open Shorts." Then they tell tall tales and sing school songs at the boat-shaped bar. One of the best diving centers along the coast, AquaVenture, is adjacent to the hotel. ⊠ *Watamu,* ☎ *0122/ 32008,* FAX *0122/32266.* WEB *www.africaonline.co.ke/ocean/location.html. 29 rooms. Dining room, pool. AE, DC, V.*

$$$ 🏨 **Turtle Bay Beach Club.** This popular all-inclusive resort has plenty of activities for families, from tennis to miniature golf. The focus is on water sports, and even novices can try their hand at windsurfing or scuba diving. Comfortable rooms are built down the slope, reached by paths through the lovely gardens. The hotel attracts German tour groups. ⊠ *Watamu,* ☎ *0123/32080,* FAX *0122/32268,* WEB *www.turtlebay.co.ke. 154 rooms. Restaurant, bar, pool, hair salon, shop. MC, V.*

$ 🏨 **Mrs. Simpson's Guest House.** Founded by Barbara Simpson, a fervent environmentalist, this guest house is one of the best-known establishments in the area. A resident of Kenya since 1923, she has run the place for more than two decades. Though in frail health, she still entertains guests with her stories. Large rooms include private baths. The two in-house ornithologists can help you locate some rare birds. ⊠ *Watamu,* ☎ *0122/32023,* WEB *www.watamu.net. 7 rooms. Dining room. No credit cards.*

Nightlife and the Arts

North of Watamu, **Pole Pole Bar** (⊠ across from Turtle Bay Beach Resort, ☎ no phone) is a pleasant watering hole where locals stop by in the early evening. Getting started a little later is **Come Back Day and Night Club** (✉ facing Blue Lagoon, ☎ no phone), which plays reggae and African music. It is a friendly place to meet other independent travelers. **Happy Night** (✉ facing Blue Lagoon, ☎ no phone) plays mostly American soul, hip-hop, and rhythm and blues. The place really gets going around 11 PM.

Outdoor Adventure and Sports

AquaVentures (✉ Ocean Sports Hotel, ☎ 0122/32420), at the Ocean Sports Hotel, offers trips on two dive boats.

Malindi

㉑ *24 km (14 mi) from Watamu.*

Malindi, the country's second-largest coastal town, has been an important port for hundreds of years. "Ma Lin De" is referred to as a stop on the trade route in ancient Chinese documents. The town battled with Mombasa for control of the coast, which explains why Portuguese explorer Vasco da Gama received such a warm welcome when he landed here in 1498. The **Vasco da Gama Cross,** made from Portuguese stone, sits on a promontory on the southern tip of the bay.

There are other historic sites worth visiting in Malindi. The 14th-century tombs beside the **Jamaa Mosque** near Uhuru Park are among the oldest in Malindi. On the seafront near the massive old baobab tree stands the **Portuguese Church.** Dating from 1542, it is one of the oldest Catholic churches still in use in Africa.

The road leading to the Malindi Marine Park leads to the **Malindi Crocodile Farm & Snake Park.** Feeding time for the more than 1,500 crocodiles in residence is 4 on Wednesday and Friday. ✉ *3 km (2 mi) south of Malindi,* ☎ *0123/20121.* 🎫 *Ksh 400.* ☉ *Daily 9–6.*

The **Malindi Falconry,** down the dirt road leading to the Catholic church, is worth the struggle to find. A knowledgeable guide tells you all about the resident birds of prey. You'll see rare creatures, such as the southern banded snake eagle. ✉ *Off Harambee Rd.,* ☎ *123/20383.* ☉ *Daily 10–6.*

Malindi Marine Park is home to an impressive variety of colorful coral. Here you'll find two main reefs separated by a deep sandy-bottom channel. There's very little commercial fishing in the area, which means the kingfish found here are trophy size. The water ranges from 25°C (77°F) to 29°C (84 °F), making this a particularly pleasant place to snorkel or scuba dive. If you want to stay dry, try one of the glass-bottom boats. ✉ *Offshore from Malindi.* 🎫 *Ksh 400.*

Dining and Lodging

$$–$$$ ✗ **La Malindina.** On a side street not far from Lamu Road, this very popular restaurant serves excellent Italian food. The setting, by a pool, makes it one of the most romantic spots on the coast. ✉ *Near Eden Roc Hotel,* ☎ *0123/20449. Reservations essential. AE, MC, V.*

$$ ✗ **I Love Pizza.** Overlooking the bay, this place is famous for its moderately priced pizza. You can also order fresh seafood. The calamari salad is excellent. ✉ *Vasco da Gama Rd.,* ☎ *0123/20672. AE, MC, V.*

$$ ✗ **The Old Man and the Sea.** Near the fishing jetty, this place is known for its fresh seafood. Sticking with the Hemingway theme, its sister restaurant north of town is called The Sun Also Rises. ✉ *Vasco da Gama Rd.,* ☎ *0123/31106. Reservations essential. AE, MC, V.*

$–$$ ✗ **La Gelateria.** This is a great place to stop by for real Italian ice cream—there are more than 30 flavors from which to choose. This pleasant restaurant, in the Sabaki Shopping Center, also serves great cappuccino. ⊠ *Lamu Rd.,* ☎ *0123/20710. No credit cards.*

$$$$ 🏨 **Indian Ocean Lodge.** This Arab-style mansion near Casuarina Point is set within a walled garden overflowing with bougainvillea. Furnished with kilims, brass ornaments, and four-poster beds, the enormous suites have sitting rooms and private balconies. Elegant meals with fine wines are served outdoors, within earshot of the surf. You are hosted by a charming couple who can arrange excursions to Gedi, bird-watching in the Arabuko–Sokoke Forest, snorkeling, or fishing trips. ⊠ *Point Casuarina,* ☎ *0123/20394, 404/888–0909 in the U.S.,* FAX *404/888–0188 in the U.S,* WEB *www.savannahcamps.com. 5 rooms. Dining room, minibars, pool. AE, DC, MC, V. Closed Apr.–May.*

$$$$ 🏨 **Silversand Villas.** Palm-shaded cottages surround a central lodge at this popular resort. Beautiful carved doors and colorful Ethiopian carpets make for a delightful stay. There is an excellent restaurant built right on the beach so you can put your toes in the sand. You can relax by either of the two pools. ⊠ *Tourist Rd.,* ☎ *0123/20407,* FAX *0123/30002. 4 cottages. Restaurant, pool. MC, V.*

$$$$ 🏨 **Tana Delta Camp.** Although its location at the mouth of the Tana River is remote, once you are here, you won't want to leave. You'll be transported to the camp by boat and will most likely spot hippos along the way. They won't be the last animals you see—hike by the river to spy bushbuck, yellow baboons, and vervet monkeys, or canoe past herons, kingfishers, and bee-eaters. Shaded by tamarind trees, the tents all have private baths and running water. The dining tent is built atop a huge sand dune, providing a view of the ocean. Book through Bush Homes. ⊠ *At mouth of Tana River,* ☎ *02/571–647 in Nairobi, 404/888–0909 in the U.S.,* FAX *02/571–665 in Nairobi, 404/888–0188 in the U.S,* WEB *www.unchartedoutposts.com. 6 tents. Dining room, pool, beach. AE, DC, MC, V.*

$$$ 🏨 **African Dream Village.** Furniture made of beautifully carved wood complements the spacious rooms at this popular resort. The service is friendly and efficient. ⊠ *Point Casuarina,* ☎ *0123/20442,* FAX *0123–20788. 120 rooms. Restaurant, bar, pool, health club. AE, MC, V.*

$$$ 🏨 **Club Che-Shale.** Near the ancient village of Mambrui you'll find this collection of a dozen bandas nestled among the sand dunes on a secluded beach. Each has a private bath and a veranda facing the ocean. You can walk along the beach, but a better means of transportation is one of the 20 camels that take visitors on half-day excursions. The restaurant is known for its excellent seafood. ⊠ *North of Malindi,* ☎ *0123/20063,* FAX *0123/21257.* WEB *www.che-shale.com. 4 rooms. MC, V.*

$$$ 🏨 **Driftwood Club.** In an attractive garden, this popular lodging is in a Swahili-style structure. Rooms are a bit basic, but the independent travelers who rave about the place don't seem to mind. The staff, always eager to see to your needs, can arrange for any type of water sports. The restaurant serves excellent seafood. ⊠ *3 km (2 mi) south of Malindi,* ☎ *0123/20155,* FAX *0123/30712. 37 rooms. Restaurant, bar, pool, dive center. AE, DC, V.*

$$$ 🏨 **Eden Roc Hotel.** This sprawling complex atop a cliff has a commanding view of the bay. Favored by package tour groups, it has comfortably furnished rooms overlooking the ocean. The friendly staff can arrange golfing trips and deep-sea fishing expeditions. ⊠ *2 km (1 mi) north of Malindi,* ☎ *0123/20480,* FAX *0123/20333,* WEB *www.kenyabeach.com/edenroc.html. 157 rooms, 6 suites. Restaurant, bar, 3 pools, 2 tennis courts, volleyball, dance club, meeting rooms. AE, DC, V.*

$$$ 🏨 **Scorpio Villas.** Thatch-roof cottages filled with handcrafted furniture are scattered around the exotic gardens of this resort near the Vasco da Gama Cross. Your cottage will have a kitchen staffed with your own

cook, although you are free to join the other guests in the restaurant. There are three pools, and the beach is just a short walk down a narrow path. ⊠ *Harambee Rd.,* ☎ *0123/20194,* FAX *0123/21250,* WEB *www. scorpiovillas.com. 17 cottages. Restaurant, bar, 3 pools, travel services. AE, V.*

$$$ 🏨 **White Elephant Sea Lodge.** Animal hides decorate the reception area of this luxurious lodge south of Malindi. Very popular with Italian travelers, it has a large pool and a great stretch of shoreline. The traditionally styled cottages are filled with hardwood furniture. The open-air restaurant is excellent, serving great seafood. ⊠ *2 km (1 mi) south of Malindi,* ☎ *0123/20528,* FAX *0123/30105. 40 rooms. Restaurant, bar, pool. AE, V.*

$$ 🏨 **Blue Marlin Hotel.** This landmark dating from the 1930s has served for years as a retreat for anglers and writers (including Ernest Hemingway, who once stayed here). The hotel is on the beach, but it's a rather long walk to the water. The adjacent Lawford's Hotel, owned by the same company, has lower rates. ⊠ *Off Harambee Rd.,* ☎ *0123/20440. 145 rooms. Bar, café, 2 pools, dance club, meeting rooms. MC, V.*

$ 🏨 **Malindi Cottages.** These thatch-roof cottages, many with room for five people, are a good choice for families. They are in the northern part of town across the street from the beach. The place is popular, so book early. ⊠ *Lamu Rd.,* ☎ *0123/20304,* FAX *0123/21071. 12 cottages. Pool. No credit cards.*

Shopping

Al Noor Gallery (⊠ Goram Mast Rd., near Uhuru Gardens, ☎ no phone) specializes in antiques in brass and silver. Beautiful beadwork on belts and sandals can be found at **Kongoni** (⊠ Goram Mast Rd., near Uhuru Gardens, ☎ 0123/20461).

Northern Beaches A to Z

To research prices, get advice from other travelers, and book travel arrangements, visit www.fodors.com.

AIR TRAVEL TO AND FROM THE NORTHERN BEACHES

Kenya Airways has flights to Malindi from Mombasa and Nairobi every day except Saturday. Airkenya also has daily flights to Malindi from Mombasa and Nairobi, as well as continuing flights to Lamu.

➤ CARRIERS: **Airkenya** (⊠ Galana Shopping Centre, Malindi, ☎ 0123/ 30808). **Kenya Airways** (⊠ Utali Parade, Harambee Ave., Malindi, ☎ 0123/20237, WEB www.kenya-airways.com).

BUS TRAVEL

Tana Express and several other companies run buses between Mombasa and Malindi. The journey takes 2½ hours. Buses arrive and depart at the main bus depot in Malindi, southwest of the center of town near Mombasa Road. At the same bus station you can inquire about taking one of the station wagons, which are safer and more comfortable. They depart when they have seven passengers. The ticket price is Ksh 250.

➤ BUS COMPANIES: **Tana Express** (⊠ Uhuru Rd., Malindi, ☎ 0123/ 20095).

BIKE AND MOPED TRAVEL

Fredlink, based in Mombasa, will deliver bicycles as far north as Malindi for an extra charge. It also rents scooters and motorbikes. Malindi Bike Rental and Sudi Sudi Safaris are both Malindi-based companies that offer reasonable rates.

➤ BIKE RENTALS: **Fredlink** (✉ Shimanzi Rd., Mombasa, ☎ 011/230–484). **Malindi Bike Rental** (✉ Harambee Rd., Malindi, ☎ 0123/31741). **Sudi Sudi Safaris** (✉ Harambee Rd., Malindi, ☎ 0123/20596).

CAR RENTAL
Given the corrosive salt-air climate and poor state of the roads, you will find car-rental prices higher here than in Nairobi. For a typical small car expect to pay Ksh 3,500 per day for a compact and Ksh 7,800 for a four-wheel-drive vehicle. At most agencies you need to be at least 23 to rent a car.
➤ LOCAL AGENCIES: **Avis** (✉ Harambee Rd., Malindi, ☎ 0123/20065).

MAIL AND SHIPPING
The main post office in Malindi is open weekdays 8–6 and Saturday 9–noon.
➤ POST OFFICES: **Malindi** (✉ Kenyatta and Uhuru Rds).

MONEY MATTERS
Barclay's Bank, near the fishing jetty in Malindi, is open weekdays 8:30–1 and 2:30–5, Saturday 8:30–noon.
➤ BANKS: **Barclay's Bank** (✉ Lamu Rd., Malindi).

TOUR OPERATORS
Abercrombie & Kent, one of the world's most respected tour operators, has an office in Malindi.
➤ TOUR OPERATORS: **Abercrombie & Kent** (✉ Harambee Rd., Malindi, ☎ 0123/21169, FAX 0123/30188).

VISITOR INFORMATION
➤ VISITOR INFORMATION: **Tourist Information Center** (✉ Harambee Rd. near Kenya Airways, Malindi, ☎ 0123/20747).

LAMU

★ ㉒ *175 km (109 mi) north of Malindi.*

The 19th-century houses in Lamu reach down to the water's edge where fishermen shout as they draw their dhows out to sea. This busy waterfront is what most visitors see when they first arrive in Lamu, as boats to the island drop their passengers here. Instantly you are transported to another world where pastel paint covers carved bows and Bob Marley's face graces many a vessel's flag. The minor chaos of collecting your luggage and getting ashore is about the only turmoil you will feel in Lamu, a place completely devoid of modern pressures. After all, donkeys are the principal form of transportation.

Lamu, with a population of 13,000, is Kenya's oldest Swahili settlement. Founded around the 13th century as one of many Swahili villages that stretched from Somalia to Mozambique, Lamu is surrounded by the ruins of even older communities. During the 16th century the Portuguese held sway over the Lamu Archipelago, but in the 19th century Zanzibar wrested control of the region.

To the east of Lamu is the smaller town of Shela. The people here emigrated from the nearby island of Manda, so the Swahili spoken here is noticeably different from that of Lamu. The sight that can't be missed in Shela is the Jamaa Mosque, a oddly conical structure set back from the beach.

Since the 1970s Lamu and the neighboring villages have been a prime destination for the rich and famous. The hotels in the region are most crowded around Christmas, when rooms may be booked a year or more in advance.

A Good Walk

Because few have the telltale minarets, the best way to find a mosque in Lamu is to look for a large collection of sandals left in a doorway. You'll find one in the northern part of town at the **Jumaa Mosque.** A few blocks south is the **Swahili House Museum.** That braying sound you hear as you approached the ocean is the **Donkey Sanctuary.** A few blocks south on Kenyatta Road, just past the **M'na Lalo Mosque,** is the **Lamu Museum.** Enter through a door embellished with brass studs that was imported from Zanzibar. Walk along the waterfront promenade to see the craftsmen constructing furniture, doors, and, farther on, dhows.

After lunch visit **Lamu Fort,** an immense edifice that once stood at the water's edge. Next door is the **Pwani Mosque,** the oldest house of worship in town. Back on Kenyatta Road you'll find the **German Post Office Museum.** To the west is the newest mosque, the **Riyadha Mosque.**

TIMING

Should you spend some time exploring the museum, this walk can take the better part of a day.

Sights to See

Donkey Sanctuary. Established by the International Donkey Protection Trust, this shelter is for abused, injured, and aged donkeys. The facility opened on July 4, 1987, so the staff celebrates July 4 as "Donkey Independence Day." ⊠ *Harambee Ave.,* ☎ *no phone.* ▣ *Donation.* ⊙ *Daily 9–12:30.*

German Post Office Museum. In the late 1870s the sultan of Witu was having problems governing Lamu. He allowed his kingdom to become a German protectorate, and the region's first German Post Office opened here in 1888. After only two years Germany relinquished its holdings in Kenya to Britain. It was reopened in 1996 as a museum. ⊠ *South of Lamu Fort on Harambee Ave.,* ☎ *no phone.* ▣ *Ksh 200.* ⊙ *Daily 8:30–6.*

Jumaa Mosque. Dating from 1511, Jumaa Mosque is among the oldest in the city. It's in the northern part of town. ⊠ *West of Harambee Ave.,* ☎ *no phone.*

Lamu Fort. Completed in 1821, the fort served as a garrison for soldiers sent by the sultan of Oman. The protection it offered the often besieged town encouraged development around the waterfront, and many of these stone structures still survive today. From 1910 until 1984 it served as a prison. Today it houses a walk-through exhibit about the country's environment. For a good view of the city, take a walk on the ramparts. ⊠ *Harambee Ave.* ▣ *Ksh 200.* ⊙ *Daily 8:30–6.*

Lamu Museum. Built in 1891 by Al-Busaidy, who served as the local representative for the sultan of Zanzibar, the two-story building that houses the Lamu Museum is one of the town's most imposing structures. It holds an unparalleled collection of artifacts from the Swahili, Oromo, and Pokomo cultures. One of its most intriguing displays is about the rituals of a Swahili bride. There are photos of Lamu taken between 1846 and 1849 by French photographer Guillain. *Siwa* horns, some of the oldest musical instruments in sub-Saharan Africa, are found here; the ones you'll see are made of ivory and brass. The staff can arrange guided tours to various archaeological sites on Manda Island and Pate Island. ⊠ *Kenyatta Rd. near main wharf,* ☎ *0121/33073 or 0121/33201,* FAX *0121/33402.* ▣ *Ksh 200.* ⊙ *Daily 8:30–6.*

M'na Lalo Mosque. In the center of town, this mosque was built in 1753. ⊠ *North of Lamu Museum,* ☏ *no phone.*

OFF THE
BEATEN PATH
MATONDONI – Facing the narrow Makanda Channel is the village of Matondoni, 8 km (5 mi) from Lamu. This is the last surviving stronghold of the boatwright craft. Basic tools are used, powered by nothing more than sweat and muscle. The community does not have any accommodations, but there is a small café selling fruit juices and fresh fish. The best way to get to Matondoni is by dhow, which can be hired in Lamu.

Pwani Mosque. The town's oldest house of worship, Pwani Mosque dates from 1370. At one time it was where most of the city's Muslim men came to pray. ⊠ *Adjacent to Lamu Fort,* ☏ *no phone.*

Riyadha Mosque. In the southern part of town, this modern mosque is one of the newest in Lamu. It's adjacent to the Muslim Academy, funded by Saudi Arabia. ⊠ *Southwest of Lamu Fort,* ☏ *no phone.*

Swahili House Museum. This 18th-century house, restored in 1986, demonstrates what life was like for a middle-class Lamu family. The three rooms are filled with furniture from the period. Outside is a garden filled with fragrant frangipani trees. ⊠ *Northwest of Lamu Museum,* ☏ *no phone.* ⌫ Ksh 200. ☉ *Daily 8:30–6.*

Dining and Lodging

$–$$ ✕ **Bush Gardens.** This lively waterfront eatery has great fresh fish, with tuna, shark, and snapper among the standouts. Entrées are served with coconut rice or french fries. If you stop by for breakfast, make sure to try the fresh fruit juices. ⊠ *Harambee Ave., south of main jetty, Lamu,* ☏ *no phone. No credit cards.*

$$–$$$ ✕ **Hapa Hapa.** With a name that is Swahili for "Here, Here," Hapa Hapa is known for its outstanding seafood. Make sure to try the barracuda. This restaurant is on the waterfront, making it a great spot to watch the fishing boats heading out into the Indian Ocean. ⊠ *Harambee Ave., south of main jetty, Lamu,* ☏ *0121/3226. No credit cards.*

$$ ✕ **Whispers Coffee Shop.** On Harambee Avenue in the same building as the Baraka Gallery, this upmarket café has a pretty courtyard where you can sip the excellent cappuccino. ⊠ *Harambee Ave., Lamu,* ☏ *no phone. No credit cards.*

$$$ ✕▢ **Peponi's Hotel.** Set amid towering palm trees, this gleaming white building has long been considered one of Lamu's finest hotels. The rooms, cooled by lazily turning ceiling fans, all have views of the water. Relax in the pool built between two baobab trees, or head out for waterskiing or windsurfing. Snorkelers and scuba divers can take a boat to the nearby reef. Set beneath great vines of bougainvillea, the restaurant ($$–$$$) serves the best seafood on the island. If you prefer, enjoy dinner as you cruise the harbor on a dhow. ⊠ *Shela,* ☏ *0121/33154 and 0121/33421,* ⚞ *0121/33029,* ▦ *www.peponi-lamu.com. 24 rooms. 2 restaurants, bar, pool, beach, shop. AE, MC, V.*

$$ ✕▢ **Island Hotel.** A good budget alternative, this guest house is popular with families. The penthouse, with lovely views, is worth the extra cost. Some of the other rooms have walls that do not reach all the way to the ceiling, so ask to see a few before you decide. On the rooftop is an excellent seafood restaurant called Barracuda ($$). Make sure to try the lobster. ⊠ *Shela,* ☏ *0121/33290,* ⚞ *0121/33568. 14 rooms. Restaurant. AE, DC, V.*

$$ ✕▢ **Petley's Inn.** Established by the eccentric Percy Petley in 1862, this small hotel is the oldest in Kenya. The nicest of the rooms face the sea. Breakfast is included in the rate. The rooftop restaurant ($$$) has expanded its menu since Petley announced he was serving only stew. Now there's a range of excellent seafood. The terrace bar can be lively in the evening because it's one of the few places in Lamu town to serve a cold mug of Tusker. Occasionally there's dancing. ⊠ *Harambee Rd., Lamu,* ☎ *0121/33107. 11 rooms. Restaurant, bar, pool. AE, DC, V.*

$$$$ 🏨 **Beach House.** Next to the windswept dunes at the end of Shela, this
★ hotel couldn't have a better setting. Each room is different, but all have comfortable beds, ceiling fans, and shuttered windows that open to exceptional bird-watching in the nearby trees. The vibrant wings of carmine bee-eaters may dazzle you. There are many spaces for dining, but the rooftop terrace, which has a white hammock, gives you an extraordinary view of the channel. The staff is on hand to prepare meals to order, and you can place orders from a small but well-stocked wine cellar. The hotel is booked far in advance for the holidays. ⊠ *Shela,* ☎ *02/442–171 or 02/445–013,* ℻ *02/445–010,* ⓦⒺⒷ *www.lamu-shela. com/beach.html. 5 rooms. Restaurant, pool. AE, DC, V.*

$$$$ 🏨 **Fish Trap House.** On the waterfront, this lovely private house has a large sundeck with a shaded baraza surrounded by three bedrooms decorated with local artifacts. Your own servants are included in the rate. Book far in advance for the holidays. ⊠ *Shela,* ☎ *02/882–973. 3 rooms. No credit cards.*

$$$ 🏨 **Kipungani Bay.** On the southern tip of Lamu Island, this lodge is for anyone seeking a truly secluded getaway. The immense cottages— a half-hour trip by speedboat from Lamu—feel removed from the rest of the world. There's not much to do here—take a walk on the sandy beach, snorkel at the nearby reef, or charter a boat to go deep-sea fishing. Excursions take you to Lamu for shopping or to Matondoni for a glimpse at the ancient art of crafting a dhow. From the freeform saltwater pool you have a stunning view of the sunset. ⊠ *Kipungani,* ☎ *011/33432. 15 rooms. Restaurant, bar, pool. AE, DC, V.*

$$$ 🏨 **Palm House.** A palm tree sways over the courtyard of this Arabic-style inn. There's a panoramic view from the covered rooftop, and a terrace on the second floor that leads to a comfortable baraza overflowing with colorful cushions. The nicest of the rooms has a four-poster bed and balconies on two sides. ⊠ *Shela,* ☎ *02/442–1171 or 02/445–013,* ℻ *02/445–010. 5 rooms. Dining room. AE, DC, V.*

$$$ 🏨 **Shela House.** Favored by families, this beautiful old house has three floors of rooms huddled around a bougainvillea-scented courtyard. There's a nursery, a playroom, and a library filled with children's books. Rooms fill up, so book far in advance. ⊠ *Shela,* ☎ *02/442– 171 or 02/445–013,* ℻ *02/445–010. 6 rooms. Dining room, library. AE, DC, V.*

$$ 🏨 **New Lamu Palace Hotel.** This Swahili-style hotel on the waterfront is run by the same owner as Petley's Inn, but it lacks the charm. The smallish rooms do have air-conditioning, however. The restaurant and bar are handy if you're looking for someplace to relax. The hotel sponsors a beach party on Manda Island on Friday and Saturday nights. ⊠ *Kenyatta Rd., Lamu,* ☎ *0121/33272,* ℻ *0121/33104. 17 rooms. Restaurant, bar. AE, DC, V.*

$ 🏨 **Casuarina Rest House.** In a former police station, this waterfront lodging has a large rooftop terrace. Rooms are spacious, and the place is well managed. ⊠ *Off Kenyatta Rd., Lamu,* ☎ *0121/33123. 17 rooms. Dining room.*

$ 🏨 **Yumbe House.** In a beautifully restored building on a side street near the Swahili House Museum, this private house is great place to stay in Lamu. The central courtyard keeps all the rooms cool. ⊠ *On street opposite Donkey Sanctuary, Lamu,* ☎ *0121/33101,* ℻ *0121/33300. 17 rooms. Dining room. No credit cards.*

Nightlife and the Arts

Nightlife in the Lamu area is largely confined to bars, although a few venues offer dancing on Friday and Saturday nights. In Lamu, **Petley's Inn** (⌂ Harambee Rd., ☎ 0121/33107) attracts a crowd on weekends. Shela's top watering hole is at **Peponi's Hotel** (⌂ Shela, ☎ 0121/33154 or 0121/33421). Both places have cold beers that taste great on a sultry evening.

On weekends those in the mood for dancing head to the **Civil Servants Club** (⌂ Harambee Ave., Lamu, ☎ no phone). If you're in the mood for staying out all night, take the shuttle from the **New Lamu Palace Hotel** (Kenyatta Rd., Lamu, ☎ 0121/33272) to the beach party on nearby Manda Island.

Shopping

Jahazi Trading Company (⌂ Shela, ☎ 0121/32201) will delight anyone with an eye for beautiful things. Some were made here, while others were imported from Pakistan. Antique kilims, cedar chests, and intricately carved doors are among the items on display. The **Wildebeeste Workshops** (⌂ Lamu, ☎ 121/32261) have beautiful locally made batik fabrics. Founded in 1989, the gallery is where locals work with artists from around the world to learn how to make prints, weave tapestries, and hand-bind books. Get your reading material at **Lamu Book Center** (⌂ Harambee Ave., ☎ no phone). In the southern part of town, it's the only good source for books beyond the Lamu Museum.

Side Trips from Lamu

Kiwayu Island

This strip of sand is 50 km (31 mi) northeast of Lamu. The main attraction of Kiwayu Island is its proximity to **Kiunga Marine National Reserve,** a marine park encompassing Kiwayu Bay. The confluence of two major ocean currents creates unique ecological conditions that nurture three marine habitats—mangroves, sea-grass beds, and coral reefs. Here you have a chance of catching a glimpse of the most endangered mammal in Kenya, the manatee. Because of its tasty flesh, this gentle giant has been hunted to the point of extinction all along Africa's eastern coast.

LODGING

$$$$ 🏨 **Kiwayu Safari Village.** One of the most romantic destinations in Kenya, Kiwayu Safari Village is a collection of thatch-roof bandas facing the northern tip of Kiwayu Island. The cottages are vast, with views of the lagoon from the hammocks hanging on the private verandas. For dinner sample local delicacies such as giant mangrove crabs or sweet rock oysters. The area is known for its deep-sea fishing—record-setting sailfish, marlin, and tuna have been caught here. The hotel is very near the Kiunga Marine National Reserve, where coral reefs offer great snorkeling. Book far in advance for holidays. ⌂ *Kiwayu Island,* ☎ *02/503–030 or 02/503–043,* ℻ *02/503–149,* 🕸 *www.kiwayu.com. 22 cottages. Restaurant, bar, shop. AE, DC, MC, V. Closed mid-Apr.– June.*

$$$$ 🏨 **Munira Island Camp.** The name is Arabic for "light of the moon," which might refer to this lodge on the tip of Kiwayu Island being lighted at night by gas lanterns. It's certainly rustic—there's no electricity, and water is delivered by donkeys. The spacious bandas, constructed of local materials, have lovely views. Many people come here for the spectacular snorkeling at nearby Kunga Marine National Reserve. Two dhows allow you to cruise along the bay, and a speedboat brings you to the

best spots for deep-sea fishing. ✉ *Kiwayu Island*, ☎ *02/512–213*, FAX *02/512–543. 10 cottages. Dining room, snorkeling, boating, fishing. AE, DC, V.*

Manda Island

Just across the channel from Lamu, the mostly uninhabited Manda Island once held one of the area's largest cities. The once-thriving community of **Takwa** was abandoned in the 17th century, and archaeologists have yet to discover why. Reached by taking a dhow up a baobob tree-lined creek, the ruins are a popular day trip from Lamu and Shela.

LODGING

$$$$ 🔝 **Blue Safari Club.** For more than two decades, word of mouth has been the only advertising this hideaway required. A line of thatch-roof bungalows on a sandy spit on the northern shore of Manda Island, the Blue Safari Club specializes in water sports, especially snorkeling and scuba diving. Sail around the ocean in the dhow, or head out in the speed boat on a deep-sea fishing adventure. The lodge is run by Bruno Brighetti, who treats you like a personal guest. Only 24 people can stay here at any given time, making this feel like a private beach. ✉ *Manda Island*, ☎ *02/338–838*, FAX *02/218–939*, WEB *www.bluesafariclub.com. 10 cottages. Restaurant, bar, fishing, shop. AE, DC, MC, V. Closed May–Sept.*

Pate Island

The island of Pate, about 25 km (16 mi) northeast of Lamu, holds the ruins of several ancient Swahili settlements. Here you'll find **Siyu,** a small fishing village where you can see the Omani-style walls of an immense fort. Cannons still rest in the grass nearby. Houses excavated in the last few decades indicate that Siyu was an important cultural center for the archipelago from the 17th to the 18th centuries.

Even older than Siyu is the 8th-century settlement of **Shanga,** which can be visited on an organized tour. Excavations suggest a sophisticated culture prevailed, as the architecturally advanced buildings show evidence of plumbing for both hot and cold water. Clothing was intricately laced with gold and silver, and furniture was inlaid with ivory. Beautifully carved doors studded with brass are testimony to their craftsmanship. The origins of Shanga are still unclear, but a legend among the people of neighboring Siyu Island is that the town was founded by traders from Shanghai, thus the name Shanga. Chinese porcelain has been found among the ruins.

On the northern tip of the island are the ruins of **Faza,** which shows signs of having been occupied in the 11th century. Note the beautiful *qibla* in the ruins of the Kunjanya Mosque.

Lamu A to Z

To research prices, get advice from other travelers, and book travel arrangements, visit www.fodors.com.

AIR TRAVEL TO AND FROM LAMU

Kenya Airways has daily flights from Nairobi. Airkenya has frequent flights to Lamu and Kiwayu from Nairobi, Mombasa, and Malindi. It also offers hops from Lamu to Kiwayu.

➤ CARRIERS: **Airkenya** (✉ Harambee Ave., Lamu, ☎ 0121/33445). **Kenya Airways** (✉ Kenyatta Ave., Lamu, ☎ 0121/32040).

BOAT AND DHOW TRAVEL

Most hotels can arrange for a trip by dhow from Lamu to Shela or Matondoni. The price should be in the range of Ksh 400–Ksh 1,500, depending on the distance. You can also head to neighboring islands such as Manta (about Ksh 300), Manda Moto (about Ksh 1,500), and Pate (about Ksh 5,000). More distant destinations, such as Kiwayu, are more expensive. A trip to that island can set you back Ksh 12,000.

BUS TRAVEL TO AND FROM LAMU
Taking a bus from Mombasa to Lamu is a risky endeavor. Because of attacks by *shiftas* (thieves), a convoy of buses forms near Garson, and the group is escorted to Lamu by armed guards. If you can't fly, try TSS Buses. At Makowe the bus will drop you at a jetty, where boats ferry you to Lamu for less than Ksh 100.

➤ BUS COMPANIES: **TSS Buses** (⊠ Digo Rd., Mombasa ☎ 011/224–541).

CAR TRAVEL
If you have a four-wheel-drive vehicle, you can take the road from Mombasa to Lamu, but beware the danger of being robbed. At Garson you should join the convoy of buses being escorted by armed guards. Talk to the police in Malindi before you venture farther north along the road.

FESTIVALS AND SEASONAL EVENTS
The Maulidi festival, marking the birth of Muhammad, has been celebrated on Lamu for more than a century. Dhow races, poetry readings, and other events take place around the town's main mosques. Maulidi, which takes place in the spring, attracts pilgrims from all over Kenya.

HOLIDAYS
October 10 is Moi Day, and October 20, Kenyatta Day. December 12 is Jamhuri (Independence Day). The period of Ramadan may cause some places to be closed until sunset. The date of Ramadan is decided by the lunar calendar, and the fasting period begins 11 days earlier every year. Try to get here toward the end of Ramadan, when a huge feast and party, the Eid al Fitr, brings everyone out to the streets.

MAIL AND SHIPPING
The main post office in Lamu is south of the jetty on Harambee Avenue. It's open weekdays 8–12:30 and 2–5, Saturday 9–noon.

➤ POST OFFICES: **Lamu** (⊠ Harambee Ave.).

MONEY MATTERS
The Standard Chartered Bank on the waterfront has terribly slow service. You're better off cashing traveler's checks at your hotel.

SAFETY
The best way to see Lamu town is on foot, but you should not walk alone at night. Crime is rare in this part of Kenya, but it's better to be on the safe side.

TELEPHONES
You'll find public phones in front of the post office on Harambee Avenue. The area code for Lamu is 0121. If you are calling Lamu from outside Kenya, dial the country code, 254, the area code, 121, and the local number.

Dar es Salaam means "haven of peace" in Arabic, and that's just what you'll find in this bustling port city on the Indian Ocean. Although it has grown to become Tanzania's most important commercial center, Dar es Salaam still recalls its origins as a fishing village. The reason is the city's inhabitants, who go out of their way to make newcomers feel at home. When someone says *"Karibu!"* when you meet, they are saying "Welcome!"

By Kim Beury

S ITTING BESIDE A SPARKLING BAY, Dar es Salaam calls to mind
its origins as a fishing village. The harbor is crowded with the
hand-hewn canoes and triangular-sailed dhows that have distinguished the region for centuries. The palm-lined shore is lively with
men selling freshly caught fish, mending giant nets, and scrubbing
down their boats, while women nearby are roasting crayfish over open
fires or stirring pots of soup.

The tiny boats now must share the harbor with mammoth tankers, as
the sleepy village has been transformed into one of East Africa's busiest ports. The country's major commercial center, Dar es Salaam has
also become its largest city, home to more than 3.5 million inhabitants.
Dar es Salaam also serves as the seat of government during the very
slow move to Dodoma, which was named the official capital in 1973.
The legislature resides in Dodoma, but most government offices are
still found in Dar es Salaam.

In the early 1860s, Sultan Seyyid Majid of Zanzibar visited what was
then the isolated fishing village of Mzizima, on the Tanzanian coast.
Anxious to have a protected port on the mainland, Majid began constructing a palace here in 1865. The city, poised to compete with
neighboring ports such as Bagamoyo and Kilwa, suffered a setback after
the sultan died in 1870. His successor, his half-brother Seyyid Barghash,
had little interest in the city, and its royal buildings fell into ruins. Only
the Old Boma, which once housed royal guests, still survives.

The city remained a small port until Germany moved its colonial capital here in 1891 and began constructing roads, administrative offices,
and many of the public buildings that remain in use today. The Treaty
of Versailles granted Great Britain control of the region in 1916, but
that country added comparatively little to the city's infrastructure during its 45-year rule.

Tanzania gained its independence in 1961. During the years that followed, President Julius Nyerere, who focused on issues such as edu-
cation and health care, allowed the capital city to fall into a decline
that lasted into the 1980s. When Benjamin William Mkapa took office in 1985, his market-oriented reforms helped to revitalize the city.
The city continues to evolve—those who visited only a few years ago
will be startled by the changes.

As more and more historic buildings such as the Old Boma are refurbished and new hotels and restaurants are built, Dar es Salaam is lur-
ing visitors that once might have scurried past on their way to the
Serengeti. It doesn't hurt that the city has a bustling waterfront, interesting
neighborhoods, and sights like the National Museum, which contains
the 1.7 million-year-old hominid skull discovered by Mary Leakey in
the Olduvai Gorge in 1959.

Pleasures and Pastimes

Beaches

The pristine beaches north and south of Dar es Salaam are irresistible
for those seeking the calm, cool waters of the Indian Ocean. Kunduchi
Beach and Oyster Bay, just north of Dar es Salaam, offer a range of
lodgings from thatch-roof bungalows to luxury high-rises. Open-air
bars, cafés, and restaurants sit so close to shore you can feel the sea
breeze. When you tire of swimming, you can snorkel around the coral
reefs or sail in dhows to small islands such as Bongoyo and Mbudya.
The coastline south of Dar es Salaam is less developed, and lodging is

more difficult to reach. However, the handful of peaceful cottages settled in the sand might be the perfect place to escape.

Dining

You can spend days sampling Dar es Salaam's remarkably varied cuisine. There's no need to spend a lot, as *hotelis* (cafés) offer heaping platefuls of African or Indian fare for less than Tsh 1,000. Typical *chakula* (food) for an East African meal includes *wali* (rice) or *ugali* (a slightly damp mound of breadlike ground corn) served with a meat, fish, or vegetable stew. A common side dish is *kachumbari*, a mixture of chopped tomatoes, onions, and cucumbers. Even less expensive are roadside stalls, such as those that line the harbor, offering snacks such as chicken and beef kebabs, roast corn on the cob, and *samosas*, triangular pastries stuffed with meat or vegetables. If you're in the mood for something sweet, try a doughnutlike *mandazi*. Wash it all down with a Safari, the local beer, or with *chai*, a hot tea served with milk, sugar, and various spices.

Should you be in the mood for something fancier, upscale hotels offer cosmopolitan meals and elaborate buffets for as much as Tsh 30,000. Even at the toniest of restaurants, reservations are rarely required. Restaurants in hotels generally are open until at least 10:30 PM, even on Sunday, while the hours of local restaurants vary.

CATEGORY	COST*
$$$$	over Tsh 13,500
$$$	Tsh 9,000–Tsh 13,500
$$	Tsh 4,500–Tsh 9,000
$	under Tsh 4,500

per person for a main course at dinner.

Lodging

Because Tanzania has been courting foreign investors, international hotel chains have been moving into Dar es Salaam. This is good news for travelers, who can now choose luxurious lodges with unforgettable views of the ocean or business hotels with high-tech conference centers. However, it has also signaled growing deterioration for some of the city's older establishments. For instance, several of Dar es Salaam's most famous hotels have either closed their doors, like the Kilimanjaro, or have become dark and dismal, such as the Embassy. There's no need to stay in a standard-issue room, however. As interest in "cultural tourism" grows, opportunities to stay with families in nearby villages are also increasing.

Rates nearly always include breakfast. Almost all rooms, even in hostels built with budget travelers in mind, have air-conditioning or at least strong ceiling fans. Most have private baths and, so they promise, hot water. There's been a strong push to modernize the city's communications system, so virtually all hotels offer access to E-mail. Advance booking is recommended, especially during the high season, which runs from June through August. Prices for hotels in the city don't vary from low to high season; some coastal resorts adjust their prices slightly.

CATEGORY	COST*
$$$$	over Tsh 135,000
$$$	Tsh 90,000–Tsh 135,000
$$	Tsh 45,000–Tsh 90,000
$	under Tsh 45,000

All prices are for a standard double room, excluding tax.

Shopping

Adventurous shoppers will have a field day in Dar es Salaam. Opportunities to shop abound, from Western-style boutiques to sprawling open-air markets where you can pick up anything from Zanzibar spices to high-heel shoes. Items to keep an eye out for include ebony carvings, batik weavings, and *kangas,* the colorful cotton wraps East African women wear as shawls or use to carry babies on their backs. You can also find Tanzania's finest coffees and teas.

Tourists and locals alike are expected to bargain with street vendors and merchants in markets and smaller shops. Keep in mind that prices generally are marked 50% above what the seller hopes to get. Try to agree on a price about 25% less than what the merchant is asking. If you are successful in paying less than that, even the merchant will be impressed. Always be courteous; bargaining here is carried out in a friendly manner. Be wary of the curio vendor pleading for your patronage with a heartrending story about the need for money—it's a sales technique used on unsuspecting tourists.

EXPLORING DAR ES SALAAM

To get your bearings, think of Dar es Salaam as being split into three sections. Central Dar es Salaam is adjacent to the harbor. To the north of the city center is the Msasani Peninsula, which holds upscale neighborhoods such as Kunduchi and Oyster Bay. Nearly all points of interest outside the city center are found here. To the south you'll find the beaches that begin past Kigamboni.

Finding your way around the Dar es Salaam area can be difficult, even with the best maps. Many major roads change names after a few blocks, and some side streets have no names at all. Businesses don't use street addresses, only post office box numbers. To avoid getting lost, it's best to know the cross streets of where you are headed, as well as some nearby landmarks.

Because of the confusing streets, as well as the heavy pedestrian traffic and lack of parking, renting a car to tour this bustling city is a hassle. Taxis, found outside larger hotels and at busy intersections, are a better option. It costs about Tsh 1,500 for a short ride within Dar es Salaam. An hour-long trip with several stops around town runs about Tsh 5,000. Hiring a cab for the day, which can include trips outside the city, can cost nearly Tsh 30,000. The easiest way to get around the city center, however, is by foot.

For destinations north of the city center, taxis are quite reasonable as well (about Tsh 3,500 to Oyster Bay, for example). Another option is taking a *dala-dala.* These minivans are crowded and slower, depart only when full, but are much less expensive than taxis (about Tsh 150 to Oyster Bay). The main dala-dala stations are New Posta, on Maktaba Street in front of the main post office, and Old Posta, on Sokoine Drive opposite the Lutheran church. Destinations are noted on the windshields. Once on board, you can ask fellow passengers when to get off.

The beach areas south of Dar es Salaam are accessed by taking a very short ferry ride from the city center harbor to Kigamboni, where taxis and dala-dalas transport you to your destination. The ferry carries both pedestrians and vehicles. The Kigamboni Ferry Terminal is on the harbor where Ocean Road meets Kivukoni Front. Another option for transport to southern beach resorts is a chartered 15-minute flight from the city, which can be arranged when you book your hotel.

Great Itineraries

IF YOU HAVE 2 DAYS

If you have just a day, explore the center of the city. Start by strolling along the harbor, stopping to check out the catch of the day at **Mzizima Fish Market.** The two spires along Sokoine Drive are the **Azania Front Lutheran Church** and **St. Joseph's Cathedral.** After stopping for lunch, discover more about the history of the region by ducking into the **National Museum.** After checking out the Swahili neighborhoods, look for souvenirs at the colorful **Kariakoo Market.**

On your second day head north along Bagamoyo Road to the **Makumbusho Village Museum,** where you can see examples of Tanzania's various traditional dwellings, and then continue on to **Mwenge Market,** where artisans carve the finest ebony figures you'll find in the area. In the afternoon drive north to the Msasani Peninsula. Here you can learn to sail a dhow, snorkel in Mbudya Marine Conservation Area, or explore uninhabited Bongoyo Island.

IF YOU HAVE 3 DAYS

With a little more time to spend you also can head up the coast to the quiet town of **Bagamoyo,** about 70 km (44 mi) from Dar es Salaam. Relax on the palm-lined shore and snorkel in the cool Indian Ocean.

When to Tour

Dar es Salaam isn't the reason many people come to Tanzania, but a lot of tourists stop here en route to Zanzibar and other destinations. Beach resorts are popular, so make reservations at least two weeks ahead. Temperatures don't fluctuate much in Dar es Salaam, thanks to the region's tropical climate. The most pleasant months are June through August, when you'll find cloudless skies and temperatures hovering around 29°C (85°F). The surrounding months are hotter, especially from October through February. The rainiest months are from March through May and from October through December.

Numbers in the text correspond to numbers in the margin and on the Dar es Salaam map.

Central Dar es Salaam

To find your way around Central Dar es Salaam, use the Askari Monument, at the intersection of Samora Avenue and Azikiwe Street as a compass. Most sights are within walking distance. Four blocks northeast on Samora Avenue you'll find the National Museum and Botanical Gardens, while about seven blocks southwest stands the Clock Tower, another a good landmark. One block southeast is Sokoine Drive, which empties into Kivukoni Front as it follows the harbor. Farther along Kivukoni Front becomes Ocean Road.

Along Samora Avenue and Sokoine Drive you'll find banks, pharmacies, grocery stores, and shops selling everything from clothing to curios. Northwest of Samora Avenue, around India Street, Jamhuri Street, and Libya Street, is the busy Swahili neighborhood where merchants sell all kinds of items, including Tanzania's best kangas. Farther west you'll find the large Kariakoo Market.

A Good Walk

Begin your walk in the center of town at the **Askari Monument** ①. Walk northeast along Samora Avenue (listed as Samora Machel Avenue on some maps) until you come to Shaaban Robert Street. Less than a block southeast is the **National Museum** ②. Return to Samora Avenue, where you'll come to the **Botanical Gardens** ③. On your right you'll see **Karimjee Hall** ④. The next street you come to is Luthuli Road, where

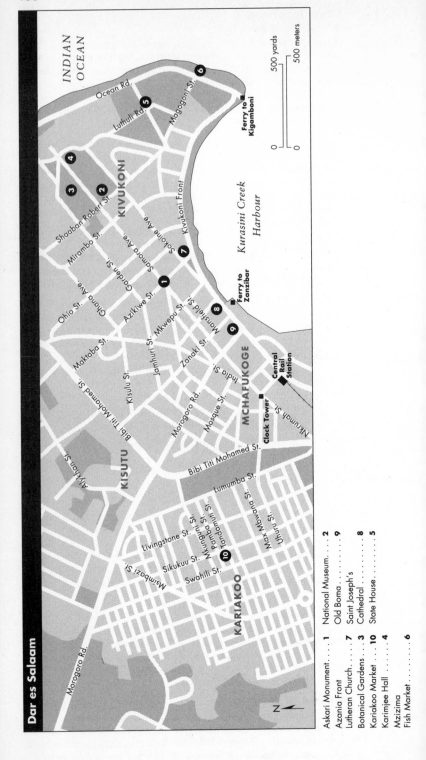

Dar es Salaam

INDIAN OCEAN

Ocean Rd.

Luthuli Rd.

Magogoni St.

Ferry to Kigamboni

500 yards
500 meters

KIVUKONI

Shaaban Robert St.

Mirambo St.

Samora Ave.

Garden St.

Sokoine Ave.

Kivukoni Front

Kurasini Creek Harbour

Ohio St.

Ghana Ave.

Azikiwe St.

Maktoba St.

Jamhuri St.

Mkwepu St.

Mansfield St.

Zanaki St.

Ferry to Zanzibar

Kisutu St.

India St.

MCHAFUKOGE

Central Rail Station

Bibi Titi Mohamed St.

Morogoro Rd.

Mosque St.

Clock Tower

Nkrumah St.

KISUTU

Aykhan St.

Lumumba St.

Livingstone St.

Mkunguni St.

Pomba St.

Tandamuti St.

Max Mwano St.

Uhuru St.

Sikukuu St.

Swahili St.

Msimbazi St.

KARIAKOO

Morogoro Rd.

N

Askari Monument....**1** National Museum....**2**
Azania Front
Lutheran Church....**7** Old Boma....**9**
Botanical Gardens...**3** Saint Joseph's
Kariakoo Market...**10** Cathedral.........**8**
Karimjee Hall.......**4** State House.......**5**
Mzizima
Fish Market........**6**

you can see the now-closed Ocean Road Hospital, built by Germany in the late 1800s. Turn right on Luthuli Road, heading south toward the harbor. You'll pass the **State House** ⑤ on your left before you reach a somewhat confusing intersection where Luthuli Street intersects with Shaaban Robert Street and Madaraka Street, on the right, and Magogoni Street, on the left. Turn left on Magogoni Street and stay on it until it runs into Ocean Road. The lively **Mzizima Fish Market** ⑥, where locals sell fresh catch from the Indian Ocean, sits on the shore.

Continue down Ocean Road until it ends at the bustling Kigamboni Ferry Terminal. Turn right and stroll along Kivukoni Front, taking note of several century-old German buildings still in use today, including those that house the country's ministries of foreign affairs and justice. On the corner of Mirambo Street and Kivukoni Front you'll see the once-grand Kilimanjaro Hotel, built just after the country gained its independence. It suffered a sad decline in the 1980s and is now shuttered. Just beyond stands **Azania Front Lutheran Church** ⑦. Farther down Kivukoni Front becomes Sokoine Drive, where you'll find **St. Joseph's Cathedral** ⑧. The Zanzibar Ferry Terminal is just across the street on the harbor. Follow Sokoine Drive until you reach Morogoro Road, where you'll see the city's oldest building, the **Old Boma** ⑨. Across Morogoro Road you'll find the handsome City Hall building.

If you're in the mood for shopping, venture into the surrounding neighborhoods, where you'll find streets lined with busy stores. Continue along Sokoine Drive until you reach the Central Rail Station. Turn right on Railway Street, and you'll reach the landmark Clock Tower. Head north on India Street until you reach Mosque Street, where you should turn left. On the next two blocks you will pass several Muslim houses of worship, including Ibaddhi Mosque and Memon Mosque. Turn right on Jamhuri Street, then left on Morogoro Road. Walk up Morogoro Road (crossing Bibi Titi Mohamed Street) until you come to Msimbazi Street. Take a left, and then take another left onto Sikukuu Street. There you'll find the large **Kariakoo Market** ⑩, between Mkunguni and Tandamuti streets.

TIMING

This walk can take as little as two hours if you stop only briefly at each sight, but it's better to budget an entire day if you have the slightest interest in wandering around the museums or perusing the markets. The walk is by no means strenuous, as the terrain is flat, but you should wear comfortable shoes. The streets are dusty, and the weather is usually hot and humid, so carry drinking water and bring a hat if you are sensitive to the sun.

Sights to See

❶ **Askari Monument.** This bronze statue was erected by the British in 1927 in memory of African troops who died during World War I. (The word *askari* means "soldier" in Swahili.) It stands on the site of a monument erected by Germany to celebrate its victory here in 1888. It stood only five years before being demolished in 1916. ✉ *Samora Ave. and Azikiwe St.*

❼ **Azania Front Lutheran Church.** With a red-tile spire that soars above the surrounding rooftops, this church was built by German missionaries in 1898. The whitewashed building is still one of Dar es Salaam's most recognizable landmarks. Its lovely gardens are a nice place to retreat from the city's crowded streets. ✉ *Kivukoni Front between Azikiwe St. and Pamba Rd.,* ☎ *no phone.*

❸ **Botanical Gardens.** Though small and sometimes in need of weeding, this collection of indigenous plants is a great respite from the dusty city. The region's first director of agriculture planted the gardens in 1893. This is one of the few places outside the Seychelles where you can see the coco de mer, a palm tree that can live for more than 200 years. ⊠ *Samora Ave. at Shaaban Robert St.,* ☎ *no phone.* ⌑ *Free.*

❿ **Kariakoo Market.** The pungent scent of spices from Zanzibar overwhelms you as you wander around this sprawling market near Mnazi Mmoja Park. Vendors here sell everything from fresh produce to kitchenware to bicycles. It's crowded, so keep an eye on your wallet or handbag. ⊠ *Between Mkunguni and Tandamuti Sts.,* ☎ *no phone.* ☾ *Daily early morning–evening.*

❹ **Karimjee Hall.** The British government constructed this impressive building to house its legislative council when it took charge of the city in 1916. Tanzania housed its own parliament here after gaining independence in 1961. The beloved Julius Nyerere was sworn in here as the country's first president. ⊠ *Between Samora Ave. and Sokoine Dr., near Ocean Rd.*

OFF THE
BEATEN PATH

MAKUMBUSHO VILLAGE MUSEUM – This outdoor museum, about 10 km (6 mi) from the center of the city, showcases several types of traditional homes found throughout Tanzania. Visitors are welcome to walk through the dwellings, where artisans can be found painting, weaving baskets, and carving figures. Traditional dances are performed Thursday and Saturday at 4. ⊠ *10 km (6 mi) from city center on New Bagamoyo Rd.,* ☎ *no phone.* ⌑ *Tsh 2,400.* ☾ *Daily 9:30–6.*

---

❻ **Mzizima Fish Market.** Everything from red snapper to barracuda is sold in this lively outdoor market right on the harbor. The air is thick with smoke from the dozens of sweating merchants frying the day's catch over open fires. You can't miss the market, as it is set amid wooden fishing boats and large nets spread out to dry. ⊠ *Ocean Rd. near Kivukoni Front,* ☎ *no phone.* ☾ *Daily dawn–dusk.*

★ ❷ **National Museum.** Originally built by the British in 1940 as the King George V Memorial Museum, the unassuming site became Tanzania's National Museum when the country won its independence in 1961. A must-see for first-time visitors to the city, the museum displays the 1.7 million-year-old hominid skull archaeologist Mary Leakey discovered in 1959 and other significant Olduvai Gorge fossil discoveries. There are also exhibits on the region's natural history, the Zanzibar slave trade, and 19th-century East Africa explorers, including Dr. David Livingstone. ⊠ *Between Samora Ave. and Sokoine Dr., near Ocean Rd.,* ☎ *022/212–2030.* ⌑ *Tsh 1,800.* ☾ *Daily 9:30–6.*

❾ **Old Boma.** The city's oldest building, the Old Boma was constructed in 1867 to serve as a lodging for guests of Sultan Seyyid Majid, whose palace stood next door. Be sure to note the coral walls and Zanzibari door. Only three years after the structure was completed, the sultan died, and the city he had constructed here fell into ruins. ⊠ *Sokoine Ave. and Morogoro Rd.,* ☎ *no phone.*

❽ **Saint Joseph's Cathedral.** Built by missionaries at the beginning of the 19th century, this Gothic-style church keeps watch over the harbor. The imposing structure still contains many of the original German inscriptions. ⊠ *Sokoine Dr. near Zanaki St.,* ☎ *no phone.*

❺ **State House.** Now the home of the president, this sprawling structure was erected by Germany in the late 1890s to house the colonial governor. It was rebuilt in 1922 after the British nearly destroyed it during World War I. Note the graceful arches, a nod to the architectural style of East Africa. ☒ *Between Magogoni St. and Ocean Rd.,* ☏ *no phone.*

DINING

$$$–$$$$ ✕ **Karambezi Café.** Set on a coral cliff, this open-air restaurant treats you to what is perhaps the area's best ocean views. A crowd that includes both locals and tourists heads to this lively establishment in the Sea Cliff Hotel for an elaborate buffet that mixes traditional African cuisine with more Continental fare. Live guitar music blends with sounds of crashing waves Tuesday, Thursday, Saturday, and Sunday nights. It's 20 minutes north of the city. ☒ *Toure Dr., Msasani Peninsula,* ☏ *022/260–0380. MC, V.*

$$$–$$$$ ✕ **Tradewinds.** In the Royal Palm, this elegant steak house offers candlelighted tables, a wide selection of wine and liquor, and attentive waiters who tend to your every need. The menu, featuring delicious imported steaks and fresh local seafood, is one of the best in Dar es Salaam. The spectacular salad bar is unmatched by any other in the city. ☒ *Ohio St. and Ali Hassan Mwinyi Rd.,* ☏ *022/211–2416. AE, MC, V. Closed Sun. No lunch.*

$$–$$$$ ✕ **Serengeti.** Sumptuous buffets have made this restaurant at the Royal
★ Palm a favorite among tourists as well as business executives. The cuisine changes nightly—Monday, Thursday, and Sunday are reserved for Asian fare, while Tuesday, Wednesday, and Friday are the nights to go for European-style meals. Saturday the chef turns his attention to the foods of East Africa. A champagne breakfast is a Sunday morning ritual among regular patrons. ☒ *Ohio St. and Ali Hassan Mwinyi Rd.,* ☏ *022/211–2416. AE, MC, V.*

$$–$$$ ✕ **Bandari Grill.** Long one of Dar es Salaam's best values, this place attracts the city's movers and shakers. Many business deals are cut over the "power lunch" served on the mezzanine. The seemingly endless buffet features traditional Tanzanian cuisine as well as selections from other countries. The beef tenderloin tips with king prawns is always a favorite. There's also a sports bar where executives kick back after a long day. Enjoy live music most evenings. ☒ *Azikiwi St. and Sokoine Dr.,* ☏ *022/211–7051. AE, MC, V.*

$$–$$$ ✕ **Sawasdee.** With a name that means "welcome" in Thai, Sawasdee
★ has a peaceful atmosphere and attentive service that make it one of the best eateries in the city. Tanzania's first and perhaps only Thai restaurant, Sawasdee serves authentic dishes—duck in brown sauce, fish in ginger, chicken in green curry—prepared by a highly esteemed chef from Bangkok. The ninth-floor dining overlooks the sparkling lights of the harbor. ☒ *Azikiwi St. and Sokoine Dr.,* ☏ *022/211–7050. AE, MC, V. No lunch weekdays.*

$$–$$$ ✕ **The Arches.** Set amid towering palms, this thatch-roof restaurant puts you within a stone's throw of the beach. The party's always in full swing, making this the perfect place to bring a group of friends. The seafood platter is especially good, but the beef curry, fish masala, and ginger chicken also receive high marks. After dinner enjoy a drink at the Oyster Bay Hotel's open-air bar. ☒ *Toure Dr., Oyster Bay,* ☏ *022/260–0352. V.*

$ ✕ **Amrapali.** Treat yourself to a truly authentic East African meal in this cozy restaurant cooled by lazily turning ceiling fans. The windows and doors of the colorful dining room are thrown open to let in the sights and sounds of the busy Indian neighborhood, about a 10-minute walk from the Askari Monument. Sample the *bilian kuku* (spiced rice with chicken) and wash it down with a favorite traditional drink, spiced coconut milk served ice cold. ⊠ *Zanaki St. near Libya St.,* ☎ *no phone. No credit cards.*

$ ✕ **Salamander Coffee House.** On one of the city's busiest corners, this lively outdoor café puts you right in the center of the action. It's a great place to watch the crowds go by as you enjoy a meal hot off the grill. It is popular among travelers looking for others with whom to share tales and tips. ⊠ *Samora Ave. and Mkwepu St.,* ☎ *no phone. No credit cards.*

$ ✕ **Steers.** The best fast-food joint in town, Steers serves up burgers and fries as well as fried chicken and pizza in an appropriately colorful atmosphere. It's filled with tourists stopping by for some comfort food. ⊠ *Corner of Samora Ave. and Ohio St.,* ☎ *022/212–2855. No credit cards.*

LODGING

Central Dar es Salaam

$$$$ ☷ **Holiday Inn Dar es Salaam.** With its eye on corporate travelers, this luxury hotel opened in the heart of the city's business district in 2001. There are plenty of amenities for traveling executives, from secretarial services to meeting rooms. Rooms have data ports and generously sized desks. The upper-floor rooms overlook the nearby Botanical Gardens. ⊠ *Garden Ave.,* ☎ *022/213–7575,* ℻ *022/213–9070,* 🕸 *www.southernsun.com. 152 rooms, 2 suites. Restaurant, bar, room service, in-room safes, pool, exercise room, shops, business services, meeting room, travel services. AE, MC, V.*

$$$$ ☷ **New Africa Hotel.** Dar es Salaam's oldest lodging, the imposing white structure once known as the Kaiserhoff was built by the Germans in 1906. More subdued in style than the Royal Palm, it has comfortably furnished rooms with views of the harbor. Within walking distance of the city's financial and governmental buildings, the hotel caters to corporate travelers. There are several meeting rooms and a business center that lets you connect to colleagues back home. ⊠ *Azikiwi St. and Sokoine Dr.,* ☎ *022/211–7050,* ℻ *022/211–6731,* 🕸 *www.newafricahotel.com. 19 rooms, 7 suites. 2 restaurants, bar, room service, casino, shops, laundry service, business services, meeting rooms, travel services, airport shuttle. AE, V.*

$$$$ ☷ **Royal Palm.** The most luxurious hotel in the city center, this well-
★   run establishment offers anything a business traveler might want. Rooms are spacious and furnished with the dark woods that call to mind the style of eras past. With relaxing afternoons spent sunning by the pool or reading on the veranda, surrounded by extravagant gardens that extend to the only golf course in the center of the city, you may forget the hustle and bustle just outside the front doors. ⊠ *Ohio St. and Ali Hassan Mwinyi Rd.,* ☎ *022/211–2416,* ℻ *022/211–3981,* 🕸 *www.royalpalmdar.com. 250 rooms, 7 suites. 2 restaurants, 2 bars, deli, room service, pool, gym, shops, business services, meeting rooms, travel services, airport shuttle. AE, MC, V.*

$$ ☷ **Peacock Hotel.** Across from Mnazi Mmoja Park, this small hotel is a good choice for budget-minded travelers. It has clean rooms and attentive service. There's a lounge on the ground floor, and the rooftop bar has the added bonus of views of the city. ⊠ *Bibi Titi Mohamed St. at Libya St.,* ☎ *022/211–4126,* ℻ *022/211-7962,* 🕸 *www.peacock-hotel.co.tz. 54 rooms, 4 executive suites. Restaurant, bar, café, lounge, room service, business services, meeting rooms, travel services. AE, V.*

$ ⊞ **Econo Lodge.** The best of the budget hotels, this comfortable little lodging is close to cafés filled with young travelers trading safari stories. Simply furnished rooms are clean and spacious. ⊠ *Band St. and Libya St.,* ☎ *022/211–6048,* 𝕱𝕬𝕏 *022/211–6053. 21 rooms. Dining room, lounge. No credit cards.*

$ ⊞ **Luther House.** Near the harbor, this little hostel is an ideal place to meet backpackers. Rooms are clean, and most have a balcony overlooking the Azania Front Lutheran Church. The friendly staff is nononsense when it comes security. ⊠ *Sokoine Dr.,* ☎ *022/212–0734. 20 rooms. Restaurant. No credit cards.*

Northern Beaches

$$$$ ✕⊞ **Golden Tulip Dar es Salaam.** Set on a coral cliff, the coast's newest luxury hotel welcomes you with a white-columned lobby with lots of windows overlooking the Indian Ocean. The bright and airy rooms are furnished in Swahili style. Nearly all have grand views. The hotel is a 15-minute drive north of Dar es Salaam. ⊠ *Toure Dr., Msasani Peninsula,* ☎ *022/260–1442,* 𝕱𝕬𝕏 *022/260–1443.* 𝐖𝐄𝐁 *www.goldentulip.com. 91 rooms. 2 restaurants, bar, room service, pool, hair salon, shops, business services, convention center, meeting rooms, travel services, airport shuttle. AE, V.*

$$$ ✕⊞ **Oyster Bay Hotel.** Only a few kilometers north of the city center, this seaside hotel feels worlds away. Set amid bamboo gardens so exquisite that many couples are married here, the buildings are topped with thatch-covered roofs. The open-air restaurant and bar, with views of the ocean, are cooled by salty breezes. Original batik wall hangings, ebony carvings, and dark-wood furnishings make each of the rooms unique. The beach itself is not as pristine as those found a little farther north, but the hotel's proximity to the city makes it popular. ⊠ *Toure Dr., Oyster Bay,* ☎ *022/260–0352,* 𝕱𝕬𝕏 *022/260–0347.* 𝐖𝐄𝐁 *www.tanzaniantravel.com. 45 rooms. 4 restaurants, bar, room service, pool, hair salon, spa, 18-hole golf course, health club, shops, business services, meeting rooms, travel services. AE, DC, V.*

$$$ ✕⊞ **Sea Cliff.** Set high on a coral cliff, this sprawling hotel on the tip of the Msasani Peninsula isn't the kind of place where you simply sit in the sun. There is a wide range of amenities, everything from a bowling alley to a health spa. Rooms, many of which face the sea, are set among lush gardens. All are beautifully furnished with the dark woods of the colonial era. ⊠ *Toure Dr., Msasani Peninsula,* ☎ *022/260–0380,* 𝕱𝕬𝕏 *022/260–0419,* 𝐖𝐄𝐁 *www.hotelseacliff.com. 86 rooms, 4 suites. 3 restaurants, 2 bars, room service, pool, massage, bowling, health club, dive shop, shops, casino, business services, conference rooms, travel services. AE, V.*

$$ ✕⊞ **Bahari Beach Hotel.** On a peaceful beach about 30 km (19 mi)
★ north of the city, this palm-shaded resort wraps around a beautiful swimming pool. Lodgings are in coral-rock chalets with balconies that overlook the ocean. The restaurant specializes in seafood as well as Asian fare. ⊠ *Kunduchi,* ☎ *022/265–0352,* 𝕱𝕬𝕏 *022/265–0351. 100 rooms. 2 restaurants, 2 bars, room service, pool, tennis court, shops, business services, convention center, meeting rooms, travel services. No credit cards.*

$ ✕⊞ **Silver Sands.** A longtime favorite among budget-minded travelers, this hotel has rooms no more than a few steps from the shore. Breakfast is served outside on heavy wood tables with views of Pangavini Island. If it intrigues you, the staff will arrange for a boat so you can get a closer look. Scuba divers can visit the reefs of nearby Mbudya Marine Conservation Area. ⊠ *Kunduchi Beach,* ☎ *022/265–0567,* 𝕱𝕬𝕏 *022/265–0428.* 𝐖𝐄𝐁 *www.silversands.co.tz. 37 rooms. Restaurant, bar,* *room service, beach, dive center, snorkeling, camping, billiards, recreation room, travel services. AE, V.*

Southern Beaches

$$$$ ⊞ **Protea Amani Beach Hotel.** Thatch-roof cottages with verandas
★   that open out to extravagant gardens are the accommodations at this
hotel facing the Indian Ocean. Only 30 km (19 mi) south of the city
center, the hotel is on a pristine stretch of shoreline. The seafood in
the Amani Restaurant is considered some of the finest in the area. ⊠
30 km (19 mi) south of Dar es Salaam, ☏ *051/600–020,* FAX *051/602–
131.* WEB *www.protea-hotels.co.za. 10 suites. Restaurant, bar, room service, pool, snorkeling, business services, travel services, airport shuttle. AE, MC, V.*

$$$$ ⊞ **Rus Kutani.** With a dozen elegant bungalows, this lodging set in a
coastal forest has been popular for more than 25 years. The ocean is
close enough that the sound of the waves might lull you to sleep as
you relax on your private veranda. The furnishings, different in each
room, reflect the region's Swahili heritage. Outdoor activities, from
snorkeling to windsurfing to fishing for tuna and marlin, are popular
pastimes. Of course, you might only want to stroll along the palm-fringed
beach. Just 35 km (22 mi) south of the city center, the hotel is a quick
trip from Dar es Salaam. ⊠ *30 km (19 mi) south of Dar es Salaam,*
☏ *022/211–3480,* FAX *022/211–2794,* WEB *www.selous.com. Restaurant,
bar, room service, snorkeling, fishing, business services, travel services, airport shuttle. AE, MC, V.*

$ ⚠ **Kipepeo Camp.** Thatch-roof bandas only a few steps from the
beach are the best accommodations at this rustic seaside campground.
If you have brought along a tent, you'll also find plenty of campsites.
The Swimming Cow Pub is popular among backpackers. ⊠ *8 km (5
mi) south of Kigamboni Ferry Terminal,* ☏ *022/212–2931,* FAX *022/
211–9272,* WEB *www.kipepeocamp.com. Restaurant, bar, airport shuttle. No credit cards.*

NIGHTLIFE AND THE ARTS

The best places to find out what's going on in Dar es Salaam are the
weekly *Advertising Dar* (best for its live music listings), the bimonthly
Dar es Salaam Guide, and the monthly *What's Happening in Dar es
Salaam.* These free publications are found in hotels, restaurants, and
other establishments catering to tourists.

Bars

At the Royal Palm, **Kibo Bar** (⊠ Ohio St. and Ali Hassan Mwinyi Rd.,
☏ 022/211–2416) is a peaceful place to stop for drinks. Seated on the
veranda overlooking the hotel's beautiful gardens, you may forget the
hustle and bustle just outside the front doors. The **Q-Bar** (⊠ Haile Selassie St., Msasani Peninsula, ☏ 022/260–2150) is a laid-back place
where you can play eight ball on three pool tables. The rooftop bar at
Smokies Tavern (⊠ Chole Rd., Msasani Peninsula, ☏ no phone) is a
great place to share stories with other travelers. There's live music on
Thursday nights.

SHOPPING

The most popular area for shopping is along Samora Street, including
the few blocks on either side of the Askari Monument. You'll most likely
find anything you need in the stationery, fabric, shoe, appliance, drug

and many other specific-item stores or from street-side vendors, who sell wood carvings, postcards, leather goods, and more.

Markets

Mwenge Market. You can chat with artists as they work at this market on Bagamoyo Road. This is the best place in the city to find ebony carvings. ⊠ *New Bagamoyo Rd.,* ☎ *no phone.* ⊙ *Daily 9–5.*

Nyumba ya Sanaa. Batik wall hangings, wood carvings, and other items can be found in this large market, whose name is Swahili for "house of art." Many of the artists work on site, so you can ask them about their latest work or commission a new piece. The market can be a bit dreary but is well worth a look. ⊠ *Biti Titi Mohamed St. and Ohio St.,* ☎ *022/133–960.* ⊙ *Weekdays 8–5, weekends 10–4.*

Shopping Centers

Casanova Shops. This upscale shopping mall on the northern point of the Msasani Peninsula is a great place to browse for clothes, cosmetics, and jewelry. Some of the shops also have interesting handicrafts. ⊠ *Toure Dr., Msasani Peninsula,* ☎ *no phone.* ⊙ *Daily 10–5.*

The Slipway. North of the city center in the Msasani Peninsula, this waterfront shopping mall has shops selling imported goods ranging from best-selling books to high-tech computer games to European wines. Some stores specialize in fine local goods, such as jewelry made from locally mined tanzanite. ⊠ *West side of the Msasani Peninsula,* ☎ *022/260–0908.* ⊙ *Daily 10–9.*

Shoppers Plaza. North of the city on Old Bagamoyo Road, this western-style shopping center offers perhaps the widest variety of stores, including a supermarket that's great for stocking up on provisions before heading out into the bush. ⊠ *Old Bagamoyo Rd.,* ☎ *no phone.* ⊙ *Daily 10–9.*

SIDE TRIPS FROM DAR ES SALAAM

Bagamoyo

Bagamoyo, Tanzania's first capital, was always a place for people heading elsewhere. It was the last stop for explorers and missionaries before they headed inland, as well as the final destination for slave-trade caravans headed to Zanzibar. Its sad legacy makes the town's name, which means "crush down your heart," all the more poignant.

A quiet town about 70 km (44 mi) north of Dar es Salaam, Bagamoyo has a history dating to the 9th century, when trading started among the coastal communities for items such as fish and salt. Later, people from the interior arrived with elephant tusks, rhinoceros horns, tortoise shells, and leopard skins.

Bagamoyo's many historic sites include the **Holy Ghost Mission,** just north of town, East Africa's first Catholic mission. The seaside church, constructed in 1873, is where explorer Dr. David Livingstone's corpse was kept before it was shipped for burial in England. The 13th-century ruins of **Kaole,** 5 km (3 mi) south of Bagamoyo, are thought to include the oldest mosque on East Africa's mainland.

Lodging

$$ 🏨 **Paradise Holiday Resort.** Only a nearly deserted beach stands between this resort and the sparkling blue ocean. Elegant bungalows in traditional Swahili style offer a peaceful retreat. An outdoor restau-

rant serves up a menu of eclectic dishes. ☒ *Bagamoyo,* ☎ *023/244–0136,* FAX *023/244–0142,* WEB *www.paradiseresort.net 32 rooms. Restaurant, bar, pool, volleyball, snorkeling, business services, meeting rooms, travel services. AE, MC, V.*

$ 🔟 **Badeco Beach Hotel.** The friendly atmosphere of this beachfront hotel is typical of what you'll find along the Indian Ocean. The accommodations are simple compared to those in neighboring resorts, but the price is quite reasonable. The restaurant is known for its excellent seafood dishes. ☒ *Bagamoyo,* ☎ *05/244–018,* FAX *05/440–154. 15 rooms. Bar, restaurant, travel services. No credit cards.*

$ 🔟 **Travellers' Lodge.** Less expensive than the nearby luxury hotels, this cluster of small bungalows is a great budget option. ☒ *Box 275, Bagamoyo,* ☎ *05/244–0077,* FAX *05/244–0154. 8 rooms. Restaurant, bar. No credit cards.*

DAR ES SALAAM A TO Z

To research prices, get advice from other travelers, and book travel arrangements, visit www.fodors.com.

AIR TRAVEL TO AND FROM DAR ES SALAAM

Many airlines fly directly to Dar es Salaam from Europe, but there are no direct flights from the United States. KLM offers the only daily flights to Dar es Salaam. Other airlines that fly here frequently are Air India, Air Zimbabwe, Air Tanzania, British Airways, Egypt Air, Emirates, Ethiopian Airlines, Kenya Airways, South African Airways, and Swissair. Air Tanzania has daily flights to Dar es Salaam from destinations within East Africa.

➤ AIRLINES AND CONTACTS: **Air India** (☎ 022/215–2642). **Air Zimbabwe** (☎ 022/212–3526). **Air Tanzania** (☎ 022/211–0245). **British Airways** (☎ 022/211–3820). **Egypt Air** (☎ 022/211–3333). **Emirates** (☎ 022/211–6100). **Ethiopian Airlines** (☎ 022/211–7063). **Kenya Airways** (☎ 022/213–6826). **KLM** (☎ 022/211–5012). **South African Airways** (☎ 022/211–7045). **Swiss Air** (☎ 022/211–8870).

AIRPORTS AND TRANSFERS

Dar es Salaam International Airport is about 13 km (8 mi) from the city center. Plenty of white-color taxis are available at the airport and will cost you about Tsh 10,000 to the city center. Most hotels will send drivers to meet your plane, if arranged in advance.

➤ AIRPORT INFORMATION: **Dar es Salaam International Airport** (☎ 0022/284–2877).

BUS TRAVEL TO AND FROM DAR ES SALAAM

Scandinavian Express operates daily bus services to destinations throughout Tanzania. A first-class ticket to Arusha, a nine-hour journey north, costs about Tsh 17,000, while a second-class ticket runs about Tsh 11,000. First-class buses are more comfortable, and the service includes coffee and snacks. Book tickets at least a day in advance.

➤ BUS COMPANIES: **Scandinavian Express** (☒ Msimbazi St. and Nyerere Rd., ☎ 022/218–4833).

CAR RENTAL

There are several car-rental companies in Dar es Salaam, and most operate through tour companies. Hotel travel services generally are equipped to arrange car rentals as well. Renters must be at least 25 and able to show a valid international driver's license.

➤ RENTAL AGENCIES: **Coastal Tours** (☒ Upanga Rd., ☎ 022/211–7957). **Savannah Tours** (☒ Ohio St., ☎ 022/211–2416).

EMBASSIES

Canada (✉ 38 Mirambo St., Dar es Salaam, ☎ 022/211–2831, ⨎ 022/211–6896). **United Kingdom** (✉ Samora Ave., Dar es Salaam, ☎ 022/211–2953, ⨎ 022/211–2669). **United States** (✉ 140 Msese Rd., Dar es Salaam, ☎ 022/266–6010, ⨎ 022/266–6701).

FERRIES

Ferries operated by Sea Ferries Express to Zanzibar depart daily at 7:30, 10:30, 1, and 4:15 from the Zanzibar Ferry Terminal on Sokoine Drive. The two-hour journey costs about Tsh 35,000. The Kigamboni ferry to the southern beaches runs continuously throughout the day and departs from the southern tip of the city center, where Kivukoni Front meets Ocean Road. The 10-minute ride costs about Tsh 100.
➤ FERRY COMPANIES: **Sea Ferries Express** (Sokoine Dr., ☎ 022/211–4026)

MAIL AND SHIPPING

Postal service in Dar es Salaam is generally reliable. A letter to the United States takes about 10–14 days. The main post office is downtown near the Askari Monument. Hotels will sell stamps and deliver mail to the post office. If you are sending something valuable, try DHL Worldwide Express.
➤ OVERNIGHT SERVICES: **DHL Worldwide Express** (Nyerere Rd., ☎ 022/286–1000; ⊙ Weekdays 8–6, Sat. 8–1).
➤ POST OFFICES: **Main Post Office** (✉ Mktaba St. between Ghana Ave. and Garden St.).

MONEY MATTERS

Tanzania's notorious black market no longer exists, but tourists occasionally are approached by strangers to change money. Don't be tempted, even if it sounds like a good deal. Banks and change bureaus buy dollars at similar rates. Hotel exchange rates are often significantly lower.

Credit cards are increasingly accepted by hotels and restaurants. In general, traveler's checks are difficult to use throughout Tanzania and always are exchanged at rates worse than cash. ATMs are becoming increasingly popular in Dar es Salaam, and they dispense both Tanzanian shillings and U.S. dollars.

SAFETY

Dar es Salaam is among the safest cities in East Africa. It's fine to wander around by yourself during the day, but after dark it's best to stick with your companions. Because taxis are cheap, it's a good idea to use them at night. The area with the most street crime is along the harbor, especially Kivoni Front and Ocean Road.

WOMEN IN DAR ES SALAAM
Foreign women tend to feel safe in Dar es Salaam. Women in Dar es Salaam never wear clothing that exposes their shoulders or legs. You'll feel more comfortable in modest dress.

TAXIS

Taxis are the most efficient way to get around town. During the day they are easy to find outside hotels and at major intersections, but at night they are often scarce. Ask someone to call one for you. Taxis don't have meters, so agree on fare before getting in. Fares run about Tsh 1,500 within the city.

TIPPING

Here's a good rule of thumb: leave a tip if the service is good. Tips are not expected, but they are greatly appreciated by workers who often earn meager salaries. Bills in most restaurants already include a 5% service charge, but leaving 10% more is appropriate in expensive restaurants, while 5% is sufficient elsewhere. Taxi drivers don't expect tips, but most people add 5%–10% to the fare. In luxury hotels tip porters about Tsh 1,000; in more moderately priced hotels, Tsh 500 is appropriate. The same amount is appropriate for room service waiters and for bellmen and maids who provide extra services such as bringing an iron or map to your room.

TRAIN TRAVEL

All Tanzania rail lines converge in Dar es Salaam. The Tazara Railway Station is at the junction of Mandel and Pugu roads, about 5 km (3 mi) from the city center. The line runs southwest through Iringa and Mbeya. The Central Railway Station is off Sokoine Drive at the corner of Railway Street. This line runs north to such destinations as Lake Tanganyika, Tanga, and Moshi.

➤ INFORMATION: **Tanzanian Railways Corporation** (Railway St. and Sokoine Dr., ☎ 022/211–0599).

VISITOR INFORMATION

The Tanzania Tourist Board has maps and information on travel to dozens of points of interest around Tanzania. The staff will discuss hotel options with you and assist you in making reservations.

➤ INFORMATION: **Tanzania Tourist Board** (✉ Samora Ave. and Zaniki St., ☎ 022/213–1555).

7 NORTHERN TANZANIA

The Africa you've dreamed about—
the Serengeti Plains, Olduvai Gorge,
and Mt. Kilimanjaro—can be found
along Tanzania's northern border. Once
a destination for those who didn't mind
roughing it, this region is now popular
among more upscale travelers who
appreciate the comfort of luxurious lodges
and tented camps. Make no mistake—this
is still an untamed territory. Many who have
traveled around East Africa prefer Northern
Tanzania because it imparts a sense of
what Africa was like a century ago.

By Delta Willis

T'S NEARLY IMPOSSIBLE TO COMPREHEND the vast expanses of land Tanzania has set aside as wildlife refuges. A total of 220,000 square km (84,940 square mi)—about a quarter of the country's total area—is protected land. And of the country's 12 national parks and 17 game reserves, some of the most sprawling are clustered around the country's northern border.

Many of these parks also number among the country's most popular destinations. Along the border you'll find the golden grasslands of the Serengeti. Every year these seemingly endless plains are the setting for the annual migration of more than 1.5 million wildebeest. The galloping herds stir up huge clouds of dust in August and September, when they move north to Kenya's Maasai Mara National Reserve in search of greener pastures. Other mammals join in the parade, including 200,000 zebras and gazelles. By November they are heading south again, reaching the region in time to give birth to a new generation between January and April.

Mary Leakey, the famous archaeologist, once suggested that humans may have been inspired to migrate by the wildebeest. The herds are, after all, a good supply of meat. The gnus also seem to have a sixth sense for imminent rains. Whether it's because they acutely hear the distant thunder or they feel the storm's vibrations, it's clear that these antelopes move toward rain before it is visible. Some scientists speculate that they once led early humans to water.

It wasn't far from the Serengeti that Leakey uncovered a 1.7-million-year-old fossil skull. This astounding discovery, as well as many others in the area, led to East Africa being called the Cradle of Humankind. Many of Leakey's other discoveries, including castings of the 3.5-million-year-old hominid footprints she unearthed, can be seen in the Olduvai Museum, found in Ngorongoro Conservation Area. This preserve attracts nearly as many visitors as nearby Serengeti National Park. Inside a volcanic crater measuring 20 km (12 mi) across you will find a breathtaking array of more than 30,000 animals. From the edge of the caldera the elephants below seem as small as ants.

For intrepid travelers, reaching the snows of Kilimanjaro is the highlight of a visit to Tanzania. Climbing to the summit of Africa's most prominent peak requires at least five days, but you should set aside six or seven days if you want to avoid the devastating effects of altitude sickness. At least one out of every four climbers never makes it to the top because of underestimating the toll the altitude can take on the body. If you would like to expend a little less effort, choose from several new paths across the Shira Plateau, on the western side of the mountain.

Mt. Kilimanjaro may be the most popular destination for climbers, but there are other mountains along the northern border that are well worth exploring. Mt. Meru, southwest of the taller peak, can also provide a very pleasant climb. If you really want to see nature but don't want to challenge your body, consider hikes in the highlands around Ngorongoro Crater.

Pleasures and Pastimes

Archaeology

The legendary Olduvai Gorge became the world's most famous archaeological site with Mary Leakey's discovery of a 1.7-million-year-old hominid skull in 1959. The achievement, featured in *National Geographic,* was the first of many in the area. Perhaps the most significant was the discovery of *Homo habilis,* or Handy Man, thought to be the first among our ancestors to make tools. The Olduvai Museum in Ngorongoro Conservation Area is small but informative, with casts of the 3.5-million-year-old hominid footprints Leakey unearthed nearby. Examples of other important archaeological discoveries can be found here as well. But there are many sites around Tanzania where you can see evidence of ancient civilizations. You can see some of these rock paintings in Serengeti National Park and Tarangire National Park.

Climbing and Hiking

Many people head to Tanzania with the goal of climbing Mt. Kilimanjaro or one of the country's other challenging peaks. Rick Ridgeway's *In the Shadow of Kilimanjaro* chronicles the journey of veteran climber Iain Allen. But there are plenty of other adventures for those with a good pair of hiking boots. The Ngurdoto Forest, near Arusha, has fascinating woodlands you can to explore. You can even enjoy walking safaris through some of the game reserves, including Tarangire National Park.

Dining

Most visitors to Northern Tanzania head to the national parks, where gourmet meals are served by the lodges and camps where they are staying. Some very good restaurants are found in hotels in some of the larger towns.

CATEGORY	COST*
$$$$	over Tsh 13,500
$$$	Tsh 9,000–Tsh 13,500
$$	Tsh 4,500–Tsh 9,000
$	under Tsh 4,500

per person for a main course at dinner

Lodging

A decade ago visitors to East Africa would have found the lodges in Tanzania less fancy and less expensive than those in Kenya. This is no longer the case. Gone are the days when travelers to Tanzania brought along their own lightbulbs, toilet tissue, and scotch. Over the past few years private developers have built extraordinary structures such as Ngorongoro Crater Lodge, so baroque that it reminded one visitor of Cher's home in Malibu. Even the clusters of tents you'll find at Klein's Camp, Maji Moto Camp, and Grumeti River Camp would not look out of place in a Calvin Klein ad.

Ecofriendly accommodations may look less expensive, but the price still hovers around $450 per person, partly because of the expense of transporting the table linens and keeping the chardonnay cold in the middle of nowhere. Wherever you stay, reservations are essential during the peak season, from October through February.

CATEGORY	COST*
$$$$	over Tsh 135,000
$$$	Tsh 90,000–Tsh 135,000
$$	Tsh 45,000–Tsh 90,000
$	under Tsh 45,000

All prices are for a standard double room, excluding tax.

Wildlife

The annual wildebeest migration may overshadow everything else, but it's certainly not the only show. With a wide variety of terrains, Northern Tanzania gives you the opportunity to view different types of wildlife. Walking through the forest you might spot a rare black-

and-white colobus monkey, or even chance upon a herd of elephants moving through the brush. You can take a game drive and see the zebras and giraffes that migrate across the open plains. Chimpanzees are the draw at Gombe Stream National Park, while Mahale Mountains National Park is home to red colobus monkeys and yellow baboons. For many people Northern Tanzania is for the birds. On the plains ground hornbills stalk about in search of an insect snack. Yellow-throated sandgrouses congregate in the grass, as do the black-throated honeyguides. The ostrich, of course, is the star here. The huge birds are easily spotted weaving across the landscape.

Exploring Northern Tanzania

The national parks along the country's northern border can easily be visited by car. When planning your trip, keep in mind that the distance between many parks is great and that most roads are not in ideal condition. A better option, especially if you hope to cover long distances, is flying. Charter planes can take you to parts of the country that were inaccessible a few years ago.

Numbers in the text correspond to numbers in the margin and on the Northern Tanzania map.

Great Itineraries

IF YOU HAVE 7 DAYS

The Northern Circuit is a classic itinerary for newcomers to Tanzania. Versions of this tour can be found in almost any travel brochure, so brace yourself for an endless parade of minivans. From **Arusha** ① head southwest to ⬛ **Lake Manyara National Park** ③, where you'll find great herds of elephants. Stay for two nights at one of the luxurious tented camps. Drive north to the ⬛ **Ngorongoro Conservation Area** ⑤ in time for a picnic lunch on the rim. Spend the rest of the day hiking in the surrounding highlands, then get up early to see the amazing array of wildlife in the crater itself. The next day you can explore Olduvai Gorge, site of many archaeological discoveries, before heading to ⬛ **Serengeti National Park** ⑥. From the Maasai word for "endless plains," this sprawling park is one of the world's great wildlife refuges. The grasslands are home to millions of animals, most notably the wildebeest that make their home here until they migrate north to Kenya.

IF YOU HAVE 10 DAYS

If you have a little more time to explore Northern Tanzania, add a visit to ⬛ **Arusha National Park** ②, where you can take two or three days to climb Mt. Meru. Compared to its more famous neighbor, the slopes of Mt. Meru are blissfully uncrowded. Wildlife abounds, including the elegant black-and-white colobus monkey. If you prefer, head to ⬛ **Tarangire National Park** ④, where you can search for rock paintings dating from the Stone Age.

IF YOU HAVE 14 DAYS

A two-week trip will allow you to see much more of Tanzania. If you're up for a challenge, spend six or seven days climbing Africa's tallest peak, at ⬛ **Kilimanjaro National Park** ⑦. Other alternatives include flying south to ⬛ **Selous Game Reserve,** then to ⬛ **Mahale Mountains National Park** to see the country's largest concentration of chimpanzees. If snorkeling is on your agenda, head to ⬛ **Mafia Island Marine Park.**

When to Tour Northern Tanzania

Tanzania is so vast that rainy seasons vary from one reserve to the next. Generally, the peak travel season is July through October, when the weather is cooler. Many people underestimate how cool it can be in

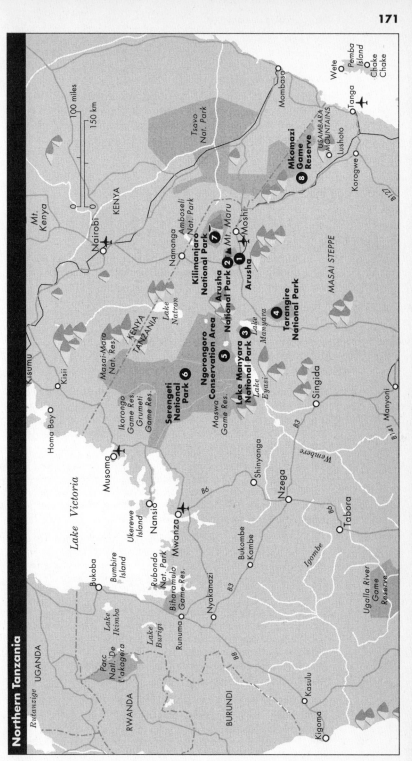

Northern Tanzania

100 miles
150 km

UGANDA
Rutanzige
RWANDA
BURUNDI
Parc Nat'l. De l'okagera
Lake Ikimba
Lake Burigi
Bukoba
Bumbire Island
Rubondo Nat. Park
Biharamulo Game Res.
Runuma
Nyakanazi
B8
B3
Kasulu
Kigoma

Lake Victoria

Homa Bay
Kisii
Kisumu
KENYA
Mt. Kenya
Nairobi

Ukerewe Island
Nansio
Mwanza
B6
Musoma
Bukombe Kambe
Shinyanga
Nzega
B6
Tabora
Igombe
Wembere
B1/1 Manyoni
Ugalla River Game Reserve

Ikorongo Game Res.
Grumeti Game Res.
Masai-Mara Nat. Res.
KENYA
TANZANIA
Lake Natron
Namanga
Amboseli Nat. Park
Tsavo Nat. Park
Mombaso
Mt. Maru
Moshi
Kilimanjaro National Park
7
Arusha National Park **2** **1**
Arusha

6 Serengeti National Park
Maswa Game Res.
5
Ngorongoro Conservation Area
Lake Manyara National Park **3**
Lake Eyasi
Lake Manyara
4 Tarangire National Park
Singida
B3
MASAI STEPPE
USAMBARA MOUNTAINS
Lushoto
8 Mkomazi Game Reserve
Korogwe
B127
Tanga
Wete
Pemba Island
Chake Chake

the higher altitudes, so bring along a sweater, hat, and gloves if you are headed to Ngorongoro Crater or other areas in the highlands. Even in the plains you might even need a sweater on game drives on chilly mornings and evenings.

From December through March can be rather hot. The long rains generally come between March and May, when many areas become inaccessible. The short rains come in October and November. This is not a bad time to visit, as you will encounter fewer people. You will see smaller concentrations of game, however, because the animals are not crowding around the few watering holes.

THE NORTHERN CIRCUIT

The most popular safari route in Tanzania is the Northern Circuit, which begins in the town of Arusha. You swing southwest to Lake Manyara National Park, then head north to Ngorongoro Conservation Area, then on to Serengeti National Park. Allot at least seven days for this overland journey. Remember, though, that for the better part of the year this is a path beaten down by most visitors to the area. Many first-time visitors don't know any better until it's too late. Take a day or two to venture into the game reserves not on your travel agent's itinerary.

Arusha

❶ *470 km (291 mi) northwest of Dar es Salaam.*

One of East Africa's fastest-growing cities, Arusha has changed enormously over the past decade. This former trading post for indigenous peoples now exhibits a marked contrast between the rows of tin houses and the massive new structures downtown like the sprawling Arusha International Conference Centre.

Almost 500,000 people live in Arusha, about 10 times as many as 50 years ago. Because of the influx of people, including some refugees from neighboring countries, the streets bustle with activity. You'll spot many older buildings undergoing renovation, as well as some newer ones where construction was halted when funds ran out.

A mere 80 km (50 mi) south of the Kenya border, Arusha is the starting point for many safaris. The city suffers from a glut of tour operators, including some "flycatchers" who hustle travelers on arrival. If you haven't selected a company before you arrive, check the "blacklist" of disreputable firms kept by the staff of the Tanzania Tourist Board.

Before heading out to the national parks, stop by the **Arusha Natural History Museum.** Inside the vast white structure, built in 1886 as a fort and later used as a prison, you'll find an exhibit on fossil discoveries in Tanzania. There is a pleasant garden in the rear with picnic tables. ⊠ *Boma Rd. near Arusha International Conference Centre,* ☎ *no phone.* ⊡ *Tsh 250.* ☉ *Weekdays 7:30–5, Sat. 7:30–4:40, Sun. 11–4.*

The **Meserani Snake Park** is 25 km (15 mi) from Arusha on the road to Ngorongoro Crater. The park has a reptile zoo and a rehabilitation center for injured birds, as well as a lively bar and barbecue restaurant. South African owner Berry Bale can also arrange camel rides to a traditional Maasai home. ⊠ *Dodoma Rd.,* ☎ *no phone.*

About 90 km (56 mi) north of Arusha is the **Longido Cattle Market.** Here you can watch cattle being auctioned in the market and observe how the Maasai people conduct business.

Dining and Lodging

$$ ✕ **Mezza Luna.** Run by an Italian family, this pleasant restaurant has
★ a menu featuring more than 200 regional specialties. Wash your meal
down with good wines from South Africa, then end the evening with
an excellent cappuccino. A local band performs most evenings. ⊠
Moshi Rd., ☎ *027/254–4381,* ℻ *027/254–4381. MC, V.*

$ ✕ **Mambo Jazz Café.** Grab one of the outdoor tables at this extremely
★ popular café near the center of Arusha. It serves sandwiches and piz-
zas, but many people return to have breakfast any time of day. The
cappuccino is excellent. ⊠ *Old Moshi Rd.,* ☎ *no phone. No credit
cards.*

$ ✕ **Mac's Patisserie.** Near the clock tower, this is a meeting place for
travelers. You can check your E-mail while you chow down on soups
and sandwiches. ⊠ *Sokoine Rd.,* ☎ *no phone. No credit cards.*

$$$ ⬚ **Dik Dik.** Near the banks of the Usa River, this modern lodging lends
a sense of privacy. Past doors carved with bold animal designs you'll
find sleek bungalows with fireplaces to keep you cozy after the sun goes
down. On warm afternoons you can relax on your veranda. From the
bright dining room you can enjoy the views of the mountain slopes
where the diminutive antelope called the dik-dik lives. ⊠ *25 km (16
mi) east of Arusha,* ☎ *027/254–8110,* ℻ *027/254–8110,* 〚WEB〛
*www.dikdik.ch. 18 rooms. Restaurant, bar, minibars, pool, shop. AE,
DC, MC, V.*

$$$ ⬚ **Mountain Village Lodge.** This sprawling complex of thatch-roofed
rondavels (round huts) is meant to call to mind a Maasai village. Gar-
dens full of colorful bougainvillea are a great place to rest after a long
day exploring the nearby national parks. If you have some energy, stretch
your legs on a guided bird walk around nearby Lake Duluti. There are
a pool and a rooftop lounge where you can see Mt. Meru and Mt. Kil-
imanjaro on clear evenings. ⊠ *Box 376, 15 km (9 mi) east of Arusha,*
☎ *027/250–4058,* ℻ *027/250–4155,* 〚WEB〛 *www.serenahotels.com. 42
rooms. Restaurant, bar, shop. AE, DC, MC, V.*

$$$ ⬚ **Novotel Mt. Meru.** This ideally located high-rise hotel sits a few blocks
from the Arusha International Conference Centre. The lobby buzzes
with activity at the Themi Grill restaurant, the Maasai Bar, and at the
shopping arcade. Many of the spacious rooms have views of the hotel's
namesake peak. ⊠ *Boma Rd.,* ☎ *027/250–2711,* ℻ *027/250–8503,*
〚WEB〛 *www.novotel.com. 168 rooms. 2 restaurants, 3 bars, pool, golf
course, tennis court, squash. AE.*

$$$ ⬚ **Rivertrees.** Set in an old farmhouse, this lovely inn is a place where
★ you feel at home immediately. There are only six rooms, so you never
feel crowded. It's run by Martina Gehrken, formerly with the Mambo
Jazz Café in Arusha, so the food is exceptional. Vegetables and herbs
are fresh from the kitchen garden. Have breakfast on the back porch
as you gaze up at Mt. Kilimanjaro. Later you can stroll through the
gardens in search of the dozens of species of birds that make their home
nearby. ⊠ *23 km (14 mi) east of Arusha,* ☎ *027/255–3893,* ℻ *027/
255–3894,* 〚WEB〛 *www.rivertrees.com. 6 rooms. Dining room. MC, V.*

$$ ⬚ **Golden Rose Hotel.** A good option for travelers on a budget, this
five-story hotel is in the middle of Arusha. Traditional meals are served
at the inexpensive restaurant. The hotel has a travel office that can arrange interesting excursions to a nearby tanzanite mine or a stay with
the Chagga people in the Kilimanjaro area. ⊠ *Colonel Middleton Rd.,*
☎ *027/250–7959 or 027/250–8860,* ℻ *027/250–8862,* 〚WEB〛 *www.gold-
enrose.20m.com. 34 rooms. Restaurant, bar, business services, meeting rooms, travel services. MC, V.*

$$ ⬚ **Hotel Seventy Seven.** Southeast of the center of Arusha, Hotel Sev-
enty Seven is the largest hotel in Tanzania. Locals know it by its Swahili
name, Hotel Saba Saba. The sprawling complex is laid out like a small

village, with about a dozen clusters of utilitarian rooms. There are a nice restaurant and bar on the premises. ✉ *Old Moshi Rd.,* ☎ *027/250–8054,* FAX *027/250–8407. 391 rooms. Restaurant, bar. AE, MC, V.*

$$ 🏨 **Impala Hotel.** This modern hotel is designed for business travelers and has secretarial services and conference facilities. Set amid landscaped gardens, the facility is close to the Arusha International Conference Centre. Rooms are clean and comfortable. ✉ *Moshi Rd. and Old Moshi Rd.,* ☎ *027/250–2398,* FAX *027/508–680,* WEB *www.impalahotel.com. 63 rooms. 2 restaurants, 3 bars, pool, hair salon, health center, shop, business services, meeting rooms. AE, MC, V.*

$$ 🏨 **Moivaro Coffee Plantation Lodge.** There are stunning views of the changing colors of Mt. Kilimanjaro from the grounds of this coffee plantation. You can explore nearby Mt. Meru by horseback or mountain bike, play a few games of tennis, or relax in the pool. Simple cottages, each with a private veranda, are warmed by fireplaces for the cool nights. Redd's African Grill House serves up barbecued meats as you enjoy traditional dances. ✉ *6 km (4 mi) east of Arusha,* ☎ *027/255–3243,* FAX *027/255–3242,* WEB *www.moivaro.com. 25 rooms. Restaurant, horseback riding, tennis court, volleyball, shop, playground. AE, DC, MC, V.*

$ 🏨 **New Safari Hotel.** This is one of Arusha's older hotels, but it is still very comfortable. On Boma Road, it's in the center of activity. There are a restaurant and bar, as well as a popular disco on weekends. ✉ *Boma Rd.,* ☎ *027/250–3842,* FAX *027/254–8628. 12 rooms. Restaurant, bar, beer garden, dance club. AE, MC, V.*

$ 🏨 **Outpost Lodge.** Near the center of town, these small bungalows set in a lovely garden are popular with expats. On the premises are a bar and a small restaurant where locals turn out for the buffet dinner. There are numerous other dining options nearby, including Mezza Luna and Mambo Jazz Café. ✉ *Serengeti Rd.,* ☎ *027/254–8405,* WEB *www.theoutpost.gq.nu. 14 rooms. Restaurant, bar, laundry service. AE, DC, MC, V.*

Nightlife and the Arts

Most larger hotels have bars where you can stop by for a drink. Some, including Hotel Seventy Seven, have dancing on the weekends. Popular with locals, **Big Y Club** (✉ Arusha-Moshi Rd., ☎ 744–477) features live Congolese music. The **Colobus Club** (✉ Jacaranda St. near Sokoine Rd., ☎ no phone) is a popular spot for singles. It has a terrace café that serves sandwiches and other light fare.

Shopping

There are plenty of shops along the streets near the clock tower at the intersection of Old Moshi Road and Boma Road. You can get carvings here at a better price than in other spots along the tourist trail. One of the city's largest dealers in tanzanite, **Cultural Heritage** (✉ Dodoma Rd., ☎ 27/250–8698) has in-house artisans producing beautiful jewelry. **Art de Afrique Gallery** (✉ Mezza Luna, Old Moshi Rd., ☎ 027/254–4381) has some fine souvenirs.

Arusha National Park

★ ❷ *32 km (20 mi) northeast of Arusha.*

With Arusha only a short drive away, it's easy to see Arusha National Park in a day. Don't overlook this tiny reserve. Despite only covering 137 square km (58 square mi), it has more to see than many much larger reserves. You'll find three distinct areas within the park: the forests that surround the Ngurdoto Crater, the brightly colored pools of the Momella Lakes, and the soaring peaks of Mt. Meru.

Established in 1960, the park was originally called Ngurdoto Crater National Park, but after the mountain was annexed in 1967 it became known as Mt. Meru National Park. Today it is named for the Warusha people who once lived in this area. The Maasai also lived here, which is why many of the names for sights within the park come from their language.

After entering the park through the Ngurdoto Gate, you'll pass through the fig, olive, and wild mango trees of the Ngurdoto Forest. Farther along is the Ngurdoto Crater, which is actually a caldera, or collapsed crater. Unlike another nearby caldera, Ngorongoro Crater, this one appears to have had two cones. There are no roads into the crater itself, so the buffaloes and other animals that make their homes in the swampy habitat remain protected. (If you feel disappointed, take a good look at the damage inflicted by too much tourism at Ngorongoro.) You can drive around the rim, where you'll find a misty landscape covered with date palms, orchids, and lichens. The grasslands to the west are known as Serengeti Ndogo ("Little Serengeti") and boast a herd of Burchell's zebras, thriving because there are no lions nearby.

Many baboons and other monkeys are found in the Ngurdoto Forest. Elegant black-and-white colobus monkeys spend most of the morning basking in the sun in the highest parts of the forest canopy, then later move lower in the branches to feed on the tender vegetation. Colobus monkeys do not drink water but get all their moisture from their food. They are endangered because their lovely fur was prized by humans.

From Ngorongoro Crater drive northeast to the Momella Lakes. Reedbuck and waterbuck are common sights near the dirt road. There are numerous observation points along the way for getting a closer look at the more than 400 species of birds that have been spotted in the area. The lakes were created by lava flow from nearby Mt. Meru; each is a distinct color because of the varying mineral content in the water. Each lake, therefore, attracts different types of birds. Keep an eye out for the flamingos that feed on the algae.

From the Momella lakes the road toward Mt. Meru leads into a forest with a profusion of wildflowers. Here you'll encounter dik-diks and red forest duikers. Rangers can accompany you on walks to the rim of Meru Crater, where you'll have a breathtaking view of the sheer cliffs rising to the summit. Keep an eye out for a diminutive antelope called the klipspringer.

Because it is not as well known, the slopes of Mt. Meru are blissfully uncrowded. Although Meru looks diminutive alongside Kilimanjaro, do not underestimate what it takes to climb to the top. You must be in good shape, and you need to allow time to acclimatize. Climbing Mt. Meru itself takes at least three days. The route begins at the Momella Gate, on the eastern side of the mountain. Huts along the way sleep 24–48 people, but inquire beforehand whether beds are available; if not, you should bring a tent. You can arrange for no-frills journeys up the mountain through the park service, or book a luxury package through a travel company that includes porters to carry all your supplies. Either way you'll be accompanied by an armed guard to protect you from unfriendly encounters with elephants or buffaloes. ✉ *Tanzania National Parks, Box 3134, Arusha,* ☎ *027/250–1930,* FAX *027/254–8216.* ✍ *$25.*

Lodging

$$$$ 🏨 **Ngare Sero Mountain Lodge.** Ngare Sero means "sweet water," ★ which refers to a spring that flows into a lake surrounded by lush trop-

ical foliage. You must cross a small footbridge to reach the beautiful estate where the lodge is located. The main house is a splendid mansion decorated with superb taste. Cottages set in the lovely garden can accommodate only 20 guests, so you never feel crowded. The staff will arrange trout fishing and other excursions. ⊠ *Near Ngurdoto Gate,* ☏ *027/254–8690. 10 rooms. Dining room. AE, MC.*

$$$$ ▣ **Safari Spa Polo.** On the grounds of the Kiliflora Rose Farm, this luxurious spa is a great place to sneak away for a day or two of pampering. You can take a dip in the tropical pool after enjoying some soothing aromatherapy, or head to the fully equipped fitness center to try the sauna, steam room, or hot tub. The owners are obviously keen on polo, and you can sign up for lessons from instructor Peter Grace or his daughter Victoria. Experienced players are invited to join in on games. Take horseback journeys into the countryside through the small villages of the Maasai. Each cottage, decorated in *Out of Africa* style, has a private bath. Book through African Encounters. ⊠ *Near Arusha National Park,* ☏ *011/880–3079 in South Africa,* 🖷 *011/447–6773,* 🌐 *www.africanencounters.com. 14 rooms. Restaurant, bar, pool, horseback riding. AE, DC, MC, V.*

$$ ▣ **Momella Wildlife Lodge.** Built for the 1962 John Wayne film *Hatari!* (the staff will screen it for you on request), this lodge still resembles a movie set. Most accommodations are in traditional rondavels, although there are a handful of cabins as well. Inside the main building is a bar as well as a vast dining room with a roaring fireplace. Outside you can walk around the nearby lakes, where you'll doubtless encounter some snorting hippos. The complex is just outside the boundary of Arusha National Park, so there are spectacular views of both Mt. Kilimanjaro and Mt. Meru. ⊠ *Near Momella Gate,* ☏ *027/225–3743. 9 cabins, 37 rondavels. Restaurant, bar. AE, DC, MC, V.*

$$ ▣ **Mt. Meru Game Lodge.** This old-fashioned lodge on the foothills of Mt. Meru is just outside Arusha National Park. The nicely furnished cottages are set in a lovely garden near a pond that attracts flamingos. The dining room in the main lodge serves excellent food. Book through Abercrombie & Kent. ⊠ *Near Ngurdoto Gate,* ☏ *027/250–8346 in Arusha, 800/323–7308 in the U.S.,* 🖷 *027/250–8273 in Arusha, 630/ 954–3324 in the U.S.,* 🌐 *www.abercrombiekent.com. 14 cottages. Restaurant, bar, hiking. AE, DC, MC, V.*

Lake Manyara National Park

❸ *130 km (81 mi) west of Arusha.*

Near the eastern branch of the Great Rift Valley, Lake Manyara National is the first stop for many safaris following the Northern Circuit. It's a small park, and more than two-thirds of it is covered by water, but it's among the country's most popular destinations because it has the greatest density of elephants in Tanzania. This area is where Iain Douglas Hamilton and his wife, Oria, lived in the 1970s, conducting the research that they would later document in their book *Among the Elephants.* They still work with elephants and today can be found in Kenya's Samburu National Park.

The park entrance is near the market town of Mto wa Mbu (Mosquito River). As the name implies, the mosquitoes can be bothersome. There are also many tsetse flies that do not carry sleeping sickness but do have a nasty bite. Make sure to bring along plenty of insect repellent. In the reserve you'll find a cool forest where towering date palms and tamarind trees grow. Baboons and several types of monkey are easy to spot here, as are guinea fowl.

In the forests of acacia trees, lions can often be found draped sleepily over the branches of trees, perhaps to escape the heat. Impalas stay close to the acacias because they browse on the tender leaves. Theses graceful creatures can be seen either in large breeding herds of females with one dominant male or in groups of bachelor males. The open grasslands are home to huge herds of buffaloes, as well as zebras, giraffes, wildebeest, bushbuck, and waterbuck. At the edge of the grassland is a large hippo pool, where marabous and other species of stork gather. There are also a few rhinos, but their number has decreased drastically because of poachers. In the marshes watch for tree-climbing monitor lizards.

In addition to the rich wildlife, there is a stunning array of birds, especially along the lakes. Pelicans perch in trees, and flamingos are sometimes found along the water's edge. In the woods, larks, swallows, and doves are abundant. ⊠ *Tanzania National Parks, Box 3134, Arusha,* ☎ *027/250–1930,* ℻ *027/254–8216.* ✆ *$25.*

Lodging

$$$$ ⊞ **Kirurumu Tented Lodge.** In a grove of acacia trees, this lodge is perfect for those who desire a bit of privacy. The thatch-roofed tents all have verandas with comfortable armchairs where you can admire the view of the lake. Mindful of its impact on the environment, the ecofriendly lodge uses solar panels to heat the water for your shower. It also contributes to a school for local children. Book through Hoopoe Adventure Tours. ⊠ *Lake Manyara National Park,* ☎ *020/8428–8221 in the U.K.,* ℻ *020/8421–1396,* ☒ *www.hoopoe.com. 20 tents. Bar, dining room. MC, V.*

$$$$ ⊞ **Lake Manyara Serena.** High on an escarpment, this lodge overlooks the southern end of the Great Rift Valley. The dining room, bar, and even the swimming pool take advantage of the view. Soaring birds that float above on thermal currents provided the inspiration for the lodge's architecture. Full of gracefully curving lines, there is scarcely a right angle in the whole place. You're sometimes greeted by singing schoolchildren when you return from a game drive. Stargazing is offered in the evening. An airstrip is nearby. ⊠ *Lake Manyara National Park,* ☎ *027/ 250–4058,* ℻ *027/250–4155,* ☒ *www.serenahotels.com. 67 rooms. Restaurant, bar, pool, shop. AE, DC, MC, V.*

$$$$ ⊞ **Maji Moto Camp.** With a name that is Swahili for "hot water," it's not surprising that this luxurious camp is situated near a mineral spring that reaches 60°C (140°F). Ernest Hemingway used this setting for his book *The Green Hills of Africa,* and it's easy to see why he was so inspired when you glance at a flocks of flamingos flying past. Acacia trees provide a canopy above the camp, which consists of ivory-color tents perched on stilts to keep them cool. Each has a small wooden deck where you can enjoy views of the lake. Meals are served in a traditional *boma,* which is an outdoor enclosure from which you can see the stars. Book through CC Africa in Nairobi. ⊠ *Lake Manyara National Park,* ☎ *02/750–780 in Nairobi,* ℻ *02/750–512 in Nairobi,* ☒ *www.ccafrica.com. 9 tents. Bar, dining room, lounge, pool, laundry service. AE, DC, MC, V.*

Outdoor Activities and Sports

Guided walks over the escarpment of the Great Rift Valley were begun here in 2001 by **Serena Active** (⊠ Lake Manyara Serena, ☎ 027/253–926). Scaling the steep cliffs is also popular, and certified instructors accompany beginners as well as more advanced climbers. Bicyclists can explore the shores of Lake Manyara, while those who prefer a less strenuous activity can canoe among the birds.

Tarangire National Park

★ ❹ *115 km (71 mi) southwest of Arusha.*

This lovely park has continued to be a well-kept secret, which is odd because during the dry season Tarangire National Park is second only to Ngorongoro Crater in concentration of wildlife. The best time to visit is from July through September, when animals flock to the watering holes. It's then that a good-size population of elephants can be seen lumbering to the Tarangire River for a drink. It also attracts large herds of elands, gnus, oryxes, and zebras. Pythons can often be seen in trees near the swamps.

There are more than 300 species of birds in Tarangire National Park, including martial and bateleur eagles. Especially good bird-watching can be had along the wetlands of the Silale Swamp and around the Tarangire River. Yellow-collared lovebirds, hammerkops, helmeted guinea fowl, long-toed lapwings, brown parrots, white-bellied go-away birds, and a variety of kingfishers, weavers, owls, plovers, and sandpipers make their homes here. A shallow soda lake attracts flamingos and pelicans in the rainy season.

Kolo, just south of Tarangire, is where you'll find some of the most accessible Kondoa rock paintings. From the last stage of the Stone Age, these illustrations on the walls of caves depict hunting scenes using stylized human and animal figures. These fragile documents of an era long past were studied by Mary Leakey, who wrote a book about them called *Africa's Vanishing Art.* At a nearby site Leakey discovered "pencils" in which ocher and other pigments had been ground and mixed with grease. Later excavations revealed that some were 29,000 years old. *Tanzania National Parks, Box 3134, Arusha,* ☎ *027/250–1930,* ℻ *027/254–8216.* ▧ *$25.*

Lodging

$$$ ▦ **Oliver's Camp.** Set among rock outcroppings, this camp is quite close
★ to the excellent birding opportunities of the Silale Swamp. It's near the major migratory routes, so you'll have a front-row seat for the wildlife heading to the Tarangire River. You might even see elephants stroll by while you're enjoying dinner. The emphasis here is on learning the region's natural history from well-informed guides. Owner Paul Oliver is often at the camp and may even join your group on a walking safari. The accommodations are luxurious, and each of the generously proportioned tents is filled with beautifully made furniture. A private airstrip lets you fly here from Arusha. ✉ *Tarangire National Park,* ☎ *027/250–8548,* 𝚆𝙴𝙱 *www.oliverscamp.com. 20 tents. Restaurant, bar, pool. MC, V.*

$$$$ ▦ **Tamarind Camp.** This semipermanent camp is pitched in a grove of
★ acacia trees overlooking a sand river where lions are frequently spotted. Handcrafted hardwood furnishings fill the large tents, where private baths include bucket showers with plenty of hot water. At night the camp is illuminated by lanterns. A percentage of the profits go toward funding a local school in a Mswakini village. Book through Hoopoe Adventure Tours. ✉ *At entrance of Tarangire National Park,* ☎ *020/ 8428–8221 in the U.K.,* ℻ *020/8421–1396,* 𝚆𝙴𝙱 *www.hoopoe.com. 20 tents. Bar, dining room. MC, V.*

$$$ ▦ **Tarangire Sopa Lodge.** Providing the only permanent accommodations within the park, Tarangire Sopa Lodge was constructed on a wooded hillside. A massive marble lobby that leads into the imposing public areas has floor-to-ceiling windows with views of millennium-old baobab trees. An attractive lounge leads to the cozy bar and dining room. Over the pool is a small bridge leading to a terrace where

you can enjoy afternoon tea. Rooms are modern and have amenities such as hair dryers. ☒ *Tarangire National Park,* ☏ *02/336–088 in Nairobi,* ℻ *02/223–843 in Nairobi,* 🆆🅔🅑 *www.sopalodges.com. 75 rooms. Bar, dining room, pool. AE, DC, MC, V.*

Ngorongoro Conservation Area

❺ *152 km (94 mi) west of Arusha.*

Measuring about 20 km (12 mi) across, Ngorongoro Crater one of the largest calderas in the world. The rim is at an altitude of 2,285 m (7,495 ft), which means the nights are cool no matter the season. The Germans called this area the winter highlands, not merely because of altitude, but because of the way clouds gather like snow on the lip of the caldera.

Around the crater is tropical forest that you'll pass through if you drive here from Lake Manyara National Park. This forest once extended much farther down the slopes, but farms slowly crept upward as the area's population expanded. Ngorongoro Conservation Area was created to protect the remaining forests, as well as Olduvai Gorge and the rest of the magnificent Crater Highlands. If you look at a map of the region, you'll notice that Ngorongoro Crater is just a fraction of the protected lands. This is where the crowds gather, however, because of the concentration of wildlife. It is estimated that more than 30,000 animals make their homes here.

On clear days you can stand on the rim of the crater and see the floor 610 m (2,001 ft) below. From this vantage point elephants resemble ants. The great beasts, including some big tuskers, wander in and out of the crater. The flat, grassy plains are home to abundant numbers of wildebeest, hartebeest, gazelles, and zebras. You might expect to see giraffes, but the crater's walls are too steep for them to negotiate. There are also no cheetahs because aggressive hyenas have chased them out.

Ngorongoro Crater is one of the best places to watch lions stalking their prey. Early morning is the most likely time. Even if you miss the actual hunt, it is not uncommon to find a pride of lions licking their chops around a half-eaten carcass. Inbreeding in the closed community has led to some intriguing problems, as documented in the film *The Crater Lions.*

Getting around inside Ngorongoro Crater is fairly easy. A network of dirt roads covers almost all parts of the crater floor, including around Lake Magadi. For years the Maasai have brought their cattle here to lick the mineral salts. The alkaline lake attracts flamingos, which sometimes can be found here in great numbers. Many other species are absent because the water is too salty for fish, but you will spot ostriches. You may see rather large groups of hippos, although their numbers were greatly diminished after a drought in 2000.

Because Ngorongoro Crater is often crowded with minivans, consider exploring other parts of Ngorongoro Conservation Area. One good destination is Ol Doinyo Lengai, known as the "Mountain of God" in the language of the Maasai. Its peak, measuring 2,751 m (9,023 ft), rises majestically from the plains south of Lake Natron. It erupted in 1983, making it the only remaining active volcano in Tanzania. The surrounding area is a great place for walking safaris. About 90 km (56 mi) from Ngorongoro Crater is Lake Ndutu; it is prime location for spotting wildebeest with their new calves.

Legendary Olduvai Gorge became the most famous archaeological site in Africa with Mary Leakey's discovery of a 1.7-million-year-old hominid skull in 1959. Her husband named it *Zinjanthropus*, from an Arabic word for East African people. The press dubbed it "Nutcracker Man" because of its huge jaws. However much he hoped this skull would prove to be a link to early humankind, it was not. Another fossil discovered at Olduvai Gorge, called *Homo habilis*, is a better candidate. The name means "Handy Man," referring to the belief that he is among the first of our ancestors to make his own tools. Thousands of stone artifacts have been found at Olduvai.

The drive to Olduvai Gorge is breathtaking, with panoramic views of volcanic peaks in the distance. Often there are wildflowers in the fields where the Maasai are herding their goats and cattle. Inside the gorge itself you can clearly see the different layers of earth piled on top of each other. The grayish lines, which indicate volcanic eruptions, are used to estimate the age of the fossils found here. If you trek down to the site of the *Zinjanthropus* discovery, you can see these layers behind the plaque denoting Leakey's discovery.

The Olduvai Museum, near where *Zinjanthropus* was discovered, is small but informative. The skull itself was moved to the National Museum in Dar es Salaam, but other exhibits, such as a plaster casting of the 3.5-million-year-old hominid footprints Leakey unearthed nearby, will delight archaeology buffs. Examples of some of the region's other prominent discoveries can be found here, such as the skeletons of extinct animals like three-toed horses and giant antelopes. Outside the building a guide will point out notable geological features.

A hurried visit to Olduvai Gorge is likely to be disappointing. Many tour groups head here at midday, when the horizon is hazy, the museum is crowded, and everyone is in a rush to get to the Serengeti. This is a place that deserves to be seen in the long shadows of dawn or discussed around a campfire in the evening. Before your trip, read Mary Leakey's autobiography *Disclosing the Past*. She conveyed the wonder of it all, explaining complex things with amazing clarity. The rough conditions in which she lived and worked will make you grateful for wherever you sleep that night.

Lodging

$$$$ ☶ **Gibb's Farm.** This coffee plantation is best known as a luncheon stop for tour groups, but it's also a lovely little lodge. Originally built in the 1930s by German settlers, Gibb's Farm is in green countryside near Karatu, halfway up Ngorongoro Crater from Lake Manyara. There is a lovely garden, so the vegetables you are served at dinner are always fresh. Lunch is a huge buffet, and dinner is a five-course meal. You can watch weaver birds near the lodge, or take a guided walk to a nearby watering hole frequented by wildlife. The farm is 40 minutes from the Lake Manyara airstrip. ✉ *Karatu,* ☎ *027/250–6702,* FAX *027/250–8310,* WEB *www.gibbsfarm.net. 15 rooms. Dining room. MC, V. Closed Apr.–May.*

$$$$ ☶ **Ngorongoro Crater Lodge.** Welcome to the Versailles of Ngorongoro Crater. Crystal chandeliers and carved wood paneling decorated with gold leaf inspired one reviewer to deem the decor "safari baroque." Designed by the same architect who did the inspired Makalai Camp in South Africa, the Crater Lodge is anything but subdued. It may have banana leaf ceilings and a thatch roof, but the only thing primitive about it is the lack of a heating system. You can wear a sweater, but that makes using the elegant bathtubs a challenge. Three separate camps are linked by a golf cart to the central dining area. Rooms, all with incredible views, are each served by a personal butler. Book through CC Africa. ✉ *Ngorongoro Crater,* ☎ *02/750–780 in Nairobi,* FAX *02/750–512 in Nairobi,* WEB *www.ccafrica.com. 30 rooms. Dining room, shop. AE, DC, MC, V.*

$$$$ 🏨 **Ngorongoro Serena.** The philosophy at this ecofriendly lodge is to let the natural environment dominate. The design of the exterior uses locally quarried stone, and a grand effort has been made to make the building blend into the contour of the crater rim. The lodge even limits the amount of light that shines across the crater at night. Every room has a great view of the landscape, which is part of the reason many tour groups head here. ✉ *Western rim of Ngorongoro Crater,* ☎ *027/ 250–4058,* ꜰᴀх *027/250–4155,* ᴡᴇʙ *www.serenahotels.com. 67 rooms. Restaurant, bar, shop. AE, DC, MC, V.*

$$$ 🏨 **Ndutu Lodge.** Near the southern border of the Serengeti, this lodge overlooks Lake Ndutu. For a long time it was the headquarters for filmmaker Hugo van Lawick, who made the Emmy-winning *People of the Forest.* This is a popular place during the annual wildebeest migration, especially when they calve in February and March. Nearby acacia trees and the lake attract 400 species of resident and migrant birds. ✉ *Lake Ndutu,* ☎ *027/253–7015,* ꜰᴀх *027/250–8310,* ᴡᴇʙ *www.ndutu.com. 32 rooms. Dining room, shop. MC, V.*

$$$ 🏨 **Plantation Lodge.** Set in beautiful gardens, this lodge is on a coffee plantation near the town of Karatu. The cluster of comfortable cottages overlooks the surrounding farmland. You can enjoy the view from the pool. The dining room serves up delicious African fare. ✉ *Karatu,* ☎ *027/255–3829,* ꜰᴀх *027/255–3830. 16 rooms. Dining room, pool, tennis court, shop. AE, MC, V.*

$$ 🏨 **Ngorongoro Rhino Lodge.** A good choice for travelers on a budget, this former youth hostel is away from the rim of the crater, so there are no views. The facility is small and spartan, and all rooms share a bath. ✉ *Ngorongoro Crater,* ☎ *022/211–1244. Dining room. AE, V.*

Serengeti National Park

★ ❻ *335 km (208 mi) west of Arusha.*

Serengeti comes from the Maasai word *siring,* meaning "endless plains." This sprawling national park, the largest in Tanzania, stretches as far as the eye can see. There are open plains in the south; a savanna with scattered acacia trees in the center; hilly grasslands in the north; and extensive woodlands and black clay plains in the west. But as large as the park might seem, it's only a small part of a larger ecosystem that covers several other of Tanzania's reserves and even extends northward to Kenya's Maasai Mara National Reserve.

The Serengeti was declared a game reserve in 1929. The area, including Ngorongoro Crater, became the country's first national park in 1951. The boundaries were altered in 1959, adding more land to the north and south to protect the annual wildebeest migration while splitting some of the land in the east to form Ngorongoro Conservation Area. The Serengeti continues to be extremely popular, attracting 100,000 visitors each year and generating enough revenue to help fund other national parks.

Throughout the Serengeti you'll find distinctive stone outcroppings called *kopjes,* a Dutch word meaning "little heads." These granite hills gained their rounded shapes from years of erosion. They attract wildlife, particularly baboons, hyraxes, hyenas, and klipspringers. The kopjes might seem to be a beautiful setting for a campsite, but beware of leopards drawn to the cool shade these rocks provide. Keep an eye out for cobras, which can often be seen sunning themselves on the exposed rocks.

In the more wooded areas in the central part of the park you find eland, giraffes, and impalas, as well as elephants and buffaloes. Lions are more

Serengeti National Park and Ngorongoro Conservation Area

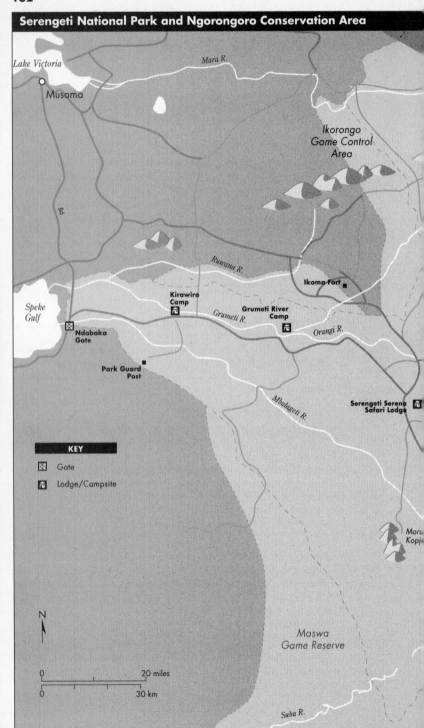

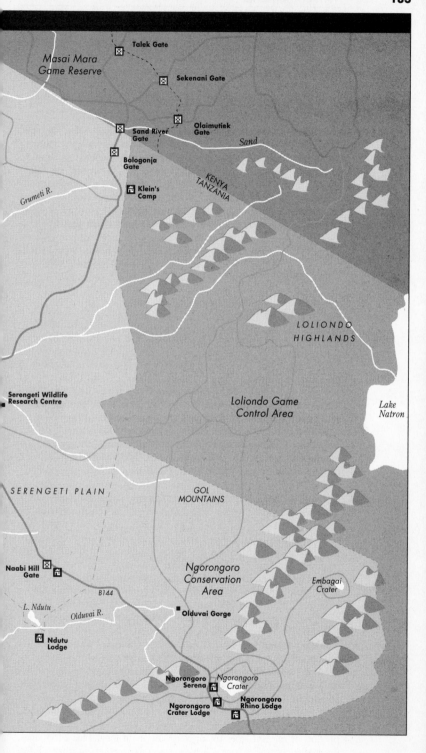

likely to be found here because they can hide when stalking their prey. In the hills to the north you can spot herds of wildebeest grazing on the grassy slopes. The plains in the south are home to a large number of gazelles. Ostriches and secretary birds skirt through the grass, and warthogs can be seen down on their front knees grubbing for roots. In the west there is less big game, but the swamps attract thousands of birds such as the crowned crane and sacred ibis. Avoid this area during the rainy season, as tracks tend to be covered by rising water.

The annual wildebeest migration, when 1.5 million white-bearded gnus search for greener pastures, is the region's biggest draw. It begins with a rut, with males marking their territory and collecting females. Competitors bump their flat heads together, but the battles are rarely violent. In June and July, when they have consumed the grasses of the Serengeti, the vast herds move north. They are accompanied by tens of thousands of antelopes, gazelles, and zebras. By November, when the short rains come to the Serengeti, they head south once again as they prepare to give birth to the next generation. From late January to mid-March they move to the Ndutu and Salei plains, where you'll see them with their new calves. ⊠ *Tanzania National Parks, Box 3134, Arusha,* ☎ *027/250–1930,* 🖷 *027/254–8216.* 🖾 *$25.*

Lodging

$$$$ 🖬 **Grumeti River Camp.** In the reserve's western spur, this secluded camp overlooks the Grumeti River, which eventually drains into Lake Victoria. Thick with hippos and crocodiles, the river is also home to black-and-white colobus monkeys. Guides will drive you into the savanna woodlands and open plains, but you also have great views at the camp itself, which looks across the Kawanga Plains. This is one of the more luxuriously decorated camps, with cream-color tents filled with lavishly carved cypress headboards and chairs in eye-popping shades of lime and scarlet. Dinners prepared in traditional *jikos* (kitchens) are served outside under the trees. The camp is incredibly peaceful, as solar panels provide quiet electrical power. Book through CC Africa. ⊠ *Near Ndabaka Gate,* ☎ *02/750–780 in Nairobi,* 🖷 *02/750–512 in Nairobi,* 🆆🅴🅱 *www.ccafrica.com. 10 tents. Bar, dining room, lounge, pool. AE, DC, MC, V.*

$$$$ 🖬 **Kiriwira Camp.** With all the charm of a bygone age, Kiriwira Camp
★ calls to mind the Victorian-era camp once on this site. A gramophone softly plays as you sink into a high-backed chair to contemplate the endless savanna. The dining room is actually in two separate tents to maintain an intimate feeling. The spacious tents are filled with antique furniture and East African art. Each has a deck with views of the reserve's western reaches. Activities include game drives, but there is plenty of wildlife right at your doorstep. The camp is 45 minutes from an airstrip. ⊠ *Near Ndabaka Gate,* ☎ *027/250–4058,* 🖷 *027/250–4155,* 🆆🅴🅱 *www.serenahotels.com. 25 tents. Restaurant, bar, shop, pool. AE, DC, MC, V.*

$$$$ 🖬 **Klein's Camp.** In a 25,000-acre private sanctuary, Klein's Camp is booked far in advance for when the wildebeest migration passes through in November. Set on a hillside, the camp has sweeping views of the plains. The common areas looked a bit tired on a recent visit, but the staff is friendly and the location superb. Because the camp is outside the reserve, you can take night game drives, set out on walking safaris, or enjoy a bush dinner served on top of a kopje. A small portion of the rate goes to support schools in local Maasai villages. Book through CC Africa. ⊠ *Near reserve's northern border,* ☎ *02/ 750–780 in Nairobi,* 🖷 *02/750–512 in Nairobi,* 🆆🅴🅱 *www.ccafrica.com. 10 tents. Bar, dining room, pool. AE, DC, MC, V.*

$$$$ ▦ **Migration Camp.** Overlooking the Grumeti River, this camp looks down on the giant crocodiles waiting for a wildebeest feast. It nearly resisted the trend toward decadence, but the brave gnu world of luxurious accommodations in the bush brought about the addition of an outdoor hot tub. Otherwise, the emphasis is on the region's spectacular terrain, which attracts animals ranging from lions and leopards to elephants and buffaloes. ✉ *Near Bolongonya Gate,* ☎ *027/254–4521,* FAX *027/254–4574,* WEB *www.halcyonhotels.co.za. 21 tents. Bar, dining room, library. MC, V.*

$$$$ ▦ **Serengeti Serena Safari Lodge.** Set high on a hill with breathtaking views of the grasslands, the Serengeti Serena Safari Lodge is ideally situated for watching the annual wildebeest migration. Inspired by a traditional African village, rondavels house the luxury rooms, each overlooking the plains. Yellow fever trees line the nearby Seronera River, where you'll doubtless see some hippos. Predators such as lions, leopards, and cheetahs are often spotted on the game drives. ✉ *Serengeti National Park,* ☎ *027/250–4058,* FAX *027/250–4155,* WEB *www.serenahotels.com. 66 rooms. Restaurant, bar, shop, pool. AE, DC, MC, V.*

Kilimanjaro National Park

❼ *126 km (78 mi) east of Arusha.*

While traveling in East Africa in 1848, missionary Johannes Rebmann reported back to colleagues in Europe that he had seen a snowcapped mountain near the equator. Understandably, his friends thought he was bonkers. Rising out of the sunbaked plains, the icy peaks of Mt. Kilimanjaro just don't seem possible. Ernest Hemingway immortalized the mountain in his book *The Snows of Kilimanjaro,* describing it as "wide as all the world, great, high, and unbelievably white in the sun."

Kilimanjaro is made up of three extinct volcanoes: Kibo, Mawenzi, and Shira. At the top of Kibo is the highest peak, 5,895-m (19,340-ft) Uhuru. The mountain's vegetation varies greatly by altitude. First, you encounter open grasslands where you can see bush babies at night. Next there is a band of rain forest where you'll find a type of scarlet-and-yellow impatiens unique to this region. Black-and-white colobus monkeys make their homes in the trees. The alpine zone is rolling moors where you'll find many birds of prey, including Mackinder's owl, Verreaux's eagle, and a rare vulture called the lammergeier. The summits have little vegetation.

The Chagga people called the mountain Kilema Kyaro, meaning "that which makes a journey impossible." They knew that anyone heading through this part of East Africa had to detour around it. Today Mt. Kilimanjaro is a destination in itself, with thousands of people heading here each year to scale its peaks. With the assistance of a guide and porters, a very fit person can make the trek up to Uhuru with no previous experience. The journey is not only for young people. The oldest person to have reached the summit was 74.

The majority of climbers choose the Marangu Route on the eastern face because it is relatively easy and has accommodations along the way, but there are also five other routes. The Rongai Route, which leads up the mountain's northern slopes, is favored by many climbers because the trails are drier and there are far fewer people. The other four—Machame, Rongai, Shira, and Umbwe—see relatively few climbers. The Machame Route may be the most scenic, but it is only for those with lots of experience. *Seven Summits,* by Dick Bass, Rick Ridgeway, and Frank Wells, has a detailed descriptions of the Machame Route.

Kilimanjaro National Park

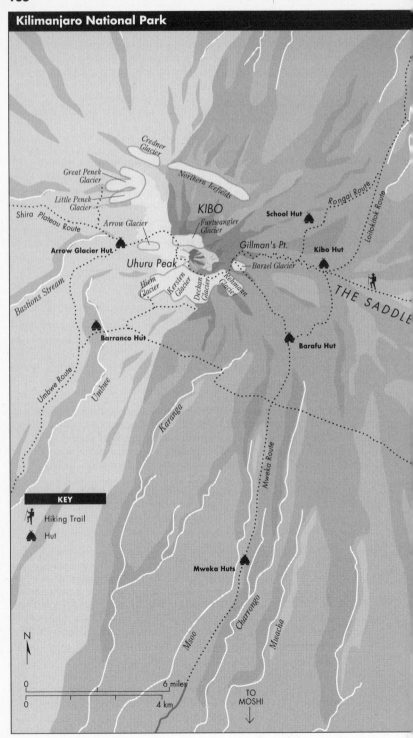

Credner Glacier

Great Penek Glacier

Little Penek Glacier

Northern Icefields

KIBO

Shira Plateau Route

Arrow Glacier

Furtwangler Glacier

School Hut

Rongai Route

Loitokitok Route

Arrow Glacier Hut

Uhuru Peak

Gillman's Pt.

Kibo Hut

Barzel Glacier

THE SADDLE

Hiem Glacier

Kersten Glacier

Decken Glacier

Rebmann Glacier

Bastions Stream

Barranco Hut

Barafu Hut

Umbwe Route

Umbwe

Karanga

Mweka Route

KEY

Hiking Trail

Hut

Mweka Huts

Charrongo

Msoo

Mwacha

N

0   6 miles

0   4 km

TO MOSHI

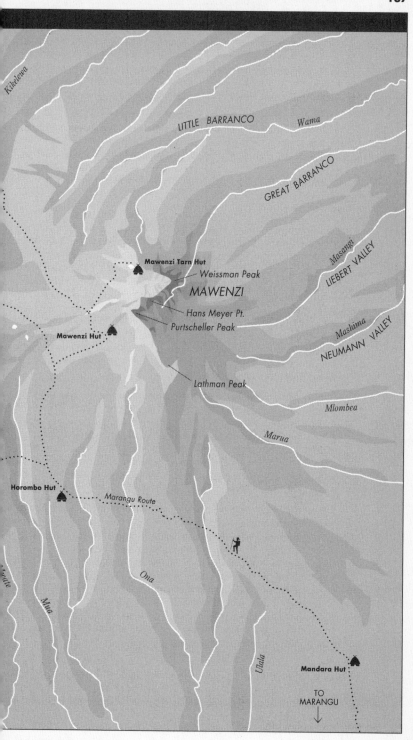

Kikelewa

LITTLE BARRANCO

Wama

GREAT BARRANCO

Masangi

LIEBERT VALLEY

Mawenzi Tarn Hut

— Weissman Peak

MAWENZI

— Hans Meyer Pt.

Mawenzi Hut — Purtscheller Peak

Mashima

NEUMANN VALLEY

— Lathman Peak

Mlombea

Marua

Horombo Hut

Marangu Route

Ona

Mua

Ulala

Mandara Hut

TO
MARANGU
↓

For those who are content to admire the peaks from below, there are new hiking trails in the Shira Plateau, near the park's Londorossi Gate. One trail leads to a volcanic ridge where you'll be treated to views of the Chyulu Hills in Kenya. A second trail takes you into the northern part of the plateau to Simba Gorge. Guides are not required at this altitude, but they are a good idea. Younger children, not allowed on the upper slopes, are welcome on these trails.

There are several regulations to keep in mind when climbing Mt. Kilimanjaro. Before you start, you or your guide must check in at the park headquarters and give details of your planned route and schedule. This is essential in case you need to be rescued. Even if you are an experienced climber, you are required to hire a guide to take you to the summit. No children under 12 are allowed above 3,000 m (9,834 ft). If you have a cold, sore throat, or fever, you should not venture above this point.

Be aware that climbing to such high altitudes can be dangerous. Acute mountain sickness, also known as altitude sickness, strikes more than 50% of those who attempt to climb Mt. Kilimanjaro. Common symptoms include headache, nausea, lack of appetite, exhaustion, and swelling of the face, hands, and ankles. The best way to relieve these symptoms is to return to a lower elevation; a change of as little as 500 m (1,640 feet) is sometimes all that is required. Make sure to get some rest and drink plenty of water. In serious cases of acute mountain sickness, fluid builds up in the brain (cerebral edema) or the lungs (pulmonary edema). Both conditions can be fatal, so descend immediately. The best way to avoid acute mountain sickness is to ascend gradually, taking an extra day to acclimatize.

Climbing Mt. Kilimanjaro is not an inexpensive proposition. You must pay the park fee of $25 per day, plus a camping fee of $40 per day and a rescue fee of $20 per trip. On top of these fees you must pay a tour company before the trip and tip the guide and porters when you're finished. Most companies include the park fees in their rate, but always check to make sure this is the case. The cheapest trips can be had for a total of $500 per person, but don't expect hearty meals or new equipment. Expect to pay closer to $1,000.

Running shoes work fine on the easier part of the climb, but sturdy hiking boots are a must for the summit. Blisters can be avoided if you use moleskin and wear thin socks inside thick ones. Light clothing, including shorts, will suffice for the first two days of a trek. Don't underestimate the frigid conditions at the top, however. Bring a down-filled parka with a hood, fleece shirts, waterproof shell pants, thermal underwear, mittens, wool hat, and a scarf. You must take two changes of clothing in case you get wet. Otherwise, you'll be in danger of hypothermia. Other essentials include sunglasses, sunblock, toilet paper, first-aid kit, water bottle, and flashlight. Nutritious snacks are a good idea to tide you over between meals.

Mt. Kilimanjaro is accessible year-round, but the best months are January, February, and September, followed by July, August, November, and December. At other times of the year you'll encounter snow on the top or rain at the base. December through February are the warmest months, although the summit will still be below freezing at night. The weather is often cooler at midday than in the morning because of the clouds that gather around the mountain. If you want to avoid the crowds, January, February, and September are ideal—you'll encounter far fewer hikers.

Marangu Route

Cameron Burns, author of *Kilimanjaro & Mount Kenya: A Climbing and Trekking Guide,* believes that the Marangu Route does not deserve its reputation as the "Coca-Cola Trail." It's not only for tourists, he insists. "One of the best things about Marangu," according to Burns, "is that it's possible to stay in huts all the way up the mountain." He also appreciates that there are bathing facilities available, as well as places to buy water and soft drinks.

The climb starts at the Marangu Gate, near the village of Marangu. After registering, which takes up to an hour, it is a three- to four-hour walk through the rain forest to the Mandara Hut, actually a group of cottages that sits at 2,700 m (8,856 ft). Spend the first night here, keeping an eye out for elephants, buffaloes, and sometimes even leopards.

The next morning you'll leave the last glades of the forest and follow a gently ascending path through alpine meadows dotted with giant lobelia. The altitude is now apparent, so make a point of not overexerting yourself. You'll reach the Horombo Hut, which sits at 3,720 m (12,202 ft), after about 5–7 hours. Spend the second night here. Good outfitters recommend that you stay an extra night at Horombo to get accustomed to the altitude. The scenery in this area is spectacular, so take advantage of the many short hikes available. It is a very good exercise for your body to go higher then sleep lower.

On day four continue past giant groundsels to the saddle between the peaks of Kibo and Mawenzi. You might see eland at this height. The Kibo Hut, at 4,635 m (15,202 ft), is where you'll spend the fourth night. It can be reached in 5–6 hours. You'll be awakened at about 2 AM because the loose gravel is frozen at this hour, making the trail easier to traverse. Once thawed, it's two steps forward, one step back. For 5–6 hours you'll climb the steepest, most demanding part of the route to Gillman's Point, on the crater's rim at 5,592 m (18,342 ft). The remaining two hours to the summit are not as steep, but you should be very alert to the effects of decreased oxygen on your body.

The descent is far less demanding. You'll spend one night at the Horombo Hut, then by midafternoon the next day you'll reach the park gate. There you'll receive a well-earned certificate proving you've climbed Africa's tallest peak.

Other Routes

The Machame, Shira, and Umbwe Routes are one-way ascents; climbers using these trails are required to descend using the Mweka Route. Those on the Rongai route must come down on the Marangu route. Many climbers describe this as a study in contrasts; very few people take the steep Rongai Route, while many are encountered on the Marangu Route.

Although Kilimanjaro lies entirely within Tanzania, it is possible to start the climb from the Kenya side with a special permit. The Rongai Route begins very near the Kenyan town of Loitokitok, which is why many maps refer to it as the Loitokitok Route. ⊠ *Tanzania National Parks, Box 3134, Arusha,* ☎ *027/250–1930* FAX *027/254–8216.* ⬚ *$25.*

Lodging

$$ ⊡ **Kibo Hotel.** The best lodging in Marangu, this hotel is full of interesting historic photographs and maps from the town's bygone era. A walled garden provides fresh flowers for the dining tables. Marina Stromvall, the general manager, has climbed Mt. Kilimanjaro and can help you organize your own journey. ⊠ *Marangu,* ☎ *027/275–1308,* FAX *027/275–2687. 75 rooms. Dining room. No credit cards.*

$$ ⊡ **Marangu Hotel.** This cluster of cottages is on a 12-acre coffee es-
tate near the park's Marangu Gate. What was once a farmhouse is now
a restaurant that serves freshly baked bread and vegetables from the
kitchen garden. Relax in the small pool or play a game of croquet on
the well-tended lawn. You'll get a discount on your room if you book
a climb with the hotel. ⊠ *Marangu,* ☎ 027/275–1307, ℻ 027/275–
0639, WEB *www.maranguhotel.com. 29 rooms. Dining room, pool,
travel services. MC, V.*

Outdoor Activities and Sports

Hoopoe Adventure Tours (⊠ India St., Arusha, ☎ 027/250–7011, ℻
027/254–8226, WEB www.hoopoe.com) leads tours up Mt. Kilimanjaro's
Machame Route. You'll be accompanied by experienced guides, porters,
and a cook. Accommodations are in mountain tents. **Wilderness Africa
Limited** (⊠ Arusha, ☎ 027/254–8182, ℻ 027/254–8320, WEB
www.wildernessafrica.com) guides climbers up the more difficult Shira
Route. Recommended by experienced climbers like Cameron Burns,
Zara Tanzania Adventures (⊠ Ghalla St., Moshi, ☎ 027/275–0011,
℻ 027/275–3105, WEB www.kilimanjaro.co.tz) offers several different
trips to Mt. Kilimanjaro.

Mkomazi Game Reserve

❽ *100 km (62 mi) north of Tanga.*

The site of one of the country's most promising wildlife conservation
projects, Mkomazi Game Reserve has completely changed in the last
two decades. Established in 1951, the park was in serious decline by
the 1980s. Heavy poaching had nearly eradicated the indigenous ele-
phants and rhinos, while slash-and-burn agriculture had taken its toll
on the landscape. Tanzanian officials had nearly given up hope when
they decided to invite the George Adamson Conservation Trust to
work to restore the park's endangered species. Tony Fitzjohn, who heads
the organization, accepted the ambitious undertaking in 1989.

Elephants are one of the reasons more and more visitors are heading to
the park. Decades of slaughter by ivory poachers decimated the great
herds once found here, so by 1987 only 11 were left. Today you'll see
scores of elephants roaming across the reserve, including some females
with their young. The population approaches 1,500 in the rainy season.

Black rhinos, prized for their horns, suffered even more losses. By the
late 1980s no more were seen in the park. In 1997, after five years of
development and construction, a 72-square-km (28-square-mi) sanc-
tuary was ready for its first rhino. Four black rhinos were flown here
from Addo Elephant National Park, in South Africa. Another five
were relocated here in 2001.

South of the Kenya border, Mkomazi forms a natural extension of
Kenya's Tsavo West National Park. Together the two parks form one
of the largest ecosystems in Africa. Mkomazi is covered with ancient
baobab trees. The bush gives way to open savanna dotted with um-
brella acacias. Migrating herds of oryxes and zebras drift south dur-
ing the wet season. ⊠ *Ministry of Natural Resources & Tourism, Box
1994, Dar es Salaam,* ☎ 022/211–1061, ℻ 22/211–6004, WEB *www.tan-
zania.go.tz/natural.htm.*

Lodging

$ ⊡ **Hilltop Tona Lodge.** Simple rooms can be found in this hotel in the
town of Mbaga. This is an ideal base for exploring Mkomazi Game
Reserve and the Pare Mountains. ⊠ *Mbaga,* ☎ 600–158. *Dining
room. No credit cards.*

NORTHERN TANZANIA A TO Z

To research prices, get advice from other travelers, and book travel arrangements, visit www.fodors.com.

AIR TRAVEL TO AND FROM NORTHERN TANZANIA

Most flights to Northern Tanzania fly into Kilimanjaro International Airport, 55 km (34 mi) east of Arusha and 56 km (35 mi) east of Moshi. Some domestic flights use Arusha Airport, 10 km (6 mi) west of Arusha.

KLM is the only European airline that has regularly scheduled flights to Arusha. It offers daily service from Amsterdam. Air Tanzania flies from other African countries, including Kenya and South Africa. Air Tanzania also has two daily flights from Dar Es Salaam, while Precision Air has one. Precision Air offers regular service to various cities in Tanzania. Regional Air flies to most national parks. Precision Air and Regional Air also offer charter services.

➤ AIRLINES AND CONTACTS: **Air Tanzania** (✉ Boma Rd., Arusha, ☎ 022/211–0245. **KLM** (✉ Boma Rd., Arusha, ☎ 027/250–6063). **Precision Air** (✉ Simeon Rd., Arusha, ☎ 027/250–6903, WEB www.precisionairtz.com). **Regional Air** (Box 14755, Arusha, ☎ 027/250–4477, WEB www.airkenya.com).

BUS TRAVEL TO AND FROM NORTHERN TANZANIA

Because Northern Tanzania is such a vast area, traveling here by bus is bound to take a lot of time. Fresh ya Shamba operates express buses between Dar es Salaam and Arusha. Scandinavian Express offers similar service. Either way the journey takes at least nine hours.

➤ BUS INFORMATION: **Fresh ya Shamba** (✉ Jogoo St., Arusha). **Scandinavian Express** (✉ Jogoo St., Arusha, ☎ 22/250–0153).

CAR RENTAL

There are a handful of car-rental companies in Arusha. Hotel travel offices are generally equipped to arrange car rentals as well. Renters must be at least age 25 and able to show a valid international driver's license.

➤ LOCAL AGENCIES: **Serena Car Hire** (✉ India St., ☎ 027/255–6593). **Takims Holidays Tours** (✉ Simeon Rd., ☎ 027/250–8026, WEB www.takimsholidays.com).

CAR TRAVEL

Because of the conditions of the roads in Tanzania, you may prefer to hire a car and driver. If you choose to drive yourself, make sure you have a four-wheel-drive vehicle for all journeys except those on the major roads. Check about your destination during the rainy season, as some roads may be impassable.

MAIL AND SHIPPING

If you need to mail a letter or package when traveling in Northern Tanzania, it's best to do it from Arusha. The main post office, near the clock tower, is open from Monday through Saturday 8–5.

➤ POST OFFICES: **Arusha** (✉ Old Moshi Rd.).

MONEY MATTERS

Arusha has several currency exchange offices operated by Forex, including one at the Impala Hotel. Some will exchange both cash and traveler's checks as well as give cash advances on credit cards, but the latter service often includes a fee of 25%. Most offices are open from 9 to 5.

You can also exchange currency at the National Bank of Commerce. The branch near the clock tower is open weekdays 8:30–3 and Saturday 8:30–noon.

➤ BANKS: **Forex** (✉ Moshi Rd. and Old Moshi Rd.). **National Bank of Commerce** (✉ Sokoine Rd. and Sinoni Rd., ☎ 027/254–8662).

SAFETY

Muggings are not uncommon in some parts of Arusha. Take a taxi rather than walking around the Arusha International Conference Centre.

TOUR OPERATORS

Make your travel arrangements before arriving in Arusha, as lodges are often booked far in advance. Beware of hucksters who prey on unsuspecting travelers arriving in Arusha. The Tanzania Tourist Board keeps a list of all the unscrupulous travel agencies, so check there before you sign on the dotted line. If you hire a tour operator in Arusha, ask to see its license from the Tourist Agents Licensing Authority.

If you want to plan you own safari though Tanzania, Justin Bell and Tor Allan of Wilderness Africa Limited have excellent reputations. Both come from families that have lived in East Africa for decades. Camps are designed with comfort and mobility in mind, enabling you to visit truly remote places while maintaining the high standards of more permanent accommodations.

Hoopoe Adventure Tours offers tours to the Northern Circuit as well as to more remote parts of Tanzania. Established by archaeologist Peter Jones, Tanganyika Film & Safari Outfitters offers trips for professional photographers and filmmakers, as well as those who just want a good shot of Mt. Kilimanjaro to show the folks back home. Francesco Pierre-Nina of Tanzania Outfitters & Safaris organizes luxury safaris for families and small groups.

Venture into the bush with Equestrian Safaris, the country's most experienced company offering horseback safaris. It offers several routes, including the Hatari Safari, which lets you "ride in the footsteps of John Wayne." Trips begins at Uto Farm, 30 km (18 mi) north of Arusha. You can see the Serengeti from a totally different perspective with Serengeti Balloon Safaris. The trips begin at dawn, allowing you to see the landscape as the sun is peaking over the horizon. Afterward is a champagne breakfast.

➤ TOUR COMPANIES: **Equestrian Safaris** (✉ Oldonyo Sambu, ☎ 00–871–761–229–074 for satellite phone, FAX 00–871–761–229–075 for satellite fax, WEB www.safaririding.com). **Hoopoe Adventure Tours** (✉ India St., Arusha, ☎ 027/250–7011, FAX 027/254–8226, WEB www.hoopoe.com). **Serengeti Balloon Safaris** (✉ Arusha, ☎ 027/250–8578, WEB www.balloonsafaris.com). **Tanganyika Film & Safari Outfitters** (✉ Arusha ☎ 027/250–2713, FAX 027/250–8547, WEB www.tanzania-safari.com). **Tanzania Outfitters & Safaris** (✉ Arusha ☎ 027/254–4051). **Wilderness Africa Limited** (✉ Arusha, ☎ 027/254–8182, FAX 027/254–8320, WEB www.wildernessafrica.com).

VISITOR INFORMATION

The Tanzania Tourist Board, near the New Safari Hotel, stocks maps and other useful information. It maintains a blacklist of tour operators that have bilked travelers.

➤ TOURIST INFORMATION: **Tanzania Tourist Board** (✉ Boma Rd., Arusha, ☎ 027/254–3842, FAX 027/254–8628, WEB www.tanzania-web.com)

TANZANIA'S OTHER GAME RESERVES

At one time the Northern Circuit was the only accessible part of Tanzania. This has changed, thanks to flights to many of the country's more remote reserves. There are many other choices, such as Ruaha National Park, in the central part of the country, and Selous Game Reserve, in the south. Taking a plane can leave you with more time for actually seeing wildlife, rather that eating dust on the road. You can also tailor your trip to your own interests, whether mountain climbing or scuba diving.

Gombe Stream National Park

16 km (10 mi) north of Kigoma.

This small park has a big reputation because of Jane Goodall's study of its chimpanzee population. The research that she began at Gombe Stream National Park continues today into its fourth decade. In 1960, at about the same time that anthropologist Louis Leakey wrote that "tool making in a regular and set pattern" defined humans, a young primatologist he had hired noted in her field diary that she had observed two chimps using a piece of straw to remove termites from a mound.

Intrigued by this behavior, Goodall found many other examples of tool making in a "regular and set pattern." One chimp used a leaf as a sponge to gather water, while another chimp used a leaf as a tissue to clean his little brother after he sneezed. Goodall contended that the genius in the use of tools was not the tool itself, but the solving of a problem.

The chimps in Gombe, given familiar first names, captured the world's attention through documentaries produced by the National Geographic Society. A few of the chimps worked their way into the hearts of viewers. When a well-known chimp named Flo died, an obituary ran in London's *Sunday Times*.

The park currently holds about 150 chimps, split between three families that maintain their own territories. Rangers can advise you about where the chimps were last spotted. They do not roam as far in the wet seasons (from February through June and from November through mid-December), making them easier to find. Photographers often prefer to visit in the dry season (from July through October and in late December) because there is less vegetation.

The park is a narrow strip of a mountainous country bounded by the escarpment of the Great Rift Valley to the east and by Lake Tanganyika to the west. Habitats vary from evergreen forests to open grasslands. Besides chimps, keep an eye out for blue monkeys, red-tailed monkeys, and red colobus monkeys. There are no roads through the park, which means you can't get here by car. Take a boat from the nearby village of Kigoma. ⊠ *Tanzania National Parks, Box 3134, Arusha,* ☎ *027/250–1930,* 𝗙𝗔𝗫 *027/254–8216.* ⊡ *$100.*

Lodging

$$$–$$ ⬚ **Kigoma Hilltop Hotel.** With a magnificent perch above Lake Tanganyika, this luxurious hotel is a great base for exploring Gombe Stream National Park and Mahale Mountains National Park. After a day with the chimpanzees you can take a dip in the pool or head out to the lake for some waterskiing or parasailing. The helpful staff can arrange excursions to the nearby village of Ujiji, where Henry Morton Stanley uttered the immortal words: "Dr. Livingstone, I presume." The Sangara restaurant serves Continental cuisine. ⊠ *2 km (1 mi) west*

of Kigoma, ☎ *028/280–4435,* FAX *028/280–4434,* WEB *www.kigoma.com. 30 rooms. Restaurant, bar, pool, health club, tennis courts, playground, meeting rooms, travel services. AE, DC, MC, V.*

$ ⌸ **Aqua Lodge.** At the western end of Kigoma, this modern hotel has rooms with balconies overlooking Lake Tanganyika. The staff is happy to arrange fishing trips. The hotel and the adjoining restaurant are near the Mahale Wildlife Research Center. ⊠ *Kokolwa Ave., Kigoma,* ☎ *028/282–586. 9 rooms. Restaurant. AE, DC, MC, V.*

$ ⌸ **Lake Tanganyika View Hotel.** The town's most venerable hotel, this beauty in decline has a lovely lawn that slopes down to the water. Rooms are basic but comfortable. There are a restaurant and a popular disco on weekends. ⊠ *Stanley Rd., Kigoma,* ☎ *028/280–2694. Restaurant, bar, shop, dance club. AE, DC, MC, V.*

Gombe Stream National Park A to Z

To research prices, get advice from other travelers, and book travel arrangements, visit www.fodors.com.

AIR TRAVEL TO AND FROM GOMBE STREAM NATIONAL PARK

Gombe Stream National Park is north of the town of Kigoma, on the western edge of Tanzania near the Burundi border. The Kigoma Airport is reached via scheduled flights from Dar es Salaam on Precision Air.

➤ AIRLINES AND CONTACTS: **Precision Air** (⊠ Ohio St., Dar es Saalam, ☎ 022/212–1718, WEB www.precisionairtz.com).

BOATS AND FERRIES

You can reach Gombe Stream National Park on the M/V *Liemba,* which serves ports along Lake Tanganyika. The former warship has a fascinating history. It was built by the Germans in 1914, two years after the sinking of the *Titanic.* It was sunk to hide it from the British, who later raised it and refitted it as a ferry. The ship is often hot and crowded. Second-class cabins are tiny and cramped. First-class cabins are much more expensive, and the added comfort makes them worth every dime. Book through the Kigoma Hilltop Hotel.

➤ INFORMATION: **M/V *Liemba*** (⊠ Kigoma, ☎ 028/280–4435, FAX 028/280–4434).

MAIL AND SHIPPING

The main post office is Kigoma is in the center of town near the main roundabout.

➤ POST OFFICES: **Kigoma** (⊠ Kiezya Rd.).

MONEY MATTERS

There are no currency exchange offices in Kigoma, so make sure you have enough cash on hand before leaving Arusha or Dar es Salaam. The National Bank of Commerce on Lumumba Road will cash traveler's checks.

➤ BANKS: **National Bank of Commerce** (⊠ Lumumba Rd., ☎ 028/280–2210).

Katavi National Park

★ *40 km (25 mi) southeast of Mpanda.*

Although it is Tanzania's third-largest national park, Katavi remains one of the least visited. One reason is its location in the western corner of the country, far off the tourist trail. Another was the dearth of decent accommodations here until a tented camp was established in 1999.

But Katavi is one of the country's best-kept secrets. Be prepared to see some of the country's largest herds of buffaloes rumbling across the horizon. It has been compared to the way the Serengeti was a half century ago, before minivans raised clouds of dust across the plains. In this unspoiled wilderness you can have a sliver of Africa all to yourself.

Palm-fringed Lake Chada, in the southeastern part of the park, has the country's highest concentration of crocodiles. When droughts shrink the lake, the crocodiles pile together in the only remaining pools. A few lucky ones retreat to small caves, emerging to browse around for a meal in the parched savanna grasses. You may never have seen a 20-ft crocodile strolling at sundown, its belly the color of jaundice, but here it's a common sight.

The grasslands near the lake attract grazers such as the southern reedbuck, the blue-flanked topi, and the seldom-seen *puku,* a honey-color antelope. These animals, in turn, bring substantial numbers of lions and leopards. There are more hippos in the swampy areas around the Katuma River than anywhere else in the country.

More than 400 species of birds have been recorded in Katavi. Here you'll see the black-browed albatross, crested lark, green sandpiper, black-faced barbet, and blue swallow. African fish eagles gather in large numbers by the river. ✉ *Tanzania National Parks, Box 3134, Arusha,* ☎ *027/250–1930,* FAX *027/254–8216.* 🖃 *$15.*

Lodging

$$$$ 🏕 **Katavi Tented Camp.** The green-canvas tents that make up this tra-
★ ditional camp are positioned on the edge of Katavi National Park. Each has a rather spacious sleeping area with a dressing area and a veranda overlooking Chada Plain. There are also great views from your private bath. A telescope is handy for game spotting or stargazing, and the campaign chairs around the campfire encourage guests to share stories. Although these tents are comfortable, the highlight of a safari here is to spend at least one evening in a simple fly camp. Owner Roland Purcell has two small planes that you can charter for your trip here. Book through Uncharted Outposts. ✉ *Katavi National Park,* ☎ *404/ 888–0909 in the U.S.,* FAX *404/888–0081 in the U.S.,* WEB *www.unchartedoutposts.com. 6 tents. Dining room. AE, DC, MC, V. Closed Nov.–mid-May.*

Katavi National Park A to Z

To research prices, get advice from other travelers, and book travel arrangements, visit www.fodors.com.

AIR TRAVEL TO AND FROM KATAVI NATIONAL PARK

Precision Air offers regularly scheduled flights to the nearby town of Tabora from Arusha and Dar es Salaam. Northern Air offers charter service from Arusha to Tabora.

➤ AIRLINES AND CONTACTS: **Northern Air** (✉ Goliondio Rd., Arusha, ☎ 027/254–8060). **Precision Air** (✉ Ohio St., Dar es Salaam, ☎ 022/ 212–1718; ✉ Simeon Rd., Arusha, ☎ 027/250–6903, WEB www.precisionairtz.com).

BOATS AND FERRIES

Take the M/V *Liemba* from Kigoma to Sumbwa or Karema, points near Katavi National Park. Arrange to have someone meet you on your arrival.

➤ INFORMATION: **M/V** *Liemba* (✉ Kigoma, ☎ 028/280–4435, FAX 028/ 280–4434).

CAR TRAVEL

Katavi is on the main road running through the western edge of Tanzania. Katavi is 390 km (242 mi) from Mpanda and 550 km (342 mi) from Mbeya.

Mafia Island Marine Park

In the Indian Ocean 120 km (75 mi) south of Dar es Salaam.

Delicate sea fans, long strands of whip coral, and gargantuan stands of blue-tipped staghorn coral draw divers from around the world to the waters surrounding Mafia Island. This amazing undersea world is protected by the Mafia Island Marine Park, the country's first marine preserve.

Chole Bay, Mafia Island's protected harbor, is popular with snorkelers. Around the island's southern tip are reefs that are home to hundreds of species of fish, from barracuda to marlin. Divers head to the pristine coral gardens surrounding Juani and Jibondo islands.

The World Wildlife Fund is active in conservation efforts here, fighting practices such as dynamite fishing. It's a difficult battle because the 38,000 people that live on Mafia Island and the smaller islands of Jibondo, Juani, and Chole make their livelihood from the sea. The organization is working with the locals to find other ways to support the islands.

Mafia Island's history goes back to the 8th century, when it was a stop along the trade routes. For 2,000 years the island was a port for Arab dhows sailing from the Persian Gulf to Madagascar. Portuguese explorer Vasco da Gama sighted Mafia Island in 1498. Europeans referred to the island as Morfiyeh, from an Arabic word meaning "archipelago." The word eventually became Mafia.

The major attractions here are diving and snorkeling, but you can also arrange to see locals building dhows or charter a boat to go deep-sea fishing. You can also take a trip to see the breeding grounds of giant turtles. Ruins of several mosques dating from the 18th and 19th centuries can be visited on Juani Island. ⊠ *Tanzania National Parks, Box 3134, Arusha,* ☎ *027/250–1930,* 𝖥𝖠𝖷 *027/254–8216.*

Lodging

$$$$ ⊞ **Chole Mjini.** Named after some nearby archaeological ruins, this island retreat is inspired. Built around towering baobab trees, these stilt houses call to mind those of the seminomadic people of the Rufiji Delta. Inside you'll find luxurious furnishings such as four-poster beds. The dining room, in an open-sided building with lovely views, serves up dishes like octopus and lobster prepared in traditional Swahili fashion. Relax with a book in the library, or chat with fellow guests upstairs in the small bar. A portion of the room rate goes toward assisting local people in building schools and clinics. Book through Africa Travel Resource. ⊠ *Chole Island,* ☎ *831/338–2383 in the U.S., 1737/241–892 in the U.K.,* 𝖶𝖤𝖡 *www.intotanzania.com. 7 cottages. Bar, dining room, lounge, in-room safe, boating. AE, MC, V.*

$$$$ ⊞ **Kinasi.** Nestled in a cashew plantation, this lodge overlooks the startlingly blue waters of Chole Bay. It's not surprising that many people come here to learn how to windsurf or earn a certificate in diving. The rooms are in bungalows covered with *makuti,* a Swahili word for palm leaves. Each has a large veranda with lovely views. All of the furniture is handcrafted, and the glassware in the dining room was created by East African artists. Entrées of locally caught shrimp, crab, and lobster are accompanied by fresh vegetables and fruits flown in from

the mainland. The staff can organize camping trips to other islands. ✉ *Mafia Island,* ☎ *404/888–0909 in the U.S.,* ℻ *404/888–0081 in the U.S.,* 🕸 *www.mafiaisland.com. 12 rooms. Dining room, pool, dive shop, boating. AE, DC, MC, V.*

$$$$ 🔟 **Pole Pole.**With a name that is Swahili for "take it easy," it's not surprising that Pole Pole is a place where you can get away from it all. The lodges are built on a hillside with sweeping views across Chole Bay. Constructed from mangrove and makuti thatch, each has handsome hardwood floors. Private verandas have daybeds where you can while away an afternoon. The dining room serves seafood cooked in traditional Swahili fashion. Good beaches are rare on Mafia Island, but Pole Pole has a nice one all to itself. ✉ *Mafia Island,* ☎ *051-843–717,* ℻ *051/116–239. 9 cottages. Dining room. No credit cards.*

Mafia Island Marine Park A to Z

To research prices, get advice from other travelers, and book travel arrangements, visit www.fodors.com.

AIR TRAVEL TO AND FROM MAFIA ISLAND MARINE PARK
Precision Air runs scheduled flights to Mafia Island from Arusha, Moshi, Stone Town, and Dar es Salaam. Eagle Air flies to Mafia Island from Stone Town and Dar es Salaam.
➤ AIRLINES AND CONTACTS: **Eagle Air** (✉ Azikiwe St., Dar es Salaam, ☎ 022/212–7411). **Precision Air** (✉ Ohio St., Dar es Salaam, ☎ 022/212–1718; ✉ Simeon Rd., Arusha, ☎ 027/250–6903, 🕸 www.precisionairtz.com).

BOATS AND FERRIES
From Kisiju, about 80 km (50 mi) south of Dar es Salaam, you can hire a dhow to take you to Kisiju Island or a motorboat to deliver you to Mafia Island.

Mahale Mountains National Park

150 km (93 mi) south of Kigoma.

In a tropical rain forest on the eastern edge of Lake Tanganyika, Mahale Mountains National Park is home to one of the world's largest populations of chimpanzees. Here you'll encounter five times as many of these primates as at Gombe Stream National Park. A team of Japanese researchers at the Kasoge Research Camp have worked here since 1965, so some of the chimps have become accustomed to humans. A few will even allow you to come within a few feet.

The region was first documented in 1877, when Verney Lovett Cameron wrote about his travels here in *Across Africa*. Since that time it has been a favored destination for many researchers, including a team from Oxford University that journeyed here in 1958. The Japanese scientists working with the chimps petitioned the government for years to protect this important region. It finally gained national park status in 1985.

Although not as famous as Gombe Stream National Park, where Jane Goodall has worked for more than 40 years, Mahale is equally as interesting. Michael Huffman, a professor at Kyoto University's Primate Research Institute, has been studying the chimps here since 1985. Huffman documented the first scientific evidence for self-medication in these animals. He noted how chimps infected with parasitic worms use plants to help keep them under control.

About 1,000 chimpanzees make their home in Mahale. They live in groups of between 30 and 80. Each group has its own territory, which is patrolled by the males. Research has focused on the 50 or so chimps that make up M group. They live in the Kasoge Forest on the lowest slopes of the Mahale Mountains, which makes them relatively easy to find. They do have a mind of their own, however. When Microsoft founder Bill Gates visited Mahale, they were nowhere to be found.

Although most people come here to see the chimps, there are plenty of other primates in the forests of Mahale. You may see yellow baboons, red colobus monkeys, and a subspecies of black-and-white colobus monkeys. Also here is a wide variety of wildlife, including brush-tailed porcupines, bushy-tailed mongooses, and Sharp's grysboks. Conservation projects have meant that lions and leopards—long absent from the park—are returning.

The bird life is unusually rich, with many West African species making an appearance. By the shore of Lake Tanganyika you can see red-collared widow birds. In stands of oil palms look for speckled mouse birds. Near Mt. Nkungwe you're likely to spot crowned eagles, bee-eaters, and rollers. Redwing starlings and violet-backed starlings live in the forest. At dusk and dawn listen for the song of white-browed robin chats. ⊠ *Tanzania National Parks, Box 3134, Arusha,* ☎ *027/ 250–1930* FAX *027/254–8216.* ⬚ *$50.*

Lodging

$$$$ ⬚ **Mahale Mountain Camp.** Roland Purcell, who served as director of Rwanda's Mountain Gorilla Project after Dian Fossey's death, founded this inspired camp on the sandy shores of Lake Tanganyika. Elegant white canvas and mahogany tents that call to mind the grandeur of the Ottoman Empire are based on a photo Purcell saw in a museum. In the large dining tent don't be surprised to find that fresh sushi is a specialty here. Treks into the forest to see the chimps are the big draw, and you must be in reasonable shape to manage the hikes through the forest. You can also enjoy sunset cruises on a 45-ft mahogany dhow. If getting to this remote camp sounds daunting, remember that Purcell himself can collect you in his six-seater plane. ⊠ *Mahale Mountains National Park,* ☎ *404/888–0909 in the U.S.,* FAX *404/888–0081 in the U.S.,* WEB *www.unchartedoutposts.com. 6 tents. Bar, dining room, fishing. AE, DC, MC, V.*

Mahale Mountains National Park A to Z

To research prices, get advice from other travelers, and book travel arrangements, visit www.fodors.com.

AIR TRAVEL TO AND FROM MAHALE MOUNTAINS NATIONAL PARK

Precision Air has regularly scheduled flights from Arusha and Dar es Salaam to Kigoma. Precision Air and Northern Air make the 40-minute flight to Mahale. You can make both these flights in the morning and get into Mahale in time for lunch.
➤ AIRLINES AND CONTACTS: **Northern Air** (⊠ Goliondi Rd., Arusha, ☎ 027/254–8060). **Precision Air** (⊠ Ohio St., Dar es Salaam, ☎ 022/ 212–1718; ⊠ Simeon Rd., Arusha, ☎ 027/250–6903, WEB www.precisionairtz.com).

BOATS AND FERRIES

In the village of Lagosa you can charter small fishing boats to take you to Mahale. Lagosa is one of the ports of call for the M/V *Liemba,* the steamer that travels here each week from Kigoma. Book through the Kigoma Hilltop Hotel in Kigoma.

➤ INFORMATION: *M/V Liemba* (✉ Kigoma, ☎ 028/280–4435, 🖷 028/280–4434).

Ruaha National Park

130 km (81 mi) west of Iringa.

Take one look at the magnificent baobob trees in Ruaha National Park and you'll know what inspired the legend that the gods mistakenly planted them with their roots in the air. Their bare branches scrape the sky most of the year, producing leaves for only three months at a time. Baobabs come closer to immortality than any other living thing on this landscape. These trees can live 3,000 years or more; many of the larger ones you see here are between 100 and 800 years old.

Although it is nearly as large as Serengeti National Park, Ruaha attracts only a fraction of the visitors. In fact, this is one of Tanzania's least traveled reserves. Yet Ruaha offers some amazing opportunities for viewing wildlife. Here you'll see more elephants than anywhere else in the country. More than 12,000 make their home here. Not so long ago you would have seen only a handful of the gentle creatures. Their numbers were dwindling in Ruaha and elsewhere because of rampant poaching. A team of nearly 100 park rangers now patrols the park between the central headquarters and seven outlying posts. Antipoaching patrols head out on foot, in cars, and in planes.

Ruaha is one of the few places in East Africa where you can still see rare African wild dogs. Packs of more than 30 have been spotted in the reserve. Cape buffaloes rumble across the plains. Greater and lesser kudus cautiously head to the Ruaha River for a drink, keeping an eye out for lions.

The variety of plants found here is astounding. There are vast tracts of deciduous woodlands, undulating plains, and even evergreen forests. One intriguing species found here is the winterthorn, which keeps its leaves in the dry season and sheds them during the rains, when other trees are lush. ✉ *Tanzania National Parks, Box 3134, Arusha,* ☎ *027/250–1930,* 🖷 *027/254–8216.* 🔊 *$15.*

Lodging

$$$$ 🏠 **Mwagusi Camp.** Nestled on the banks of the Mwagusi Sand River,
★ this small tented camp overlooks a watering hole that attracts much wildlife. Seeing a few thousand buffaloes while relaxing on your veranda or as you share stories in the dining room is not uncommon. The thatch-roof bandas have thoughtful touches, such as spacious wardrobes and dressing tables. Hurricane lamps provide lighting at night. Game drives are in open-sided four-by-fours filled with reference books so you can read about the game you have spotted. Walking safaris, accompanied by an experienced guide, are one of the appealing parts of staying here. ✉ *Ruaha National Park,* ☎ *831/338–2383 in the U.S., 1737/241–892 in the U.K,* 🌐 *www.intotanzania.com. 8 bandas. Bar, dining room, hiking. AE, MC, V.*

$$$$ 🏠 **Ruaha River Lodge.** Overlooking the Great Ruaha River, this venerable lodge is built around a large kopje. It's owned by the Fox family, British expatriates with loads of expertise about the bush. Accommodations are in bandas made of locally quarried stone covered with thatch. From your veranda you can watch the elephants and other animals that come quite close to the camp. A nearby farm supplies fresh vegetables and dairy products for meals, which are served in an open-sided structure with views of the river. The camp has four-by-fours for game drives and for transfers from the nearby airstrip. ✉

Ruaha National Park, ☎ *0811/327–706,* WEB *www.ruahariverlodge.com. Bar, dining room, hiking. MC, V.*

Ruaha National Park A to Z

To research prices, get advice from other travelers, and book travel arrangements, visit www.fodors.com.

AIR TRAVEL TO AND FROM RUAHA NATIONAL PARK

Coastal Air and Precision Air both offer scheduled flights to Ruaha National Park. You can also charter a flight through Northern Air. There's an airstrip near the park headquarters.

➤ AIRLINES AND CONTACTS: **Coastal Air** (✉ Upanga Rd. at Ohio St., Dar es Salaam, ☎ 022/211–7959, FAX 022/211–8647, WEB www.coastal.cc). **Northern Air** (✉ Goliondi Rd., Arusha, ☎ 027/254–8060). **Precision Air** (✉ Ohio St., Dar es Salaam, ☎ 022/212–1718; ✉ Simeon Rd., Arusha, ☎ 027/250–6903, WEB www.precision-airtz.com).

Selous Game Reserve

★ *350 km (217 mi) from Dar es Salaam.*

Noted naturalist Richard Bonham described Selous Game Reserve as "the heart of Africa." The raw wilderness is characterized by its many rivers. The Great Ruaha and the Kilombero flow into the Rufiji, which in turn empties into the Indian Ocean near Mafia Island. Far off the beaten path, you won't run across any minivans full of picture-snapping tourists here. What you will see are great herds of buffaloes on the savanna.

Tanzania's largest game reserve, Selous even dwarfs Serengeti National Park. It was named for Frederick Selous, who chronicled his adventures in East Africa in his book *A Hunter's Wanderings in Africa.* He later gave up hunting almost entirely, preferring to lead safaris through the region. He even escorted U.S. president Theodore Roosevelt on a trip through the bush in 1909. Selous came out of retirement in 1917 to join the British forces in World War I, and while scouting in the area was killed by a German sniper. He is buried on a bluff overlooking the Beho Beho River. Nearby is a more recent grave, belonging to Elizabeth Theobald, who was devoted to protecting black rhinos. She died of malaria in 1997.

The only part of the Selous Game Reserve readily accessible is north of the Rufiji River. The area boasts an impressive variety of wildlife. Hundreds of thousands of elephants, including some big tuskers, once roamed Selous. Many were killed by poachers, but the elephant population is now on the rise. There's no shortage of hippos—you will see hundreds along the Rufiji River. ✉ *Ministry of Natural Resources & Tourism, Box 1994, Dar es Salaam,* ☎ *022/211–1061,* FAX *22/2110–6004,* WEB *www.tanzania.go.tz/natural.htm.*

Lodging

$$$$ 🏨 **Rufiji River Camp.** Built on the banks of the Rufiji River, this camp is within sight of the elephants along the shores. You can watch snorting hippos from the dining room or bar. The dinner menu may include impala and warthog. ✉ *Selous Game Reserve,* ☎ *022/277–5164,* FAX *022/277–5165,* WEB *www.coastal.cc. 10 tents. Bar, dining room, hiking. MC, V.*

$$$$ 🏨 **Sand Rivers Selous Lodge.** With stunning views of the Rufiji River,
★   Sand Rivers Selous Lodge has Africa at its doorstep. The cottages are spacious and comfortable. The beautifully designed dining area, con-

structed of local stone and mahogany, has a massive fireplace to keep you cozy on cool evenings. Swim in the pool shaded by a great baobab or grab a beer at the large open bar. In addition to game drives in custom-designed vehicles, you can set out on a walking safaris, drift silently past hippos on the river, or sleep beneath a billion stars in a fly camp in Steigler's Gorge. ⊠ *Selous Game Reserve,* ☎ *02/882–521 in Nairobi,* FAX *02/882–728 in Nairobi,* WEB *www.richardbonhamsafaris.com. 8 cottages. Bar, dining room, hiking, boating, private airstrip. AE, DC, MC, V.*

$$$$ ⌂ **Selous Safari Camp.** This camp has catered to royalty—Britain's Prince Charles and his sons trekked to the remote lodge in 1997. Designed to blend in with the natural environment, Selous Safari Camp is on the Rufiji River. Raised on a wooden platforms, the tents have verandas with easy chairs so you can sit outside and watch for the animals that wander into the camp. Walking safaris with a knowledgeable guide are a big draw. You can even stay overnight at a mobile camp. Children under 12 are not welcome. ⊠ *Selous Game Reserve,* ☎ *022/ 213–4802,* FAX *022/211–2794,* WEB *www.selous.com. 12 tents. Bar, dining room, hiking, private airstrip. MC, V. Closed Apr.–May.*

Selous Game Reserve A to Z

To research prices, get advice from other travelers, and book travel arrangements, visit www.fodors.com.

AIR TRAVEL TO AND FROM SELOUS GAME RESERVE

Coastal Air offers daily flights to Selous Game Reserve from Dar es Salaam.

➤ AIRLINES AND CONTACTS: **Coastal Air** (⊠ Upanga Rd. at Ohio St., Dar es Salaam, ☎ 022/211–7959, FAX 022/211–8647, WEB www.coastal.cc).

CAR TRAVEL

It's possible to drive to the Selous Game Reserve, but it's a long trip, and the roads are not always paved. If you decide to take a car, be sure to bring along enough gas for your return trip.

TOURS OPERATORS

Nick van Gruisen, owner of Worldwide Journeys & Expeditions, organizes first-rate safaris throughout Africa. He knows the Selous very well.

➤ TOUR COMPANIES: **Worldwide Journeys & Expeditions** (⊠ 8 Comeragh Rd., London W149HP, ☎ 020/7386–4646, FAX 020/7381–0836, WEB www.worldwidejourneys.co.uk).

8 ZANZIBAR

This ancient isle once ruled by sultans and slave traders served as the stepping stone into the African continent for missionaries and explorers. Today this jewel in the Indian Ocean attracts adventurers intent on discovering its sandy beaches, pristine rain forests, or boldly colored coral reefs. Once known as the Spice Island for its export of cloves, Zanzibar has become the most exotic flavor in travel, better than Bali or Mali when it comes to beauty that will make your jaw drop.

By Delta Willis

FEW PLACES ARE MORE EXOTIC than Zanzibar, where the heady scent of clove trees hangs heavy in the air. The name of this tiny archipelago off the coast of Tanzania is thought to come from the Persian phrase *zayn zal barr,* which means "fair is the island," or *zinj el barr,* an Arab term for the region that translates as "land of the black people." Either way, the name reflects a culture and architecture that, like the Swahili language spoken by most people here, is a combination of Africa and Arabia.

Separated from the mainland by a channel only 35 km (22 mi) wide, this tiny archipelago in the Indian Ocean was the launching base for a romantic era of expeditions into Africa. Sir Richard Burton and John Hanning Speke used it as their base when searching for the source of the Nile. It was in Zanzibar that journalist Henry Morton Stanley, perched in a penthouse overlooking the Stone Town harbor, began his search for David Livingstone.

Six degrees south of the equator, Zanzibar consists of two major islands, Unguja and Pemba. Although Stone Town can rightly be called a city, much of the western part of the larger island of Unguja is a slumbering paradise where cloves, as well as rice and coconuts, still grow. Imported from Southeast Asia in the early 1800s, cloves brought much prosperity to the region and led to the introduction of other crops such as cinnamon, vanilla, cumin, nutmeg, cardamom, ginger, and black pepper. Disaster struck in 1872 when a severe storm destroyed most of Unguja's trees. Pemba became the main producer of cloves, but not before great palaces were erected on Unguja from the profits of large plantations. Ivory and slave traders such as Tippu Tip also built mansions, with floors of black-and-white marble and carved doors heavier than those of a bank vault. Today many of these homes serve as hotels or museums, including the People's Palace, Salome's Garden, and the House of Wonders—at a towering four stories it is Zanzibar's tallest building.

About the same color as cloves are the rare monkeys that make their home in Unguja's Jozani Forest Reserve. Named Kirk's red colobus after Sir John Kirk, the British consul in Zanzibar from 1866 to 1887, the species is known for its white whiskers and rusty coat. Many animals here are endangered because 95% of the original forests of the archipelago have been destroyed. Reserves have been established to harbor such species as the blue duiker, a diminutive antelope whose coat is a dusty bluish-gray.

The first ships to enter Unguja's harbors may have belonged to the Phoenicians, who are believed to have sailed in around 600 BC, and since then every other great navy in the eastern hemisphere has dropped anchor here at one time or another. But it was Arab traders who left an indelible mark. Minarets punctuate the skyline of Stone Town, where more than 90% of the residents are Muslim. In the harbor you will see dhows, the Arabian boats with triangular sails. Islamic women with their faces covered by black boubou veils scurry down alleyways so narrow their outstretched arms could touch buildings on both sides. Stone Town received its odd name because most of its buildings were made of limestone, which means exposure to salty air has eroded many foundations. Flat rooftops, perfectly suited for the deserts where many of the oldest inhabitants originated, merely collected rain. After more than a few roofs collapsed from the standing pools, residents started changing their construction methods. As you gaze out upon the rooftops in the evening, you may notice a few vaulted A-frames, the better to drain the water during monsoons.

The first Europeans who arrived here were the Portuguese in the 15th century, and thus began a reign of exploitation. As far inland as Lake Tanganyika, slave traders captured the residents outright or bartered for them from their own chiefs, then forced the newly enslaved to march toward the Indian Ocean carrying loads of ivory tusks. Once at the shore they were shackled together while waiting for dhows to collect them at Bagamoyo, a place whose name means "here I leave my heart." Although it's estimated that 50,000 slaves passed through the Zanzibar slave market each year during the 19th century, many more died en route.

Unguja has lured adventurous travelers for years. Newer on the tourist map is Pemba, to the north of Unguja. For many years Arabs referred to this island as Al Khudra, or the Green Island, and indeed it still is, with forests of king palms, mangos, and banana trees. The 65-km-long island is less famous than Unguja except among scuba divers, who enjoy the lush coral gardens with colorful sponges and huge fans. Archaeology buffs are also discovering Pemba, where sites from the 9th to the 15th centuries have been unearthed. At Mtambwe Mkuu coins bearing the heads of sultans were discovered. Ruins along the coast include ancient mosques and tombs.

In the 1930s Pemba was famous for its sorcerers, attracting disciples of the black arts from as far away as Haiti. Witchcraft is still practiced, and, odd enough, so is bullfighting. Introduced by the Portuguese in the 17th century, the sport has been improved by locals, who rewrote the ending. After enduring the ritual teasing by the matador's cape, the crowds drape the bull with flowers and parade him around the village.

Beyond Pemba, smaller islands in the Zanzibar Archipelago range from mere sandbanks to Changdu, once a prison island, and Mnemba, a private retreat for guests who pay hundreds of dollars per day to get away from it all. To the west of Pemba, Misali Island reputedly served as a hideout for the notorious Captain Kidd, which makes visitors dream of buried treasure. In reality it is the sea turtles that do most of the digging.

Tanganyika and Zanzibar merged in 1964 to create Tanzania, but the honeymoon was brief. Zanzibar's relationship with the mainland remains uncertain as calls for independence continue. "Bismillah, will you let him go," a lyric from Queen's "Bohemian Rhapsody," has become a rebel chant for Zanzibar to break from Tanzania. (Freddie Mercury, lead singer of Queen, was born Farouk Bulsara in Stone Town.) The archipelago also has tensions of its own. Accusations of voting irregularities during the elections in 2000 led to violence that sent scores of refugees fleeing to the mainland. Calm was quickly restored. As the old proverb goes, the dogs bark and the caravan moves on.

Zanzibar's appeal is apparent to developers, who are intent on opening restaurants, hotels, and even water-sapping golf courses. But so far the archipelago has kept much of its charm. It retains the allure it had when explorer David Livingstone set up his expedition office here in 1866.

Pleasures and Pastimes

Architecture
You can easily get lost on the narrow streets of Stone Town, but it's a pleasant experience; the architecture of this ancient city captivates the eye. Arab doors are ornately carved, some with pointed brass bosses, a design meant to discourage soldiers riding elephants from getting too close. More modern doors are curved at the top, while the truly old

Zanzibar Archipelago

0   10 miles
0   10 km

Ngezi Forest — Verani

Pemba Island

Njao Island

Fundo Island

Wete

Kojani Island

Uvinje Island
Kokota Island
Funzi Island

Ras Mkumbuu Ruins ■

Chake Chake

Misale Island

Pemba Channel

Mkoani

Makongwe Island

Matumbini Island
Kisiwa Panza Island
Yombi Island
Kiweni Island

0   10 miles
0   10 km

N

Nungwi

Kidoti

Puopo Island

Mnemba Island

Tumbatu Island

Shirazi Ruins ■

Matemwe

Mkokotoni

Pwani Mchangani

Makoba

Unguja Island

Kiwengwa

Bumbwini

Mahonda

Pongwe

Mangapwani Caves ■

Uroa

Chuini

INDIAN OCEAN

Kibweni Palace ■

Kibandiko Island

Kidichi

Bambi

Michamvi

Chunguu Island

Mtoni

Dunga

Chwaka Bay

Bawe Island

Stone Town

Maruhubi Palace ■

Dunga Ruins ■

Chwaka

Murogo Island

Pange Island

Charawe

Mbweni

Fuoni

Jozani Forest

Bwejuu

Mbweni Ruins ■ ✈

Chukwani

Kombeni

Ukanga Island

Pete

Muungoni

Kitogani

Chumbe Island

Jambiani

Fumba

Kiwani Bay

Miwi Island

Uzi Island

Zanzibar Channel

Nianembe Island

Kwale Island

Menai Bay

Muyuni

Makunduchi

Vundwe Island

Shirazi Mosque ■

Mtende

Kizimkazi

N

ones are square. Symbols on the doors express the hope of the household—a fish for fertility, for example—but in most cases the doors have outlived their original owners. There are hundreds of carved doors in Stone Town; some of the most impressive are found at the palace of Beit el-Ajaib. Homes built by Indian merchants have a shop on the ground floor, with a dwelling above that has verandas with lattice work on the balconies.

History

There are so many layers of history in Zanzibar that you often find startling juxtapositions. The Anglican Cathedral in Stone Town was built over the former slave market, its high altar on the site of the whipping post. The Marahubi Palace, built by the third Omani Arab sultan for the 99 women in his harem, became the province of grazing cows. Head in any direction and soon enough you'll encounter the past. At Kidichi, 15 km (9 mi) northeast of Stone Town, are the ruins of a Persian bath built by Sultan Seyyid Said in 1850. They are remarkably well preserved, the domed buildings still standing. The Mangapwani Caves, 20 km (12 mi) north of Stone Town, were once used as holding pens for slaves. At Chukwani, 10 km (6 mi) south of Stone Town, are the ruins of an opulent summer palace.

Ask questions about the past, and the region's history really comes alive. For example, the notorious slave trader known as Tippu Tip was really named Hamed bin Mohammed el Marjebi. He earned his sobriquet because his red-rimmed eyes resembled those of a small bird.

Dining

Zanzibar was the legendary Spice Island, so it's no surprise the cuisine here is flavored with lemongrass, cumin, and garlic. Even the beverages have an extra kick; cinnamon enlivens tea and coffee, while ginger flavors a refreshing soft drink called Tangawizi. Zanzibar grows more than 20 types of mangos, and combining them with bananas, papayas, pineapples, and passion fruit makes for great juices. When it comes to dinner, seafood reigns supreme. Stone Town's seaside fish market sells skewers of kingfish and tuna. Stop by in the early evening, when the catch of the day is hauled in and cleaned. Make sure to try the prawn kabobs, roasted peanuts, and corn on the cob at the outdoor market at Forodhani Gardens. A few regional dishes eschew fish, however. Try the vegetarian Zanzibar pizza for breakfast; it's more like an omelet.

Gratuities are often included in the bill, so ask the staff before adding the usual 10% tip. Credit cards are not widely accepted, so make sure you have enough cash. Lunch hours are generally from 12:30 to 2:30, dinner from 7 to 10:30. Dress is casual for all but upscale restaurants, where you should avoid T-shirts, shorts, and athletic shoes.

CATEGORY	COST*
$$$$	over Tsh 13,500
$$$	Tsh 9,000–Tsh 13,500
$$	Tsh 4,500–Tsh 9,000
$	under Tsh 4,500

*per person for a main course at dinner

Diving

When it comes to underwater wonders, Unguja and Pemba are unrivaled. Huge schools of chevrons, barracudas, and eagle rays cruise around divers as they explore immense caverns, while hundreds of unicorn fish circle snorkelers paddling past untouched coral formations. The shallow reef at Chumbe Island is known for its brightly colored anemone fish, while dolphins and humpback whales have been spotted near

Mnemba Island. Unguja, especially around Kizimaki, is where you can find companies offering the experience of swimming with dolphins in captivity, but it can't compare to the unplanned encounters you can have with these creatures off Pemba Island.

Lodging

Depending on your taste, there are plenty of places to stay in Zanzibar. In Stone Town you can pick an unprepossessing guest house or a luxurious hotel. Been there, done that? Try a hunting lodge with stuffed wildlife staring at you from the walls or a sultan's palace surrounded by fragrant orange and lime trees. If you travel a bit farther afield, you can stay at a thatch-roof resort reachable only by boat or a beachfront hideaway where you'll have an unobstructed view of the sunset from your veranda.

The most popular accommodations are booked well in advance, so make sure to call ahead during the high seasons of June through August and mid-November through early January. During these periods many hotels increase their prices. During shoulder season, however, you can negotiate a better rate.

CATEGORY	COST*
$$$$	over Tsh 135,000
$$$	Tsh 90,000–Tsh 135,000
$$	Tsh 45,000–Tsh 90,000
$	under Tsh 45,000

All prices are for a standard double room, excluding tax.

Shopping

There are plenty of distinctive items for sale in the many markets of Zanzibar. Full-length caftans in white cotton, known as *khanzus,* are very comfortable for lounging. Colorful *kangas* and *kikois* make ideal sarongs for covering a bathing suit. Zanzibar chests—wooden jewelry boxes trimmed in brass—are cumbersome to pack but make distinctive souvenirs. And what sailor can leave these shores without purchasing a wooden eye that allows a boat to see reefs and other dangers?

Most shops are open from 8 to 6, although some close for lunch. Bargaining is acceptable everywhere that prices are not marked. Do not buy polished seashells, coral, and tortoise-shell products, as they are illegal. You can be fined for bringing them into the United States or the United Kingdom.

EXPLORING ZANZIBAR

There's no better way to end a safari to Kenya or Tanzania than with a trip to tropical Zanzibar. Many tour companies send you here for a day or two at the end of your journey. But the archipelago's two large islands and the dozens of smaller ones are well worth exploring further. It's an especially appealing destination for water sports, as the coral reefs are some of the best in the world.

Great Itineraries

IF YOU HAVE 2 DAYS

Explore Stone Town on your first day, either on your own or with a guide who can point out the architectural treasures such as the palaces of **Beit el-Ajaib** and **Beit al-Sahed.** With or without a guide, you won't be able to miss the massive **Old Fort,** a landmark definitely worth a visit. On your second day take a spice tour, where your guide will explain how the region grew rich-smelling cardamom, cinnamon, cloves, and nutmeg.

After two days in Stone Town, hit the beach on your third day. For a glimpse of life in a traditional fishing village, head to the eastern side of Unguja to **Bwejuu Beach.** Women here still used coconut fibers to make the nets. If you're intrigued by the triangular-sailed dhows, visit **Nungwi,** on the island's northern tip. If you're fortunate, you'll arrive on a day when a newly finished dhow is being launched.

If you're here for underwater adventures, take a few days to explore Stone Town, then fly to **Chake Chake** on the nearby island of Pemba. Head north to **Wete,** where you can sleep in a yacht right on the Indian Ocean. Swim with manta rays, eagle rays, and barracudas at the nearby Mesali Island Marine Reserve. When you're in the mood for exploring the island itself, just north of Wete is the **Ngezi Forest Reserve.** This rain forest has an amazing array of animals found nowhere else, including a fruit-eating bat called the Pemba flying fox.

When to Tour Zanzibar

From June through October is the best time to visit Zanzibar. These are the coolest months, when the temperature averages 26°C (79°F). Spice tours are best during harvest time, July and October, when cloves (unopened flower buds) are picked and laid out to dry. Zanzibar experiences a short rainy season in November, but heavy rains can fall from March until the end of May. Temperatures soar during this period, often reaching over 30°C (90°F). Most travelers come between June and August and from mid-November to early January. During these periods many hotels add a surcharge.

Zanzibar observes Ramadan for a month every year—in 2002 it begins November 6, and in 2003 it starts October 27. During this period Muslims are forbidden to eat, drink, or smoke between sunrise and sunset. Although hotels catering to tourists are not affected, many small shops and restaurants are closed during the day. If you plan to arrive during Ramadan, aim for the end, when a huge feast called the Eid al-Fitr (which means "end of the fast") brings everyone out to the streets.

UNGUJA ISLAND

Often called Zanzibar Island, Unguja is separated from the mainland by a channel measuring little more than 35 km (22 mi) at its widest point. Measuring 96 km (60 mi) from end to end, the island still has much land devoted to growing the cloves that once gave it the name Spice Island. The ruins of opulent palaces built by the sultans line the island's west coast, while beautiful beaches are found on the east coast as well as the northern tip.

Stone Town

Stone Town is a maze of narrow streets lined with houses that feature magnificently carved doors studded with brass. It's surrounded by the sea on three sides, reflecting its history as an important port. Many of its grand buildings are crumbling, but a joint undertaking by private and public organizations has restored some of the city's landmarks to their original splendor. To help protect the city's unique character, UNESCO designated Stone Town a World Heritage Site in 1994. Things are slowly changing, however. Dusty shops and rambling bazaars are competing with modern shopping centers, and traditional restaurants are next door to sophisticated eateries serving international fare. Young people are just as likely to greet you with "ciao" as with "jambo," even

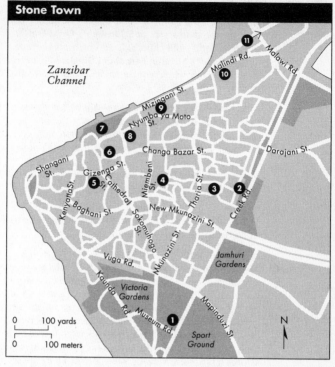

Stone Town

though Zanzibar is a major center for the study of the Swahili language, said to be spoken here in a purer form than on the mainland.

Walking is the best way to see Stone Town. Although this may be the most fascinating place in the world to get lost, make sure to bring along a good map to help you find your way. Don't forget to take the number and address of your hotel in the event you should become truly frustrated and want to take a cab. A little patience, however, is usually all that is needed to figure out where you are, as most roads lead to the harbor.

The streets can be dusty or muddy, depending on the weather. When it rains, poor drainage makes getting around a challenge. Should you hear the excited shout of "Hodi! Hodi!" (which means "Am I welcome?" in Swahili), it may be the driver of an overloaded cart asking you to step aside.

Although Stone Town is much safer than Dar es Salaam or Nairobi, it's a good idea to take a taxi when you go out in the evenings. The area around the harbor, as in most port towns, is best avoided at night.

Numbers in the text correspond to numbers in the margin and on the Stone Town map.

A Good Walk

To learn a bit about Zanzibar, begin your tour at the southern tip of Creek Road at **Beit el-Amani** ①, a pair of museums with displays about the region's fascinating history. Head north along Creek Road to a sprawling bazaar called the **Darajani Market** ②. A block or so west of Creek Road you'll find the **Anglican Cathedral** ③, a local landmark built on the site of the old slave market. On Hamamni Street, a few blocks west, are the ruins of the **Hamamni Baths** ④. Inside you can still see the polished marble floors of the opulent facility. At this junction you are getting close to the harbor, but if you need a point of reference, look for the twin spires of **St. Joseph's Cathedral** ⑤. After a tour inside the century-old church, head north on Cathedral Street toward the **Old Fort** ⑥. Stroll in **Forodhani Gardens** ⑦, near the Old Fort on the waterfront, where your nose will lead you to freshly caught fish sizzling on the grill.

After lunch you can explore **Beit el-Ajaib** ⑧, a four-story palace known as the House of Wonders because it was the first building in town to install electric lights. Make your way north on Mizingani Road to the palace of **Beit al-Sahed** ⑨. Pass the Ijumaa Mosque on your way to the **Old Dispensary** ⑩, now full of shops and galleries. Farther along Mizingani Road is **Dhow Harbor** ⑪, where you can watch sacks of cloves being loaded onto waiting ships.

TIMING

This walk will easily take an entire day. Remember to dress conservatively if you want to enter a mosque.

Sights to See

❸ **Anglican Cathedral.** The crucifix of this landmark was carved from the tree under which explorer David Livingstone's heart was buried in the village of Chitambo. Built in 1887 to mark the end of the slave trade, the cathedral's high altar was constructed on the site of a whipping post. Nothing of the slave market remains, although nearby are underground chambers in which slaves were forced to crouch on stone shelves less than 2 ft high. Ask to take the stairs up to the tower, which affords a bird's-eye view of Stone Town. There are services in Swahili every Sunday and in English once a month. ⊠ *Off Creek Rd.,* ☎ *no phone.* ☎ *Ksh 1,800.* ◷ *Daily 8–6.*

❾ **Beit al-Sahed.** This structure was known as the People's Palace, but for a long time the name was a bitter irony. It was here that sultans and their families lived from the 1880s until the revolution of 1964. It now has a museum inside that exhibits collections of furniture and clothing from the days of the sultans. A room is dedicated to Princess Salme, daughter of Sultan Said, who eloped with a German businessman in the 19th century. On the grounds outside are the tombs of Sultan Said and two of his sons. ⊠ *Mizingani Rd.,* ☎ *no phone.* ☎ *Tsh 4,000.* ◷ *Tues.–Sat. 10–6.*

❽ **Beit el-Ajaib.** Known as the House of Wonders because it was the first building in Zanzibar to use electric lights, this four-story palace is still one of the largest buildings in the city. Built in the late 1800s for Sultan Barghash, it was bombarded by the British in 1886, forcing the sultan to abdicate his throne. Today you'll find canons guarding the beautifully carved doors at the entrance. In the marble-floored rooms are exhibits detailing the battle for independence. ⊠ *North of the Old Fort,* ☎ *no phone.* ☎ *Free.* ◷ *Daily 10–6.*

❶ **Beit el-Amani.** Actually two museums within a block of each other, the Peace Memorial Museum holds exhibits on Zanzibar's cultural heritage. In the domed main building is explorer David Livingstone's medicine chest, a display about the harvesting of cloves, relics from the days of the slave trade, and an exhibit about a World War I steamer called the *Königsberg* that sunk at the Rufiji Delta. Giant tortoises roam the grounds of the natural history museum next door, which features dusty displays of butterflies and small mammals like the Zanzibar leopard. You can also see the skeleton of a dodo. ⊠ *Creek Rd. and Museum Rd.,* ☎ *no phone.* ☎ *Tsh 800.* ◷ *Mon.–Sat. 9:30–12:30 and 3:30–6.*

② **Darajani Market.** This gable-roofed structure built in 1904 houses a sprawling fruit and vegetable market. Goods of all sorts—colorful fabrics, wooden chests, and all types of jewelry—are sold in the shops that line the surrounding streets. To the east of the main building you'll find spices laid out in colorful displays of beige, yellow, and red. On Wednesday and Saturday vendors arrive for an antiques fair. The market is most active in the morning between 9 and 11. ⊠ *Creek Rd., north of New Mkunazini St.,* ☏ *no phone.* ☑ *Free.* ⊙ *Daily 8–6.*

⑪ **Dhow Harbor.** The scent of cloves hangs heavy in the air as stevedores load and unload sacks of the region's most valuable crop. Every day you'll spot dhows arriving from the mainland with deliveries of flour and other goods not available on the islands. Fishermen deposit their catch here early in the morning. This is a seedy area, so be cautious. ⊠ *Malindi St., north of Malawi St.*

⑦ **Forodhani Gardens.** This pleasant waterfront park is a favorite spot for an evening stroll. Dozens of venders sell freshly grilled fish under the light of gas lanterns. ⊠ *Mizingani St.*

④ **Hamamni Baths.** Built in the late 19th century by Sultan Barghash, these public baths still retain the grandeur of a past era. Although they are now closed, you can get the key from the shopkeeper next door and explore the maze of marble-floored rooms leading to the ornately tiled tubs. ⊠ *Hamamni St.,* ☏ *no phone.*

OFF THE BEATEN PATH

LIVINGSTONE HOUSE – Now housing to the Zanzibar Tourist Board, this former base camp for missionaries and explorers was built in 1860 for Sultan Majid. David Livingstone stayed here in 1866 before his last safari. Other explorers—Burton, Speke, Cameron, and Stanley—resided here while preparing for their expeditions. The living quarters are not open to tourists. ⊠ *Bububu Rd., east of Creek Rd.,* ☏ *024/223-3485.*

⑩ **Old Dispensary.** With intricately carved wood balconies that make it resemble a wedding cake, this former dispensary shines again after being renovated by community groups. Built at the turn of the last century, it was donated to the city by an Indian merchant named Tharia Topan. Today it houses shops, galleries, and a small café. ⊠ *Mizingani Rd., near Malindi Rd.,* ☏ *no phone.* ☑ *Free.* ⊙ *Daily 9–6.*

★ **⑥** **Old Fort.** Built by the Portuguese in 1560, this bastioned fortress is the oldest structure in Stone Town. It withstood an attack from Arabs in 1754. It was later used as a jail, and prisoners who were sentenced to death met their ends here. It has undergone extensive renovation and today is headquarters for many cultural organizations, including the Zanzibar International Film Festival. Performances of traditional dance and music are staged here several times a week. The Neem Tree Café is a good place to stop for lunch. ⊠ *Creek Rd. and Malawi Rd.,* ☏ *no phone.* ☑ *Free.* ⊙ *Daily 10–6.*

⑤ **St. Joseph's Cathedral.** Built by French missionaries more than a century ago, this ornate church is based on the basilica of Notre Dame de la Garde, in Marseilles, France. It's now one of the city's most recognizable landmarks, with twin spires that will be one of the first sights you'll see as you arrive in Stone Town. ⊠ *Cathedral St. near Gizenda St.,* ☏ *no phone.*

Dining

$$$ ✕ **Tower Top.** With stunning views past the city's minarets to the harbor where dhows are setting out to sea, this rooftop restaurant is a great place to watch the sun sink into the Indian Ocean. It only holds about 20 people, who dine on fish or chicken accompanied by spice-scented

rice while reclining on soft cushions. You'll feel more a part of the scene if you wear something loose-fitting, perhaps even the local caftans known as *khanzus*. ⊠ *Hurumzi St.,* ☎ *024/223–0171,* FAX *024/223–1038,* WEB *www.zanzibar.org/emegre. Reservations essential. No credit cards.*

$–$$ ✕ **Blues.** Formerly known as the Floating Restaurant, this terrace restaurant is built on a pier jutting out into the Indian Ocean. Enjoy the breezes off the water as you sample the fresh local seafood. ⊠ *Off Miningani Rd. near Old Fort,* ☎ *0811/320–413. AE, MC, V.*

$–$$ ✕ **Fisherman's Restaurant.** The lobsters are certainly fresh at this long-time favorite—two scrappy ones tried to make a run for it during a recent visit. Besides tasty seafood, there are also good salads and soups. The whitewashed walls in the dining are decorated with light fixtures fashioned from old lobster traps. ⊠ *Shangani St., across from the Tembo House Hotel,* ☎ *no phone. V.*

$–$$ ✕ **Zanzibar Serena.** Grand views from the terrace are a highlight of this restaurant in the Zanzibar Serena. Inside, the wooden windows in the lovely tile-floored dining room are flung open to catch the breeze. Seafood is the specialty here, with fresh fish prepared with local herbs and spices. ⊠ *Shangani Rd.,* ☎ *024/223–3587,* FAX *024/223–3019,* WEB *www.serenahotels.com. AE, DC, V.*

$ ✕ **Neem Tree Café.** Tucked inside the Old Fort, this little café serves up great light lunches. Also popular is the local yogurt. ⊠ *Creek Rd. and Malawi Rd.,* ☎ *024/232–321. No credit cards.*

$ ✕ **Sambusa Two Tables Restaurant.** So named because there are only two tables, this eatery is on the balcony of a private home. The couple who own it prepare traditional Zanzibari food, usually a set meal. There is also traditional dancing. ⊠ *Off Kaunda Rd., near Victoria Hall,* ☎ *024/223–1979. Reservations essential. No credit cards.*

Lodging

If you stay in a hotel in the center of town, you may be awakened by the muezzin calling Muslims to prayers at dawn. If you're a light sleeper, bring earplugs. The biggest drawback to staying in Stone Town—the lack of a beach—has been addressed by shuttles taking tourists to sandy retreats.

$$$$ 🖫 **Emerson & Green.** This sprawling old mansion, artfully restored by
★ New Yorker Emerson Skeens and partner Tom Green, is the city's most romantic lodging. Each room is a different size and configuration, but they all are draped with yards of colorful fabrics. The Lavender Room, for example, has blue and violet silks hanging over a handsome brass bed. The Crystal Room has a bath where sun shines through hand-painted windowpanes. The rooftop West Room has two walls of elegant latticework laced with passion fruit, allowing glimpses of Beit el-Ajaib in the distance. Some rooms are large enough for families, but children under 12 are not welcome. ⊠ *236 Hurumzi St.,* ☎ *024/223–0171,* FAX *024/223–1038.* WEB *www.zanzibar.org. 9 rooms. Restaurant, bar. MC, V.*

$$$$ 🖫 **Shangani Apartment.** This hunting lodge on a beachfront in a quiet corner of Stone Town is a great place to stay if you can bear all the stuffed wildlife staring at you from the walls. The apartment has two large bedrooms and a kitchen complete with an espresso machine, making it a good choice for families. An enormous double bed is constructed of tree trunks, chairs are carved from logs, one table is made with an elephant leg, and a stool consists of whale vertebrae. A large balcony overlooks the sea. ⊠ *Shangani St.,* ☎ *831/338–2383 in the U.S., 1737/ 241–892 in the U.K. 1 room. Dining room. AE, MC, V.*

$$$$ 🖫 **Zanzibar Serena.** Two historic waterfront buildings were combined
★ to create this luxury hotel on the tip of the Shangani Peninsula. The rooms, furnished with canopy beds, all overlook the azure waters of

the Indian Ocean. With its professional polish, this is the only hotel in Stone Town that meets the exacting standards of business travelers. On the down side, business travelers are the only visitors you're likely to meet here. A nice amenity is the free shuttle to a private stretch of Mangapwani Beach, where you can enjoy water sports or set sail on a sunset cruise. The chef at the beachfront restaurant prepares seafood dishes any way you like. ⊠ *Shangani Rd.,* ☎ *024/223–3587,* FAX *024/223–3019,* WEB *www.serenahotels.com. 51 rooms. Restaurant, pool, business center, convention center, airport shuttle. AE, DC, V.*

$$$–$$$$ 🏠 **Salome's Garden.** Built by sultans in the 19th century, this palace is embraced by brilliantly colored bougainvillea. One of the only royal residences to survive intact, this enchanted place surrounded by fragrant orange and lime trees holds a maximum of 10 guests. The Princess Salome Room has high ceilings, views of the gardens, and a hidden stairwell into a catacomb bathroom. A veranda with views across the bay towards Stone Town makes the Sultan Majid Room fit for a king. ⊠ *8 km (5 mi) north of Stone Town,* ☎ *831/338–2383 in the U.S., 1737/241–892 in the U.K.* WEB *www.salomesgarden.com. 4 rooms. Dining room. AE, MC, V.*

$$–$$$ 🏠 **Mtoni Marine Center.** On the site of one the island's first clove plantations, this resort north of Dar es Salaam is an ideal base from which to explore Unguja's western coast. The *Umande,* a traditional dhow, takes you on sunset cruises and trips to the nearby islands. Should you wish to dip below the surface, there's an excellent dive shop on the premises. Stay in the palm-shaded main building or in one of the large bungalows, each with a kitchen and two or three bedrooms. In the evening you can dine barefoot on the beach on dishes like lobster tail and vanilla bisque. Make sure to finish with the cardamom crème brûlée. ⊠ *4 km (2½ mi) north of Stone Town,* ☎ *024/225–0140,* FAX *024/225–0496,* WEB *www.onward.to/mtoni. 25 rooms, 3 bungalows. Restaurant, bar, dive shop. MC, V.*

$$ 🏠 **Beit al-Amaan.** This private apartment in the Vuga neighborhood of Stone Town is near the President's Palace. Three bedrooms surround a living room overlooking a park. You can book rooms individually, or rent the whole floor. Breakfast, cooked by your own servant, is included in the rate. Bring your earplugs so you won't be awakened by a local turkey. Don't gobble back; it only encourages him. ⊠ *Vuga Rd.,* ☎ *831/338–2383 in the U.S., 1737/241–892 in the U.K.,* WEB *www.allaboutzanzibar.com. 3 rooms. Restaurant. No credit cards.*

$$ 🏠 **Narrow Street Hotel.** Don't be put off by the plain exterior, as this is one of the city's sweetest hotels. Embroidered sheets and pillowcases grace the hand-carved four-poster beds. The rooms may seem small, but that's because they have so much ornate furniture. If you feel cramped, head to the balcony and enjoy a view of the rooftops of Stone Town. ⊠ *Kokoni St., off Creek Rd.,* ☎ *024/232–620,* FAX *024/230–052. 13 rooms. Restaurant, bar. No credit cards.*

$$ 🏠 **Tembo House.** A unbeatable location on the tip of the Shangani Peninsula makes this landmark hotel one of the island's most popular accommodations. Ask to stay in the older wing, where you'll find a salon ringed with stained glass and a balcony overlooking the ocean. All rooms are decorated with traditional Zanzibari antiques, including hand-carved beds draped with netting. The Bahari Restaurant serves local and international cuisine, but no alcoholic beverages. ⊠ *Shangani St. near Kenyatta Rd.,* ☎ *024/233–005,* FAX *024/233–777,* WEB *www.zanzibar.net/tembo. 34 rooms. Restaurant, minibars, pool, shop. AE, MC, V.*

$ 🏠 **Malindi Guest House.** Near the dock where boats arrive from the mainland, this well-maintained guest house has rooms that wrap around a spacious courtyard filled with greenery. The best room is a penthouse kept cool by a ceiling fan. The Funguni Bazaar is a short walk away. Rates include breakfast. ⊠ *Malindi Rd. near Malawi Rd.,* ☎ *024/230–165,* FAX *024/233–030. 17 rooms. Restaurant, bar. No credit cards.*

Nightlife and the Arts

Because of its history as an important stop on the trade routes, Stone Town has an unusually vibrant cultural community. It's an African city, but it draws heavily on Arab and Indian influences. To obtain information on arts events, see the listings in local newspapers. Also try *Recommended in Zanzibar,* a free bimonthly publication available at Stone Town hotels and restaurants.

The Arts

DANCE

Inside the Old Fort, the **Zanzibar Cultural Centre** (⊠ Creek Rd. and Malawi Rd., ☎ 024/232–321 or 0812/750–969) holds an arts festival each July. The organization also sponsors regular performances of traditional dances.

FILM

The world-famous **Zanzibar International Film Festival** (⊠ Creek Rd. and Malawi Rd., ☎ 024/223–3135) is held in Stone Town each July. The organization also stages the Festival of the Dhow Countries in the first week of July. This annual celebration features art, film, and music from the countries that surround the Indian Ocean.

With an unmistakable art deco facade, **Cine Afrique** (⊠ Malawi Rd. at Funguni Rd., ☎ no phone) runs nonstop kung fu and kickboxing flicks. The adjoining café is also popular.

MUSIC

Stone Town's lively music scene revolves around *taarab,* traditional music that is a fusion of African, Arabic, and Indian styles. Taarab, an Arabic word for "joy," was also influenced by the British. The several dozen members of the orchestra usually dress in black tie. Newcomers will recognize instruments like the violin, but the *kanun* (similar to the dulcimer) and the *nay* (a wooden flute) are less familiar. Singers such as Siti Binti Saad and Bi Kidude are very popular. To hear taarab, check the schedule for music performances at the Zanzibar Cultural Centre.

Modern taarab, which mixes in more contemporary sounds, is the forte of a group known as East African Melody. The group often performs at the **Bwawani Plaza Hotel** (⊠ Funguni Rd., ☎ 024/230–200).

Nightlife

If you decide to sample Stone Town's bars and clubs, do not walk anywhere at night. Always ask your hotel to call a taxi for you.

BARS AND PUBS

Established in 1888 as a men's club, **Africa House** (⊠ Kaunda Rd. and Kenyatta Rd. ☎ 024/223–0708) saw its share of handlebar moustaches. Even older than the legendary Mombasa Club, it had a library, billiard room, and dining room. Its location near the water means the bar still has a marvelous view of the harbor, which is why people flock here for a view of the sunset. It's popular with travelers, so don't be surprised if you meet someone from your past at the ritual cocktail hour. Simple meals are served on the second floor.

Inside Baghani House Hotel is a late-night hangout called the **Livingstone Bar** (⊠ off Kenyatta Rd., ☎ 024/235–654). It's popular with young expats.

People start arriving late in the evening at **Fuji Beach Disco** (✉ 10 mi (6 mi) north of Stone Town, ☎ 024/233–939). It's right on the ocean, so you can step outside to cool off after dancing for hours. It's busiest on weekends. In the Bwawani Plaza Hotel, the **Komba Disco** (✉ Funguni Rd., ☎ 024/230–200) is packed on Saturday night.

Outdoor Activities and Sports

BEACHES

Off the coast near Stone Town, **Changuu Island** has a lovely white beach that makes it an ideal getaway. Bordered by a colorful coral reef, the island also has great snorkeling. You might think for a moment you are in the Galápagos Islands, but Changuu's giant tortoises were brought here from the Seychelles in the late 19th century. The island has an interesting history. Also called Prison Island, it's the former site of a jail for rebellious slaves. Also boasting a beautiful beach is nearby **Chapwani Island.** This islet is home to a herd of tiny dik-diks.

Near the town of Bububu is **Fuji Beach,** a stretch of sandy shoreline that is popular with day-trippers from Stone Town. At night the town is hopping with discos, favored by young people from the area.

DIVING

Although the best diving is around the islands of Pemba and Mnemba, there are some good sites near Stone Town. One interesting wreck, thought to be the remains of the *Pegasus,* a British ship sunk by the Germans in 1916, is just offshore. Even closer to Stone Town is the wreck of the tugboat *Bahari,* which was scuttled during World War II. The nearby reefs of Bawe Island, with dramatic examples of staghorn and brain coral, are home to octopuses and stingrays.

Considered one of the best dive shops in Zanzibar, **One Ocean Zanzibar Dive Center** takes you out in two dhows, the *Henya* and the *Ana,* for shorter trips, as well as custom-built dive boats for more far-flung destinations. Most excursions are double dives, with a traditional meal included in the cost. ✉ *Below Africa House, Kaunda Rd. and Kenyatta Rd.,* ☎ *024/223–8374,* WEB *www.zanzibaroneocean.com.*

Shopping

MARKETS

If you're looking for some of the island's beautiful fabrics, you can find kangas and kikois at the city's many markets. The stalls along **Mlandege Street** have some of the best values. Going for $20 at many hotels, the colorful cloths can be found here for less than half the price. The vendors around the **Darajani Market,** on Creek Road north of New Mkunazini Street, are another source.

SHOPS

A wide selection of books and periodicals can be found at the **Gallery Zanzibar** (✉ Gizenga St., ☎ 024/223–2244, FAX 024/223–6583, WEB www.galleryzanzibar.com), including the fascinating *Slaves, Spices & Ivory,* a history of Zanzibar written by Abdul Sheriff of the University of Dar es Salaam. The shop also stocks a wide variety of antiques, jewelry, and locally made oils and perfumes. Especially nice are the beautiful postcards by the owner, artist Javed Jafferji.

Paintings by local artists can be found at the **Orphanage Shop** (✉ Forodhani Gardens, ☎ no phone). Choose from bolts of brightly colored fabric, which a tailor can sew into any style of garment you choose. The profits help support children who have lost their families. **Memories of Zanzibar** (✉ Kenyatta Rd., ☎ 024/223–3078) sells lovely carved wooden boxes.

Side Trips from Stone Town

Jozani Forest. This small reserve is home to the endangered red colobus monkey, a species found only in Zanzibar. These primates, as well as blue vervet monkeys, can also be seen at very close quarters just outside the boundaries of the reserve. Other rarities include the small but ornate Zanzibar leopard, which has double or triple the number of spots, or rosettes, of those on the mainland. These cats are extremely rare, and because they are nocturnal, they are seldom seen. The Jozani Forest has an excellent nature trail and informative guides. ⊠ *24 km (15 mi) east of Stone Town,* ☎ *no phone.* ◎ *Tsh 1,200.*

Mangapwani Caves. These caves were used for hiding slaves when the trade was abolished in 1876. A path runs down to the ocean, where dhows filled with human cargo came ashore. Rain collects in the caves, and until recently they were visited by locals in search of fresh water. ⊠ *25 km (16 mi) north of Stone Town,* ☎ *no phone.*

Maruhubi Palace. Built by Sultan Barghash for his harem of 99 women, this palace was opulent when it was finished in 1882. Largely destroyed by a fire in 1899, the pillars and aqueducts remain, alongside towering palms. Guides serve up stories about how the women performed for the sultan, as well as about the sweets with which he rewarded them. A look at the palace ruins is often included in tours of the spice farms. ⊠ *3 km (2 mi) north of Stone Town,* ☎ *no phone.*

Mbweni

6 km (4 mi) south of Stone Town.

At Mbweni are the ruins of the first Anglican Christian missionary settlement in East Africa. Here you'll find the stone walls of St. Mary's Girls School, established in 1871 to educate girls whose parents died in the slave trade. Nearby are botanical gardens that invite a variety of birds.

Lodging

$$$$ ⊞ **Mbweni Ruins Hotel.** This Victorian-style hotel has only a dozen
★ rooms, each with a veranda overlooking the ocean. Rooms are furnished in a traditional style, with four-poster beds draped with mosquito nets. The best room is the Baobab Suite, which has its own rooftop terrace. The thatch-roofed Raintree restaurant is set high on a cliff with a fabulous view. The chefs make good use of local fish and the exotic fruits and vegetables of the island. ⊠ *Mbweni,* ☎ *024/235–478, 0812/781–877,* 🆑 *024/230–536,* 🅆🅴🅱 *www.mbweni.com. 12 rooms. Restaurant, bar, pool.*

Chumbe Island

4 km (2 mi) from Mbweni.

This tiny island, a tangle of lush mangroves, is surrounded by what marine biologists consider the world's best shallow-water coral reef. To protect this treasure, the area was named the country's first marine sanctuary in 1994. **Chumbe Island Marine Sanctuary** is home to such odd looking creatures as the blotched porcupine fish, black-spotted puffer fish, and potato groupers.

The island itself, where a pristine rain forest grows, is home to the endangered coconut crab, which climbs up to the top of palm trees and cracks coconuts with its powerful claws. Also found here is Ader's duiker, a small antelope now extinct on the mainland. A working lighthouse, built by the British in 1904, crowns the island. The lighthouse keeper's home has been converted into a visitor center.

Lodging

$$$$ **Chumbe Island Eco-Bungalows.** Winner of several ecotourism awards, this group of seven bungalows is the only place to stay on Chumbe Island. The lodge is committed to making sure the facilities don't have a negative impact on the adjacent marine park. Rainwater is collected, filtered, and stored for future use. Hot water comes courtesy of solar panels. The bungalows, all overlooking the sea, have dramatically sloped thatch roofs. The rate includes meals, walks with park rangers, snorkeling in the reef, tours of the historic lighthouse, and transportation to the island. ⊠ Chumbe Island, ☎ 024/223–1040, WEB www.chumbeisland.com. 7 rooms. Restaurant, bar. MC, V.

Bwejuu

65 km (40 mi) southeast of Stone Town.

On Unguja's southeastern shores, Bwejuu faces an ocean that alternates between shades of jade and aquamarine. In this coastal village, the men set out each day in their dhows, while the women bury coconuts in the sand to soften the fibers for making the twine that holds together the fishing nets. The children come by with baskets full of hot potatoes or shells to sell.

Lodging

$$$ 🏨 **Breezes Beach Club.** Relax on your own palm-shaded terrace at this beachfront resort. The rooms, inside tile-roof bungalows, have lovely hand-carved furniture. If you're in the mood for adventure, try windsurfing or sailing, or head to the Rising Sun Dive Center, which organizes dives and offers courses. If you just want to stay cool, sip a frozen drink by the pool. In the evening sneak off to the Safari bar for live jazz, or dance the night away at the Spices disco. ⊠ *Pingwe Beach, south of Bwejuu,* ☎ *0741/326–595,* FAX *0741/333–151,* WEB *www.breezes-zanzibar.com. 10 bungalows, 6 rooms. 3 restaurants, 2 bars, in-room safes, refrigerators, pool, tennis, health club, dance club, shop, meeting rooms. MC, V.*

$–$$ 🏨 **Palm Beach Inn.** This little beach house with a shady veranda has a
★ few double rooms with private baths, as well as two dormitory-style rooms with shared bath. This is roughing it—there's no running water or electricity. Fresh water comes from barrels complete with coconut-shell ladles, and light is courtesy of kerosene lanterns. A new restaurant on the premises features fresh fish and curry. ⊠ *Bwejuu Beach,* ☎ 024/232–733, FAX 024/233–886. *15 rooms. Restaurant, bar. AE, MC, V.*

$–$$ 🏨 **Twisted Palm.** These spacious and clean bungalows, a longtime favorite of budget travelers, are on an isolated stretch of sand north of Bwejuu. The restaurant serves up excellent fish dishes. The owner knows the best spots for diving and is happy to take you. Like many smaller establishments, it has no phone. The best way to secure a reservation is through the Zanzibar Tourist Office in Stone Town. ⊠ *2 km (1 mi) north of Bwejuu Beach,* ☎ *no phone. 15 rooms. Restaurant, bar. No credit cards.*

Kiwengwa

50 km (31 mi) northeast of Stone Town.

On Unguja's northeastern coast, Kiwengwa is popular with Italian tourists. Weekly charter flights from Milan head here for some of the best beaches on the island. There are also excellent water sports, especially deep-sea fishing trips that depart from the village of Chakwa, to the north.

About 19 km (11 mi) from Kiwengwa, the splendid **Dunga Palace** was built around 1850 by the island's *mwinyi mkuu* (supreme ruler). You can still see the massive walls that once supported an extensive roof garden. Slaves are rumored to have been buried alive within the walls. In 1914 some skeletons were discovered inside the structure.

Lodging

$$$$ **🖸 Mapenzi Beach Resort.** Named for the Swahili word meaning "love," this seaside retreat is set among tropical gardens. Popular among European travelers, it makes use of traditional architecture from the coast. Nap on your veranda overlooking the ocean, relax in the hot tub, or swim a few laps in the pool. The beachfront restaurant, which emphasizes Italian cuisine, serves a buffet-style breakfast and lunch. ✉ *North of Kiwengwa*, ☎ *0811/325–985*, FAX *0811/325–986*, WEB *www.tanzania-web.com. 87 rooms. Restaurants, 2 bars, in-room safes, pool, disco, library, travel services. MC, V.*

$$ **🖸 Kiwengwa Club Village.** Amid acres of coconut palms, this Italian-
★ owned complex has rooms spread among three two-story structures. The thatch-roof bungalows are a treat after a day of exploring, as they have air-conditioning, hot water in private baths, telephone, and verandas with views of the sea. The main restaurant serves Italian and American fare but is especially known for freshly grilled fish. There's plenty to do here, from bicycling and canoeing to snorkeling and diving. There's also a health club where you can join in an aerobics class. ✉ *Kiwengwa*, ☎ *024/232–6205*, FAX *024/232–5304. 102 rooms. 3 restaurants, 2 bars, café, tennis courts, health club, dive shop, bicycles. MC, V.*

$–$$ **🖸 Shooting Star Inn.** These bungalows, with gleaming white walls
★ washed with lime, let you gaze at the sea from your private veranda. You have the luxury of space here—the generously proportioned rooms have wood-beamed ceilings and large windows that let in lots of light. For the "barefoot" traveler, there are also three rustic bandas. The open-air restaurant and bar have views over a tropical garden. The chef, known for his excellent smoked-fish dishes, uses traditional African recipes. ✉ *Kiwengwa*, ☎ *047/415–365*, WEB *www.zanzibar.org/star. 12 rooms. Restaurant, bar. MC, V.*

Matemwe

15 km (9 mi) northeast of Kiwengwa.

On an isolated stretch of coastline, the traditional fishing village of Matemwe goes on much as it has for centuries. The lagoon here is lovely, but it doesn't compare with that on nearby Mnemba Island. Surrounded by 16 km (10 mi) of coral reefs, the island is a breeding area for green sea turtles, which come to shore to lay their eggs between December and May. Humpback whales have been seen traversing the channel in July and August.

Lodging

$$$$ **🖸 Mnemba Island Retreat.** On a private island, Mnemba Island Re-
★ treat is one of Zanzibar's most exclusive resorts. It's never crowded, as no more than 20 guests can stay here at any given time. Set around a secluded lagoon, cottages constructed of locally designed palm matting are separated from one another by lush tropical vegetation. Inside, they are surprisingly luxurious, with leather chairs and beds with scrolled headboards. All have private baths. Dinner is often served on the beach, where the waves lap gently at your feet. The favored recreational activities here are snorkeling and diving. If you're a novice, courses are available. Rates includes all meals and two dives a day. ✉ *Mnemba Island*, ☎ *024/233–110*, WEB *www.mnemba-island.com. 10 rooms. Dining room, shop, snorkeling, boating. AE, DC, MC, V.*

$$$ ⌂ **Matemwe Beach Village.** Set amid foliage so thick you can hardly see the thatch-roof bungalows, this lodging is truly secluded. Each room is furnished in a comfortable Zanzibari style with a veranda overlooking the sea. The restaurant serves freshly caught seafood, delicately flavored with Zanzibar's famous spices. The resort is heaven for snorkelers and divers, who flock here for the fabulous coral reef. *Matemwe,* ☎ *024/ 223–9340. 17 rooms. Restaurant, bar, boating. AE, MC, V.*

$$$ ⌂ **Matemwe Bungalows.** With large verandas overlooking the Indian Ocean, these bungalows are a great place to relax. Shaded by palm-leaf roofs, the rustic lodgings sit right on the beach. Seafood, caught daily, is the specialty of the house. Instead of the speedboats offered by other resorts, here you can sail on *ngalawas,* the wooden fishing boats used by locals. The dive shop on the premises offers a range of courses. You can even swim with the dolphins. ⊠ *Matemwe,* ☎ *024/ 223–789,* FAX *024/231–342,* WEB *www.matemwe.com. 16 rooms, 12 with bath. Restaurant, bar, dive center, boating. AE, MC, V.*

Nungwi

56 km (35 mi) north of Stone Town.

On the northern tip of Unguja, the Ras Nungwi Peninsula has beautiful beaches with water that is a little cooler than on the eastern shore. In Nungwi you can watch as locals practice the ancient art of building dhows. With a little luck you'll stumble on one of the graceful boats being launched or a ceremonial goat feast when the mast is raised.

In 1993 villagers built a sanctuary where injured hawksbill turtles and other marine creatures are coddled before being released back into the wild. The **Mnarani Aquarium,** 1 km (½ mi) south of Nungwi village, lets you see these creatures up close.

Near Nungwi are some fascinating historic sites, including the 16th-century **Fukuchani Ruins,** constructed of coral bricks. They're known locally as the Portuguese Ruins, although they were almost certainly built by Swahili people. From the Fukuchani Ruins is an excellent view of Tumbatu Island, which has the oldest Swahili villages in all of East Africa. The **Tumbata Ruins** include 40 houses of a 12th-century village. Near the Fukuchani Ruins are the **Mvuleni Ruins,** so named for the local Mvule trees.

Lodging

$$$$ ⌂ **Ras Nungwi Beach Hotel.** On the northern tip of Unguja, this diving resort has rooms with handcrafted four-poster beds and intricately carved doors. You can snorkel at the nearby reefs or learn to scuba at the fully equipped dive center. Waterskiing, windsurfing, and deep-sea fishing are just a few of the activities available. The large colonial-style dining room serves everything from calamari to coconut curries. ⊠ *Nungwi Island,* ☎ *024/223–3767,* FAX *024/223–3098,* WEB *www.rasnungwi.com. 32 rooms. Restaurant, pool, masseuse, water sports. AE, MC, V.*

$–$$ ⌂ **Amaan Beach Bungalows.** Right on the beach, this lodging is a good
★ budget option. Rates include breakfast—including fresh mango and pineapple—served in the restaurant overlooking the beach. There's a great dive shop on the premises. ⊠ *Nungwi,* ☎ *024/224–0026. Restaurant, 2 bars, dive shop, bicycles. No credit cards.*

PEMBA ISLAND

Welcome to underwater heaven. Off the coast of Pemba, the second-biggest island in the Zanzibar Archipelago, are lush coral gardens with colorful sponges and huge sea fans. From October through March the visibility is unparalleled—views of 60 m (200 ft) are not uncommon. In general, diving off the west side of the island is easier. Favorite dive sites include those around Njao and Fundu Islands (Njau Gap, Fundu Gap, Manta Point, Swiss Reef) and Mesali Island (Mesali West, Chiles Wall, and Attaturks Wall). Diving off the east coast requires more experience because of the strong currents.

Although most people who fly into the largest city of Chake Chake are in search of great diving, Pemba is also a mecca for mountain bikers. That's because Pemba is extremely hilly, with some peaks 1,000 meters above sea level. The island was formed millions of years ago from rising blocks of stratified rock. It emerged from the ocean long before Unguja, and is separated from its sibling and the mainland by a deep rift.

On Pemba's northern tip is the Ngezi Forest Reserve, where 1,500 acres are dominated by pristine rain forest. Here you'll find the Pemba flying fox—which doesn't really fly and isn't a fox. The fruit-eating bat is found nowhere else on earth. Also making their home in this reserve are red colobus monkeys, blue vervet monkeys, and the Pemba blue duiker, a diminutive antelope. Beyond this reserve, much of the indigenous forest on the island was felled to grow groves of cloves. During the June and October harvests nearly everyone on Pemba works from dawn till dusk. Cloves are dried on the roads and in front of houses, filling the air with the pungent scent.

Chake Chake

Pemba's largest town, Chake Chake is a lively Arab settlement where thatch-roof huts stand side by side with stone buildings in the Moorish style. Carefree evening strolls are one of the highlights of a visit to Chake Chake, which sits on a ridge overlooking a harbor. In the evenings local men can still be seen dressed in flowing white robes known as *kanzus*.

About 10 km (6 mi) southeast of town, the **Pujini Ruins** include the remains of a mosque dating from the 13th century. Visitors who seek this place out are told a legend that the palace was built by a tyrant who was given the Swahili moniker Mkama Ndume ("milker of men") because he whipped his workers while they were carrying heavy stones. Head west of Chake Chake for about 20 km (12 mi) and you'll reach the **Ras Mkumbuu Ruins,** an ancient Swahili settlement. This was one of the largest towns in East Africa during the 11th century. Remains include a large mosque, and some pillarlike tombs. For nature lovers, offshore of Chake Chake is **Misali Island,** a sanctuary for sea birds and turtles.

Dining and Lodging

$ ✕ **Balloon Brothers.** Fish cooked on a charcoal grill is the specialty of this little restaurant south of the mosque on main street. Dining is outside on a banda-shaded patio. ⊠ *On the main street,* ☎ *no phone. No credit cards.*

$$$$ ⊞ **Fundu Lagoon.** Reachable only by speedboat, this resort on the Wambaa Peninsula brings new meaning to the word "secluded." There are 20 thatch-roof bungalows, each with a private balcony where you can enjoy the sea breeze. The retreat has a fully equipped diving center, water sports, and canoe safaris into the mangroves. The rate includes snorkeling trips, canoe trips, and sunset cruises on romantic old dhows. ⊠ *Wambaa Peninsula,* ☎ *024/223–2926,* FAX *024/223–2926,* WEB *www.fundulagoon.com. 20 rooms. Restaurant, 2 bars. Closed mid-Apr.–mid-June. No credit cards.*

$ ⛺ **Old Mission Lodge.** Located in a restored Quaker mission, this friendly guest house is set back from the road in a grove of trees. The upper balcony overlooks the Indian Ocean. The lower balcony holds a small restaurant where local spices reign supreme. You can arrange diving and snorkeling trips through Swahili Divers, found on the premises. ⊠ *North side of Chake Chake,* ☎ *024/452–786,* WEB *www. swahilidivers.com. 7 rooms. Restaurant, dive shop, boating.*

Mkoani

38 km (24 mi) from Chake Chake.

Most people who arrive on Pemba by boat come through Mkoani, the island's most important port. Almost all of them pass through quickly, but there are a few diversions if you find yourself here with a few hours to kill. South of the dock you'll find a market, a small café, and a bakery where you can watch bread being prepared in a traditional oven. The local Ibazi Mosque, near the town's bandstand, has an impressive carved door.

Dining and Lodging

$ ⛺ **Jondeni Guest House.** The friendly and informative staff—providing assistance in booking diving excursions, mountain bike journeys, and fishing expeditions—make the difference here. Located uphill from the port, it also has an unbeatable location. The restaurant has great views and is a good value. ⊠ *Mkoani,* ☎ *024/223–2190,* FAX *024/ 223–2926. 20 rooms. Restaurant, bar. Closed Apr.-June. No credit cards.*

Wete

30 km (18 mi) north of Chake Chake.

As you drive here from Chake Chake, you pass through tiny villages and hillsides dotted with banana trees. Wete is a port that is mainly used for exporting cloves, so it is busiest during the harvest times of June and October. The village, on a hill overlooking the port, has some lovely colonial architecture.

Dining and Lodging

$$ ✕⛺ **Pemba Afloat.** Two yachts moored in a calm lagoon at the northern tip of Pemba are the accommodations at this unusual lodge. Each can sleep up to a dozen people. All your food is prepared on board by the resident chef, who cooks up seafood that was caught earlier in the day. Don't think this will be roughing it; onboard amenities include everything from hot showers to CD players. Day trips to Mesali Island Marine Reserve offer clear waters for snorkeling or diving, plus glimpses of sea turtles and nesting sea birds. Your hosts can arrange fishing in deeper waters for barracuda, kingfish, wahoo, and tuna. ⊠ *Pemba lagoon,* ☎ *0743/330–904,* WEB *pembaisland.com. Snorkling, boating. AE, MC, V.*

$$ **Sharook Guest House.** A well-known meeting place in Wete, this lodging has a knowledgeable owner who can provide tips on traveling in the area. Meals are served with advance notice, and most people say they are the best for miles around. ⊠ *Wete,* ☎ *024/454–386. Restaurant. No credit cards.*

Verani

20 km (12 mi) northwest of Wete.

★ The **Ngezi Forest Reserve** harbors a spectacular display of flora and fauna, with some species that are found nowhere else on earth. Half of the 3,558-acre reserve is covered in thick rain forest, with a coastal belt consisting of thick brush growing in coral rag. Mangrove tributaries become brakish wetlands at high tide, but in a sandy area in the center of the reserve you'll find a type of heather that grows only here and on nearby Mafia Island. Birding can be rewarding, especially if you catch sight of an African goshawk, palm nut vulture, malachite kingfisher, or Pemba white eye, a species unique to the island. The large fruit-eating bat, Pemba's flying fox, is active at dusk, although you might spot one hanging like a dirty sock from a tree branch at midday. Red colobus monkeys and blue vervet monkeys are the main primates found here, while mammals include blue duiker antelopes and tree hyrax. The only indigenous carnivore is a marsh mongoose, most often seen in the wetlands. A nature trail begins near the information center. ⊠ *North of Wete between Tondooni and Konde,* ☎ *no phone.* 🖃 *$5.*

Lodging

$$$$ 🏨 **Manta Reef Lodge.** This secluded resort on the Ngezi Peninsula has rustic cabins raised on stilts to give you an unobstructed view of the sea. The lodge is designed for divers, and in a single day you may head out to beautiful spots such as Manta Point, Mandela Wall, and Fundu Gap. If you like, lunch can be a picnic on a deserted beach. This lodge also books for a luxurious live-aboard yacht called the *Jambo,* which takes you to reefs you cannot reach on day trips. ⊠ *Verani,* ☎ *011/471–771 and 011/471–772 in Mombasa,* 📠 *011/471–349 and 011/474–194 in Mombasa,* 🌐 *www.africa-direct.com. 11 rooms. Restaurant, bar, dive shop. Closed May–July. AE, MC, V.*

ZANZIBAR A TO Z

To research prices, get advice from other travelers, and book travel arrangements, visit www.fodors.com.

AIR TRAVEL TO AND FROM ZANZIBAR

There are no direct flights from the United States. Generally you need to connect through a city on the mainland, the easiest being Dar es Saalam. From Dar es Saalam to Stone Town, there are regular flights in small twin-engine aircraft operated by Precision Air and Coastal Air. The flight takes around 20 minutes. From Nairobi and Mombasa, you can fly to Stone Town on Kenya Airways.

You can also hop between the two main islands of Zanzibar. Zan Air, a local charter company, flies between Stone Town and Chake Chake three times a week. The flights take 20 minutes, and give you a spectacular aerial view of the islands and the coral reefs. Coastal Air flies every day except Saturday from Dar es Salaam to Stone Town to Chake Chake.

Visitors from the the United States and Europe require visas to enter Tanzania. Zanzibar is a semi-autonomous state within Tanzania, so you don't need a separate visa to visit, but you do need to show your passport.

➤ DOMESTIC CARRIERS: **Coastal Air** (⊠ Shangani Rd., Stone Town, ☎ 024/233–489). **Kenya Airways** (⊠ Creek Rd., Stone Town, ☎ 024/232–041). **Precision Air** (⊠ Kenyatta Rd., Stone Town, ☎ 024/234–521). **Zan Air** (⊠ Malawi Rd., Stone Town, ☎ 024/233–670).

AIRPORTS AND TRANSFERS

After arrival in Unguja you will be approached by taxi drivers. Be sure to agree on a price before getting in, as taxis do not have meters. The fare to Stone Town should be around Tsh 4,000. Your driver may let you out several blocks before you reach your hotel because the streets are too narrow. Ask the driver to walk you to the hotel. Be sure to tip him if he carries your luggage.

BIKE AND MOPED TRAVEL

Bikes can be rented from shops near Darajani Market. Mopeds and motorcycles are another great way to get about the island.

BOAT TRAVEL TO ZANZIBAR

Several hydrofoil ferries travel between Dar es Salaam and Stone Town. The fastest trip, lasting about 75 minutes, is on hydrofoils operated by Sea Express and Azam Marine. Sea Express has daily departures from Dar es Salaam at 8, 10, noon, 2:30, and 4:30, with returns at 7, 10, noon, 2:30, and 4:30. Azam Marine departs from Dar es Salaam at 8, 1:15, and 4, returning at 7, 1:30, and 4.

Tickets can be purchased on the spot or in advance from the row of offices next to the port in Dar es Saalam. Timetables and prices are displayed on boards outside each office.

➤ FERRY COMPANIES: **Azam Marine** (✉ Stone Town port, ☎ 024/233–046. **Sea Express** (✉ Stone Town port, ☎ 024/233–013).

CAR RENTAL

If you have reserved a rental car in Stone Town, you can arrange to have your vehicle waiting for you at the airport. Make sure to tip the driver who drops it off for you. To rent a car in Zanzibar you must have an international driver's license, and most agencies require you to be at least 23. A four-wheel-drive vehicle will cost between $40 and $50 a day.

➤ CONTACTS: **Chemah Brothers** (✉ Shangani Rd., Stone Town, ☎ 024/233–385). **Sama Tours** (✉ Changa Bazaar St., Stone Town, ☎ 024/233–543). **Partnership Travel** (✉ Main Rd., Chake Chake, ☎ 024/452–278).

CAR TRAVEL

The roads in Zanzibar are fairly decent, but drive with caution. Traffic in Stone Town can be chaotic, especially to and from the airport. Accidents are frequent, so be on your guard. Proceed *pole pole,* which means cautiously. Drive on the left side of the road, yield to the right at roundabouts, and pass on the right.

ELECTRICITY

The current is 220 to 230 volts, 50 cycles alternating current. Converters may be needed to use appliances in the 3-prong, triangular sockets. Many hotels on the beach do not have electricity, so don't count on being able to recharge your laptop or other electrical devices.

EMERGENCIES

Zanzibar Medical & Diagnostic Center provides 24-hour emergency services. Ask for Dr. Mario Mariani. The main hospital in Stone Town is the state-run Mnazi Mmoja Hospital.

➤ HOSPITALS: **Mnazi Mmoja Hospital** (✉ Kaunda Rd., Stone Town, ☎ 024/223–1071). **Zanzibar Medical & Diagnostic Center** (✉ Vuga Rd. near Makunazini St., Stone Town, ☎ 024/233–113).

ENGLISH-LANGUAGE MEDIA

The East African is a good weekly newspaper that can also be found online. Dar es Salaam's *Daily News* is flown in every day. You may be able to find the *International Herald Tribune, Time,* and *Newsweek* at larger hotels.

HEALTH

Visitors to Zanzibar are required to have a yellow fever vaccination certificate. You should also talk with your doctor about a malaria prophylactic. The best way to avoid malaria is to avoid being being bitten by mosquitoes, so make sure your arms and legs are covered and that you wear plenty of mosquito repellent. Always sleep under a mosquito net; most hotels and guest houses provide them. The sun can be very strong here, so make sure to slather yourself with sunscreen.

Drink bottled water, and plenty of it—it will help you avoid dehydration. Avoid raw fruits and vegetables that may have been washed in untreated water.

MAIL AND SHIPPING

Stone Town's main post office is located east of town near Amani Stadium. A more convenient branch office is located on Kenyatta Road. On Pemba Island, the Post Office at Chake Chake is on the main road towards the police station.

➤ POST OFFICES: **Chake Chake** (✉ Main Rd.). **Stone Town** (✉ Kenyatta Rd. near Gizenga Rd.).

MONEY MATTERS

Visa is the most widely accepted credit card, followed by MasterCard and Diner's Club. American Express does not enjoy the popularity it does in other parts of the world. Hotels, shops, and airlines may tell you that using a credit card will add a percentage to your cost, then ask if you would rather pay in cash. Most larger hotels only accept U.S. dollars; some budget hotels will also accept Tanzanian shillings.

There are handy currency exchange booths in Stone Town that offer good rates. The best rates are at Forex Bureau around the corner from Mazson's Hotel on Kenyatta Road, and the Malindi Exchange across from Cine Afrique. Mtoni Marine Center, also in Stone Town, will give a cash advance on your Visa or MasterCard. It charges a commission as well as a processing fee. Currency exchange offices can also be found on Pemba in Chake Chake and in Wete.

SAFETY

While the best way of experiencing Stone Town is to wander around its labyrinthine streets, you should always be on your guard. Don't wear jewelry or watches that might attract attention, and keep a firm grasp on purses and camera bags. Leave valuables in the safe at your hotel. Always take a taxi when traveling at night.

Muggings have been reported at Nungwi and other coastal resorts, so never carry valuables onto the beach.

TAXES

The 20% value-added tax is not always included in the quoted price of goods and services, so be sure to inquire.

TELEPHONES

The country code for Tanzania is 255, and the regional code for Zanzibar is 024. The "0" in the regional code is used only for calls placed from other areas within the country. To call from abroad, dial the international access number 011, then the country code 255, then the area code 24, and then the telephone or fax number, which should have six or seven digits. If you run across a number with only five digits, it's a remnant of the old system that was changed in 1999. Because telephone communications are difficult, many people in the travel business have mobile phones, indicated by an 811 prefix.

TIPPING

Tips are often included in restaurant bills; inquire if your bill does not make it clear. If not, 10% is sufficient. Many tour operators include tips for hotel staff in their packages; otherwise porters should be tipped Tsh 750. If you stay in a private home, it is customary to tip the cooks, maids, and gardeners about Tsh 750 a day. Taxi drivers do not expect a tip unless they carry your luggage or serve as a guide.

TOUR OPERATORS

Spice tours are a very popular way to see Zanzibar. Guides take you to farms in Kizimbani or Kindichi, teaching you to identify plants that produce cinnamon, turmeric, nutmeg, and vanilla. A curry luncheon will undoubtedly use some of the local spices. Any tour company can arrange a spice tour, but the best guides are those who work for Mr. Mitu, a renowned guide who has his own agency and a battalion of guides trained by him. The average price for a spice tour is $15, including lunch. Most depart around 9:30 AM.

Fisherman Tours is an experienced operator based in Stone Town that offers general city tours. There are many types of tours available. John da Silva, a local artist, gives tours of the architecture in Stone Town.
➤ OPERATORS: **Fisherman Tours** (✉ Vuga Rd., Stone Town, ☎ 024/223–8791). **John da Silva** (✉ Stone Town, ☎ 024/232–123). **Mr. Mitu** (✉ Malawi Rd., Stone Town, ☎ 024/223–1020).

VISITOR INFORMATION

Web sites such as www.africaonline.com and www.allaboutzanzibar.com have excellent information about the region. You should do your online research before you get to Tanzania, as local connections are sluggish between 8 and 8. The free tourist magazine *Recommended in Zanzibar,* found in hotels and shops, lists cultural events, as well as tide tables that are very useful for divers. There is a Tourist Information Center north of Stone Town. Although not very useful for information about the city, it does book rooms in inns in other parts of the island.
➤ INFORMATION: **Tourist Information Center** (✉ 2 km north of Stone Town, ☎ 024/223–3485).

9 PORTRAITS OF KENYA AND TANZANIA

Call of the Wild

Swahili Glossary

CALL OF THE WILD

YOU RISE SHORTLY BEFORE DAWN, instinctively aware that creatures out there in the darkness are doing the same. After a quick cup of coffee you and your fellow adventurers climb into the back of a four-wheel-drive vehicle. By midday the lions you heard last night will be seeking the shade, and so will you. Early morning is one of the times when these hunters are on the move, and that's why you're heading out as the sun starts to rise.

The chance to see a pride of lions pursuing a wildebeest is one of the main reasons people flock to East Africa. The vast array of wildlife, much of it found nowhere else on earth, entices some to return to the region again and again. They need not even visit the same place twice, as Kenya has a total of 57 national parks and reserves spreading for 35,000 square km (13,500 square mi). Tanzania, its neighbor to the south, has only 29 parks and reserves, but they cover more than 140,000 square km (86,940 square mi). The scale is almost incomprehensible. Kenya's Tsavo National Park is the size of Wales. Tanzania's Selous Game Reserve is far bigger than Belgium or the Netherlands. If you added those European countries together, then threw in Austria, you'd have something close to the size of all the game reserves in Kenya and Tanzania.

Some of these parks are so famous their names are instantly familiar. With more lions than any other park in Kenya, Maasai Mara Game Reserve is one of the country's most popular destinations. It's justly celebrated for its annual wildebeest migration. This parade of more than 1.5 million gnus is one of Africa's longest-running shows. It's superbly cast, with sharp-toothed predators honing their hunting skills when this movable feast arrives in their territory. Crocodiles that spend much of their life imitating logs on the banks of the Mara River barely submerge their deadly intentions. Tree branches bend with the larder of leopards, their neck and jaw muscles robust from the chore, their eyes gleaming with that keen golden sparkle of the wild that distinguishes them from caged cats.

Also extremely popular is Kenya's Amboseli National Park, home to great herds of elephants and caravans of ivory-color minivans that rush to see everything as if the store were about to close. Maybe it is. The dust devils of Amboseli sing of desert conditions. Lone cheetahs, frequently surrounded by a dozen vehicles, show their ribs with every breath they take. It's a sad irony that their hunt for a meal has often been halted by the people who have come to admire them. It became all too clear in the 1980s that Amboseli and other national parks were too popular for their own good. Rules against straying from the roads were more strictly enforced to diminish the damage to fragile grasslands, and higher entrance fees were implemented to nudge visitors toward parks farther off the beaten path.

Kenya's parks also have battled other pressures, not the least of which is rampant poaching. The herds of rhinos that once roamed Tsavo National Park were decimated. Elephants were nearly wiped out of Maru National Park. In 1990 Kenya Wildlife Service director Richard Leakey led a war against poachers, implementing a shoot-to-kill policy to discourage the lucrative practice. The campaign's greatest success was achieving a moratorium on the international ivory trade. But although poaching was greatly curtailed, a burgeoning human population continued to encroach on areas once reserved for wildlife. Previously nomadic peoples settled down to cultivate their own *shambas* (small farms), which meant fences suddenly appeared in the traditional paths of migrating animals. Elephants and other animals could no longer move across Kenya's vast plains. Borders were ignored when tribes whose herds were facing droughts found the grass was greener in the parks than in the surrounding areas. Conflict was inevitable.

Some of the pressure has been eased by the establishment of private game reserves. The country's wildlife, which has adapted to this harsh landscape over millennia, flourishes on grasslands that can barely support cattle. Ranchers in Kenya's central plains, realizing the intrinsic value of their land doesn't come from cattle, have created their own wildlife sanctuaries. To protect the animals found there, including endangered species such as the black rhino, these ranches have funded their own antipoaching teams. Lewa Downs is perhaps the best-known private sanctuary, but the Mukutan Retreat, founded by Kuki Gallmann, gained international attention from her bestselling autobiography, *I Dreamed of Africa*. The accommodations on these reserves are small, making you feel like a guest in someone's home (which is often the case). You won't run into hordes of travelers, as most of these reserves host fewer than a dozen guests at any time.

Many private reserves have been built with the cooperation of the indigenous peoples. Ol Donyo Wuas, a 300,000-acre retreat in the Chyulu Hills, occupies land owned by the Maasai people. The Sarara Camp, in the Mathews Range, is run by the Saburu people, which means all the profits benefit the local community. One of the biggest success stories is Lewa Downs, which not only has provided employment for locals but has set up schools and clinics as well.

In the meantime, several of Kenya's national parks are enjoying a renaissance. For a couple of decades the two reserves that make up Tsavo National Park had to rely on their impressive landscapes rather than animals. Hammered by poachers and droughts, they drew visitors to unique vistas such as Mzima Springs, Lugard's Falls, the Yatta Plateau. Now herds are slowly recovering, partly due to the success of the Sheldrick Animal Orphanage, near Nairobi, which by 2002 had returned 30 mature elephants to the wild. They now wear the red dust characteristic of this landscape.

Also making a comeback is Meru National Park, to which more than 50 elephants were moved in 2001. The nearby triumvirate of the Samburu National Reserve, Buffalo Springs National Reserve, and Shaba National Reserve is also home to more wildlife than a decade ago. Like Tsavo National Park, these areas were crawling with poachers, who in the late 1980s turned their weapons on one of the bravest figures ever to walk this landscape, naturalist George Adamson. The story of this confrontation is told in a magnificent movie, *To Walk With Lions*. Richard

Harris portrays Adamson, who looked very like a lion with his white beard and wild silver mane. These northern parks contain species not seen in southern Kenya: the thinly striped Grevy's zebra, the blue-shanked Somali ostrich, and the Beisa oryx. The landscape, dotted with doum palms, is so expansive you can see the curvature of the earth.

There is also good news in Tanzania, where the country has set aside nearly a quarter of its total area as wildlife preserves—the largest percentage in East Africa. A portion of Kilimanjaro National Park was designated in 2001 as Tanzania's first "wilderness area," providing a higher level of protection. It's needed because Mt. Kilimanjaro is among the areas of Tanzania most disturbed by tourism. The popular Marangu Route has been described as the "tissue trail" because of garbage left behind by hikers. The boundaries of Katavi National Park were extended in 2000, doubling the size of that truly wild park from 2,253 square km (870 square mi) to 4,471 square km (1,726 square mi). The nation's first marine reserve, around Mafia Island, was established in 1995.

Several regions of Tanzania that were once declining are becoming robust, among them the fascinating rain forests of the Usamabara and Pare mountains. Mkomazi Game Reserve has not only reintroduced black rhinos and wild dogs, but also helps protect the great elephant herds that meander across the border from Kenya's Tsavo National Park. Although private reserves are not blossoming as fast in Tanzania as they are in Kenya, the Ndarakwai Ranch, near the base of Mt. Kilimanjaro, expanded to cover 10,263 acres in 2001. Those on a recent horseback safari reported spotting a herd of seven giraffes, the national symbol of Tanzania, in this once heavily poached area.

Despite these signs of progress, Tanzania has many of the same problems as its neighbor to the north. The construction of lodges on the rim of Ngorongoro Crater has continued, taxing water supplies and adding to traffic problems. The famous caldera now sees more than 100,000 visitors each year. For the better part of the year it is covered with vans that may make you feel as if you're part of a parade. A single day in 2000 saw 20 vehicles wait-ing at a spot where rhinos are known to cross the road. Even the vast Serengeti can sometimes seem crowded during high season. Near the lodges you may find a half dozen vans encircling a lion. And although poaching has decreased, other dangerous practices continue. For instance, dyna-mite fishing up and down the Tanzanian coast, including around Mafia Island, is killing coral and other marine life.

Tanzania National Parks, the organization charged with protecting these reserves, is coming up with ways to make sure they are still here for future generations. In Gombe Stream National Park, made fa-mous by the studies of naturalist Jane Goodall, it has increased the entrance fee to $100 to limit the number of people who visit Tanzania's smallest park. The or-ganization is also open to the potential of adventure travel, cautiously increasing opportunities for safaris that head out on horseback, canoe, mountain bike, or even on foot. Many of these options are avail-able in Lake Manyara National Park and around the Ngorongoro Crater.

Even wilder adventures outside the con-fines of four-wheel-drive vehicles can be found in isolated areas of Selous Game Re-serve and Katavi National Park. At night there is nothing between you and the stars but a simple mosquito net held aloft by a tree branch. In parks like these you will see no minivans—in fact, you're not likely to encounter other people. The accom-modations are compact, allowing a max-imum of about six or eight people. As Roland Purcell, owner of Katavi Tented Camp, proclaimed one recent evening, "This is the only dinner party for a mil-lion square acres."

Almost everywhere in Kenya and Tanza-nia you will encounter at least a few of the Big Five. Buffaloes, elephants, leopards, lions, and rhinos were originally selected because they were considered big scores among hunters. When hunting was banned in 1977, the Big Five continued to top the list for photo safaris. But this rather su-perficial focus has changed. You can now find safaris that delve into botany or bird-watching. There are more than 1,000 species of birds in Kenya, and more than 450 of those can be found in Nakuru Na-tional Park. Many people head to spots like Kenya's Aberdare National Park, where they can experience a jungle so thick it seems like twilight at noon. Others dive under the sea to take advantage of some of the best snorkeling and diving on the planet.

The geographical spread of East Africa makes it necessary to plot your safari care-fully. It's a big region, more than three times the size of California. It would take months to glimpse all the reserves in the two coun-tries, and even then you'd be rushing. Don't plan too tight a schedule—what you want here is a nice long soak, not a quick shower. Give yourself at least two nights at each destination. It is always good to combine a variety of habitats, making sure to see the lush rain forests as well as the golden grasslands. Alternate the types of accommodations you choose, staying in tents as well as lodges. Meet more local people than just your bartender, and take time to visit a local home or school.

Even if your primary goal is riding over the plains of Kenya's Maasai Mara Na-tional Reserve or scaling the peaks of Tan-zania's Mt. Meru, you should consider combining both countries in your itinerary. Visiting both has become increasingly popular since the border between them was opened in 1984. Because of improved air service between Nairobi and Arusha, it is much easier to travel from Nairobi to Tanzania's Serengeti National Park or Arusha National Park than to Kenya's Marsabit National Reserve or Lake Turkana.

— Delta Willis

SWAHILI VOCABULARY

Although scholars trace its origins back at least 2,000 years, Swahili is constantly evolving. When they began trading with Middle Eastern merchants, the people living along the Indian Ocean incorporated Arabic words and phrases into their language (even the word for the language itself comes from the Arabic word *sawahil*, which means "coast"). The arrival of the Portuguese in the 16th century meant some Portuguese words came into common usage. For instance, the word for table in Swahili is *meza*, from the Portuguese word *mesa*. The British also left behind a few key words. If you want to travel somewhere, you can ride a *baisikeli* (bicycle), drive a *gari* (car), or hop on a *basi* (bus).

More than 130 million people in Kenya, Tanzania, and other East African countries speak Swahili. Because it is spread over such a wide area, there are regional differences in usage. The words and phrases below will be understood by most Swahili speakers.

Basics

English	Swahili
Hello	Jambo *or* hujambo
Good-bye	Kwaheri
Excuse me	Samahani
How are you?	Habari?
Fine	Mzuri
Bad	Mbaya
So-so	Hivi hivi
Please	Tafadhali
Thank you	Asante
Thank you very much	Asante sana
You're welcome	Karibu
Yes	Ndio
No	Hapana
Man	Bwana
Woman	Bibi
Infant/child	Toto
Elder	Mzee
May I come in?	Hodi?
Come in	Karibu
Wait	Ngojea
Where?	Wapi?
When?	Lini?
How?	Vipi?
What?	Nini?
Who?	Nani?
Which?	Ipi?

Useful Phrases

What is your name?	Jina lako nani?
My name is . . .	Jina langu ni . . .
Where are you from?	Unatoka wapi?
I come from America/Australia/ England/Canada.	Mimi ninatoka amerika/australia/ uingereza/kanada.
Do you speak English?	Una sema kiingereza?
I don't speak Swahili.	Sisemi kiswahili.
I don't understand.	Sifahamu.
How do you say this in English?	Unasemaje kwa kiingereza?
How many?	Ngapi?
How much is it?	Ngapi shillings?
May I take your picture?	Mikupige picha?
Where is the bathroom?	Choo kiko wapi?
I need . . .	Mimi natafuta . . .
I want to buy . . .	Mimi nataka kununua . . .
Doctor	Daktari
Hospital	Hospitali
Bank	Benki
Market	Sokoni
Police	Polisi
Post office	Posta
Shop	Duka

Numbers

1	Moja
2	Mbili
3	Tatu
4	Nne
5	Tano
6	Sita
7	Saba
8	Nane
9	Tisa
10	Kumi
11	Kumi na moja
12	Kumi na mbili
13	Kumi na tatu
14	Kumi na nne
15	Kumi na tano
16	Kumi na sita
17	Kumi na saba
18	Kumi na nane
19	Kumi na tisa

20	Ishirini
30	Thelathini
40	Arobaini
50	Hamsini
60	Sitini
70	Sabini
80	Themanini
90	Tisini
100	Mia
1,000	Elfu
Half	Nusu
Quarter	Robo

Days of the Week

Sunday	Jumapili
Monday	Jumatatu
Tuesday	Jumanne
Wednesday	Jumatano
Thursday	Alhamisi
Friday	Ijumaa
Saturday	Jumamosi

Months of the Year

January	Mwezi wa kwanza
February	Mwezi wa pili
March	Mwezi wa tatu
April	Mwezi wa nne
May	Mwezi wa tano
June	Mwezi wa sita
July	Mwezi wa saba
August	Mwezi wa nane
September	Mwezi wa tisa
October	Mwezi wa kumi
November	Mwezi wa kumi na moja
December	Mwezi wa kumi na mbili

Time

Now	Sasa
Soon	Sasa hivi
Yesterday	Jana
Today	Leo
Tonight	Leo usik
Tomorrow	Kesho
Morning	Asubuhi
Day	Siku
Week	Wiki

Month	Mwezi
Year	Mwaka
Daytime	Mchana
Afternoon	Alasiri
Late afternoon	Jioni
Night	Usiku
What time is it?	Saa ngapi?
The time is 2 o'clock.	Saa mbili.
The time is a quarter past 8.	Saa nane na robo.
The time is a quarter to 1.	Saa moja kasa robo.
The time is 9 in the morning.	Saa tisa asubuhi.
The time is 10 at night.	Saa kumi jioni.
What day of the week is it?	Leo siku gani?
Today is Sunday.	Leo jumapili.
What is the date?	Tarehe gani?
The date is January 2.	Tarehe kumi mbili mwezi wa kwanza.

Accommodations

Where is a hotel?	Wapi hoteli ya kulalia?
Do you have a room?	Kuna rumu?
How much is the room?	Rumu ni shillingi ngapi?

Food and Drink

Where is a restaurant?	Wapi hoteli ya chakula?
Bring me hot water, please.	Lete maji moto, tafadhali.
How much is the bill?	Deni yangu ngapi?
Breakfast	Kifungua kinywa
Lunch	Chakula cha mchana
Dinner	Chakula cha usiku
Food	Chakula
Water	Maji
Coffee	Kahawa
Tea	Chai
Milk	Maziwa
Beer	Pombe
Wine	Muinyo
Soft drink	Soda
Ice	Baratu
Meat	Nyama
Beef	Ngombe
Chicken	Kuku
Fish	Samaki
Fruit	Tunda
Goat	Mbuzi

Lamb	Kondoo
Pork	Nguruwe
Plantains	Matoke
Porridge	Ugali
Cold	Baridi
Warm	Moto
Hot	Ya moto
Finished	Quisha
Fork	Uma
Spoon	Kijiko
Knife	Kisu
Napkin	Kitambaa
Plate	Sahani
Glass	Bilauri
Cup	Kikombe

Transportation

How much is the fare?	Nauli ni kiasi gani?
I am going to Nairobi.	Mimi nakwenda Nairobi
One ticket to Mombasa, please.	Tikiti moja kwenda Mombasa, tafadhali.
When does it leave?	Inaondoka lini?
When does it arrive?	Tutafika lini?
Ticket	Tikiti
Airplane	Ndege
Airport	Kiwanja cha ndege
Bus	Basi
Bus station	Stesheni ya basi
Bus stop	Kituo cha basi
Train	Treni
Train station	Stesheni ya treni
Car	Gari
Bicycle	Baiskeli

Safari

Animal	Mnyama
Baboon	Nyani
Bird	Ndege
Buffalo	Nyati
Cheetah	Duma
Chimpanzee	Sokwe
Elephant	Tembo
Giraffe	Twiga
Hippo	Kiboko
Hartebeest	Kongoni

Hyena	Fisi
Leopard	Chui
Lion	Simba
Monkey	Kima
Ostrich	Mbuni
Python	Chatu
Rhinoceros	Kifaru
Warthog	Ngiri
Zebra	Punda milia

Vocabulary

INDEX

NOTES

NOTES

NOTES

NOTES

NOTES

NOTES

NOTES

NOTES

NOTES